Political Communciations: The General Election Campaign of 1987

POLITICAL COMMUNICATIONS: THE GENERAL ELECTION CAMPAIGN OF 1987

Edited by

IVOR CREWE
Professor of Government,
University of Essex
and
MARTIN HARROP
Senior Lecturer in Politics,
University of Newcastle upon Tyne

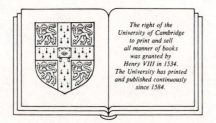

The right of the
University of Cambridge
to print and sell
all manner of books
was granted by
Henry VIII in 1534.
The University has printed
and published continuously
since 1584.

CAMBRIDGE UNIVERSITY PRESS

Cambridge
New York   Port Chester
Melbourne   Sydney

Published by the Press Syndicate of the University of Cambridge
The Pitt Building, Trumpington Street, Cambridge CB2 1RP
40 West 20th Street, New York, NY 10011, USA
10 Stamford Road, Oakleigh, Melbourne 3166, Australia

First published 1989

Printed in Great Britain at The Bath Press, Avon

British Library cataloguing in publication data

Political communications: the general election campaign of 1987
1. Great Britain. Parliament. House of Commons. Members.
General elections. Campaigns
I. Crew, Ivor
II. Harrop, Martin
324.941

Library of Congress cataloguing in publication data applied for

ISBN 0 521 36403 5

Contents

Contributors

Barrie Axford is Senior Lecturer in Politics, School of Business, Oxford Polytechnic.

Denis Balsom is a Senior Research Assistant in the Department of Politics, and International Affairs, University College, Aberystwyth.

Jay G. Blumler is Professor and Research Director, Centre for Television Research, University of Leeds. He has collaborated with Michael Gurevitch and Tom Nossiter on research on the production of BBC-TV News during election campaigns during the 1979, 1983 and 1987 elections. His many publications include *Political Television* (1968), *The Challenge of Election Broadcasting* (1978) and *Communicating to Voters: Television in the First European Parliamentary Elections* (1983).

David Broughton was a Research Assistant on the British Election Campaign Study, University of Glasgow.

Roger Carroll is a financial journalist for *The Sunday Telegraph* and was a member of the SDP's campaign team in 1987.

Ivor Crewe is Professor of Government, University of Essex. He was co-Director of the 1974 and 1979 British Election Studies and is an election commentator for BBC-TV and *The Guardian*. He is the author (with Bo Särlvik) of *Decade of Dealignment* (Cambridge University Press, 1983), *British Parliamentary Constituencies* (Faber, 1984) (with Anthony Fox) and, with Martin Harrop, co-edited *Political Communications: the General Election Campaign of 1983* (Cambridge University Press, 1986), the predecessor to this volume.

Sir Robin Day is a television and radio journalist. He was a newscaster, parliamentary correspondent and roving reporter for ITN from 1955 to 1959; since 1959 he has presented numerous current affairs and election programmes for the BBC, including (on BBC TV) *Panorama*, *Gallery*, *People to Watch*, *Daytime*, *24 Hours*, *Midweek*, *Tonight*, *Sunday Debate*, *Talk-in*, *Newsday* and, most recently, *Question Time*. On BBC Radio he has presented *It's Your Line* (1970–76), *Election Call* 1974, 1979, 1983 and 1987 and *The World at One* (1979–87). In recent election campaigns he has conducted major, full-length television interviews with each of the party leaders. An early advocate of televising Parliament.

Nina Fishman is a Lecturer in Industrial Relations at Harrow College of Higher Education and was Campaign Coordinator for TV87 in the 1987 election campaign.

Marian Fitzgerald is a researcher on race and politics in Britain. She has worked as a Research Fellow for the Runnymede Trust and the Centre for the Study of Community and Race Relations, Brunel University and is currently working for the Home Office. She is the author of *Political Parties and Black People* (Runnymede Trust, 1984).

Bob Franklin is a Senior Research Fellow at the Centre for Television Research, University of Leeds.

Philip Gould is Managing Director, Gould Mattinson Associates Ltd. He was a leading member of the shadow communications agency that designed the Labour Party's advertising campaign in the 1987 election.

Michael Gurevitch is Professor and Director of the Center for Research in Public Communication at the College of Journalism, University of Maryland. He has collaborated with Jay Blumler and Tom Nossiter on research on the production of BBC-TV News during election campaigns during the 1979, 1983 and 1987 elections. He is co-author (with Jay Blumler) of *The Challenge of Election Broadcasting* (Leeds University Press, 1978) and co-editor of *Mass Communication and Society* (Edward Arnold, 1977) and *Culture, Society and the Media* (Methuen, 1982).

Martin Harrop is Senior Lecturer in the Department of Politics, University of Newcastle upon Tyne. He is the co-author with William Miller of *Elections and Voters: A Comparative Introduction* (Macmillan, 1987) and author of the chapters on the press in the 1983 and 1987 'Nuffield' election studies. He was co-editor with Robert Worcester of *Political Communications: The General Election Campaign of 1979* (1982) and co-editor with Ivor Crewe of *Political Communications: The General Election Campaign of 1983* (Cambridge University Press, 1986) – the two predecessors to this book.

Peter Herd is Business Director of Boase, Massimi, Pollitt and was a member of the shadow communications agency that designed the Labour Party's advertising campaign in the 1987 election.

Alastair Hetherington is Professor of Media Research in the Department of Film and Media Studies, University of Stirling and a former editor of *The Guardian*.

Patricia Hewitt was the Press and Broadcasting Secretary in the Opposition Leader's Office during the 1987 election campaign and is now Campaigns and Policy Coordinator in the Opposition Leader's Office.

Dennis Kavanagh is Professor of Politics, University of Nottingham. He has co-authored with David Butler each of the 'Nuffield' series of election studies since February 1974 and has recently published *British Politics: Continuities and Change* (Oxford University Press, 1985) and *Thatcherism and British Politics: The End of Consensus?* (Oxford University Press, 1987).

Chris Ledger was a researcher on special projects for the Broadcasting Research Department of the BBC during the 1987 election. He now works for Central Television.

Brian MacArthur is a former editor of *The Times Higher Education Supplement* and *Today* and now writes on the media for *The Sunday Times*.

Robin McGregor is Acting Head of Special Projects in the Broadcasting Research Department of the BBC.

Peter Madgwick is Professor and Head of the Department of Law, Politics and Economics in the School of Business, Oxford Polytechnic.

Peter Mandelson is Director of Campaigns and Communications for the Labour Party.

Duncan McLean was a Research Assistant on the British Election Campaign Study, University of Glasgow.

William L. Miller is Edward Caird Professor of Politics, University of Glasgow, and Director of the British Election Campaign Study. His recent publications on British elections include *The End of British Politics?* (Clarendon Press, 1981), *The Local Government Elector* (HMSO, 1986) and, with Martin Harrop, *Elections and Voters* (Macmillan, 1987).

Lewis Minkin is Senior Lecturer in the Department of Government, University of Manchester. He is the author of *The Labour Party Conference* (Manchester University Press, 1980) and numerous articles on trade union and Labour Party affairs.

Pippa Norris is a Lecturer in the Department of Politics, University of Edinburgh. She is the author of *Politics and Sexual Equality* (Wheatsheaf, 1987) and numerous articles on elections and public opinion especially in relation to women. In the 1987 election campaign she assisted Vincent Hanna in the conduct of polls of marginal seats for BBC-TV.

Tom Nossiter is a Senior Lecturer in the Department of Government, London School of Economics. He has collaborated with Jay Blumler and Michael Gurevitch on research on the production of BBC-TV News during the 1979, 1983 and 1987 elections.

John Pardoe is Managing Director of Sight and Sound Education Ltd. He was Liberal MP for Cornwall North from 1966 to 1979 and was Chairman of the Alliance Campaign Committee and a member of the Alliance Planning Group during the 1987 election campaign.

Michael Pinto-Duschinsky is a Senior Lecturer in the Department of Government, Brunel University. He is an authority on party finance. His publications include (with David Butler) *The British General Election of 1970* (Macmillan, 1971) and *British Political Parties, 1830–1980* (American Enterprise Institute, 1981).

Chris Powell is Managing Director and Chief Executive of Boase, Massimi, Pollitt. He was Chairman of the shadow communications agency that designed the Labour Party's advertising campaign during the 1987 election.

John Sharkey is Joint Managing Director of Saatchi & Saatchi Compton Ltd.

Andrew Shaw was a Research Assistant in the Department of Political Theory and Institutions, University of Liverpool, and was Research Officer for TV87.

Niels Sonntag was a Research Assistant on the British Election Campaign Study, University of Glasgow. He has recently completed a doctoral thesis at the University of Stirling on the media's coverage of the European Parliament.

Michael Svennevig is a social psychologist specialising in mass media research, currently employed by the Independent Broadcasting Authority. He is the co-author of *Television Coverage of the 1983 General Election* (Gower, 1986).

The Rt Hon. Norman Tebbit, CH, PC, MP has been Conservative Member of Parliament for Chingford since February 1974 (Epping, 1970–February 1974). He was Minister of State,

Department of Industry, 1981; Secretary of State for Employment, 1981–83; Secretary of State for Trade and Industry, 1983–85 and Chancellor of the Duchy of Lancaster, 1985–87. He was Chairman of the Conservative Party from 1985 until the autumn of 1987.

Robert Waller is a former Prize Fellow of Magdalen College, Oxford and currently Director of Social and Political Research, Harris Research Centre. He is a regular radio and television commentator on elections and public opinion and is the author of *The Atlas of British Politics* (Croom Helm, 1985), *The Almanac of British Politics* (Croom Helm, 3rd edition, 1987) and *Moulding Political Opinion* (Croom Helm, 1988).

Mallory Wober is a social psychologist and Deputy Head of Research at the Independent Broadcasting Authority. He is the co-author of *Television Coverage of the 1983 General Election* (Gower, 1986).

Preface

This is the third book in a continuing series examining political communication in British general elections. Like its predecessors on the 1979 and 1983 campaigns, this volume has a dual purpose: first, to analyse the role of the media, the parties and the polls in the campaign and, secondly, to make available the reflections of some of those who participated in it.

The book is based on a conference held at the University of Essex in October 1987. The book is inevitably a selective record of the proceedings and we indicate here some points that emerged in the discussion.

In introducing the conference, David Butler noted the 'professionalisation' of British election campaigns. This is seen in the efforts made by the major parties to integrate all their key communications – speeches, press conferences, party election broadcasts, paid advertisements – around their own agenda. Looking back to 1979, we note that Peter Kellner had called for party advertising to be brought into the political cut and thrust, only to be told that organisationally this was not tenable. Clearly the art of the possible has advanced since then.

Election campaigns are agenda-setting games. The object is to concentrate the attention of television and newspapers on your strengths (and their weaknesses), thereby deflecting attention from your weaknesses (and their strengths). In 1987, by common consent, Labour had considerable although not complete success in the battle of agendas. Yet there was substantial agreement at the conference that while Labour's tactics were outstanding, its strategy was flawed. By concentrating on social issues such as health, education and pensions, the Party detached itself from the election-winning economic issues. There was no dissent from Norman Tebbit's observation that 'perceptions of economic well-being are the master card in all this'. Indeed, there were some claims at the Conference that in 1987 the Labour Party sought not to win but to finish a convincing second. Certainly integrated communication cannot disguise a faulty product. 'Policies', said one practitioner ruefully, 'count for 85 per cent'.

The professionalism of modern campaigns is one reason why electoral volatility is not reflected in dramatic shifts of opinion during the campaign itself. As David Butler observed, by sticking to their game plans, the professionals neutralise each other. Butler suggested that this was a desirable development, allowing the outcome to be determined by long-term factors rather than short-term tactics. Certainly in discussing the campaign at the conference, party managers concentrated as much on the twelve-month build-up as on the four-week campaign. In the run-up a successful party conference or a good by-election enables a party to develop that most critical of campaign resources – momentum. Peter Riddell suggested that in 1987 the media were more attentive to the run-up than in previous elections.

The Alliance campaign is the glaring exception to David Butler's thesis of the growing professionalism of election campaigners. Conference discussion centred on where, not whether, the Alliance went wrong. In his chapter John Pardoe points to the difficulties of the dual leadership although, as Winston Fletcher noted, the Alliance managed 26 per cent with two leaders (albeit one of whom was described as a prime minister designate) in 1983. There was more support for the view, also advanced by Pardoe, that the Alliance should have concentrated its fire on one party – and in particular on the Labour Party. This lack of clear purpose underlay the Alliance's tactical failings in the campaign.

As any good advertising man should, Fletcher also attributed the Alliance's problems to its relative lack of paid advertising: 'if one is not throwing heavy advertising at people, then irrespective of content people infer you are not interested in their custom'. The question of the impact of paid advertising has surfaced at all the conferences in this series, testifying that the legitimacy of this communication channel is still not completely accepted. But two points are clear. First, the millions of pounds spent by the major parties on advertising in the national press made a mockery of the expenditure limits at constituency level. Secondly, parties spend the money not because they know it makes a difference but because they fear it might do. The Alliance spent least only because it had least to spend. Party chairmen cannot be expected to repeat Cecil Parkinson's courage in cancelling advertising in the final week of the 1983 campaign because he was so sure of victory.

As advertising expertise moves to the heart of campaigns, so the question of its impact becomes hypothetical. 'Silly question, isn't it?', commented Chris Powell, 'you might as well ask if the campaign made any difference.' The effect of professional communication skills is seen much more in party election broadcasts than in press advertising. The 'Kinnock' election broadcast, directed by Hugh Hudson and written by Colin Welland, was the foremost example of this. The film energised Labour's 'sales force'; it was undoubtedly the major communications event of the campaign (see pp. 52–3).

There is complete agreement among advertising people that political advertising is more effective when it is negative rather than positive. At the 1979 conference, Barry Day described this as 'the technique of What We Are Not': the politics of fear. Sometimes it is the fear of the Unknown Alternative; sometimes the fear of 'More of the Same'. In 1983, Labour's advertising man Johnny Wright struggled with 'Think Positive, Act Positive, Vote Labour', only to conclude ruefully that 'knocking is what it is all about'. In 1987 Winston Fletcher observed 'how hard it is to make positive points without sounding like motherhood and apple pie'. Certainly the one press advertisement from 1987 which will outlast the campaign – Labour's defence policy symbolised by a soldier with his arms high in a surrendering posture ('Labour's arms policy', p. 69) – is a classic example of knocking copy. Perhaps someone might explain at the next conference why the best advertising is negative when opinion polls consistently report that people say they want an end to slanging matches.

We are grateful to Anglia Television, in particular Malcolm Allsop; the Independent Broadcasting Authority; the Nuffield Foundation; and the Political Studies Association for their generous support. We thank Ilse Mochan and Mike Saward for their help in organising the conference. The facilities provided by the Department of Government at the University of Essex and by the Department of Politics at the University of Newcastle are gratefully acknowledged. We again owe a special debt to Bob Worcester of MORI for his role in helping to arrange the politicians' panel and the advertising panel for the conference. We are grateful to Craig Dearden for compiling the index. Finally, we would like to thank all the conference speakers, even though pressure of space has meant that not all contributions could be included in these proceedings.

Ivor Crewe
Martin Harrop

PART I

The electoral setting

DENNIS KAVANAGH

1 The timing of elections: the British case

The dissolution of a legislature raises several interesting political and constitutional issues. Traditional studies of the subject have largely concentrated on the legal and institutional aspects of dissolution. More recently, constitutional experts have regarded the power of calling an election as a device which can shape the conduct of parties and politicians and produce more effective government. The contrast usually drawn was between the stable British governments, which possessed the power of dissolution, and the unstable governments in many West European states (notably France) which usually lacked such an effective power. Interestingly, in recent years in Britain a growing number of critics have argued that vesting the control of dissolution in the hands of the government actually produces an imbalance in the constitution, allows the government unfair advantage over the opposition in manipulating the economy for its own gain, and opens the way for executive dominance.

This paper examines the political and economic circumstances surrounding a British government's decision to call an election. It proceeds in five parts. First, it presents a brief list of the conditions in which elections have been held this century. Second, it studies the extent to which prime ministers alone decide to dissolve. Third, it considers whether the government's control over timing, and its ability to manipulate the economy, virtually guarantee electoral success. Fourth, it discusses the relationship between a government's popularity in the opinion polls and its economic performance. Finally, it discusses Mrs Thatcher's decisions about timing in 1983 and 1987.

Dissolutions

Dissolutions in the British parliament in the twentieth century have fallen into one of five categories.

The first consists of elections called because the parliament is at or near the end of its life. In this case the element of choice for the prime minister is virtually non-existent. The elections of 1906, 1918, 1929, 1945, 1950 and 1964 fall into this category.

The second is where the government lacks an assured parliamentary majority or has such a small one that it can no longer be confident of conducting business. The elections of 1951, 1966 and October 1974 were examples of appeals to the voter to produce a party majority sufficient to allow for losses in by-elections, absence of members from key votes, and possible defections. In many West European states coalition or minority government is frequent and the lack of a majority for one party is not regarded as furnishing an adequate pretext for a dissolution. In the twentieth century, however, the view has grown that a British government must have a majority sufficient to 'run' parliament.

The concept of a 'working' majority, however, has altered in recent years. In 1951 Mr Attlee regarded a majority of six as inadequate and in 1964 Mr Wilson's majority of four (later whittled down to two) was similarly regarded. But in October 1974 Mr Wilson's initial majority of three (which had disappeared by 1976) allowed the government to continue for nearly five years. The major change between 1950 and October 1974 was the fragment-ation of the opposition, so that the Labour government's lead over the Conservative Party was a comfortable forty-two compared with seventeen in 1950.

The third category is the defeat of the government on a vote of confidence or on a major measure in the House of Commons. Although a frequent occurrence in the nineteenth century, such defeats are now regarded as abnormal, because of the governing party's control of the House of Commons. The only occasions in the twentieth century when the government has lost such a vote and then dissolved have been in 1924 and 1979 – and both were minority Labour governments. Such an occasion is the classic justification of the dissolution power – to end parliamentary deadlock, clarify electoral choice, and produce a working majority. But, as in the first category, the prime minister of the day has little effective choice over timing.

The fourth category occurs when a changed political situation, perhaps the emergence of a salient new issue or a change of prime minister, prompts a government to seek a fresh mandate. In 1910 Asquith dissolved parliament, seeking a mandate to reform the House of Lords; in 1923 Baldwin did so because he wanted to introduce a protective tariff, contrary to the policy promised by his party in the 1922 election. In 1931 the leaders of the newly formed National government also called an election to seek 'a doctor's mandate' to tackle the economic crisis. In 1955 Eden wasted little time after his appointment in calling an election. One might also want to add Mr Heath's dissolution of parliament in February 1974. The oil crisis and miners' strike made it essential, in his view, for the government to make a fresh start backed by a clear expression of public support. But, as Asquith, Baldwin and Heath found, there are dangers in calling single-issue elections.

The fifth and final category is where a prime minister calls an election because he judges that this is the most opportune moment to maximise an already comfortable parliamentary majority. It is important to note, however, that a prime minister will want to time a dissolution well into the second half of the parliament for fear of being accused of 'scuttling'. In the dissolutions of 1959, 1970, 1983 and 1987 the parliaments still had about a year or a little more to run, there was no significant change in the political situation requiring a fresh mandate, and the government had a comfortable parliamentary majority. The 'political' aspects of such a decision are discussed further below.

Prime ministerial choice?

The right of the prime minister to recommend a dissolution of parliament to the monarch is frequently advanced as an illustration of, among other things, his or her power. Acknowledgement that the decision is exclusively the prime minister's prerogative is a recent constitutional development. In the nineteenth century the cabinet usually made a collective decision to approach the Crown. Lloyd George was an innovator in this as in other respects, with his unilateral request for dissolution in 1918. Baldwin's request for a dissolution in 1923 was much criticised but it was already recognised that it was the prime minister's decision.[1]

In a general election a prime minister always has the most to lose – office itself. It is one of the loneliest decisions he can make. He can lose all or his government may simply be returned. The responsibility cannot be shared. If the party loses, his position will be damaged, while that of his rivals for the leadership may improve. The loss of office by Sir Alec Douglas-Home in 1964, Mr Heath in 1974 and Mr Callaghan in 1979 effectively terminated their leaderships of their respective political parties and Mr Wilson's defeat in 1970 undermined his authority in the party.

Not surprisingly, prime ministers frequently seek the advice of heavyweight colleagues – particularly chancellors about the likely state of the economy – and have generally sought to dilute their own personal responsibility.[2] In 1945 an election was already five years overdue and after Labour withdrew from the war-time coalition a speedy dissolution was almost inevitable. Churchill invited ministers to write to him with suggestions for a suitable date and conducted a semi-public debate on the matter. In 1950 and 1951 Mr Attlee consulted most of his senior cabinet ministers. However, Eden's decision in 1955 was largely his own, and in 1959 Mr Macmillan shared his thoughts with very few ministers. In April 1964 Sir Alec Douglas-Home sought the advice of party officials and ministers over timing. The cabinet was split between June and October, but officials were overwhelmingly in favour of the later date. As a result Sir Alec publicly stated that there would be no election before October 1964. By then he had no option. In 1970 Mr Wilson invited the cabinet to Chequers in April to discuss his idea of a summer election.

In December 1973 and January 1974 Mr Heath listened to the views of ministers, Central Office directors, regional officials, and backbenchers. Most of the advice suggested an early election, timed for 7 February. In early January the party's private opinion pollster, Opinion Research Centre, suggested that a late January or early February election would offer a good chance of victory but that a later one would be more risky, as the issue of the miners' challenge to the government might be overtaken by other issues. Mr Heath listened to the advice, ignored it, dissolved later, and lost.

In the summer recess of 1978 there was general expectation of an autumn election. Mr Callaghan expressed his willingness to listen to the views of colleagues on the matter. Some of the input, notably about the bad state of Labour's organisation (hardly unusual) and private opinion poll reports about Labour's position in the marginals, were discouraging. At the end of August Mr Callaghan sought the views of the cabinet about election timing: a majority favoured October. When the cabinet met again on 17 September it expected Mr Callaghan to name the date. Instead, he declared that there would be no election. The decision to delay was clearly his own but he had already discussed his views with two prominent ministers, Mr Foot and Mr Healey, neither of whom dissented from his view that Labour was unlikely to improve its position in an October poll.[3] When the election was announced on 29 March 1979, after a defeat in the Commons, Mr Callaghan had little control over the date.

In 1983 and 1987 Mrs Thatcher consulted widely with key party officials and senior ministers. From May 1982, in the wake of the Falklands, the government enjoyed a handsome lead in the opinion polls. In March 1983 the party chairman Cecil Parkinson effectively persuaded Mrs Thatcher of the case for June 1983, when inflation was likely to be at its lowest and the unemployment figures not boosted by the summer-school-leavers. In late March 1987 Mrs Thatcher and the cabinet discussed possible election dates and the choice was effectively between June and October (see below).

The record seems clear. Although the decision is ultimately the prime minister's, most prime ministers are concerned to consult and to be seen to consult senior colleagues. As far as possible a prime minister wants to arrive at a consensus. The decision about timing is tied up with problems of party management and cabinet management.

Prime ministers are also increasingly concerned to prepare public opinion for an election. In 1983 and 1987 speculation among the media was allowed to develop to such an extent that the outcome was widely expected for a month or so in advance of the actual decision. On both occasions Mrs Thatcher was able to announce her request for a dissolution by mentioning the need to curb the speculation and uncertainty, features which she and her office had done a good deal to encourage, and little to dampen.

Incumbency advantages

The main resource a British government possesses is control of election timing. In theory this allows it to adopt a more efficient scheduling of pre-campaign efforts, such as purchasing poster sites and press advertisements. In 1959 the Conservative government had a massive advertising campaign six weeks ahead of the dissolution. In opposition, the Labour Party machine wrongly anticipated an election in 1963 and spent heavily on advertising for this. But even in office a party may throw away the advantage of timing. In 1970 the Labour machine mistakenly planned its publicity (and spending) for an October, not a June, election. In 1978 the Labour Party confidently expected Mr Callaghan (on the grounds that he had not said anything to the contrary) to call an election in the autumn, and spent £200,000 in advertising over the summer.

A second political advantage of incumbency is the ability to make news. In the run-up to the 1987 election the government's position was strengthened by a tax-cutting budget in March, increased spending on health and education and buoyant economic statistics. In 1983 and 1987 Mrs Thatcher made eve-of-election overseas tours which gained extensive publicity. In January 1983 she visited the Falklands, evoking memories of the successful war nine months earlier. Between March 28 and April 1987 she was given a triumphant reception by Mr Gorbachov in the Soviet Union, confirming her position as a successful international stateswoman. Both visits created numerous photo opportunities. This is something of an old trick. In 1959 Harold Macmillan, wearing the mantle of international statesman, also made a well-covered visit to the USSR. Mr Gaitskell tried to follow suit in 1959 but he had to cut the tour short when Mr Macmillan called an election. During the summer recess of 1974 the minority Labour government constantly made headlines – and conveyed an impression of activity of a sort – by publishing a series of White Papers outlining its plans for industry, land, pensions and devolution. In the first four months of 1983 Mrs Thatcher gave sixteen interviews, compared to the usual four for such a period.

A British government can also time an election to take advantage of events and announcements that are bound to occur in the campaign. Ever since the 'bad' news of the balance of payments deficit two days before polling day in June 1970, and the series of unfavourable official statistics released during the February 1974 campaign, government election advisers have been careful to make a prior assessment of the dates of routine monthly statistics on prices, unemployment and trade, and of their possible electoral impact. Party headquarters are now expected to have calendar charts for different target election dates, covering the dates of key events and publication of key statistics. Election planning means 'no surprises'. A notorious attempt to 'manage' these statistics was made in September 1974 by the Labour Chancellor of the Exchequer, Denis Healey. He used the 2.2 per cent increase in retail prices between the May/August quarter to claim that the annualised inflation figure was only 8.4 per cent. This took account of one-off factors such as the government's July reductions in VAT, rate relief for householders and the seasonal fall in foodstuffs. In 1982 and 1983 the Conservative government reduced the official unemployment figures by omitting those looking for work but not claiming benefit and then removing from the register those aged sixty or more.

Government ministers time their economic measures to have maximum electoral impact and, where they are able, choose the date of the election to coincide with economic 'good times'. The effects of the electoral-economic cycle are seen in the general tendency for rates of unemployment and inflation to level off or fall in election years and for real wages to increase sharply in the six months before general elections. Compared to previous years in the parliament, inflation was kept down in the election years 1959, 1966, 1979 and 1983. It was rising gently in 1964, 1979 and 1987 and rising steeply in 1970 and February 1974. In Britain there have been sharp increases in real disposable incomes in most election years; usually followed by a sharp slowdown or even decline in mid-parliament. This was the pattern in 1954–55, 1958–59, 1970, 1983 and 1987. Only in February 1974, an unexpected election, was the run-up accompanied by a fall in real disposable incomes.[4] There was also a sharp increase in 1978, a good launch for an October 1978 election, but not for the May 1979 one. Richard Crossman, a minister in the 1964–70 Labour governments, confessed in 1971: 'The main fact is that we won the 1966 election by choosing the moment of wage inflation before the prices had really been felt to rise and obviously we were seeking to do it again in 1970.'

The record of post-war general elections hardly supports the thesis that incumbents are overwhelmingly favoured or the contrary claim that there is a swing of the pendulum against the government. Of the twelve cases of dissolution since 1945 the government has won seven and lost five. Sir Alec Douglas-Home, Mr Heath and Mr Callaghan each dissolved once and lost. Sir Anthony Eden, Mr Macmillan, and Mrs Thatcher (twice) were successful. Mr Attlee won one and lost one, and Mr Wilson lost one and won two. But of the seven successes, Attlee's 1950 victory was indecisive and he dissolved again after nineteen months, and Wilson's two election successes in government were consolidations of earlier knife-edge results. Mrs Thatcher's clear victories were in large measure due to the divisions in the opposition parties. The

Table 1.1. *Fate of incumbents in British general elections 1950–87*

Election year	Incumbent Party	Change in per cent vote
1950	Labour	−2.2
1951	Labour	+2.7
1955	Conservative	+1.7
1959	Conservative	−0.3
1964	Conservative	−6.0
1966	Labour	+3.8
1970	Labour	−4.9
1974 (Feb)	Conservative	−8.6
1974 (Oct)	Labour	+2.1
1979	Labour	−5.3
1983	Conservative	−1.5
1987	Conservative	−0.1

record hardly bears out the claims that the dice are very heavily loaded in the government's favour.

In the seven cases of a successful post-war dissolution, governments saw their share of the popular vote increase in only four elections – 1951 (+ 2.7 per cent), which Labour lost, 1955 (+ 1.7 per cent), 1966 (+ 3.8 per cent) and October 1974 (+ 2.1 per cent). The average change in share of the vote for incumbents has been a decline of 1.5 per cent, with the biggest falls being in February 1974 (8.5 per cent), 1964 (6 per cent) and 1979 (5.3 per cent) (see table 1.1).

During the 1960s and 1970s the trend clearly worsened for the government. In part this was a consequence of the decline in support for each of the two main parties and the country's relatively declining economic performance. Of the four dissolutions in the 1970s the government of the day lost three and suffered an average fall of 4.5 per cent in its share of the vote compared with the previous election. Holding office was a disadvantage and between 1959 and 1983 no government was able to gain re-election after a near full-term of office. Of course, without the control of timing the losing governments might have done even worse. This probably applies to the Conservative dissolution in 1964 – so nearly a victory. But in February 1974 and 1979, the prime minister of the day simply got it wrong. Mr Heath's personal view after the election was that his mistake had been less in not going earlier than in calling an election at all.

An international comparison shows a mixed pattern. In the 1970s and early 1980s the dismissal of long-established government parties in Sweden, Norway and France encouraged speculation that governments everywhere were finding it more difficult, with the slow-down of economic growth, to get re-elected. Keynesian techniques of producing pre-election booms no longer worked. In fact, examination of the elections across Western states before and since 1968 show that governments were still as likely to be re-elected, although with a fall in their share of the vote. In the coalition governments of many West European states the election is usually more significant as a verdict on the relative standing of the parties in the governing coalition.[5]

Systems of proportional representation often have the effect of stabilising the legislature; they produce smaller changes in the parties' relative share of seats and governing parties have a better record of holding on to office.[6] By contrast, a swing of the pendulum against the government is more often found in Westminster systems which have the first-past-the-post electoral system. Note also that it is only in Westminster-type models that the prime minister effectively has the right to dissolve parliament.

Cycles in popularity

Before deciding to call an election, governments have traditionally taken soundings about the public mood. Until recently they relied largely on by-elections, local elections and information from party organisers. Disraeli misread two successful by-elections in 1880 and Winston Churchill wrongly assumed that Lord Beaverbrook, as a press proprietor, would have expert knowledge of the public mood in 1945.

Since 1959 the major new factor has been the development of public and private opinion polls, although the party leaders are careful to consider them along with other sources of information. The gloomy opinion polls in 1963 were certainly important in convincing Sir Alec Douglas-Home to delay going to the country. When the polls turned around in favour of the government of the day in early 1970 and January 1974 they had some effect in convincing Mr Wilson's and Mr Heath's associates to call an election. In both cases, however, the government enjoyed only a short-lived (and therefore perhaps fragile) lead in the polls. Private polls in the marginals by MORI in the summer of 1978 persuaded Mr Callaghan to soldier on and the pro-election advice (in spite of qualifications) from ORC failed to persuade Mr Heath to go earlier in January 1974. In both these cases the opinion polls were acting to reinforce the inclinations of the prime minister of the day.

Study of the opinion polls in the past two decades shows that there is something of a cyclical pattern in the popularity of a government.[7] Between 1947 and 1956 the electorate was fairly steady in its allegiance to the two main parties and the coming of a general election did little to disturb this pattern. Since then, however, governments have usually experienced a significant loss of support with corresponding huge leads for the opposition – regardless of how the economy performs – followed by a recovery as the election approaches. There were spectacular collapses in support for the government between 1957 and mid-1958, between late 1962 and mid 1964, and between December 1967 and December 1969. The Labour government trailed by double figures for most months between October 1976 and August 1977, recovered, and then fell away again in the first four months of 1979. The same happened to the Thatcher government between the end of 1980 and April 1982. In each of these cases there was a swing-back of support to the government of the day as the election approached. The one exception to this trend was Mr Callaghan's forced dissolution in 1979. The regular swing-back had occurred in 1978 but support fell away again at the turn of the year with the onset of the industrial disruption in the winter of discontent. The Falklands success in April 1982 helped to accelerate the recovery of support for the government of the day.

A good lead in the opinion polls may still not be sufficient to reassure a prime minister. An increasingly volatile electorate and the ability of election campaigns to switch votes can quickly change the poll readings. In 1970 the poll predictions were confounded and in every subsequent election until 1987 the party that started the campaign with a handsome lead saw it significantly reduced by election day. 1987 is an exception in that the government preserved its big lead to polling day.

But one may make too much of the influence of the electoral–economic cycle on the governing party's popularity. Other influences disturb a pure one-to-one relationship between changes in economic conditions and changes in the levels of party support. Voters' expectations of economic benefits may be scaled down, a foreign crisis or another issue may become important, or the public's tolerance of levels of inflation or unemployment may change over time. The small changes in economic conditions in the 1960s and 1970s were accompanied by big changes in the parties' standing in the polls.

What seems more significant for the standing of the government than absolute levels of employment or inflation is the direction of the trends and how these affect the mood of the electorate. Robert Worcester of MORI reports an impressive positive correlation between Labour's lead over the SNP and Scottish voters' feeling of optimism about the future of the economy in the late 1970s. In the run up to the election in 1983 the Conservative government gained from such optimism. During the forty-eight months of the 1983 parliament (between June 1983 and May 1987) there was a positive correlation of .450 between the government's popularity (MORI) and economic optimism, and between August 1986 and May 1987 it reached .938. In January 1987 a net 27 per cent expected economic conditions to improve over the next twelve months, rising to 38 per cent in April and 44 per cent in June.

The 1987 dissolution

The background to Mrs Thatcher calling the election in 1987 was remarkably similar to that in 1983. There was the same popular March budget, a successful overseas trip, good local election results, a big lead in the opinion polls, a favourable set of economic indicators, and a general expectation that June was the 'right time' to call an election. The encouragement of media speculation about an election was again important both in preparing public opinion for the event and testing (*via* opinion polls) the likely public mood. There was the same meeting of Mrs Thatcher and senior ministers at Chequers on the Sunday after the local elections, to confirm the decision.

The Alliance gain at Greenwich in February had certainly caused some Conservatives to think in terms of an election no earlier than October 1987. But when the Alliance bandwagon was not maintained, June became a popular option again. Although the favourable news in the opinion polls and on the economy encouraged party pressure for June, Mrs Thatcher refused to commit herself without the evidence of 'the biggest poll of all' – the local elections. Some ministers, including Lord Whitelaw, John Moore and Nigel Lawson, were believed to favour October but by the time local results were out, they switched.

Mr Tebbit was widely credited with advocating an early (May or June) election. He was, however, more concerned with the party regularly scoring 40 per cent or above in the polls and having a lead of 6 or 7 per cent over the second party, and with gaining reassurance that an Alliance upsurge would not threaten too many Conservative seats. A consequence of the arrival of the Alliance as a significant third electoral party is that parties, particularly the Conservatives, have to make more complex calculations about electoral trends.

When senior ministers met Mrs Thatcher at Chequers on May 10 they were presented with a Central Office computer prediction – based on an analysis of local elections and private polls – for a ninety-four seat Conservative majority. Even allowing for an Alliance upsurge and some Conservative defections, it seemed impossible to lose. June it was to be. There was little discussion among ministers over the exact date; 4 June was excluded because of problems of clearing essential legislation through parliament and because it was a Jewish holiday; 18 June was also ruled out because the campaign would be too long and might allow an Alliance momentum. The natural date seemed to be 11 June; it would complete four years in the administration, the benefits of the budget tax cuts would be in voters' pockets, house mortgage cuts would be in effect, and the impression of the Moscow triumph would still be present.

As in 1983 the government called an election against a background of a remarkably favourable set of economic and political indicators. The five national polls, (NOP, Gallup, Marplan, Harris for *Weekend World* and Harris for TV-AM) reporting in May, before the election date was announced, averaged Conservatives 42 per cent, Labour 30.5 per cent and the Alliance 25.5 per cent. On Friday 10 May the bank rate was reduced to 9 per cent, the fourth cut in two months, and there were much publicised and optimistic reports about the economy from the CBI and Institute of Directors. Wage settlements were running at an annualised average 7.5 per cent compared to inflation at 4 per cent – representing a substantial increase in living standards for those in work. Interest rates were coming down and the unemployment figures fell for the eighth month in succession.

The prime minister's control of the dissolution is central to the claim that Britain has prime ministerial government. Lord Hailsham portrays the prime minister 'with his hand on the lever of dissolution, which he is free to operate at any moment of his choice'. The lever, combined with the opinion polls and manipulation of the economic electoral cycle, allegedly loads the electoral dice too heavily in favour of the government of the day.[8]

I am sceptical. The post-war record, with the exception of the Thatcher victories in 1983 and 1987, hardly bears it out. It is worth adding that the government was well placed for most of the 1983 parliament and its successes in 1983 and 1987 were in part a consequence of the divided opposition parties. Timing was not as crucial as participants have made out.[9] Even with fixed calender elections there would still be scope for economic pump-priming and news management. There would still be electioneering in the last year of the parliament, the government tempted to postpone unpopular measures, and investors and others would hold off making decisions until the election was decided.

What calender elections might prevent is the increasing tendency for government to tease the electorate with the prospect of an election. Ministers then plead that they call the election to put an end to the 'intolerable' uncertainty which holds up investment and other decisions. Anthony Bevins protested in *The Independent* in February 1987 that Mrs Thatcher was 'neutering' the parliament: 'This parliament is wasting away, dying before our eyes. The prime minister should be ashamed of herself.' Speculation about timing makes for good journalistic copy. Apart from that I am not sure that the absence of calender elections makes much difference.

In a world of uncertainty, and with a lot to lose, prime ministers might follow certain guidelines in deciding when to seek a dissolution:

1 Prepare public opinion: the expectation of an election seems to produce a recovery in government popularity before an election.
2 If more than a year of the parliament remains and you have a good majority, justify your decision in terms of the national interest, e.g., the need to end uncertainty or to cope with changed circumstances.
3 Consult colleagues, so that they are implicated in the final decision. If you lose, the blame will be yours but the appearance or reality of consultation may help to deflect some of the criticism.
4 Ensure that the economic indicators are moving in a positive direction, but above all rely on the electorate's optimism that the economy will improve over the next six to twelve months.

5 Have a substantial lead in the opinion polls, over the opposition, for six months or more, so that the lead is not a flash in the pan.

According to the above guidelines the dissolutions of 1983 and 1987 were timed to perfection.

Notes

1 J. Mackintosh, *The British Cabinet* (London: Stevens, 1962), p. 449.
2 See R. K. Alderman and J. A. Cross, 'The prime minister and the decision to dissolve', *Parliamentary Affairs*, 28 (1975), 386–404.
3 See B. Donoughue, *Prime Minister* (London: Cape, 1987) and 'The winter of discontent', *Contemporary Record*, 1 (1987), 34–44.
4 J. Alt, *The Politics of Economic Decline* (Cambridge University Press, 1978), p. 136.
5 See S. M. Lipset, 'No room for the ins: elections around the world', *Public Opinion* 5 (October/November 1982), 41–3.
6 See R. Rose and T. Mackie, *Incumbency in Government: Asset or Liability?* Studies in Public Policy, no 54 (Glasgow: University of Strathclyde, 1980).
7 W. L. Miller and M. Mackie, 'The electoral cycle and the asymmetry of government and opposition popularity', *Political Studies*, 21 (1973), 263–79.
8 'The elective dictatorship', *The Listener*, 21 October 1976, p. 497.
9 At the Essex Conference Mr Tebbit claimed: 'The timing of an election is as important as the final campaign.' For Labour, Peter Mandelson stated: 'We could not overcome the problem of timing, enjoyed exclusively by the Conservatives.'

2 Financing the British General Election of 1987

Thanks to the generous help given by officials of all the main parties as well as by civil servants and trade union officials, it is possible to give a broadly accurate picture of the funding of the 1987 election campaign. Nevertheless, it must be stressed that the statistics given in the following pages are based on early, unaudited figures of expenditures by the central party organisations and, in the case of certain Liberal–Social Democratic Alliance funds, on approximate estimates.

The fact that some of the party headquarters have not yet finalised their election accounts combined with the fact that accounts for routine central party spending in the months preceding the election are not yet available makes it even more difficult than usual to make accurate or consistent distinctions between campaign spending – the main concern of this chapter – and routine spending. The distinction between routine and campaign spending is, in some cases, unclear. For example, it is hard to determine whether opinion polling in the months before the election date was announced or advertising by party organisations for the local government elections of 7 May, 1987 were really parts of the run-up to the general election campaign and ought therefore to be treated as general election expenses. The political party headquarters use somewhat different conventions in classifying expenditure as either routine or campaign. Moreover, party accounts are not always consistent between one general election and the next.

In addition, it is still too early (July 1988) to assess campaign contributions by companies. Directors' reports for the period of the election (in which political contributions over £200 must be revealed, according to company law) have yet to be issued. There will also be a delay before the Certification Office issues statistics of trade union political levy funds during 1987.

For these reasons, the figures given below will be subject to revision and clarification as further information becomes available.

Central campaign finance

Conservative

Although Conservative Central Office spent some £3.8 million on the 1983 election campaign (including pre-campaign items) and succeeded in 1983–4 in raising £0.8 million more than it spent, the financial problems which had faced the party since the 1970s were apparent again during the two years following the election. In 1984–5 and 1985–6, the party's central income fell short of expenditure by £1.8 million. Between 1978–9 and 1985–6, the accumulated excess of expenditure over income amounted to £5.3 million. By 1985–6, Conservative central income was hardly greater than Labour's. Within Central Office, there were divisions of opinion between those who saw the use of direct mail as a solution to the party's fund-raising problems and others who feared that new fund-raising methods would merely antagonise the party's traditional givers and produce 'donor fatigue'.

In 1986–7, the prospect of another general election led to a dramatic improvement in Central Office finance, largely as a result of a 90 per cent rise in 'donations' from companies and individuals. The realisation that the Labour Party was preparing a far more professional campaign than in 1983 may also have boosted Conservative fund-raising. Income rose from £5.0 million in 1985–6 to £8.9 million in 1986–7 and expenditure grew from £5.5 to £7.5 million.

As the prospect of a June 1987 election became more likely, the party treasurers appear to have given a green light for a high-spending campaign. In the penultimate week before the poll, growing alarm about the apparent impact of the Labour campaign and about a falling Conservative lead in some opinion polls led to a heavy increase in spending. It was decided to commission three pages of advertising each day in the national newspapers at a total cost of about £3 million. Because of this spending in the final stage of the election, the central cost soared to over £9 million.

Unlike the Labour Party, which planned its campaign on the basis of its income, the Conservative Central Office seems to have sanctioned spending well beyond the sum it had raised. This was partly on the assumption that donors would be persuaded to give more generously when they saw how heavily the party was spending on its advertisements and partly on the view that, even were the money not raised, it was better to go into deficit than to risk losing the election. In the words of one senior Conservative officer, 'I'd hate to be the [official] who balanced the books and lost the election'. It appears that money to cover the costs of the campaign was still being raised months after the poll. The decision to step up the level of spending as the campaign was in progress owed much to the party treasurers, in particular to Lord McAlpine, and seemed to reflect the view that the main function of the

Table 2.1. *Conservative Party central campaign expenditure, 1987, in thousands of pounds (unaudited estimates)*

		£000
Grants to constituencies		137
Advertising: press	4,523	
posters and leaflets	1,834	
		6,357
Political broadcasts (production costs)		366
Opinion research		219
Leader's tour and meetings		417
Publications		714
Staff and administration costs		818
Total		9,028

Note: Includes spending by area offices.
Source: Conservative Central Office.

central party organisation was to win election campaigns and that the routine financial needs of the machine were a less pressing consideration. In this respect, Conservative priorities differed from Labour's.

The pattern of Conservative central spending in the 1987 campaign was similar to that in 1983. As before, grants to constituency campaigns amounted to less than 2 per cent of the total. By far the largest items were those handled by the party's advertising agency, Saatchi and Saatchi, Garland Compton. They amounted to £6.4 million compared with £2.6 million devoted to the same items in 1983. This constituted an increase of 106 per cent in real terms.

Labour

The determination of Labour Head Office to fight a professional, modern campaign and to employ sophisticated advertising techniques was matched by its determination to raise far more money for the election than Labour had raised in the past. Despite the use of direct mail fund-raising, the party still relied overwhelmingly on trade union contributions. The main story of Labour Party fund-raising during 1983–7 and in the 1987 campaign was the success in attracting money from the unions. This was achieved despite the sharply falling membership of trade unions and despite legislation enacted by the Conservative government in 1984 which obliged unions to hold a ballot of members every ten years if they wished to raise political levies. By 1986, all such ballots had resulted in votes in favour of these levies, even though a majority of members of many unions opposed the Labour Party, to which almost all the political levy funds were forwarded.

Between 1984 and 1987, trade union affiliation fees to Labour Head Office increased from £2.9 million to about £4.2 million a year (an increase of 21 per cent in real terms). Labour's general secretary, Larry Whitty, who had been a trade union official in 1983 and had coordinated a body called Trade Unionists for a Labour Victory (TULV), received strong support from a similar organisation led by Bill Keys of the Transport and General Workers' Union called Trade Unionists for Labour. In 1986, TUFL undertook to attempt to raise nearly £5 million from trade union political levy funds for the forthcoming Labour campaign. This total was to be raised in instalments and was based on the assumption that the election would be held in October 1987. The fact that the election was called earlier meant that less was contributed. At the start of the campaign, a revised target of a £3.5 million minimum contribution from unions was adopted. However, this total was surpassed. A total of £3,775,228 was contributed by the unions to Labour's central campaign in 1987. This compared with £2.1 million in 1983 (an increase of over 50 per cent in real terms). As in earlier elections, the trade unions were the only significant source of Labour's central campaign income. Less than £0.3 million was raised from other sources. In addition, the party was able to draw on the reserves of its general election account, which stood at £341,000 at the start of 1986. Total campaign expenditure by the Labour Head Office amounted to £4.2 million (compared with £2.1 million in 1983). Unlike the statistics for the Conservative Party, these figures exclude income and expenditure of regional Labour parties. If these are included, total campaign spending probably reached about £4.5 million. Labour's central spending was at the same level in real terms as in 1964. Labour's expenditure in these two elections was a record for the party.

The breakdown of Labour expenditure is broadly similar to that of 1983. Nearly £400,000 was allocated for grants to constituencies. This sum was considerably larger than that of the Conservatives for the same purpose. The largest item was advertising, which accounted for over half of the total. However, it was in the area of advertising that Labour's disadvantage as compared with the Conservatives was most apparent. Conservative advertising was three times as expensive as Labour's. A source of economy for Labour was its use of volunteer advertising advisers, which saved the fees which the Conservatives paid to their agency. Labour's production costs for party election broadcasts were also considerably lower than those of Conservative Central office (£143,000 compared with £366,000).

Alliance

When the SDP was created, its central fund-raising far outpaced that of the Liberals. In 1981, central SDP income was four times as large as Liberal income. This was largely because of the notable success of the SDP in

Table 2.2. *Labour Head Office campaign expenditure, 1987, in thousands of pounds (unaudited estimates)*

		£000
Grants to constituencies		388
Advertising: press	1,862	
posters	313	
		2,175
Political broadcasts (production costs)		143
Opinion research		148
Leader's tour and meetings		233
Publications		269
Staff and administration costs		838
Total		4,194

Note: excludes regional party spending.
Source: Labour Head Office.

collecting individual membership subscriptions. However, the party found it hard to maintain the enthusiasm of its opening year. In 1986–7, SDP income from membership subscriptions was £469,000 compared with £760,000 in 1981–2. By 1986–7, the SDP's central income was still larger than the Liberals' but the margin was smaller (£991,000 compared with £488,000). The Liberal Party, although still the poorest of the central party organisations, succeeded in raising its routine income from £383,000 in 1983 to £727,000 in 1987. (These totals all exclude the Liberal and SDP shares of the 'Short' money allocated to opposition parties in the House of Commons.)

As far as campaign spending is concerned, some gaps in accounting still remain at the time of writing this chapter. However, two main points are clear. In 1987 as in 1983 there was little coordination between campaign spending by the two parties of the Alliance. Once again there were at least four separate central funds – the Liberal Party Organization campaign fund, the Liberal leader's fund, the Social Democratic general election fund and an Alliance fund (controlled by the former Liberal MP John Pardoe and by the SDP politician Lord Diamond). Secondly, the largest fund was again that of the SDP. Central Liberal campaign spending amounted to approximately £0.2 million. The Liberal leader's fund spent approximately £80,000. About £50,000 was raised for this special fund by the sale of places to journalists on the leader's 'Battlebus' and on his aircraft. Most of the remainder was provided by the Joseph Rowntree Social Service Trust Ltd. The SDP general election fund spent a total of £1,290,000. This included £217,000 spent on election preparations and £1,074,000 spent during the campaign. The Alliance fund's expenditure amounted to about £0.25 million. Also, David Sainsbury reportedly made some additional direct payments. Total Alliance central election spending (including all four funds mentioned) was at least £1.75 million and may have reached £2 million. In 1983, total Alliance spending was £1.9 million. Thus, compared with 1983, the gap between Alliance spending and that of the Conservative and Labour parties widened. Alliance spending fell, in real terms, while that of the Conservatives and Labour rose.

The largest single item of SDP expenditure consisted of grants to constituencies. The party spent £617,000 for this purpose. Every SDP candidate received a grant of £1,000 and larger sums went to candidates in target seats.

The Alliance Fund received £105,000 from the Joseph Rowntree Social Service Trust Ltd and a matching sum from Sainsbury Associates. The balance of its income came largely from company donations. The main item of expenditure from the fund was on the production costs of party election broadcasts (over £100,000). Estimated costs of other items were Ask the Alliance Rallies £50–65,000, advertising (including a full-page advertisement in *The Independent*) £20–25,000, press conference costs £25,000, manifesto and materials £15–20,000, Alliance regional offices £10–15,000. Apart from the Alliance Fund, further expenditure, funded by Sainsbury money, appears to have been incurred in the period shortly before the opening of the campaign. This apparently covered the production costs of two party political broadcasts as well as additional newspaper advertisements.

The profusion of funds and the fragmentation of fund-raising and spending is symptomatic of the lack of coordination that plagued the Alliance in 1987.

Sources of central party income

Party organisations have no obligation to reveal the identity of individual donors. Consequently, it is only the Labour Party, which appears to receive little from individual donations, for which relatively adequate information is available.

Labour's general election fund was raised mainly by a handful of large trade unions. Of £3.8 million contributed by the unions, half came from two unions and two-thirds from the five largest union contributions. The contributions were as follows (1983 figures are in brackets): Transport and General Workers £1,279,000 (£508,000); General and Municipal Workers £631,000 (£307,000); Public Employees £260,000 (£220,000); Engineering Workers £250,000 (£217,500); Mineworkers £207,000 (£234,000). Other large contributions were Railwaymen £162,000, Communication Workers £158,000, ASTMS £115,000, COHSE £111,000. Labour's heavy reliance on the Transport and General Workers' Union, which organised Trade Unionists for Labour, and on the General and Municipal Workers, for which Larry Whitty formerly worked, emerges clearly from these statistics.

These trade union payments to the central Labour general election fund formed only part of their contributions to Labour Party politics in 1987. Unions contributed over £4 million in affiliation fees to Labour Head Office as well as payments to regional Labour parties, constituency Labour parties and for a variety of other purposes. The Transport and General Workers alone paid a total of £2.3 million to Labour Head Office in 1987 in affiliation fees and contributions to the general election fund.

The increase in routine and campaign contributions to the Labour Party by most trade unions reflected the surprisingly healthy state of their general and political levy funds. Falling membership meant that the number contributing to trade union political levy funds fell from 8.1 million members in 1979 to 5.6 million in 1986 (the last year for which figures are currently available). During this same period, the income of the political levy funds rose from £4.7 million a year to £10.3 million in current prices. Income per member almost doubled in real terms. During 1987 the total income of political levy funds was probably about £11 million and there was £12.4 million in the political levy fund reserves at the start of the year (compared with £6.6 million at the start of 1983). The unions were thus capable of spending £13–15 million during 1987 while still leaving an adequate reserve. Nearly four-fifths of political levy expenditure is normally devoted to Labour Party purposes. On this basis of calculation, union contributions to Labour, centrally and locally, probably amounted to at least £10 million during 1987.

As directors' reports for 1987 become available, it will become possible to review the pattern of company contributions to political parties (although it will not be possible to distinguish between payments for routine and campaign purposes). At present, the latest available figures are for contributions made during 1986, during the start of the run-up to the campaign. A recent study by the Policy Development Directorate of the Labour Party reviewed the reports of over 1,500 of Britain's major public companies. These revealed contributions in 1986 totalling £2.1 million to the Conservative Party and to related fund-raising organizations such as British United Industrialists. There were ten contributions of £40,000 or more, totalling £536,000. The largest contributions were British and Commonwealth Shipping £91,000, United Biscuits £75,000, Allied Lyons £55,000, Trust House Forte £51,000, Hanson Trust £50,000, Kleinwort Benson, £50,000, Newarthill £43,000, Willis Faber £40,000, Trafalgar House £40,000 and Taylor Woodrow £40,000.

The Labour Party study also discovered seven companies which contributed a total of £33,947 to the SDP (including £10,000 from Coates Viyella), eleven companies which contributed £28,100 to the Alliance, and a single contribution from Pearson of £5,000 to the Liberals (alongside a £25,000 payment to the Conservatives).

The survey undoubtedly misses other payments by smaller or private companies. Moreover, contributions to Conservative funds are always greater during election years. The list of company payments for 1987 can therefore be expected to include larger sums than those given below. Nevertheless it seems unlikely that the Conservatives, and still less the parties of the Alliance, will be shown to have raised their central funds almost exclusively from corporate sources.

Although it is not possible to find firm evidence, it seems likely that the Conservatives are tending to rely increasingly on individual payments as a supplement to company donations. Occasional personal donations of at least £250,000 have been made and cheques from individual partners or directors of firms of stockbrokers, lawyers or bankers are, reportedly, frequent. As much as 15 per cent of total Conservative central income may come from legacies. Recent economic developments have made it possible for more individuals to make substantial charitable or political donations. Only occasionally do the names of large political donors become known. For instance, it has been confirmed that David Sainsbury was again the largest SDP contributor in 1987. In general the identity of party benefactors has remained a matter of speculation (including one frequent rumour about an important private contributor to the Labour cause).

Apart from institutional payments by unions and companies, and apart from large and medium-sized payments by individuals, there were frequent reports before the election about the use of American-style techniques of direct mail fund-raising. The Conservatives sent appeals to those listed as shareholders of British Telecom. The direct mail drive had to be abandoned at the start of the campaign because of legal advice that the continued despatch of letters would risk contravening the regulations about expenditure limits for parliamentary candidates. By June 1987, the Conservatives had made a profit of £0.75 million from direct mail, about 5 per cent of the income the party needed to raise for routine and campaign purposes in 1987. Labour's 'National Fund-raiser' effort to raise money by direct mail and other means produced a surplus of £34,000 in 1985 and £121,000 in 1986. This constituted 2 per cent of revenue. By June 1987, some of the most successful direct mail fund-raising efforts were still those of the SDP which reportedly raised £700,000 of the £1.1 million it spent during the general election campaign from the profits of a direct mail election appeal. The success of this appeal resulted largely from the party's earlier efforts in building up a list of members and donors.

Independent political expenditure

The four largest party organisations were not the only bodies which were active in the election. A full picture of the 1987 national campaign would also need to take account of the activities of independent (or supposedly independent) organisations which campaigned for or against particular parties.

Table 2.3. *Largest company donations to the Conservative Party and to allied bodies during the pre-election year, 1986*

British and Commonwealth Shipping	£91,500
United Biscuits	75,500
Allied Lyons	55,000
Trust House Forte	51,000
Hanson Trust	50,000
Kleinwort Benson	50,000
Newarthill	43,000
Willis Faber	40,000
Trafalgar House	40,000
Taylor Woodrow	40,000

Table 2.4. *Largest Trade Union payments to Labour Head Office in the election year, 1987*

	Affiliation fees	Contributions to General Election Fund	Total
Transport Workers	£998,625	£1,279,000	£2,277,625
General and Municipal Workers	487,500	630,750	1,118,250
Public Employees	450,000	260,000	710,000
Engineering Workers	502,500	250,000	752,500
Mineworkers	86,250	207,000	293,250
Railwaymen	98,000	161,800	259,800
Communication Workers	134,738	158,120	292,858
Shopworkers	261,750	62,150	323,900

In the Labour Party camp, trade union contributions were not limited to payments to various organs of the Labour Party. The unions also campaigned directly on the Labour Party's behalf. For example, Trade Unionists for Labour produced its own campaign posters and leaflets, spending £202,000 for this purpose between April and June 1987. This sum, together with £45,000 spent on the administration of TUFL, was additional to the £3.8 million contributed by unions, through TUFL, to the Labour Head Office general election fund. Individual unions also produced anti-Conservative literature during the campaign.

Advertising in the week before polling by the London Strategic Policy Unit, a body connected with the London Borough of Camden, also appeared to bear a clearly anti-Conservative political message.

Anti-Labour propaganda also appeared. The Committee for a Free Britain sponsored national newspaper advertising attacking education under Labour-controlled education authorities in London.

It is difficult to monitor these fringe campaigning activities or to assess how much was spent by the various organisations involved. Moreover, it is not always simple to define the boundary line between 'political' and other forms of publicity. Some advertising avoided a direct appeal to vote for or against a party (probably for legal reasons) but nevertheless had an obviously partisan intent.

My preliminary impressions are, first, that the scale of independent advertising by pro-business groups seemed to be smaller than in some previous campaigns. For example, in 1964, a campaign in which Central Office spent more than in any other since the Second World War, there was also large scale anti-Labour advertising by companies threatened by Labour's proposals for nationalisation. According to a study by Richard Rose, the anti-nationalisation campaign cost £1.9 million, which is equivalent to no less than £15 million at June 1987 values. Nothing on this scale emerged in 1987. Consequently, if independent advertising is added to that of the political parties, far less was spent in 1987 than in 1964 by interests opposed to Labour.

Secondly, it would appear that the trade union movement was particularly well mobilised during 1987 and that independent spending on anti-Conservative literature and activities may have exceeded spending by anti-Labour groups.

Some comparisons

(1) The most striking feature of central Conservative and Labour funding in 1987 is the large sums which were spent. For Labour Head Office the campaign was, in real terms, a record equalled only by the cost of its effort before the 1964 election. For Conservative Central Office, 1987 was the most expensive for over twenty years and was probably the third most expensive in its history. Only 1935 and 1964 appear to have been more costly.

(2) The 1987 campaign confirmed an important new trend, started in 1983, in the timing of campaign expenditure. In the past – notably in 1963–4 – a high proportion of the central campaign budget was devoted to advertising in the months or even years preceding the announcement of the election date. This was partly because it was feared that national press advertising during the campaign period itself would be considered to violate the spending limits for parliamentary candidates set out in the Representation of the People Acts, and partly because it was felt that voters' allegiances were formed over the medium and long term, and not just during the actual campaign. However, the Liberal Party was not taken to court after it launched a £25,000 national press campaign during the February 1974 election. This opened the door for similar short-term advertising efforts, albeit on a far larger scale, by the two main parties. In 1983, both the Conservative and Labour

headquarters concentrated almost all their press advertising into the period between the announcement of the election date and the poll. The same happened in 1987. In 1983 Labour Head Office commissioned 27.25 pages of newspaper advertisements in the three weeks before the poll. In 1987, this rose to no less than 130 pages. In 1983, the Conservative placed a total of 67 pages, a figure far exceeded in 1987 when, as mentioned above, most national newspapers included three full pages of Conservative advertisements on each of the last four days of the election.

(3) At the centre, the ratio of Conservative:Labour:Alliance spending was approximately 12:6:3. This compares with a Conservative:Labour:Alliance ratio of 12:7:6 in 1983 and a Conservative:Labour:Liberal ratio of 12:7:1 in 1979. In other words, the Conservatives slightly increased their edge over Labour. The Alliance, whose central spending approached Labour's in 1983, fell well behind in 1987, although they still performed far better than the Liberals in 1979.

(4) Because of the weakness of its local organisations the Social Democratic party had to devote a much higher proportion of its central budget to grants to local candidates. On the other hand, the Conservatives, who spent less than 2 per cent of their budget on such grants, were able to devote the highest proportion of their budget to advertising.

(5) Central campaign spending was equivalent to about one-and-a-half year's routine spending for Conservative Central Office, and for the SDP; about a year for Labour; and about six months for the Liberals. (This calculation assumes that half the spending of the Alliance fund was attributable to the SDP and half to the Liberals). The Conservatives were more willing than in 1983 to concentrate spending on the campaign as opposed to the routine maintenance of their headquarters. In 1983, Conservative campaign spending was equivalent to only nine to ten months' routine spending.

(6) The Conservative concentration on the campaign also emerges from a comparison with the Labour Head Office. Whereas Central Office spent twice as much as Labour on the 1987 campaign, it outspent Labour by only 20 per cent in the preceding period of electoral peacetime (1984–6). The Conservative advantage over Labour in the 1987 campaign resulted partly from the Conservatives' greater willingness to risk incurring deficits and from their greater stress on election rather than routine spending.

Constituency campaign finances

Legal limits on spending by parliamentary candidates were raised in May 1987 in line with inflation by a Statutory Instrument, in accordance with the provisions of the Representation of the People Act. In the 1987 election candidates in county constituencies were permitted to spend £3,370 plus 3.8 pence per elector and candidates in borough seats were limited to £3,370 plus

2.9 pence per elector. This meant that the limit in most constituencies ranged between £5,000 and £6,000.

Official statistics for spending by parliamentary candidates have been analysed by David Butler and Dennis Kavanagh in their study of *The British General Election of 1987*.[1] Conservative candidates spent an average of £4,400 (a total of £2.8 million), Labour candidates £3,900 (a total of £2.5 million) and Alliance candidates £3,400 (a total of £2.15 million).

The ratio of spending by candidates of the three main parties was the same as in 1983. In all the parties' constituency campaign spending in 1987 was about 10 per cent higher in real terms than in 1983.

The value of subsidies in kind

The three main subsidies in kind are (1) free postage for candidates; (2) free hire of halls for candidates' election meetings; (3) free broadcasting time. Assuming that the first two remained the same in real terms as in 1979, and using the same method of calculation as given in my 'Financing the British general election of 1979'[2] local-level subsidies (free postage and free hire of halls) were worth £0.7 million to each party.

By far the most important subsidy in kind is the free allocation of time to the political parties on television and radio for party political broadcasts during electoral peacetime and, during campaigns, for party election broadcasts. For the first time the Alliance received in 1987 the same allocation as the two established parties. Conservative, Labour and Alliance all received five slots of up to ten minutes each on all television channels.

The dramatic use made by the Labour Party of its opening party election broadcast demonstrates the value of this facility. The allocation of equal time to the Alliance provided an important, free opportunity which could have been used to far greater effect.

The fact that television advertising rates increased far faster than inflation greatly increased the notional value of these free broadcasting facilities. In 1979, advertising on the Independent Television network cost about £40,000 a minute; by 1987 costs had quadrupled. In practice, the value to the party organisations of free broadcasting time is somewhat limited by the fact that it has to be taken in large slices of up to ten minutes each. I have therefore assumed for purposes of calculation that a ten-minute slot is equivalent in value to the parties of four minutes of commercial advertising. I have also assumed that the value of a broadcast on commercial television is equal to the value of free time on the BBC channels. On this basis, each party had free broadcasting time during the campaign worth £7 million. If the last four party political broadcasts before the campaign are also counted as pre-election subsidies, then the value of free broadcasting facilities rises to £12.5 million. These totals exclude the value of free time on radio.

Table 2.5. *Estimated total Conservative, Labour and Alliance campaign spending (including subsidies), 1987*

	Conservative	Labour	Alliance
	(in millions of pounds)		
Central campaign spending (excluding grants to parliamentary candidates)	8.9	3.8	1.0–1.2
Local spending including grants from central party organisations	2.8	2.5	2.2
Total (excluding subsidies in kind)	11.7	6.3	3.2–3.4
Estimated value of subsidies in kind	13.2	13.2	13.2
Total campaign costs (including subsidies in kind)	24.9	19.5	16.4–16.6
Votes received (in millions)	13.8	10.0	7.3
	(in pence per vote)		
Expenditure per vote (excluding subsidies in kind)	85p	63p	44–47p
Expenditure per vote (including subsidies in kind	180p	195p	225–227p

Summary

Table 2.5 gives a preliminary and approximate estimate of total spending in the 1987 campaign. It shows that the financial advantage enjoyed by the Conservatives was greatest at the level of central campaign spending. When local spending and the value of free television broadcasts and other subsidies in kind are included in the reckoning, the gap between the parties is seen to be considerably smaller.

Including subsidies in kind, the cost per vote was 180 pence for the Conservatives, 195 pence per vote for Labour and 225–227 pence per vote for the Alliance.

Did political spending affect the outcome?

While it is possible to analyse the impact of spending by parliamentary candidates on votes gained by relating amounts spent to votes obtained in different constituencies and by controlling for other factors, there appears to be no similar way of measuring the impact of spending by the national party organisations. Judgements must necessarily be unscientific.

It is easy to exaggerate the advantages gained by the Conservatives for their heavy spending. The main use to which the money was put was to purchase poster sites and newspaper advertisements on a scale Labour failed to match. The Conservatives were forbidden by law from purchasing radio or television time for paid advertising. On the other hand all the main parties received an agreed allocation of free broadcasting time. Since television is probably the most important medium of communication, the ban on paid advertising severely limited the uses to which the Conservatives could put their financial muscle. Moreover, the legal limitations on local spending restricted the scope for advertising on behalf of particular candidates.

Compared with all the other forms of communication which were not available for purchase, press advertisements and commercial hoardings were arguably of relatively limited importance. According to some observers the Conservatives' final media blitz achieved nothing other than to give a psychological reassurance to party officials. Post-election polls gave only limited support to the view that there was a significant swing to the Government in the last days of the campaign. Moreover, they indicated that few voters felt they had been influenced by press advertisements.

On the other hand, self-assessments by voters of the factors that influenced them can be unreliable. Even if the Conservative advertising blitz did not lead to a major last-minute swing to the Conservatives it may at least have performed the function of preventing the late swing against the governing party that has been a feature of past elections.

In my view, its advertising, although not decisive, was useful to the Conservative campaign. It enabled the party strongly to reinforce the messages, particularly about the Conservative economic record and the way Labour would threaten it, that were also being made during the final stages of the election in the party's press conferences and in Mrs Thatcher's speeches. If this assessment is correct, the election result was probably influenced by the financial superiority of Conservative Central Office.

Notes

1 David Butler and Dennis Kavanagh, *The British General Election of 1987* (London: Macmillan, 1988), p. 236.

2 In Howard Penniman (ed.), *Britain at the Polls, 1979* (Washington, DC: American Enterprise Institute, 1981), pp. 230–3.

3 Some updated statistics appear in the author's article on 'Trends in British party funding, 1983–1987', *Parliamentary Affairs*, 42, 1989, 197–212.

3   Ancient and modern: innovations in electioneering at the constituency level

Background

The centre of electoral gravity has shifted over time. Where once the individual constituencies and candidates were dominant in an election, it is now the national campaigns and party leaders that make the running. As Butler and Kavanagh proclaimed in 1974,

> Developments in the mass media, opinion polling and public relations have by-passed electioneering at the local level. They have been exploited by the national campaigners in a way that has undermined the constituency campaign. Party leaders are now able to communicate directly with voters via the mass media whereas in the 19th century they relied largely on the candidates in the constituencies to convey their message to the electorate.[1]

As a description of the trends in electioneering up to and including 1983, this is plausible enough. But some commentators seem to want to go further than this: they suggest that there is nothing more to be said on the matter, that constituency campaigning can do nothing now but wither further and die, and with unwarranted determinism they give the impression that the end of the story has been reached.

Changes in the nature of electioneering practice are driven to a large extent by the twin engines of law and technology, and at any stage in history what the parties do to win support has to happen within limits set by these factors. As it so happens, almost all of the most important changes affecting elections over the course of the last century, in both the legal and technological spheres, have tended to favour the development of the national campaign. However, this does not mean that future developments will continue to aid the nationalisation of politics, or work consistently toward any other historical end. Juro-technological factors have given the national campaigner greater campaigning scope than his constituency colleague, but it is quite possible that the balance between the national and local levels of campaigning might, to some extent, be redressed by future technological developments or by reform of the election law.[2]

Campaigners in an election can achieve two things: they can persuade and they can organise. National campaigns are wholly oriented toward persuasion, whereas local campaigns may contain elements of each. However, local campaigners' attempts to do these things in recent years have been neither efficient nor efficacious. Efforts to persuade are usually on an insignificant scale, haphazardly directed and ridiculously amateur. Attempts to organise the electorate suffer from corrupt and patchy data and chronic shortage of, mainly human, resources.

But for all their immense communicating power, the mass media are not without problems for the electioneer. Television, in particular, is in some respects a pretty blunt instrument: although it allows politicians nightly access to the majority of the nation's living rooms, they can do no other than say the same thing to everyone. The nature of the medium allows for no *differentiation* of message between one sort of voter and another. In theory, campaigners at the local level could do much to make up for this deficiency by tackling voters directly and in more personal terms. But constituency campaigning is often quite a nominal activity, and, in the main, the electorate is too large to be dealt with in such a sophisticated way. In practice only rather feeble efforts are generally managed. Occasionally, in the parties' key seats, one finds a well-organised and well-resourced campaign, which is planned and has clear objectives in view. Much more often, however, a constituency's campaign will amount to nothing more than a handful of enthusiasts performing a shadow of the traditional routines: the canvassing, the leafleting, and the public meetings.[3]

There is thus no lack of *scope* for a modernisation of electioneering in the constituencies, and it is in this context that the new campaign techniques employed in the general election of 1987 are potentially so significant. In particular, the introduction of computer technology to the constituency campaign is one of the first really positive developments for the best part of a century. In respect of both persuasion and organisation, the computer opens up many possibilities, some quite exciting, to the local electioneer, and as a result 1987 appears to have been a landmark year in the development of electioneering.

The possibilities

There is little in principle that computers can do in a campaign that could not be done manually, but they are significant in practice because of the speed and power of data manipulation that they give the campaigner; there are some things that have been done, but which the computer can do more efficiently, and other activities (perhaps involving sorting, which is easy for a computer) that were simply not practical before its arrival. A computer is no more than a tool, but it is a powerful and sophisticated one and can be put to many different uses. So far, computers have been used for routine constituency and membership management, internal party communications, the 'donkey-work' of electoral organisation, and campaign communication with the electorate using direct mail.

The 1987 election could mark the start of the rehabilitation of the constituency campaign in other respects too. While ever less seems to happen in seats that are safe for one or other of the parties, there appears to have been a divergence of trends between the pattern of campaigning in these seats, and in the marginals. Indeed, in some of the parties' key constituencies there was more campaigning, more canvasssing, and more money being spent than in other recent general elections. Ironically, the impetus for these stirrings in the hitherto cadaverous local campaign, and for constituency computerisation, came largely from the centre. The organisation departments at the parties' London headquarters encouraged constituency agents and activists to take a fresh, more business-like, approach to campaigning in their key seats.

Targeting was an important part of the parties' electoral strategies. Parties have always had target seats, but this often meant little in practical terms. In 1987, however, it involved direct, daily contact and advice from members of the parties' national or regional staff, special training and guidance before the election, and, in some cases, substantial financial grants. As well as the concentration of effort and resources on particular seats, resources can be aimed at individual voters within seats; by spreading their efforts unevenly it is possible for parties to give that extra bit of attention to their marginal supporters. Neither the targeting of constituencies nor the targeting of voters is a new idea, but practical problems, in the case of the latter, have prevented it being done on any scale. As we will see in more detail below, the new availability of cheap and powerful personal computers allowed campaigners in some constituencies in 1987 to focus special attention on particular voters.

Earliest applications

A few computers were used for constituency electioneering in the general election of 1983, but only by a small band of computer fanatics, for very limited purposes, and using a variety of home-produced software. The use of computers in constituency politics has grown rapidly since 1983, and it was mainly in the by-elections of the 1983–7 parliament that the parties' electoral applications of computer technology were tested, and where they were considerably developed. A computerised polling day effort was organised for part of the constituency by Tony Benn's son in the Chesterfield by-election. The real watershed, however, was the Brecon and Radnor by-election of 4 July

1985. The Labour Party again used computers on polling day, and the Liberals used their computers to send direct mail to special groups such as farmers. The farmers were extracted from the electoral register manually in Brecon and Radnor, but by the time of the West Derbyshire and Ryedale by-elections, in May 1986, they could be identified through the computer itself, by asking it to go through the electoral register picking out all addresses with the word 'farm' in them. Perhaps the most important use of computers in Brecon and Radnor was the printing of the Liberal Party's canvass cards. In many of the rural parts of the constituency the electoral register was organised in alphabetical order, but the Liberals' computer was able to sort the register on a geographical basis. The Conservative Party's computer journal, *Micro News*, attributed the Liberals' narrow victory over Labour to this factor.[4] After Brecon and Radnor, the Tyne Bridge, Fulham and Greenwich by-elections were all minor landmarks in the growth of computerised electioneering. In all of these, the ability of the computer to send local targeted direct mail was exploited, and the communications produced in this way became more and more sophisticated. The Fulham by-election in April 1986 marked Labour's entrance into the direct mail game, and after the Newcastle-under-Lyme by-election of July 1986, the Conservatives were also in on the act.

Because by-elections are national events as much as they are local ones, the national party organisations have inevitably had a central role in the development of computerised electioneering. At all by-elections since Brecon and Radnor the parties have had national computing staff in attendance. The party HQs have been important in the development and dissemination of election management software packages (such as Labour's Elpack or the Alliance's Polly) and as the general election approached they were energetic in sponsoring computerisation in their target seats. Computers can be complicated machines and new users often need a lot of guidance; the parties centrally have attempted to provide this, as well as providing services (such as the conversion of computer tapes) which local parties could not do for themselves. The computer departments of both the Conservative and Labour parties grew out of their need to service their national headquarters organisations in the late 1970s; campaign applications, and the task of advising local parties on computers, have been secondary and much more recent developments. The SDP's first use of computers was for the storing of its national membership records, and from late 1984 the party had a computer manager encouraging local parties in the use of new technology. The poorest of the four main parties, the Liberals, had no similar national officer advising on computers, but they have made good use of computer-literate volunteers. In all of the parties there have also been local activists pressing for computerisation. For people using computers in their professional lives, the campaign potential of the computer was obvious. The parties have all established user groups (such as MicroLib and Labour's CAG) which have often played important advisory roles.

Applications in 1987

Some press accounts during the election greatly exaggerated the role and significance of computers in 1987. Some gave the very misleading impression that they had become the norm. This is very far from the truth. Most constituencies did not use computers in a campaigning context at all, and the vast majority of those which did failed to exploit their full potential; indeed, in many instances they probably just got in the way. Nonetheless, responses to the Nuffield College post-election questionnaire indicate that most of the candidates who used computers were happy with them, and a number of candidates who did not use them in 1987 expressed an intention to use them next time.[5]

Replies to the Nuffield questionnaire suggest that something like a third of all constituency campaigns used a computer in some role or other, but that the pattern of use differed between the parties. Conservatives were most likely to mention constituency management applications (such as appeals letters to members); for Labour, electronic mail between Walworth Road and the constituencies was most often mentioned; and amongst Alliance campaigns which were computerised, targeted direct mail was the most common use. A computerised electoral register, as we shall see, is a prerequisite for the more sophisticated uses a computer can be put to in an election. The Conservatives claim that 'about 90' Conservative associations were computerised in this way,[6] Labour HQ says that it did '50–60' tape conversions for the use of local parties; and 'roughly 80' Alliance campaigns had tape conversions and the Polly program, breaking down 30/50 between the SDP and Liberals.[7]

The computerisation of local parties is not always done with the electorate as a whole in mind. The Conservatives, especially, have devoted considerable effort and substantial resources to persuading constituency associations to buy computers, primarily for local membership records. Their programme of computerisation suffered a temporary setback early in 1985 when the suppliers of their recommended hardware went bankrupt, but at the time of the 1987 election about half their associations were computerised in this way. They use computers to keep track of activists, chase up renewals, and make financial appeals to members, but all of these applications are very simple compared with the sort of systems that are used for electoral purposes, and the two classes of use are quite distinct. The other parties have only computerised in this way on an *ad hoc* basis. However, the Conservatives have generally a much larger constituency membership than the other parties, and they claim computerisation has made the management of local associations a great deal more efficient.

Computers can also be used to facilitate internal party communications. The Alliance parties used Telecom's Prestel service in 1983 to keep its target seats in touch with London, but in 1987 Labour made the running in this area. Indeed, for Labour this was probably the most important use they have made of computers so far. Target constituencies, national headquarters, and area offices were all linked by micro-computers tied into the telephone system by a device known as a modem. It was thus possible for them to keep in constant touch with one another, and 125 of Labour's 144 target constituencies, as well as a number of non-target seats, had the ability to send and receive electronic mail. In their efforts to coordinate the election nationally, Labour headquarters was able to send out messages either to individual seats or to all seats at once using Telecom Gold 'mailboxes' – sometimes at the rate of three a day. One computer executive compared it to being able to telephone every constituency with an urgent message simultaneously. Texts could be sent for speeches and leaflets, and candidates could be warned of problems, emergency issues and so on. Peter Mandelson has stressed the coordination of campaign messages – at every level and across every media – as being vitally important to modern electioneering. Electronic mail is certain to play a big role in this respect in the future.[8]

The computerised register

Most other applications of computers in elections involve storing data on voters. This can be done in an unsophisticated way; for instance, by setting up data-bases of a party's own supporters simply as they are identified in the canvass. But most often it means computerising the electoral register, either for whole constituencies or for geographical sub-groups. On occasions, this has been done manually. However, the availability of electoral registers on computer tape has greatly encouraged computerisation. Since the 1985 Representation of the People Act, local authorities have been obliged to supply political parties with this, for a regulated cost of about £100 per constituency. But the Act did not specify that councils have to provide tapes in any particular format, so the parties' computer departments have had to assist in the expensive and complicated business of converting the tapes into a form compatible with the hardware requirements of the constituencies.[9] After some early diversity, IBM compatible machines have emerged as standard in all of the parties, especially following the launch of the cheap Amstrad PC in 1986.

Once the electoral register has been stored on a campaigner's computer a variety of repetitive and clerical tasks can be done straight away. Even if this were all a computer could do, the savings to be gained in time and effort spent on routine organisational chores would still be a powerful incentive to computerise. Computers were used in some constituencies in 1987 for tasks such as the preparation of canvass cards, doing away with the traditional cutting and pasting of an electoral register, and allowing campaigners to choose precisely the sort of cards they wanted; some wanted lists with columns to be ticked, while others got the computer to print adhesive address lebels for each elector to be stuck on smaller, more detailed, one-per-elector cards. Computer-generated labels can also be used for addressing electoral communications; the automation of this job makes the management of the Post Office's freepost facility much less time consuming than in the past, as well as making the envelopes more legible than when handwritten by party workers. [10]

The mass media, as we noted above, do not allow campaigners to treat one sort of elector differently from another. Selectivity, by contrast, is the computer's greatest asset; at the touch of a button it can divide the electorate into all sorts of different target groups, and all sorts of invaluable lists can be compiled, according to any criterion that the parties have data for. Data have become as important as any other resource to the modern electioneer, for the more information that is held, the more specifically electors can be targeted. Among the sorts of information that the parties might wish to store on the computers alongside electors' names on the electoral register are: data relevant to the management of the campaign; political data gathered in the canvass and inputted nightly by volunteers; and personal data about electors, with which the parties can form a rough view about people's *likely* interests and concerns. The addition of any of these sorts of data make the computerised electoral register a very useful organisational tool indeed.

The computer makes the data manageable and manipulable, even with a mass electorate, in a way it has never been before, and allows the campaigner to do things that previously would not have been at all practical. Computers may be used for the production of campaign working documents such as delivery lists for target leaflets, transport lists for polling day, lists of a party's own firm supporters as possible poster sites, and, perhaps in the future, lists of voters for telephone 'call-backs' and knocking-up. Special canvass cards can also be produced, perhaps just containing the names of electors not yet called upon, or the names of wavering opponents for a second canvass. Adhesive labels can be printed on a selective basis too. Another organisational task a computer can do quickly and accurately, if it has the data, is to analyse a party's canvass returns, and in much more detail than could be achieved by manual effort.

Finally, with computerised canvass data, the chores associated with polling day can be considerably reduced. In particular, campaigners can use their computers for the printing of polling day knock-up sheets. This can either be done on the eve-of-poll to use in the traditional way described above, or as part of an on-line polling day operation. In the latter case, the electoral registration number of electors who have voted are fed directly into a computer, the computer marks these off against a list of known supporters, and lists are printed only of those who have not voted. When this is attempted, so far, shortages of hardware have usually meant it happening in just a part of a constituency and not the whole.

Direct mail

In terms of persuasive campaigning, too, the ability of the computer to utilise more sophisticated data is having a significant impact on campaign practice. The advent of the computer and targeted direct mail, as well as three-party politics, has caused a change in the sort of data the parties seek to collect. In some constituencies the parties have become a lot more sophisticated in their canvassing, and they ask their canvassers for more specific answers about electors' voting intentions than the traditional 'For', 'Against' and 'Doubtful'; sometimes they are asked to estimate the strength or weakness of electors' support for their chosen party. Once data about an elector's likely voting behaviour are stored on the computer, he or she can be concentrated on as a possible convert, argued with as a potential tactical voter, or dropped from any further effort as a no-hope case. As we have noted, personal details allow the parties to narrow down the electorate in other ways, in an attempt to approach people in relevant terms.[11] In 1987 there were constituencies where party workers were requested to record electors' sex, age, and type of housing. Targeting with this sort of data, in the future, will mean that the elderly can be told about the parties' plans for pensions, and young families about the policy on pre-school education, with no effort wasted talking to people about things they are probably not interested in.

Although direct mail has played a regular part in election campaigns in the United States at all levels of government since the late 1960s,[12] and commercial organisations such as Readers' Digest have used personalised packages to sell their products here for some considerable time, it is only very recently that the technique has been employed by political campaigners in Britain. In the United States, the term 'direct mail' is used almost exclusively for fund-raising communications – hard-hitting political letters, but always requesting a donation. In Britain, however, the term has come to be used by the parties in a more generic way, to refer to letters sent from a number of different sources and with a number of different intentions. Because it has been developed in Britain by the parties centrally, direct mail has also been used (outside the period of the official election campaign) as a fund-raising medium. But the parties also apply the term to a class of campaigning communications sent out within particular constituencies during election campaigns.

Local direct mail communications differ from more traditional election leaflets in three respects: they take the format of a letter, they are generally personalised, and they are often targeted. In all these respects they emulate the parties' national direct mail output. Although the purposes of national and local direct mail are different, the techniques share many similarities, and have grown up alongside one another in a process of constant cross-fertilisation. In the case of the Conservative Party, the national direct mail programme and the party's efforts to sponsor computerisation and direct mail at the local level are both controlled from within the same Central Office department. Like direct mail at the local level, national direct mail has only taken off on any scale since the 1983 election.

Before the 1987 election, the SDP and the Conservative Party planned to use national direct mail during the period of the election campaign as a *campaigning* medium, i.e., not just for the mailing of known supporters for fund-raising purposes, but also 'cold' mailings to electors in their target seats. On legal advice, however, they abandoned this latter plan. Like the Labour Party, the SDP only mailed electors already on their lists of supporters. The legal objection was that the cost of letters sent to electors in a particular constituency might reasonably be taken as promoting the election of the party's candidate, and should therefore count against the official limits imposed on the expenditure of parliamentary candidates. Unless the law is changed, national direct mail looks set to remain a fund-raising medium, and it is local direct mail that will become important for the purposes of campaign communications.

Cheap dot-matrix printers are quite satisfactory for adhesive labels and campaign working documents, but for letters to electors better quality is required. If the letter format is used at all, the final product should look like a letter. The local direct mail that the Labour Party produced in 1987 was likely to be a pre-printed letter with personalising details of electors' names and addresses added to it by the computer. The Alliance, on the other hand, invested large sums of money on high quality laser-printers, which combine computer technology with that of the photo-copier. These can produce very slick-looking personalised letters (printed completely every time) which look type-written. They are flexible enough to allow personalising details, such as the name of the elector's street or polling place, to be incorporated within the text of the letter.

The preparation of texts for direct mail letters can be a highly sophisticated business. The parties' national fund-raising appeals are produced by pro-fessional copy-writers and the central organisations have sent out draft model letters for the use of constituency direct mailers. The parties believe that the personalisation of direct mail communications is important: 'There is nothing so sweet as the sound of one's own name', says one manual produced by the SDP.[13] The recipient of a direct mail letter, signed by a national party leader, appears to have been selected by external authority to join a special group. 'People do not realise how automated it is, imagining that substantial effort has been invested in tracing and reaching them. Technology has become deceitfully adept at lending a personal gloss to a highly impersonal process.'[14]

Unlike national direct mail letters, which are sent through the post, constituency letters are delivered by hand by party volunteers, or are sometimes sent using the Post Office's free delivery service. Even without the cost of postage, direct mailing is not cheap. It is not the real costs that are the problem, so much as the artificial limits set on party spending by election law. Constituency associations which used direct mail on any scale in 1987 were almost certain to have been running very close to the legal limits. However, more than one constituency agent has confided that 'the beauty of direct mail (because it is targeted) is that you don't mail everyone, so it's almost impossible to prove how many letters have been sent'.

Conclusions

The technologies behind the scenes of television, which is the foremost tool of electioneering at the national level, continue to become more and more sophisticated. However, the growth in the medium's influence would seem to have topped-out. Legal rather than technological change (perhaps allowing paid advertising) is probably necessary for television to become more important in a British general election than it was in 1987. By contrast, there is no shortage of room for growth in campaigning at the constituency level. Computers certainly do not represent some vague and mystic panacea, and they are not going to transform constituency electioneering overnight. But they are likely to change the nature of elections at the local level in time – and some of their applications could be dramatic. Computers have already emerged as the new 'ideal' of efficient campaigning, and, whether they actually do any good or not, their use is bound to grow in the future.

However, the 'whether they do any good or not' qualification is far from being an idle one, for as yet there is no hard evidence (merely anecdotes) to suggest that they do. It is not wholly fanciful to believe that computer facilities could render a constituency electorate a more manageable campaigning unit than it has been since the extension of the franchise in 1918. Certainly, computers can 'cope' with the size of the electorate, and with 'talking to' people in more direct and meaningful terms. But as for winning extra votes and seats in elections, it is quite possible that computer technology will bring no net benefits at all.

But setting aside its campaign effects, the advent of computerised electioneering is interesting because the practitioners of politics clearly believe that they are going to make a difference and because vast resources and effort will be expended as a consequence of their beliefs. It is true that some electioneering practices may survive because of inertia, but innovations count as acts of will. It is significant that belief rather than proof that an activity or a technique does some good is usually enough to make party managers adopt it.[15] Computerisation is also interesting, and will happen more and more, because the sort of techniques and technologies a party employs says a lot about the sort of organisation it is. Parties will not generally wish to be identified with low-tech or old-fashioned methods, whereas hi-tech is glamorous and gives the appearance of efficiency.[16] Perhaps there is a feeling that the way parties campaign gives voters a glimpse of the way they would govern.

Notes

1 David Butler and Dennis Kavanagh, *The British General Election of February 1974* (London: Macmillan, 1974), p. 201.

2 Alterations in the legal framework of elections could work in any direction. The proposal to put a ceiling on national electioneering expenditure, analogous to the one imposed on constituency campaigns, has been argued for a considerable time.

3 Apart from the distribution of literature, it is the canvass that makes most demands on manpower in a constituency campaign, and it is the canvass that is its centrepiece. For both the persuasive and organisational aspects of the local campaign, the canvass is held to be of key importance by electioneers, but the primary rationale for canvassing is traditionally organisational, with canvass data collected in order to achieve the maximum turnout of a party's supporters on polling day. The details have altered, but the essence of the exercise as it is practised by all of the parties has remained unchanged for at least a hundred years: party workers visit electors at their homes and try to identify which are likely supporters and which likely opponents; a record is kept of who is voting on polling day, and any electors recorded as supporters who have not voted are 'knocked-up' and sent to vote. (See M. Ostrogorski, *Democracy and the Organisation of Political Parties* [London: Macmillan, 1902], pp. 458, 459.) In a perfect campaign every house would be visited and the likely voting behaviour of every elector recorded, but the reality falls far short of this. On the efficacy of canvassing, see my 'Doorstep electioneering in Britain: an exploration of the constituency canvass' in *Electoral Studies*, 7 (1988), 41–66.

4 'Di IT give Liberals Welsh win?', *Micro News*, Autumn 1985. See also, Riddell, 'A vote of support . . . ', *Financial Times*, 29 November 1985.

5 These questionnaires, which ask about various aspects of local campaigning as well as local perceptions of the national campaign, are sent to selected candidates by David Butler in the preparation of the Nuffield Election Studies. I am very grateful to Dr Butler for allowing me to use them.

6 Like Conservative agents, some of their computers were in places that had the money for them rather than where they would have been most useful. In the key electoral battleground of the West Midlands, the best example of a computerised campaign that their Regional Office could give was Burton, a constituency which had a Conservative majority of 11,647 in 1983.

7 These figures, along with much of the other information used in this essay, are derived from interviews with relevant staff at the parties' national headquarters.

8 See p. 53.

9 As well as converting computer tapes for constituencies to use locally, Labour Party headquarters used computer tapes for the printing of about 4.3 million address labels for other seats.

10 The new technology liberates some volunteers from humdrum office work for other tasks such as canvassing, but it makes other sorts of volunteer – the ubiquitous 'little old ladies' of British electioneering – redundant. As election management software becomes increasingly 'user friendly', computer whizz-kids will not be vital, but there will be a premium on helpers with key-board skills and common sense.

11 In by-elections, and for the purposes of national direct mail, there have also been experiments with geo-demographic data. Less specific than information about individuals, classifications of neighbourhoods nonetheless allow parties to tailor their campaigning to local needs. They could be useful, too, at the earliest stages of targeting, for making an assessment of which parts of a constituency are likely to be worth more detailed attention.

12 See Larry Sabato, *The Rise of Political Consultants: New Ways of Winning Elections* (New York: Basic Books, 1981), pp. 220–63.

13 *Campaigning in the 80s* (Social Democratic Party, 1985), p. 49.

14 Nicholas O'Shaugnessy and Gillian Peele, 'Money, mail and markets: reflections on direct mail in American politics', *Electoral Studies*, 4 (1985), 115–24.

15 See Richard Rose, *Influencing Voters: A Study of Campaign Rationality* (London: Faber & Faber, 1967), p. 216.

16 See the election poster reproduced on the inside front cover of David Marquand's biography *Ramsay MacDonald* (London: Jonathan Cape, 1977) for an interesting illustration of the way politicians like to be associated with new technology.

PART II

The 1987 campaign: the view from the parties

4 The Conservative campaign

In planning our campaign, like the other parties we had to maximise our strengths, minimise our weaknesses – and do the reverse to our opponents. But of course our strengths and weaknesses were very different from those of our opponents. In many cases they were mirror images. As a consequence our campaign started earlier and emphasised the past eight years in a way that was not open to the other parties. Mr Kinnock, for example, was the fourth Labour leader in four elections and he was trying to sell policies with at least a gloss if not a substance very different from those of Mr Foot, Mr Callaghan and Lord Wilson. We had a record on which to fight as well as proposals for the future.

So our election campaign began as soon as I entered Central Office. I came to one key decision, about which little has been written, very early on, and in advance of our opinion research. That research confirmed my intuitive view that in the eighth or ninth year of government the electorate might be tempted to respond to the old cry of 'time for a change'. I therefore concluded that we had to offer a policy of change and to strengthen our image of a radical government, managing change, knowing where it was going and what it was doing. Again our research showed that this was attractive to voters and confirmed my belief that we could gain at least respect and often support from people who did not entirely agree with our policies if they saw us as knowing our own minds, purposeful and on the move. That was not the image we presented when I became chairman in September 1985. I also concluded that we were more likely to lose support to the Alliance than to Labour, so our most likely hazard was a hung parliament in which Labour would take office in another Liberal–Labour deal of some kind.

Out of those conclusions was born the political campaign not just of the final four weeks but of the previous twenty months. On the organisational front, like Cecil Parkinson before me – and our opponents too – I carried out my audit of the constituencies in which the election would be lost or won. To select those constituencies we carried out a wider and deeper audit than had been made in the past, concerning not just majorities or shares of the poll, but assessments of social change and strengths or weaknesses of organisation and indeed candidates or members.

As is now widely known, *that* resulted in the categorisation of seats. Within the extremes of those we would win or lose only in a landslide of unprecedented dimensions, the classification centred upon those which we would have to carry to achieve a satisfactory working majority – a figure I took to be in excess of 50. Beyond that were the seats we were defending to maintain our 140 plus majority and those which we were seeking to gain – such as Ryedale, Fulham, Isle of Wight and Cambridge North East, for example. Each of those seats was then strengthened in terms of organisation and equipment to ensure that if the margins were narrow then we would have maximised our chances of carrying the day.

But that, of course, was only part of our organisational preparations – and organisation was only part of the overall scheme of things. The whole scheme was set out in what has become known as 'The War Book'. The details of the book were not all brought together until Christmas 1986 – some 15 months after I took over at Central Office and five or six months before the election. The details in 'The War Book' run to the names of the individuals employed within Central Office at that time, and others, including volunteers, who would be drafted in and assigned to tasks set out in the Book. More importantly, it sets out the strategy and tone of both the campaign and the run-up to it, and of course, the considerations to be taken into account in the timing of the election.

By Christmas 1986 – indeed, well before in my view – the possible election dates had selected themselves leaving a short list of spring, early summer or late autumn 1987 and spring or early summer 1988. The War Book set out all the known data, drew attention to the unknowns and reminded us that there might well be unknown unknowns. Let me illustrate what I mean. Bank Holidays, religious festivals and the like are known data. The trend of unemployment and inflation is reasonably predictable data, the monthly trade figures are unknown. But then, just suppose we had gone for polling day on 29 October – the stock market crash would have been a perfect example of an unknown unknown! In politics – just as in anything – it does no harm to be lucky. In my view the timing of an election is as important as the final campaign – and in '87 as in '83 we got it right.

But let me return to the political theme. After eight years in government we had to stand on our record. The opposition parties had to try to obliterate theirs. In September '85 we were lagging badly in the polls:

MORI: *Evening Standard, 30 September 1985*

Conservative	30
Labour	33
Alliance	35

Some vigorous defence of the government's policies in the late autumn helped put us in a better position by the turn of the year:

MORI: *December 1985*
Conservative 35
Labour 35
Alliance 28

However, Westland, Libya, Range Rover and Sunday trading hit the government where it hurt most.

I am convinced that a party suffers most, not when it confirms its negative image in the eyes of its detractors, but when it damages its positive image in the eyes of its admirers. Let me explain. The unpopularity of the Callaghan government amongst Conservative supporters was predictable. Its defeat was not because a Labour government is expected to be good at handling the economy, nor because it was split and squabbling. All that is expected. The strong suit of a Labour government should be its ability to get on with the unions and to deliver the 'caring issues', the NHS and all that. So the Winter of Discontent – the strikes, the closure of hospitals and schools – was more damaging to a Labour government than it would have been to a Conservative one.

Similarly, Conservative governments can, and did, ride out teachers' strikes, but the Westland affair and the other problems in early 1986 were doubly damaging because they disappointed the public expectation of unity and competence in Conservative governments. This was no surprise to us. But it did mean we had to work all the harder, so on my return from hospital in February 1986 we began to plan the political build up.

It had two parts: the attack on the opposition, and the rebuilding of confidence in the Government. I saw Labour and socialism as the prime enemy but the Alliance as most likely to weaken us enough to let Labour in so, whilst keeping up some brisk fire against Labour, we set out to hit the Alliance really hard. That needed some thought. Conservative-inclined voters were more likely to defect to Owen and the SDP than to Steel and the Liberals. The reverse was true for Labour voters. Clearly, our target had to be Steel and the Liberals and by discrediting them to discredit the Alliance.

Our Torquay Central Council in the spring of 1987 gave a platform for both the Prime Minister and me to deliver attacks on the Alliance and particularly the Liberals. We were criticised – but we were right. It may be of interest that the Prime Minister and I neither discussed nor coordinated our speeches. As she told a meeting of Conservative agents at the 1987 Party Conference in Blackpool we never did, because we had found that our speeches always dove-tailed and never clashed. On that occasion at Torquay perhaps the attacks seemed especially vigorous because we followed such similar lines.

From Torquay we moved on to my celebration of the 10th anniversary of the Liberal–Labour pact. Again this caused some raised eyebrows. Some critics said it was overkill – 'Labour not the Alliance is the enemy', said some. 'Don't draw attention to the Alliance', said others. Oddly enough, few people noticed, or realised the significance of, the tactic of concentrating the fire on the Liberals and Mr Steel, not the SDP and Dr Owen. The fact is that wobbly Tory voters were attracted by Dr Owen and the SDP far more than by Mr Steel and the Liberals. We therefore hit the Alliance by hitting at its weakest point – so far as our voters were concerned – and avoided giving offence by attacking Dr Owen, whom they thought to be rather a nice man.

Perhaps the most effective blow to the Alliance was the summer 1986 opinion poll of their candidates which revealed how deep were the policy differences between the Liberals and SDP – particularly, but not only, on defence. I believe that up until then most members of the Alliance believed the differences could be resolved. From then on, it became clear to the Alliance itself that the policy gap could not be bridged, only fudged.

The Alliance had a bad conference season while, superficially at least, Labour had a good one. But we had been at work to ensure that our 1986 conference would put the party and government into a position from which we could select our time for a successful final campaign between spring 1987 and summer 1988. With the theme of 'the next move forward', devised with the help of Saatchi & Saatchi, we gave to the conference a coherence which had not before been achieved. It satisfied the voters' appetite for change, and ours for continuity. It played to our strength by emphasising government and party unity, purposefulness and competence. It also projected the government's plans and actions through and beyond the forthcoming general election.

From then on we never looked back. As is well known, we had prepared a very advanced computer analysis of the local election results of May 1987. What is less well known is that we also had organised a remarkable system of reporting in not just results but also voting figures, so that by the early hours of Friday morning we had a clear picture of the national, regional and constituency swings which by Saturday was completed in great detail. That gave a central prediction of a general election majority of 97.

The Prime Minister did not agonise over her decision and we were not slow to move into the final stage of the campaign. Even such details as the arrangements for the issue of press passes, the organisation of helicopters and aircraft and the Prime Minister's 'battle bus' were complete. The latter I might say is a unique vehicle and fulfilled its purpose perfectly.

So much for preliminaries. By 9 May it was my firm view that we were on track to win, and that only a terrible error on our part could defeat us. We did not make any serious mistakes, and the opinion polls – Vincent Hanna and other rogue polls apart – remained rock solid. The Alliance did make serious tactical errors – and lost votes to Labour in the process. On the timing of our campaign, we made a deliberate decision to keep it as short as possible. It did not seem to us that an over-long campaign, as Labour and, more particularly, the Alliance, were planning, would be of any benefit whatsoever. Indeed, we thought the reverse was probably true. And besides there was still government business to complete.

We worked on the basis that our campaign should be a positive one on balance. We had something like a 60:40 or 70:30 positive/negative ratio in mind – to the extent that we could measure such things. We also took the view that, if at all possible, any potentially negative issues should be brought out early rather than late in the campaign. Unemployment, for example, was defused early on. Defence, a strong issue for us, we intended to play strongly in mid-campaign, with a strong finish on economy. And Nigel Lawson's sheer perseverance on the issues of the economy and on tax made sure that the initiative remained with us right to the end. Timing was important as in my view it took at least a week from raising the profile of the issue to seeing an effect in the published opinion polls.

From a presentational point of view, there was a feeling that more should have been made of the Prime Minister herself, who was undoubtedly one of our greatest assets.

However, there were severe restrictions placed on her tours by the demands of security. What is more, although the 'War Book' proposed that the programme of tours should have a clear theme, that intention was never carried out. However, in accordance with the plan we saved the Prime Minister's major impact through television and radio interviews for the last phase of the campaign for the best effect.

On the whole, the campaign went very much as we had planned and expected with two exceptions. First, the Alliance challenge never materialised, so we had no need to use the material we had ready to deal with that. Second, we decided to intensify our press advertising over the last week. We did so because, rightly or wrongly, we believed the Labour Party to be planning a major press campaign. Whether such a campaign would have been directly effective or not, there was no doubt in my mind that a heavy press advertising campaign would have demoralised our party workers. For us it was imperative that the Labour Party should not be seen to be leading us in press advertising in the final week. Interestingly enough, Cecil Parkinson cut press advertising in the final week of the 1983 campaign because we were riding high. That was a sensible decision but as you will know, whereas our poll exactly matched the opinion poll forecasts in 1987 it fell a couple of points short in 1983. Thus, the intensive press campaign may have made a significant difference.

Apart from a number of advertisements targeted against the Alliance, some negative, some positive, which never saw the light of day, we had some other advertisements – directed more at Labour – which were controversial to such a degree that I would have used them only if the contest looked close.

They remained firmly in the locker. At the end of the campaign we also had an extra PPB in the can – which was perhaps better than one of the ones we used. One other unusual feature of the campaign and the manifesto was that it made no attempt to appeal to particular interest groups. The manifesto did not have sections of promises to blacks, women, the old, the young and so on. It was an appeal to the nation as a whole, in terms of what united people rather than of what divided them. I do not think we lost by that tactic.

I have no doubt that by stressing the key issues of the economy and defence we won over many working-class voters who had voted Labour before 1979. We lost some support among middle-class public sector workers, but we had to accept that that was a risk inherent in the tactic of not singling out particular groups for special attention. The biggest weakness in our campaign was a lack of a Director of Communications. Cecil Parkinson had such a man. We could and should have done so. We did not and I had to fulfil the roles of Larry Whitty, Peter Mandelson and Bryan Gould. But perhaps the professionalism of Labour's campaign appealed more to advertising and political professionals than to my old friends, the man in the pub and his wife.

I said earlier that we did not make any serious mistakes during the campaign. I do not think the importance of that can be over-emphasised. We did present brand new targets to the other parties, because we set out radical new proposals in our manifesto, rather than dishing up something bland and uncontroversial and just sitting tight. And throughout the campaign I was rigorous about the accuracy of all the claims we made on our behalf and charges we made against the opposition. We went to great lengths to provide the sources of the quotes and policy statements which we used in our PPBs and our advertising. I only wish that the other parties had observed the same standards. But this is all water under the bridge now. So far as we were concerned, there was no need for a post mortem, no need to pick over the bones of the campaign, because there was no corpse in the first place.

But, as politicians always say, there is no cause for complacency. We will have many lessons to learn for the next time, not least that too many cooks can always spoil the broth – especially if some of them are intent on trying their own recipes without telling the chef. But the party has already begun the work for 1991 or 1992 because elections are more about four years than four weeks.

5 The Labour campaign

We entered the 1987 election with a rather bitter past to live down and heavy odds to overcome. We had spent four years, since 1983, under the shadow of the worst election results since 1931, having fought one of the worst led, most unprofessional campaigns of our history. Our position was complicated by the rise of the SDP/Liberal Alliance dividing the opposition but our view is that we emerged from the 1987 election a stronger and fitter party; indeed, as the principal contender for power. It was the vitality of Neil Kinnock's leadership, in our view, and the party's response to the new direction he set that were responsible for Labour's revival after 1983 and our re-emergence in 1987.

Immediate policy changes banished the incredible aspects of the 1983 manifesto. Neil Kinnock's overhaul of the central party machine created a new professionalism in the party and the expulsion of Militant ringleaders reassured voters that breaches of the constitution would not be tolerated, and that, indeed, the leadership was in control. On all three sides of the electoral triangle, policy, party and leadership, Labour's image experienced a huge jump.

The achievement by the end of 1986 was considerable indeed. In one month of that year – April – the success of the Fulham by-election, and the launch of the new-look Freedom and Fairness campaign, resulted in a 15-point jump in response to Gallup's proposition, 'Labour's got its act together and is strong again.' As the effects of Westland and the US air strike on Tripoli took their toll, Labour benefited in the polls. In the fourth quarter of 1986, following the conference launch of the party's new red rose corporate image, we gained a 40 per cent polling average.

In the first quarter of 1987, however, this performance crucially slipped for two fundamental reasons. One was the Conservatives' success in re-launching the government as a caring, united, economically successful administration. The other was, of course, the rekindling of the Labour negatives of defence and extremism.

The ground could not have been better laid for our opponents when our failure in the Greenwich by-election in February 1987 occurred, giving a classic illustration of the law of political unknowns. The by-election had been preceded by the Conservatives' offensive against Labour's so-called 'loony left', which was trumpeted by most newspapers and echoed by the broadcasters, or in the case of ITN actually kicked-off by *News at Ten* following one of Mr Tebbit's lurid speeches one autumn evening.

It was a trenchant campaign: despite our highly competent fight in Greenwich, we could not overcome the media portrayal of our candidate in the by-election. But if the result was bad its aftermath was disastrous. Most of the press and broadcasters competed to give the most shrill and sensational account of every foot we put wrong in March and April. For by then Fleet Street had decided a June election was on its way: every tea-room tiff, every difference over defence, black sections, every malevolent White House briefing was elevated so as to knock Labour down further. They were wretched months for us and however hard we tried to organise good publicity and a positive image, the polls showed we were entering the election campaign in a severely weakened state.

By now we had only the strength of our meticulously planned campaign to overcome some appalling perceptions of the party – 67 per cent saw us as too extreme, 73 per cent as split and divided, 55 per cent had little confidence in our economic competence. Worse still, the press was shaping up for a campaign in which the result would be a foregone conclusion and which would be fought around one issue alone: will Labour be pushed into third place; indeed, can Labour survive?

Initial polls seemed to confirm this as the basic question. We were placed behind the Alliance in the first week by May's Gallup and we averaged 28 per cent in the first three polls. Our campaign objectives were clear: we had already set our aim to become the largest single party and relegate the SDP and Liberals to a poor third place. Now, in the light of these polls, we had to mount a good, fast start to the campaign so as to put an end to the third place story. Then we could resume our campaign plan, which was to project the party's policy strengths and values, culminating in a powerful, 'preparing for government' challenge as the final theme of the campaign.

Given the inauspicious context of the election we owed our campaign success to the unprecedented degree of pre-planning devoted to it. It was this planning, rooted in the strength built up in the years after 1983, and in disciplined execution, that produced the campaign's unique quality.

Work began in earnest in 1985 with the establishment of a staff planning group which later became the Campaign Management Team. It was chaired by the shadow cabinet co-ordinator, Robin Cook, and then Bryan Gould, and this brought together Larry Whitty and his directors, and Charles Clarke and Patricia Hewitt from the Leader's office. Initially, the campaign team reported directly to Neil Kinnock. Then, from the end of 1986, it presented proposals to a Leader's Committee of Shadow Cabinet and NEC members and leading trade unionists, which advised on the direction and organisation of the campaign.

When the campaign proper began, the Leader's Committee became the formal campaign committee. The team had two tasks: firstly, to ensure that the leader and his colleagues had coherent proposals for the campaign's political strategy, based on comprehensive quantitative and qualitative research; and secondly, to establish an organisation which could manage the campaign professionally and efficiently.

As in previous campaigns, survey research was carried out for the party by MORI. Instead of starting only weeks before the election as in 1983, however, this work began immediately after the 1983 election itself. At the beginning of 1986 the survey programme was stepped-up with the establishment of a panel of voters who were questioned repeatedly over the next 12 months in order to detect shifts in voter attitudes. The panel survey was complemented by fast, omnibus polling and, a major new development for us, a substantial qualitative research programme in which strategic concepts and creative ideas were tested through small group discussions.

Qualitative research and development of a communications strategy and its creative execution were the responsibility of our own shadow communications agency. Eighteen months before the election, the agency brought together many of the most gifted planners, researchers and creative talents of several London advertising agencies on a voluntary basis.

In the first three months of 1987 intensive research and analysis confirmed our view that the government was most vulnerable to attack on what voters saw as the decline in their quality of life. Improved living standards for those in work did not compensate, our research indicated, for the decline in Britain's schools and hospitals, the growing divisions in the country, evidenced by record unemployment and greater poverty – pensions being of most concern – and the rise in crime. That finding was the basis for a communications strategy which attacked the government's economic performance on unemployment, its waste of resources and the state of the real economy as the basis for focussing on the social issues. It was a strategy designed to play to Labour's greatest strengths in a way which was most attractive to target voters, particularly those tempted to vote Liberal or SDP.

By the end of April, the communications strategy and the campaign line had been agreed with the Leader and his colleagues; creative work for print material and advertisements was substantially advanced, drafts finalised for a range of direct-mail letters, treatments for five Party Political Broadcasts had been agreed, and much of the filming started. Hugh Hudson had agreed the previous autumn to direct the leading party political broadcast featuring Neil Kinnock and was working on this with Colin Welland. By April, too, the campaign management team had established most of the organisational structure which we had begun to plan in 1986.

Central to the management team's work in 1986 and early 1987 was the campaign schedule. We knew that we could hope to stick to our communications strategy, avoid being drawn onto our opponents' ground and cope with the demands of the news media only if we had a backbone of ruthless planning to take us across the campaign and through each day. Well in advance of the election we agreed a theme for each day of a 28-day campaign, designed to carry our story forward to the final week. Throughout each day, the theme was to be carried by a press conference, campaign visits, photo opportunities and a selection of key speakers and subjects for the evening rally with, on occasion, publication of a leaflet and a party political broadcast. Locations for campaign visits by the Leader and other key spokespeople were carefully researched in advance to show Labour policies in action, while at the same time providing good interview opportunities, strong human interest and attractive, relevant pictures. An innovation was a series of Leader's question-time events where Neil Kinnock would meet an audience provided by a local school or community organisation, and deliberately not vetted for political affiliation. Once the basic campaign plan was approved it was converted into detailed schedules for the Leader and for over 40 other front-bench campaigners, ensuring that every media region of the country was visited by a prominent Labour campaigner on virtually every day of the campaign. Thus, press conferences in and outside London, campaign visits throughout the country, evening rallies in every major city, and major national and regional TV and radio interviews were integrated into one massive campaign plan.

Support staff were recruited and briefed for each senior campaigner. Never again would senior figures such as Denis Healey be expected, as they were in 1983, to drive themselves across the country in an unplanned scramble of visits and speeches. A separate women's campaign with support staff was established to ensure that in addition to the other programmes a woman campaigner would be in every region on every day of the campaign. A central campaigners' unit was established at Walworth Road to ensure that every form of national, regional and local media was integrated into this mammoth programme of visits. Thus the campaign plan we took into the election had three main legs to it: (1) the strategy by which we could concentrate on our key areas of strength, namely, jobs, health, education, crime and pensions; (2) the single-minded use of all communication elements, so as to create consistent presentation of the campaign; and (3) wholly disciplined implementation from the party Leader downwards.

It has been suggested that this plan produced a presidential campaign by Labour. It is certainly true that our research indicated that Neil Kinnock's qualities were, indeed, a major asset for the party but the idea of presidentialism was true only in the sense that he was the most effective exponent of the values and hope offered by Labour, and the media circus following each leader ensured that all the leaders' tours were the principal device for telling the story of the campaign. This was the case in the Hudson broadcast as much as anything else. It was not simply a biographical tract about Neil Kinnock; it was using him as the vehicle – in fact, as the device – for saying something about the Labour Party. We could not have predicted before the campaign that Neil Kinnock's evening speeches would have had such an impact and created such good television. The famous Llandudno speech undoubtedly turned the first week of the campaign in our favour. Such was its strength that its impact was still being felt four months later in the American presidential primaries as Senator Joe Biden discovered to his amazement. Indeed, for the remainder of the campaign, no matter what he did, the Kinnock ratings remained high.

Whilst the Leader's tour became the flagship of the election, it was not the sole key to the success of Labour's campaign. The chief feature was the coherence and discipline of the campaign day. Of course, our message would be diluted by the force of our opponents' communications (this competition between rival agenda-setting is at the heart of election campaigning) but, equally, this disciplined execution was essential in creating an image – a much-needed image in the case of the Labour Party – of a united party, fit to govern. It is a lesson, indeed, which applies not only in election time. But the other lesson of good campaigning is wherever possible to create genuine news stories. We managed to combine all the ingredients of good campaigning on a number of days, most memorably on 4 June, a week before polling day. Two months before, we had determined that this day would be one of those devoted to the National Health Service, and in our campaign plan it was simply dubbed 'Health Shock'. As the day drew near, we were undecided which illustration of the state of the NHS we would use at the morning news conference. Then the case of Mark Burgess, who had been waiting so long for a heart operation, was drawn to our attention. We made a quick decision to accept the Burgesses' offer to feature Mark's case. That morning Neil Kinnock visited nurses coming off duty at St Thomas's Hospital, creating news pictures for all the bulletins for the remainder of the day. We then linked Mark's case to the hospital waiting-list crisis at the morning news conference. The rest of the story we left to Mrs Thatcher and her memorably insensitive quote contrasting Mark's experience with her own insistence on seeing the doctor of her choice, when she wanted, on the day of her choosing. We immediately signalled this quote, following the press conference, to our candidates by Telecom Gold to use on every doorstep throughout the country, having already sent our information about the Burgess case and the general state of hospital waiting lists two days before. This facilitated effective constituency campaigning that day, and Mrs

Thatcher's quote also provided us with excellent advertising copy for the following Sunday's newspapers.

In the event, this campaign day crowned a favourable Gallup poll (rogue as it subsequently turned out), and Conservative Central Office spent a very wobbly Thursday.

Although this was a particularly successful day, it is important because it demonstrates the value of advance planning, good orchestration, quick decision-taking, and sound management, and it was a slight lapse in these essentials which, in hindsight, was responsible for our not fully maintaining momentum in the final week. We knew from analysis of earlier campaigns that a significant proportion of key voters would be making up their minds in the final week. From the outset Neil Kinnock had insisted that we plan for a fresh rocket launch on the weekend before polling, although we deliberately left the detailed decision-making until midway through the campaign. In the event, we agreed on a direct appeal to Alliance supporters to join Labour in an anti-Thatcher majority to get the Conservatives out. But our communications were too weak for that purpose, probably because we had not prepared the ground sufficiently and, like everyone else, we were perhaps feeling the pressure of the campaign by then.

So what should we say about the campaign in conclusion? Labour's brilliant campaign became the cliché of 1987 but it did not prevent the Conservatives being returned with a barely reduced majority. Detailed analysis in the four months following the election does not alter the basic judgement that Labour's 1987 election campaign was one of the most effective pieces of disciplined communication of modern British politics. Not only did the campaign enhance the standing of the Leader to an extent which no one could have predicted at the end of April, but the campaign itself became, according to our private polling, a significant reason for inclining to a Labour vote. In other words, the professionalism of the campaign and the enthusiasm which Neil Kinnock and his colleagues generated went a very long way to changing deeply ingrained perceptions of the Labour Party. But no four-week campaign can do everything. We were able to win the battle of the opposition but not dislodge the government. In particular, we could not overcome the advantages of timing exclusively enjoyed by the Conservatives and the campaign could not hope to reverse completely the problems which had their roots deep in the years before 1983 and of which the electorate were reminded in the first four months of 1987. So we won the campaign, yes, but it could not win the election for us, unfortunately.

6 The Alliance campaign

The general election campaign of 1987 was the most dispiriting experience of my political life, until the weekend that followed. There *were* good things about it: personal friendships, for example, and close working relationships between Liberals and Social Democrats at local and national level (though these did not extend to the leaders). But that is not enough. As I will show in this personal account of the campaign, politics is about rather more than being good chaps.

The Alliance Planning Group was formed in October 1986. It met at least once a week, and sometimes twice-weekly, during the pre-election period. As you might expect, it was chaired alternately by the two leaders, playing box and cox so no one was ever quite sure who was in charge. Although I was a member of this group, and shared responsibility for the pre-election planning, I did not take over the chair until the election was announced. I took the job because I was the only Liberal acceptable to David Owen whom David Steel was prepared to countenance – a unique qualification!

The problem I faced was lack of common ground between the Liberals and the SDP. The two parties had much less in common than they believed and far less than they claimed. This became apparent in the major split on defence in the autumn of 1986, just as our planning got under way. It became even more obvious during the course of the campaign itself. Lack of common ground explains why we ended up with a tedious manifesto, no money, competing leaders and unclear tactics. In turn these visible weaknesses reflected a deeper misconception at the heart of the Alliance concept. This was David Steel's strategy of using the SDP as a lever for detaching people from the Labour Party. But before I come to this fundamental flaw, I will describe the campaign symptoms.

The Alliance manifesto was one instance of the two-party problem. It was the least exciting, least stimulating, least credible document it has ever been my misfortune to campaign on. Liberal policy was never boring, neither was

SDP policy as enunciated by David Owen, yet the product displayed between the covers of the manifesto was a disgrace to any kind of political party whatsoever. If you read it, you have a damned hard job finding anything positive in it. Yet the moment we strayed from the manifesto we went into uncharted territory. I had accepted David Owen's invitation to join the Alliance Planning Group because I believed any campaign led by him would be intellectually exciting. And so it would have been. Unfortunately, whenever he tried to jazz the thing up a bit, to make it sound just a little more exciting, every Liberal in the land started to splutter down the telephone at me. Frankly, it is impossible to run a constructive, stimulating campaign if your manifesto is a compromise.

Looking at our market research in 1983 and before the 1987 campaign, I had concluded that the only way to solve the two-party problem was to make a virtue of necessity. We had to say that we were two parties not because we could not unite but because we did not choose to do so. We could easily become one, couldn't we? It was ever so simple: we agreed on everything and we loved each other dearly. No, we were going to remain separate, obstinately and intentionally, in order to drive a political message into the thick heads of the British electorate. The message was that government by two parties was more effective than by one. In support of our case we would reveal the hidden glories of multi-party government in foreign parts: France would be a telling example, Italy even more so.

The public knew better. Opinion polls may well show that people support proportional representation but these same polls show opposition to its inevitable consequence, coalition. Everything we did to test the concept of coalition showed that the electorate felt it was a recipe for weakness and indecision. In other words, fudge and mudge.

The only hope of selling our proposition was to launch a major campaign on constitutional change. We had to maintain that the reason Britain had not been successful was because our method of government was wrong. At any rate, a group of us within the Alliance came to that conclusion and we thought we had won the argument by persuading our leaders to major on the issue. We wrapped it up in the Great Reform Charter and launched the theme quite successfully at our first press conference. Constitutional change was our issue, nobody else had it and the polls showed it was the one area where the public recognised we had a unique contribution to make.

However, the idea that we should major on constitutional change began to dwindle immediately after that first conference. The trouble was that constitutional change emerged as a very low priority when electors were asked what made them vote one way or the other. The leaders were beset by opinion polls showing that the public wanted them to talk about the economy and social issues such as the health service and pensions. The whole issue of constitutional change disappeared and once it had gone it could not be resuscitated.

Finance was an important element of the two-party problem. There is no doubt that the Alliance campaign was an organisational shambles and that lack of central funding was one reason for this. I was a trustee of something called the 'Alliance Fund' which had been set up (long before my time) to solicit donations from industry. I suppose the original idea had been to steal Tory gold but we ended up with just a few droppings from the rich man's table. The fund never exceeded £85,000 at any one time. In the pre-election period we decided to spend all of that on the Barbican Rally and two supporting party political broadcasts. So when the general election campaign arrived we faced a very serious financial problem. Liberals and the SDP had their own budgets and expenditures; neither wanted to siphon the money off to support the campaign at the centre. We estimated we needed a minimum of £650,000 to run the central campaign; in round figures, we ended up with £150,000 plus £100,000 for party election broadcasts.

You cannot afford to look poor. I think we did look poor; in particular our party election broadcasts on television looked appalling. Confronted with the shortage of money, my advice to my colleagues was: 'Don't worry, we don't need to spend any money at all. It is perfectly possible to go into the BBC studios, use their facilities and get by with two talking heads. We'll make a virtue out of necessity by showing the voters we're not tied to the City.' Unfortunately we had just enough money to give some creative people the idea they could create something. They did; they created an absolute mess. At the very last minute we were offered large sums specifically for advertisements in the national press, none of which I really wanted. That injection was too late to be useful; it was largely wasted.

We tried to deal with the problem of two leaders by keeping them together at major events. Why did we do this? First let me explain why we told the leaders we were doing it. We said it was because they were so awfully good together. I am not sure whether they believed it but I think they did. The real reason for keeping them together was that we were stark staring terrified of what they would say if we allowed them to speak separately. We had seen this happen in 1983 when Roy Jenkins would be grabbed by a microphone in Aberdeen while David Steel was being interviewed in Penzance. The rest of the day would be spent on the telephone trying to sort out the differences which inevitably arise when you have two mobile press conferences continuing through the day. We concluded that the only way to overcome this problem was to lock the leaders together physically so that if they did disagree, they could sort out the problem themselves.

I had in fact lectured both leaders before the campaign about how to treat journalists, not that I thought it was necessary. I had said, 'journalists are not your friends. They are shits. Worse, they are professional shits: they are paid good money to be shits. So you must never, ever talk to them as though they are your lifelong buddies.' Not long after, David Steel said publicly how unfortunate it was that the leaders were locked together in television studios looking like Tweedledum and Tweedledee. I could not believe such an experienced politician had said this. When I talked to David on the telephone, he was profusely apologetic. I emphasised that we were sticking with the policy of keeping the leaders together. The next morning I discovered that on a broadcast later the same day he had said, 'Well, perhaps not Tweedledum and Tweedledee but we do look a bit like two garden gnomes.' If you want to give cartoonists a gift, this is the way to do it!

One consequence of keeping the leaders together was that they were set up to compete against each other. We spent two horrific Fridays trying to stop major weekend stories to the effect that the Alliance had only one leader. We ended up trying to silence the one in order that the other could appear to be in command as well. This is not a criticism of either. Both have very considerable talents. David Steel has shown he is a wonderful political fixer with a very good television manner and I have long believed David Owen to be the most exciting political prospect of my generation. Yet because the press inevitably alighted on the question of who was the real leader, we never succeeded in getting the leaders to complement each other. In fact each diminished the other during the course of the campaign. By the end, I was forced to admit to myself that I did not much want to be governed by either and the thought of being governed by both was too appalling for words.

Leaders of the third force in British politics have always had to face the questions: who are you for and who are you against? Under the first-past-the-post system the issue has always been conceived in terms of one versus t'other. Jo Grimond had the only answer; he invariably refused to choose between the devil and the deep blue sea. In 1987 either leader might have been able to handle this problem à la Grimond but two were hopeless. David Owen understood the need to win over Conservative voters; he felt strongly, and I believe correctly, that the Alliance should not give the impression it was part of a campaign to sink the Tories at any cost. David Steel's appeal, on the other hand, has an instinctively anti-Conservative, pro-Labour feel. So both leaders were constantly trying to correct the other's apparent emphasis on one side or the other. As a result the whole thing fell apart.

This problem reflected a deeper ambivalence within the Alliance. I suspect that under first-past-the-post there is only room for two-and-a-bit parties. If the object is for the bit to become one of the two, then one of the two must become the bit. In my view Labour must become the bit. I come from the Labour Party and I joined the Liberals because I believed socialism was in long-term decline. I felt there was a need for the non-socialist alternative which could take over on the left. Unfortunately neither leader had extended this argument and neither party had accepted it. For example, in winding up the Barbican Rally in January 1987, I had agreed with Mrs Thatcher's objective of burying socialism but said that we were going to do it by supplanting the Labour Party. Unfortunately David Owen had to spend the next day at the SDP Conference defending me against massive attacks from Social Democrats who said, 'You must tell Pardoe not to use "socialism" as a disparaging term.' I telephoned one of these critics, an elderly SDP peer, and asked him 'when did you last think of yourself as a socialist?' He replied, 'I still do.' So I must confess I did not know exactly where I stood in the political firmament; neither, crucially, did the Alliance.

This lack of strategic conviction showed in the campaign itself. In the first week we were badly side-tracked by a poll from Gallup which put Labour in third place. It was obviously a rogue but you know how it is – you grasp at straws. We said, 'Ah, we're back in second place. We don't have to worry about Labour any more; let's go after the Tories.' And that's when David Steel was lured into saying, 'We dismiss the Labour Party. They're not going to win. They've had it.'

Many people say that the campaign we fought was a lie. We did not think so at the time, but if it was a lie, the lie was born at that infamous dinner party back in the dim and distant past when Roy Jenkins came back from Europe and told David Steel that he was coming to Britain to re-enter politics and would like to join the Liberal Party. 'Oh, don't do anything foolish like that, Roy', said David, 'very few Labour MPs or activists will leave Labour for the Liberals. But if you start a new party and call it something else, you will be able to detach a lot of Labour politicians, and once detached you can all join us later. They'll have nowhere then to go anyway.' I think that was a lie, and it was the lie at the heart of the whole concept of the Alliance. That lie was the greatest single tragedy of my political life. It was a betrayal.

The major trend in British politics since the war has been the decline in the hold of the two major parties on the affections of the British electorate. Their combined share of the vote has gone down while the third force has gained strength. Until the 1987 election campaign I believed there was some kind of inevitability in that trend. I am no longer so sure.

PART III

The selling of the parties

7 Saatchi's and the 1987 election

We at Saatchi and Saatchi have ended our eight-year-old position as the advertising agency of the Conservative Party. During this time, we have helped the party fight three elections, and win three elections. And also during this time we have worked with four remarkable party chairmen – and one utterly remarkable party leader.

From the very beginning, we have supported Margaret Thatcher's vision of a renewed and vigorous Britain. We have supported it with all our talents, all our energies. While we have worked hard for Thatcher's Britain, it is also true that we have benefited greatly from it. When we were called in by the Conservatives in 1978, we were the sixth largest agency in Britain. We are now the largest in the world, and advertising is only part of our business. Our involvement in an increasing number of businesses makes it more and more difficult to play the part of a disinterested advertising adviser. Hence the parting of the ways.

When you read a newspaper account of something you have been involved in, you can choose to be surprised at how much seems right, or by how much seems wrong. What most of you know about the 1987 election is almost certainly based on what you have read in the newspapers, or in a book published on behalf of Tim Bell. In this chapter, I'd like to present a definitive account – by the people who were not on the fringes, but in the centre.

The starting point for this account is not, of course, the day the election was called. The starting point is 12 months earlier, when – as you may remember, with some surprise now – the Conservatives were in third place in the polls, behind Labour, behind even the Alliance. We, the agency, decided we had to know the reasons why. Accordingly, we commissioned a research study that led directly to the turn in the party's fortunes. The findings were only too clear. People felt that the government had lost its way and run out of steam. The victories over inflation and the trades union bosses were now taken for granted. With the lack of new battles to fight, the Prime Minister's combative virtues were being perceived as vices: her determination was perceived as stubbornness, her single-mindedness as inflexibility, and her strong will as an inability to listen.

It was these findings that I had to present to the Prime Minster at Chequers – not without some nervousness. But the message was listened to; the messenger, I am glad to say, was not shot – at least, not mortally – and our recommendations were accepted. Obviously, we said, there was no need for the Prime Minister to change. Indeed, she shouldn't ever. What was required were new targets for her phenomenal energies. The research had identified the current prinicipal areas of public concern: unemployment, the health service, education, law and order. We said that new goals had to be set within each of these – and the ways for achieving them be announced. This programme was to be placed in the context of what had already been achieved, as the proof that 'we do what we say'.

The launching pad for this new initiative was the October Conservative Conference. Our theme for the conference was, 'The next move forward'. We, the agency, were involved to an unprecedented degree in planning and staging the conference, designing the publicity material – and even in drafting the outlines for the ministers' speeches. The result was spectacular. Despite Labour's own successful conference at the same time, by the end of October we had bounced right up alongside Labour in the opinion polls, and by the end of the year we had opened up an eight-point lead.

We were in a position to deliver to the Prime Minister, as a Christmas present, a detailed campaign plan for a general election. She just had to name the day. We were ready when she was. The critical decision day became the local elections. Conservative voters did not disappoint the Prime Minister. They turned out to vote with enthusiasm, and gave us an even better result that we had hoped.

The election was on. But few people realise how much courage it required to call the election. Let me demonstrate this. Our lead was fragile. It was only six-months old – and a mere eight points. In both 1979 and 1983, our lead had slipped during the election – this time, even a small slip could mean a hung parliament. We could not afford for that to happen. Our objective was not just to win – but to win handsomely. Because although a great deal had been accomplished since 1979, some of the most radical work was still ahead – work that required another powerful mandate.

The second restraint flowed also from our narrow lead. We could not open the campaign with a heavy attack upon Labour. There were two good reasons for this. The first was the danger of the effects of an early attack wearing off before polling day, the second was that the attack could shift Labour voters to the Alliance – causing a bandwagon to start rolling that could then attract soft Tories. The danger was a hung parliament. And for this reason we were determined that the Alliance should stay ignored.

Our remaining difficulty was that we were seeking a third election victory, when the British public very seldom gives its governments even a second victory. It had been 13 years since Labour had last been elected. A quarter of the electorate was new since then. They were too young to remember how poor the last Labour government had been. The fear was that the country might welcome change to policies that seemed newer and fresher. But, as it transpired, it was the Conservatives' eight-year-old Government that provided the freshest, most radical manifesto.

Labour, with no new policies to offer, chose to offer the country a new, presidential-style prime minister, curiously styled – for a so-called egalitarian party – 'the Right Honourable' in every one of his PEBs. Certainly, Labour's first week offered plenty of fizz. And the media picked it up with enthusiasm. On 11 May the media had been presented with an election campaign in which the outcome was totally predictable. Kinnock had just returned from a disastrous visit to the States, his party's morale and standing was low, almost as low as the Alliance. That opening position was not one that the media could hope to whip up into a cliff-hanger that would sell newspapers and glue people to *News at Ten*. Then, on the Thursday evening, the film 'Kinnock' burst onto the screens. This gave the media what they wanted. If not a party, at least a candidate who could make the election interesting. The media hype did for Kinnock what it had done for the Alliance the election before. Labour moved forward in the polls – but totally, and only, at the Alliance's expense. With two strong contenders in the running, the Alliance fell through the gap between. They offered to be everything to everybody, and proved dramatically that they were thus interesting to no one.

At the end of the first week, we were facing several problems we had not faced in previous elections. The prime minister had had the courage to publish an extremely radical manifesto. This had caused some agitation amongst even Conservatives – particularly the proposals to provide new management for schools and council homes. But of course it was the right manifesto to publish. Margaret Thatcher was not going to hide what her government planned to do when re-elected. And the weeks that followed made clearer and clearer that we were the only party able to spell out exactly what we were going to do, and how we were going to achieve it. The second problem we faced was that the Alliance had now been given equal time with the two main parties. So for every minute we had, we had two minutes' worth of opposition. Until, of course, the Alliance decided to attack Labour – and then it worked the other way round.

These were the two new problems. But at least one problem had resolved itself. We now knew whom to attack, Labour, and how hard to go for them – with every gun blazing. We based this attack on Labour's three most vulnerable points: extremism, their inability to run the economy, and defence. Labour never recovered. The advance in the polls was stopped dead in

NOW WE'VE THE FASTEST GROWTH OF ANY MAJOR ECONOMY IN EUROPE.

CONSERVATIVE ☒

Figure 1.

its tracks. We kept our final attack to the end. Over £2m spent in the press in just one week hammered home our successes – and the fact that Labour would wreck them. The Prime Minister, who had been held back, dominated the media in the final week. In her own words, 'Always finish strong'. She did just that, as those who saw her, for example, with Robin Day on the Monday before election day, will always remember. The Labour fizz had gone flat. Whatever people had told the pollsters during the weeks before ('he's a nice man, I'll vote for him') went straight out of the window when they had to choose a government for the next five years.

The election period had had plenty of thrills and spills. The worst had been Nervous Thursday – when the Gallup poll showed a sudden and dramatic narrowing of the Conservative lead to just 4 per cent. The agency Young and Rubicam chose to involve themselves, telling Downing Street that their own research confirmed the Gallup result – namely that the Conservatives were losing support fast. But both the Gallup poll and Young and Rubicam's fancy research proved to be wildly inaccurate. New polls that very evening showed our lead was the same solid 10 per cent it had been all along. This significant fact, enough to totally demolish Young and Rubicam's contribution, was of course ignored in *The Times* account (13 June) in which Banks rings up Downing Street on the Monday to say excitedly, 'The changes we suggested are working, our research shows we are coming back up the polls.'

The Gallup poll, then, had been a rogue. Yet the flurry of nerves provoked by its sudden dip benefited our campaign – by doubling the Prime Minister's determination for a strong finish. It's worth mentioning another reason why the Gallup poll caused the ripples it did. Vincent Hanna on *Newsnight* had been publishing polls that suggested narrow leads for the Tories. After the election, the BBC admitted that these polls had been inaccurate – and poorly controlled. They did not mention Vincent Hanna but a *Times* leader discussing the BBC's report did:

> If parties are not changing voters' minds on particular issues, the next best they can hope for is to start a movement in their favour in the polls in the hope that this will start a 'band-wagon' effect and multiply. Lingering in the public mind must be the memory of Mr Vincent Hanna and *Newsnight* . . .

While we are on the thornier issues, I'd like to say something about the advertising the Conservatives ran, particularly because of what some accounts would like you to believe. Every single advertisement that ran was first seen and vetted by the Prime Minister. It was the Prime Minister who briefed us for what I can only describe as a very intense three hours before the election was even called. It was the Prime Minister who saw two presentations from us – the first presentation alone covered 80 different advertising pieces. She told us how she wanted the advertising revised, and it was she who chose the final

THE BASIC RATE OF INCOME TAX IS DOWN TO ITS LOWEST FOR NEARLY 50 YEARS.

Labour would put it up again.

**BRITAIN IS GREAT AGAIN. DON'T LET LABOUR WRECK IT.
VOTE CONSERVATIVE ☒**

Figure 2

LABOUR'S POLICY ON ARMS.

CONSERVATIVE ☒
THE NEXT MOVE FORWARD

Figure 3

30 pieces that were to become the deck of cards we would hold concealed in our hand – waiting for the right moment to play each as timing dictated.

I have referred already to how vital it was that our lead never slipped. Of course Nervous Thursday had its repercussions. The Prime Minister, not helped by an inflamed tooth, did become unsettled. She did consult advertising friends from the past. And it did have effect. It meant an instruction to alter the balance of the advertising we had planned for the last week, from being very aggressive, to being what is called 'positive'. Let me illustrate. Instead of an advertisement headlined, 'Every Labour government since the war has put inflation up', and supported with, 'Today Britain has the lowest inflation for twenty years. Keep Britain great, vote Conservative', we had to reverse the advertisement: 'Today Britain has the lowest inflation for twenty years' became the headline, and 'Every Labour Government since the war has increased inflation' became the body copy.

Which version is better? One could argue about it. What one cannot argue with is that the facts, whichever way round they are presented, were very telling. 'We succeed where Labour fail', or, 'Labour fail, but we succeed'. It does not matter which way round. Inflation, strikes, defence, take-home pay, home ownership . . . on vital subject after vital subject, the Conservatives held the strong cards. The final week proved to be a barnstorm, ending with the achievement of a 101-seat majority. The Conservative campaign, popularly condemned in the press, proved to be highly successful. And Labour's campaign, popularly praised, proved to be totally ineffective: Labour ended the campaign exactly where they had started: with 31 per cent of the votes, their second worst result in history.

What were Labour's mistakes? They chose to make their party the party of the 'have nots', ignoring the fact that, under the Conservatives, the number of 'haves' (on the basis of average income, home ownership, share ownership) had been greatly increased, whilst Labour's traditional bases (the working class, and union members) had dramatically decreased. Kinnock's picture of a Britain in penury, failure and misery was clearly not true – and lost him credibility. The tasteless attack on Thatcher, which reached its lowest point in the final week's broadcasting, proved counter-productive. The party that wanted to claim for itself care and compassion, proved to run on hatred and jealousy. It was not a pretty sight. Kinnock promised plenty – but was never able to explain how any of it would be, or even could be, achieved. He also pretended the militant left were under control – when clearly this was not the case. Worst of all, Kinnock wanted – and apparently even expected – the British to vote for a defence policy which was indefensible. Those were the tactical errors – obvious to everyone.

Kinnock himself, led on by the hype in his own party, the media, and the *Newsnight* polls, undoubtedly thought he had a chance of winning. But there were other people, running his campaign, who are far shrewder than he is.

They had their own secret agenda – which was to make sure that Labour came in second, well ahead of the Alliance and secondly, to secure Kinnock's position as party leader and with this, his chances for next time around.

In this they succeeded. It is ironic that it is Labour, not the Conservatives, who sold their product as if it were a soap-powder. Though may I add, with all the authority of an agency that has the world's largest detergent manufacturer as a client, that to describe their campaign as a soap-powder campaign is an insult to soap-powder advertising. Procter and Gamble insist that every one of their advertisements conveys a benefit to the consumer – and one that can be readily and visibly substantial. Labour's promotions failed on both these counts. The foam was there, but no cleaning power.

PHILIP GOULD, PETER HERD and CHRIS
POWELL

8 The Labour Party's campaign communications

It all started back in October 1985 when Peter Mandelson, Labour's newly-appointed director of campaign communications, commissioned Philip Gould to produce a blueprint for communications development. Work had, of course, gone on before then but Peter wanted a complete, comprehensive review of communications. Nearly all the recommendations which emerged from that audit were put into effect over the next two years but none was more important than the decision to initiate the shadow communications agency.

The basic core of the organisation was a management group. In 1986, this consisted of a dozen or so people meeting monthly. In 1987, it became a smaller group meeting weekly, and during the campaign itself the group met on a daily basis at 7.00 a.m. So it maintained a continuous core while narrowing its scope as the election approached.

The management group was supported by numerous sub-groups covering such areas as creative work, research, planning, design, broadcasting and print journalism. Here we were able to draw on the services of more than 200 people who offered to work for the party at no charge. Within the communications industry, Labour's support is strongest in research and planning – and this proved to be a key sub-group within the shadow communications agency.

One innovation in research and planning was the decision to set up a coordinated system of quantitative and qualitative research. As usual, quantitative research was handled by MORI. In addition, and of crucial importance, we conducted over 200 qualitative group discussions before and during the campaign, focussing on lapsed Labour voters. These discussions added a qualitative understanding to MORI's statistics. By the time of the election we had a highly organised system of overnight feedback in place. A network of qualitative researchers provided overnight information which was fed into the morning meeting of the management group and there translated into decisions which were implemented during the day.

One key finding from this qualitative research emerged well before the campaign. A majority of voters perceived the election as substantially more important than others they could recall. People felt that here was an election which was going to alter the quality and nature of life in this country over the next ten years. Now this rise in the political temperature may occur before any election but we think it was a real finding. For many people, the election meant a more highly-charged decision than they could remember making before.

We also found that people felt strongly about the social, caring issues. This was the area where Labour was strongest and the Conservatives most vulnerable. If we could tap into the intensity of popular emotion about social issues, that would lay the groundwork for success. An emotional campaign would identify us as the real opposition to the Conservatives, our primary objective being to gain the largest number of seats in the new parliament. Our feeling was that the best way to deal with the Alliance was to ignore them. If we could show *we* were the real opposition, the Alliance would become less relevant as the campaign progressed. And that is how it turned out.

That was the strategy; how did the advertising go about implementing it? Election advertising operates with very little time and money in a fast-moving political environment. This means three things:

1   Election advertising must concentrate on setting the agenda. Political advertising is too weak a tool to change people's minds. What it can do is influence what is on people's minds – and it is the political agenda which largely determines the election outcome. If our brand was 'caring', our product areas were jobs, health, education and pensions. This portfolio became the nitty-gritty of our campaign; it formed our agenda.

2   Election advertising must be single-minded. It must concentrate on hammering home the key quality of the 'brand'. There are other media and different ways of addressing the innumerable political considerations which arise during the course of the campaign. Our advertising concentrated solely on the social/emotional area. Consistency is a matter of tone of voice as well as content. Labour's advertising had wit and an element of looking like winners.

3   The advertising must be coordinated with other campaign features which are driving home the same message. The advertising must be tied in with press conferences, visits and speeches. The advertising must be used as a series of tactical jabs to sieze the agenda and come out on top on a day-by-day basis. Advertising is best at attacking the enemy rather than putting forward a considered viewpoint. Our theme was 'we care'; our advertising said the Conservatives did not.

Now we move on to a blow-by-blow account of how the campaign went for us:

Week 1: 11–17 May

Third place in the Gallup poll and only a few points clear of the Alliance in all the others. The Alliance, starting early, is looking good. In that first week, there appeared to be a real possibility that Labour would come third, and be displaced as the true alternative to the Conservatives. The qualitative research conducted that week was among the most pessimistic ever reported to the shadow communications agency. Voters saw the result as a foregone conclusion, with Labour at its lowest ebb and an Alliance upsurge likely. This was the point where one began to reconsider being a voluntary member of the Agency!

Then came Neil Kinnock's Llandudno speech. This was a vital turning-point because it showed that there was going to be a real fight. Although there was no effect in the polls at this stage, the speech gave enormous confidence to everyone involved in the campaign. It stirred up the 'sales force'.

Week 2: 18–24 May

This was the week when the manifestos were launched and the advertising began to happen. Our first advertisement was aimed as much at our supporters as anybody else. It was about letting everyone know that this time the Labour Party had got its act together.

This week also saw the famous advertisement based on Norman Tebbit's rash comment about unemployment.

The important point here is that for two days, the media coverage reflected our priority issue of employment. In contrast to the previous campaign, Labour rather than the Conservatives was dominating the daily agenda. We kept hammering away at the issue of jobs in our advertising and that constant jab, jab, jab helped the confidence of our supporters. We were presenting ourselves in a professional manner.

All in all, it was a successful week. The 'Kinnock' party election broadcast boosted the leader's ratings and we were able to push our caring theme by exploiting weaknesses in the Conservative manifesto. The press commented favourably on our campaign, the polls flipped up and people in our qualitative research were responding positively. We were creating an impression of unity, confidence and coherence.

Week 3: 25–31 May

This was the week the agenda moved away from us. We came under attack on defence from both the Conservatives and the Alliance. The 'Dad's Army' accusations were reinforced by the Conservatives with their best advertisement of the campaign (see p. 69). At the same time extremism in the

IF THE TORIES HAD A SOUL, THEY'D SELL IT.

THE COUNTRY'S CRYING OUT FOR CHANGE. VOTE LABOUR.

Figure 4

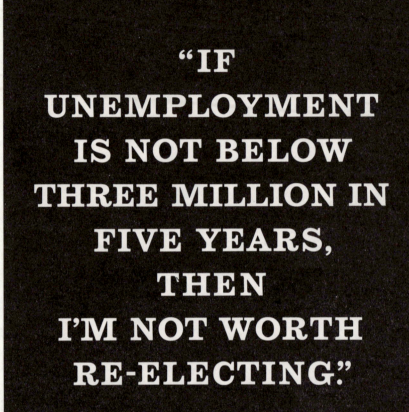

"IF UNEMPLOYMENT IS NOT BELOW THREE MILLION IN FIVE YEARS, THEN I'M NOT WORTH RE-ELECTING."

Norman Tebbit 1983

NO WONDER THEY'VE CALLED THE ELECTION A YEAR EARLY.

THE COUNTRY'S CRYING OUT FOR CHANGE. VOTE LABOUR.

Figure 5

THE TORIES SAY UNEMPLOYMENT IS FALLING. (IT MUST BE ELECTION TIME AGAIN.)

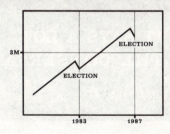

3M

ELECTION

ELECTION

1983   1987

Don't be taken in by Friday's drop in the jobless total. The Tories have been tampering with the figures.

Remember, they announced a similar fall before the 1983 election. And that didn't last long, did it?

THE COUNTRY'S CRYING OUT FOR CHANGE. VOTE LABOUR.

Figure 6

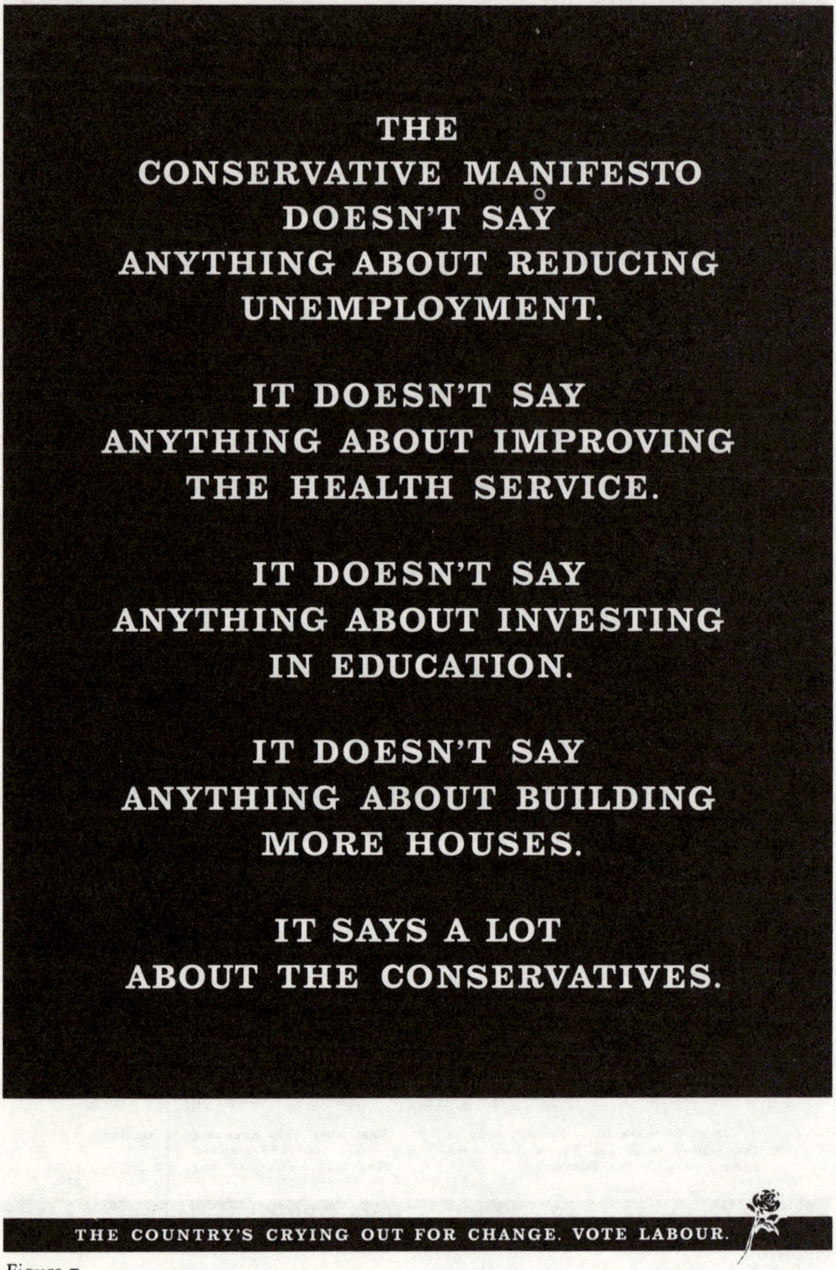

THE
CONSERVATIVE MANIFESTO
DOESN'T SAY
ANYTHING ABOUT REDUCING
UNEMPLOYMENT.

IT DOESN'T SAY
ANYTHING ABOUT IMPROVING
THE HEALTH SERVICE.

IT DOESN'T SAY
ANYTHING ABOUT INVESTING
IN EDUCATION.

IT DOESN'T SAY
ANYTHING ABOUT BUILDING
MORE HOUSES.

IT SAYS A LOT
ABOUT THE CONSERVATIVES.

THE COUNTRY'S CRYING OUT FOR CHANGE. VOTE LABOUR.

Figure 7

INVESTMENT AS PERCENTAGE OF GROSS DOMESTIC PRODUCT.		%
1	JAPAN	27.5
2	FINLAND	23.4
3	AUSTRIA	22.3
4	LUXEMBOURG	22.2
5	PORTUGAL	21.8
6	NORWAY	21.7
7	ICELAND	21.5
8	IRELAND	20.9
9	WEST GERMANY	19.5
10	SPAIN	19.1
11	SWEDEN	19.1
12	GREECE	19.0
13	FRANCE	18.9
14	DENMARK	18.8
15	NETHERLANDS	18.6
16	CANADA	18.6
17	UNITED STATES	18.6
18	TURKEY	18.5
19	ITALY	18.2
20	UNITED KINGDOM	17.2

IF A FOOTBALL TEAM PERFORMED THIS BADLY, WOULDN'T YOU GET RID OF THE MANAGER?

Since the Tories came to power, investment in industry has gone down by a fifth.

Manufacturing output is down by 5%.

And for the first time ever, we're actually importing more than we export.

The Tories are fond of saying that Britain should reclaim its rightful place in the world.

Yet how can we hold our own when our manufacturing industry is being systematically run down?

THE COUNTRY'S CRYING OUT FOR CHANGE. VOTE LABOUR.

Figure 8

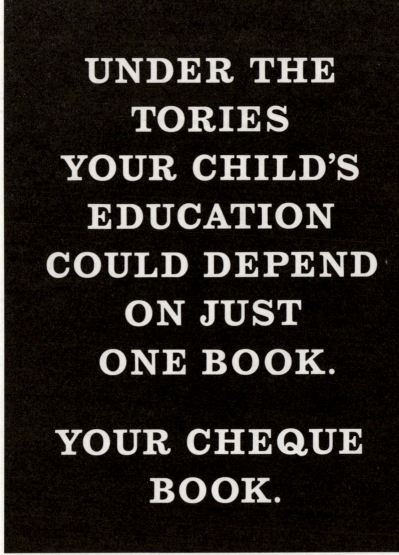

Figure 9

Table 8.1. *Evaluation of party communications in the campaign ('Which, if any, have made you more or less favourable to the . . . Party?')*

	% saying more favourable minus % saying less favourable		
	Labour Party	Conservative Party	Alliance
Party election broadcasts on TV	+8	−6	+4
Party election broadcasts on radio	+6	−6	−3
Political advertisements on billboards and hoardings	+1	−5	−3
Party political leaflets through the letterbox	+1	−3	−1

Source: MORI.

Labour Party emerged as an issue. We hit back with advertisements on education and economic policy. Neil Kinnock held his poll ratings well and the Alliance continued to falter. But our advance had been halted.

Week 4: 1–7 June

Now that the defence storm had blown over, we were able to put the Conservatives under real pressure on health. This led to Mrs Thatcher's gaffe over private treatment which we were able to exploit with an advertisement contrasting her position with Mark Burgess's. Our tactical jabs were beginning to pay off. Our pressure, plus a *Newsnight* poll pointing to a hung parliament, contributed to confusion in the Conservative campaign – Wobbly Thursday. The agenda had swung back our way; we were buoyant again.

Week 5: 8–11 June

The Conservatives fought back. The Venice Summit was a public relations success and the taxation row boiled up. It was exploited by the Conservatives in a massively expensive series of three- and four-page advertisements. We ran our own four-page block-buster two days before the election, based on the caring issues of health, education and pensions. And, finally, on election day itself, we ran an advertisement (in those papers which would accept it) saying, 'If You Are Thinking of Voting Conservative, Here's A Final Cheque List.'

Looking at the campaign as a whole, there is no doubt that we made a favourable impact on the voters, as table 8.1 shows.

800,000 PEOPLE ARE WAITING TO GO INTO HOSPITAL. THEY'RE BEING HELD UP BY THE PRIME MINISTER'S HEART PROBLEM.

The Conservative Party's cold-hearted policies are crippling the National Health Service.

221 hospitals have been shut down since they came to power, and spending on the rest has been cut by millions.

If this Government doesn't give a damn about the thousands of people waiting for operations, then the country urgently needs one that does.

THE COUNTRY'S CRYING OUT FOR LABOUR.

Figure 10

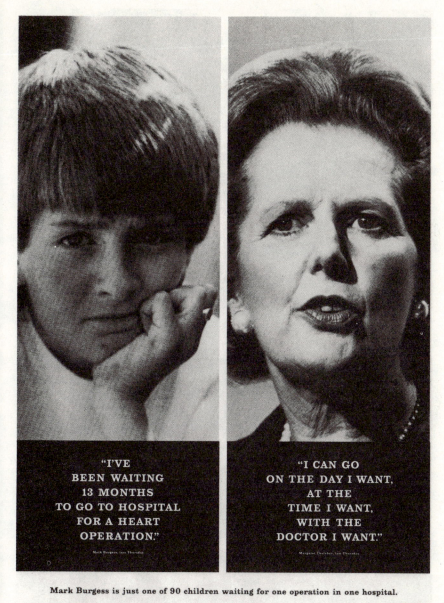

Figure 11

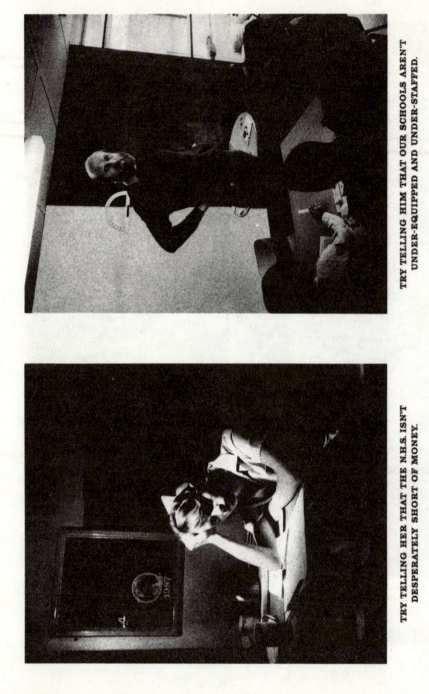

TRY TELLING HIM THAT OUR SCHOOLS AREN'T UNDER-EQUIPPED AND UNDER-STAFFED.

TRY TELLING HER THAT THE N.H.S. ISN'T DESPERATELY SHORT OF MONEY.

Figure 12

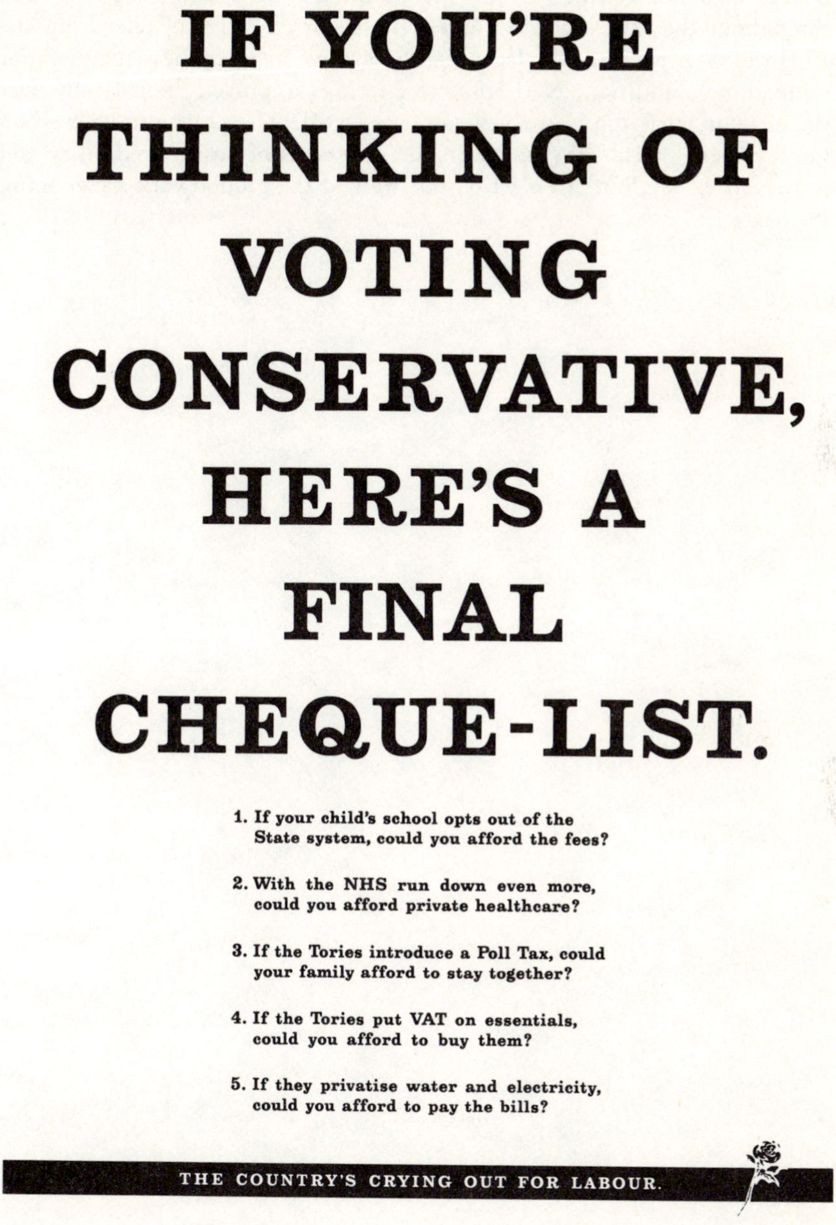

IF YOU'RE THINKING OF VOTING CONSERVATIVE, HERE'S A FINAL CHEQUE-LIST.

1. If your child's school opts out of the State system, could you afford the fees?

2. With the NHS run down even more, could you afford private healthcare?

3. If the Tories introduce a Poll Tax, could your family afford to stay together?

4. If the Tories put VAT on essentials, could you afford to buy them?

5. If they privatise water and electricity, could you afford to pay the bills?

THE COUNTRY'S CRYING OUT FOR LABOUR.

Figure 13

But we failed to cut into the Conservative vote which remained solid throughout the campaign. We did achieve our objective of relegating the Alliance to a poor third place; that was the crucial achievement of our campaign. In addition, Neil Kinnock's ratings improved dramatically over the election; that too was a key campaign goal. The polls also showed an improvement in Labour's image in the core areas of unity, credibility and competence. We lost this election but we laid the groundwork for winning the next.

9 The Alliance's non-advertising campaign

I have been asked to speak, I assume, because while the trait of a journalist is to separate the wheat from the chaff and give you the chaff, the trait of a politician, endearing or exasperating according to taste, is that they really like to believe their own propaganda. One of the abiding myths which they believe and propagate is their skill in communicating to the nation. It stems from the 'man of destiny' syndrome, best illustrated by Eamonn de Valera when he said 'when I want to know what the Irish people think I look into my own heart'. Yet, from the perspective of someone with access to, indeed bombarded by, the communications of nearly all the major industrial companies and the financial institutions, the efforts of the political parties are, I suggest, mediocre.

The minor reason why their communications are so poor compared with big companies today is that companies, certainly the efficient ones, the multi-nationals, are marketing-driven whereas the politicians, some more than others, are forced by their internal party requirements into futile gestures. This is perhaps less true of Labour now than of the Alliance, and certainly less true of the Conservatives than of Labour. Even so, few entrepreneurs would consent to work within the party-imposed constraints of any of them.

When I wrote speeches for the then prime minister, Jim Callaghan, in the 1979 campaign, the schedule imposed on us by the party machine was so geared to visiting constituencies rather than catching television that frequently we had to begin with the 'peroration' – I mean the newspoints – if we were to make television time at all. Only my saintly forbearance prevented me from starting a speech with the words 'and therefore in conclusion'. In that electoral episode the left – the hard left I suppose – controlled the National Executive Committee and would not, for example, release money, certainly not adequate money, for opinion polls. Eventually some unions paid for polling out of a quite separate budget – I hope that the excellent people who did the work were insulated from all that. But it was all hopelessly inadequate and hopelessly late in the day.

In the 1987 election, the Alliance, despite its reputation as a media play-thing, foisted on David Owen and David Steel the dreaded 'hydra' – the two-headed leadership popping up together all over the place as if they would topple over if they ventured out separately. If Sir Geoffrey Howe can be said to have negative charisma, then I suppose the negative apotheosis of the two-headed hydra came on regional television in Liverpool, where there was only one camera and so only the shoulders of the great men appeared on centre screen with their heads exiting left and right. After that, Owen and Steel did fewer joint interviews, certainly fewer regional ones. The organisational flaw in the Alliance's election planning was that far too much authority flowed in the preparation of the campaign to committees of politicians or more precisely power politicians who were not themselves standing for election, and not enough was left with the professionals. This is a standard gripe of professionals in all the parties in most campaigns, but I think it had more legitimacy in the case of the Alliance this time.

Why? I suppose the extent to which leaders put up with inefficiencies of this sort varies in direct relationship with their assessment of whether they are going to win or lose. If you feel confident you can tell the colleagues to cut out the nonsense; if you fear an inquest afterwards you may wish to diffuse responsibility and avoid making unnecessary enemies. This is less true again, I think, of the Conservatives, largely for historical reasons. They were a parliamentary party before they had to graft on an extra-parliamentary machine once the franchise was extended a hundred years ago, whereas the other parties have always allowed far more power to reside outside the party leadership and the House of Commons. Also foisted on the Alliance leadership was the requirement, an echo of Labour in 1979, for both leadeers to be physically present in just about every seat that on the most optimistic scenario could be judged marginal. I think we travelled about 12,000 miles in the Owen entourage. The Steel battle bus criss-crossed the country in much the same way. As an exercise in logistics it was very efficient. As an exercise in addressing the nation it put too much weight on the regional and local appearances and insufficient weight on the national media: a classic, old-fashioned, mistake.

But the Alliance's approach to communications in the election was put together by sophisticated people with decent motives. And if they are judged to have been in error in not seeking to insulate themselves from spontaneous interaction with the media and the public, and if the Conservatives and Labour were right to insulate themselves very ruthlessly, then some serious consequences follow.

Now let us turn to the major reason for the inefficient communication of the political parties. In three words, it is: lack of money. It is as simple as that.

Now, £10 million is big potatoes even for the Conservatives but a simple unit trust launch – one unit trust by one insurance company – will spend quite a lot more than that in a single month. For the best in research, presentation, advertising, PR – every aspect of marketing – one has to pay. A multi-national's marketing budget will be ten times that of the Conservatives over a five-year period (or less), twenty times that of Labour and fifty times that of the Alliance – and I am talking about a single company. Senior people, not in Saatchi's but in other companies, who have worked with the Conservatives on their accounts have said that it costs the companies money. They do it as a loss leader to raise their profile. Labour's problem is worse. And as for the Alliance, most of its election team worked for no pay (and we are worth twice as much as that, at least!).

When I used to think about communications in politics from a purely political perspective, I thought that in terms of relative resources the Conservatives versus Labour was the equivalent of tanks against the cavalry. Nowadays, I would compare companies with tanks, the Conservatives with the cavalry, Labour with the foot soldiers and the Alliance with infantry men with their legs tied together. Elections, unlike wars, are not contests and blunders so much as contests in degrees of being under-resourced. The participants imagine that by carrying around portable telephones they are in the star-wars league. In reality, they are in mouse-wars. Just like an old smoke-stack company the parties tend to be product-oriented rather than marketing-led. Labour is trapped in a declining market, which yet they chose to address in the election campaign. Maybe they were working out how to fight for second place so they thought they had lost before they began. The marketing director, Bryan Gould, suggested new products to attract the floating consumer, but got booed by the producers at their annual works' conference. The Alliance's great error was that by failing to segment its market it was everybody's second choice and not enough people's first choice. The Tories, I fear, only looked good because the other teams could not get their boots on.

The consequences of elections, however, are infinitely more important than selling one unit trust or car rather than another. If we get the democracy we have paid for, this really is not a triple-A democracy. But there is one factor, touched on earlier, which transforms in some respects the under-resourcing; and the politicians exploit it ruthlessly. It also lies at the heart of the difference between the Alliance approach, mistaken though it was in this election, and the other parties. To pay advertising rates for the time given free to politicians on television and radio would cost a large fortune. The parties regard television from their under-resourced standpoint as the great equalizer. Of course there are newspapers which have sweetheart relationships with them and give them uncritical coverage. The Conservatives have the lion's share of newspapers whose proprietors force them to address Mrs Thatcher from the genuflecting position. Labour has the *Daily Mirror* Group, and the list of national papers cheering for the Alliance is as follows: [silence]. But all the politicians recognise that television is what is crucial. Where I differ from the argument in the previous chapter is that we must look not only at the party election broadcasts but at all the television time that they command. Now both Labour and the Conservatives ruthlessly exploit the fact that each of them has aeons of time on television every day as of right, *regardless of news value* or even the truthfulness of what they choose to say. They realise that, given the enormous amount of time on news programmes and on features programmes (which need to be brought into one's calculations) one is dealing with very large amounts of time indeed. They realise that if they stop debating with each other or with the Alliance and if they stop making themselves available as far as possible to the public and to media questioning, then they would still receive the same amount of air-time, *regardless of news value*, because air-time is not determined during an election campaign on news value. So, by participating each day in only a severely limited number of highly artificial 'events' they can control to a considerable degree the perceptions of the voters who mistakenly imagine they are watching news rather than propaganda. Their mentors in this, of course, are President Reagan's 1984 election fixers.

By contrast the Alliance chose to hold genuine press conferences, genuine encounters with the electorate after the Alliance rallies (which were more like seminars) and a general accessibility to, and frankness with, the media. It did wonders for our souls but it was no good for our standing in the polls. The Labour and Conservative strategy of imposing their own agendas on the electorate via captive time during the campaign on television and radio, will be judged by both parties to have been sufficiently successful to make it worthwhile to attempt to advance still further the frontiers of manipulation. In this parliament, especially in the run-up to the next election, the pressure on the broadcasters will be very fierce. Some will resist, some will not. Given the importance of the advertising battle in supposed news and feature time, the main agency services are not shoving advertisements up on hoardings but preparing so that the right politicians are saying the right thing at the right time in the right way, on television and, to a lesser extent, on radio.

Finally, a brief checklist of some aspects of the Alliance's marketing, of which advertising is one part. First, unlike the others we did not represent (I suppose the past tense is realistic) large interest groups. We started from a smaller bedrock; we relied disproportionately on detachable voters from the other parties. Therefore, we had more volatile support and had to plan to hit a series of moving targets.

Secondly, our support was fairly level throughout the country. That is another handicap in a 'first-past-the-post' system. Thirdly, six years was not a long time to build up political name-awareness or brand loyalty among people, at least those who are lukewarm about politics. Fourthly, having few

MPs and no newspaper magnate cheering for us gave us relatively little media exposure before the campaign. Fifthly, lack of money meant our resources were so severely stretched that in spite of formidable personal efforts by such people as David Abbott, John Cleese and Sarah Horack, to talk of an Alliance advertising campaign is to mislead. We fired scattered shots; like the Mujaheddin, we staged guerrilla raids from the hills.

Sixth, the famous 'hydra' itself was a problem, not because we had two leaders but because it reflected an unresolved contradiction. Were we two parties in partnership or were we virtually one party? This helped lead on to the great marketing failure of the Alliance. Were we to position ourselves as a left-of-centre, anti-Thatcherite party? Or as a social-market party disagreeing with the Conservatives in detail over social justice but disagreeing with Labour in principle over socialism versus the market? Or were we to float down the middle as a bit of this and a bit of that? Because we failed to make this admittedly immensely difficult choice, we failed to target a market narrow enough to be winnable. Instead we were everybody's second choice.

My checklist of problems pinpoints here how hard it is for a third brand in politics to establish a niche in what is a two-brand market in a two-brand system. Yet, in two general elections within five or six years of its founding, the Alliance built up its support to around a quarter of the electorate. By contrast, even with a charismatic leader, an intelligent campaign and a consigning of its extremist personalities and policies to the attic like the first Mrs Rochester, Labour was unable to win back many of its lost votes from us. And while we failed to lay a glove on the Conservatives this time, it was the last North Sea oil election. Next time, they will not have this once-in-a-century free gift to bolster their economic record. If the Alliance had stayed in play, enough Conservative voters might easily have come our way next time if, as is very likely, the economy is more rocky. Yet, in a brief madness after the election, the Alliance, I believe, committed casual suicide. It is irrelevant whose finger was on the trigger. Suffice to conclude with the fact that Alliance supporters all over the country are now scouring the medical books in the hope of finding evidence of the medical condition known as 'temporary rigor mortis'.

PART IV

The performance of the media in the 1987 campaign

10 The national press

The national newspapers got the election result that most of them wanted and many had used every trick of journalism to achieve – a resounding Thatcher victory. Twelve of the daily and Sunday papers supported the Conservatives, five endorsed Labour (three of them owned by Robert Maxwell), and one – *Today* – the Alliance. *The Independent*, in its first general election, refused to endorse any party. *The Observer* defied all categorisation by opting for 'a Thatcherless Conservative party, supported by the Alliance'.

What this demonstrated was that the more things change, the more they stay the same. The three Express Group newspapers, the two *Telegraphs* and the three Mirror Group newspapers each had a different owner from 1983 (respectively, Lord Stevens, the Canadian Conrad Black and Maxwell). There were also three newly-created newspapers (four in London with Maxwell's short-lived *London Daily News*). Yet there was no significant difference in the political preferences of Fleet Street in 1987 compared with 1983. Judged by circulation, 67 per cent of Fleet Street voted for the Tories, a few points lower than the all-time high of 75 per cent in 1983, but well up on the average of just over 50 per cent of the eight post-war elections to 1970.

There was one intriguing paradox; all the new newspapers were the beneficiaries of the comprehensive Thatcher union reforms introduced since 1979. They were able to raise capital to enter the market at a fraction of the costs associated with the past only because of those reforms. Indeed the most plaintive comment of the election came from *The Independent*, which pointed out in one leading article that it would never have raised the money for its creation but for Mrs Thatcher, adding in its fastidious style that it would be loath to see Mr Kinnock, as he was promising, turn the clock back.

Yet none of the new papers supported the Conservatives, suggesting that Mrs Thatcher has enabled the new papers of the 1980s to flourish – and then oppose her. Two, *The Independent* and *Sunday Sport*, supported no party, although one could detect in *The Independent* a predilection for an Owenite social market philosophy, while *Sunday Sport*, a soft-porn all-colour comic for which politics is not a preoccupation, published an Alliance statement from its owner and a Tory one from its editor. *Today* and *Sunday Today* (until its short life was ended midway through the election) were the only outright supporters of the Alliance, while *News on Sunday*, struggling to survive after a difficult launch, was an even more committed supporter of Labour than the *Mirror* papers.

Critics of the concentration of ownership of British newspapers, 11 of which are now owned by three proprietors, Murdoch, Maxwell and Stevens, had hoped that the creation of new papers would add diversity to the range of political opinion in the British press. At least in 1987, that was true: none of the three new nationals endorsed the Tories and the new *London Daily News* supported Labour. Yet each of the new papers had achieved only small circulations, which meant that the overwhelming bias towards the Conservatives was hardly dented. However, at least voters could shop around for different sets of views.

As ever, two very different elections were 'fought' in the national press. On the one hand, there were the serious quality papers, *The Financial Times, The Times, The Guardian, The Independent* and *The Daily Telegraph*, whose reporting was thorough, analytical, by and large fair to all sides, and which published opinions and comment from all sides. Coverage ranged from some 500,000 words in the *Telegraph* to nearly 750,000 in *The Guardian* and *The Times*. What was most notable at this end of the newspaper world was the lukewarm endorsement of the Tories by *The Financial Times* (four out of five of whose readers voted Conservative) and which obviously tried hard to find merit in the Alliance's policies; the more liberal Conservatism of the two *Telegraphs* under new editors; and *The Guardian*'s support for Labour instead of the Alliance. It was *The Sunday Times* which first suggested that David Owen might become the Enoch Powell of the 1980s and Peregrine Worsthorne in *The Sunday Telegraph* who warned the Tories against the danger of 'bourgeois triumphalism', a phrase that has now entered the political coinage. At least, however, three of the 'heavies' – *The Guardian, The Financial Times* and *The Observer* – kept us waiting for their final endorsement, and each when it came was a surprise. There was, however, one area where standards among the serious papers deteriorated. In the past, all the 'heavies' usually published the party manifestos in full, an invaluable service expected by the readers of 'papers of record'. At this election, only *The Financial Times* published all three manifestos in full – an expensive total of 1,200 column inches, compared with 220 in the *Telegraph* and 147 in *The Times*.

At the other end of the market were the tabloids which always fight a propaganda war for the party they support. What they publish is bigoted, biassed, and often vicious – but even the party professionals admit that it is brilliant and telling popular journalism. Among the tabloids, there are two approaches. The *Mirror, Star* and to a lesser extent *The Sun* worry that their readers are bored by politics and play down election news until voting day approaches. The *Mail* and the *Express* fight wholeheartedly for a Tory victory from the start of the campaign.

The inner struggle between boredom and desperation to secure the desired result was seen at its most tortuous in *The Star* and the *Mirror* and the four Sunday papers which managed to survive the election without once mentioning a poll on the front page. *The Star* led its front page on the election on only three occasions in 22 days, compared with 19 in the *Mirror* and 11 in *The Sun*. Against that, the *Mail* led on the election on 15 days, compared with *The Times* and *Telegraph* (16), the *Express* and *The Guardian* (18), and *The Independent* (19). The *Sun, Mirror* and *Star* had significantly fewer column inches on the election than the other tabloids. Among the serious papers, the *Telegraph* devoted the least space on its front page and the fewest column inches to the election.[1]

Within its tabloid format, the *Mail* was the most political of all the papers, devoting 63 per cent of its front pages to election news, with *The Financial Times* the least political at 17 per cent. Among the serious papers, the *Telegraph* devoted significantly fewer column inches to the election than its rivals, most of whom gave nearly half the front page. This also demonstrated to the satisfaction of Robert Worcester, chairman of MORI, that front pages were not dominated by opinion polls. Polls were nevertheless the lead story on front pages on 24 occasions (tables 10.1 and 10.2).

As the day-by-day propaganda of the tabloids unfolded, it was tempting to think that the bias is so obvious, so blatant, that it cannot – ought not to – have any effect. Every headline, every comment, every cartoon, every front page is devoted to exploiting the alleged weaknesses of Labour (with the exception of the *Mirror* which uses the same tricks against the Tories). If it was not Red Ken (Livingstone) or black candidates such as Linda Bellos or Bernie Grant, it was robber baron trade unions or Labour threats of higher taxation and a defenceless Britain. There were also several unpleasant personal attacks. David Steel, Roy Hattersley, a Labour official and Mrs Thatcher were each the subject of damaging smears.

What appears on the front pages may not be news, it may not be fair, but it has one more important effect. Although newspapers have now given way to television as overwhelmingly the main medium of news, debate and opinion (too much so, if some polls are to be believed), it is newspapers that create the issues as much as the parties, newspapers which define the daily agenda for the party press conferences and radio and television phone-ins, newspapers which legitimise the questions that the broadcasters, bound by strict obligations of impartiality, are set free to explore.

Even before the election was declared, Labour's attempts to create a new, more rosy image for itself had been mortally wounded by its sensational defeat

Table 10.1. *National daily newspaper coverage of polls, politics and everything else, 1987 general election campaign*

Newspaper	Polls		Politics		Other		Total	
	Space	%	Space	%	Space	%	Space	%
Qualities								
Times	609	5.6	4003	37.1	6188	57.3	10800	100
Guardian	746	6.9	3693	34.2	6361	58.9	10800	100
Telegraph	581	5.4	2833	26.2	7386	68.4	10800	100
Financial Times	370	3.6	1331	12.8	8699	83.6	10400	100
Independent	590	5.5	3695	34.2	6515	60.3	10800	100
Total/average	2896	5.4	15555	29.0	35149	65.6	53600	100
Pops								
Today	164	4.2	1602	41.1	2134	54.7	3900	100
Daily Express	596	11.9	2372	47.2	2054	40.9	5022	100
Daily Mail	256	6.8	2129	56.3	1395	36.9	3780	100
Daily Mirror	58	1.3	1178	25.5	3381	73.2	4617	100
The Sun	172	3.7	1202	26.0	3243	70.2	4617	100
The Star	128	2.7	927	19.5	3697	77.8	4752	100
Total/average	1374	5.1	9410	35.3	15904	59.6	26688	100
Total/average qualities and pops	4270	5.3	24965	31.1	51053	63.6	80288	100

Note: space in column inches.
Source: MORI.

Table 10.2. *Sunday newspaper coverage of polls, politics and everything else, 1987 general election campaign*

Newspaper	Polls		Politics		Other		Total	
	Space	%	Space	%	Space	%	Space	%
Sunday Times	208	13.0	602	37.6	790	49.4	1600	100
Observer	330	20.6	528	33.0	742	46.4	1600	100
Sunday Telegraph	154	9.6	586	36.6	860	53.8	1600	100
Sunday Express	123	7.7	401	25.1	1076	67.3	1600	100
News of the World	0	0.0	146	26.1	414	73.9	560	100
Mail on Sunday	0	0.0	197	36.5	343	63.5	540	100
Sunday Mirror	0	0.0	100	14.6	584	85.4	684	100
News on Sunday	111	21.1	285	54.3	129	24.6	525	100
People	0	0.0	363	49.9	365	50.1	728	100
Sunday Today	0	0.0	121	23.2	401	76.8	522	100
Total	815	10.0	2560	31.3	4809	58.8	8184	100

Note: space in column inches.
Source: MORI.

by the Alliance at the Greenwich by-election on 26 February. That set off an inquest on the reasons for Labour's defeat. That was followed by another major row over the selection of black candidates which ended in the de-selection of Sharon Atkin. All this had been reported and analysed in gory detail and had undermined morale in the party and created precisely the image that Kinnock had tried to kill: Labour was reverting to type. But more banana skins were waiting.

The first slid almost unnoticed under Labour at breakfast on a Sunday and became the first of at least three major issues where newspapers projected stories that the broadcasters went on to exploit and which then exploded into big election debates. None helped Labour.

1   *Frost on Sunday* is broadcast on ITV at 8.30 am when most of the nation is still asleep and is not usually a programme that excites news editors. Nor did it on 24 May in most of Fleet Street, when Frost was interviewing Neil Kinnock and questioning him closely on whether he would send British conventional forces into battle in Europe against an enemy armed with nuclear weapons. Kinnock dismissed the idea that the British army fighting in Europe could be defended by nuclear weapons on the argument that the weapons would kill as many British as Soviet troops. Frost then asked if the choice would be between an unfair battle or surrender. Kinnock appeared to agree (as the *Telegraph* reported), that the alternatives were between the 'gesture, the threat, or the use of their nuclear weapons, or surrender'. He then said: 'In those circumstances the choice again is posed – and this is the classical choice of either exterminating everything that you stand for and I'll use the phrase the flower of your youth or using the resources that you've got to make any occupation untenable.'

Here was an opportunity that some newspapers had been longing for, the opportunity to raise Labour's defence policy, even though several were obviously asleep at the time. Three papers, however, had been awake. The next morning, the Kinnock interview was the front page lead, in journalistic parlance 'the splash', in the *Telegraph*, the *Express*, and *Today*. 'If the enemy comes – by Neil', said the *Express*, 'It's a surrender policy says defence supremo'. *Today*'s front page said: 'How Kinnock would meet the Soviet nuclear threat – fight them in the streets'. The *Telegraph* said: 'Take to the hills jibe by Tory, guerilla war a deterrent, says Kinnock.' Once given this prominence, Kinnock's defence policy became the issue of the week. On Tuesday, it was the lead story in *The Times*: 'Kinnock arms policy savaged by opponents.' 'Thatcher scorns "some kind of guerilla band"'; and the *Mail* – 'Dad's Army Kinnock under fire.' The *Mail* again led on the story on Wednesday under the headline 'Kinnock: the man with a white flag.' So, too, did the *Express* and *The Times*, with the *Express* using the same white flag theme as the *Mail*.

On Tuesday night, ITN's *News at Ten* led with 'Mrs Thatcher says: Labour's defence policy would leave Britain helpless.' The next night it led with President Reagan on Labour's 'grievous defence errors'; and even on Thursday Kinnock was again the lead item on ITN: 'Mrs Thatcher says Mr Kinnock would crack the Nato alliance.'

2   On Monday 1 June, defence was followed as an issue by taxes, when the *Express* led on an exclusive interview with Nigel Lawson, the Chancellor. 'Exclusive: Lawson raps plan for £10 grab. Kinnock's tax threat to 12 million', its front page declared. 'Labour were accused of fraud last night for hushing up a plan which would leave six million married couples £10 a week worse off.' This story again dominated both the *Express* and *Mail* on 5 June. 'Tax shock the price you'd pay for Labour', said the *Express*, 'A family earning £14,560 a year will have to pay £13.57 more tax every week. A single man earning £25,000 a year will have to pay £71.68 more tax every week.' The details were given across the paper's centre spread, the main platform where a tabloid can give a story real projection.

On the following Friday, the *Mail* exposed 'another secret of the iceberg manifesto': 'Labour's lies on taxation. Millions who earned anything from £9,000 a year would be worse off under Labour', it said. Again the details were set out across the centre spread and tax had become the central issue of the weekend, with neither Kinnock nor Roy Hattersley, the shadow chancellor, willing to give detailed answers to questions from television or newspapers. So both the *Mail* and *Express* again led on the tax theme the next day. The *Mail* splashed on 'Labour's incredible attack on pensions' and the *Express* on 'Labour's tax fiasco'.

3   On Tuesday, 9 June, two days before polling day, the *Sun* had an election 'exclusive': 'Private op for Healey wife, Labour's Edna had a hip joint replaced.' It reported that Denis Healey's wife had had an operation several years previously in a £250-a-week PRIVATE hospital. Edna Healey, it said, had avoided National Health Service queues to have her hip replacement done quickly. Yet only a week earlier Michael Meacher, the Labour health spokesman, had 'branded' Margaret Thatcher callous and uncaring for using private medicine. This became an identikit example of how newspapers can set the agenda for broadcasters.

The story was the third item on ITN that evening. Healey was then invited to a breakfast interview with Anne Diamond on TV-am to discuss the *Sun* exclusive. As the interview progressed, Healey became more and more angry. He accused the programme of a classical dirty trick by inviting him to discuss the Venice economic summit and then questioning him about his wife's operation. Once the interview was over the irascible Healey turned on Diamond and called her a 'shit'.

He was to regret the loss of his temper. This was a heaven-sent issue for the

Tory tabloids and was exploited for all its worth. The other papers seized on it gleefully. Next day both the *Express* and *Mail* devoted all their front page to Healey. 'Healey the Hypocrite', said the *Express*: 'Four letter outburst over wife's private op.' The outburst got the same treatment in the *Mail*: 'Labour attack on private medicine boomerangs in four-letter row over wife's cash operation: Healey's gift to the Tories', said the grateful *Mail*.

These are three specific examples of how newspapers set and legitimised the agenda for the broadcasters. Yet the relentless barrage of reporting of other perceived Labour weaknesses, such as the policies of loony left councils, the behaviour of union bosses and Kinnock's obvious uneasiness about aspects of the manifesto, were equally important. On these issues the *Mail* and *The Sun* were the most creative and inventive (or spiteful, bigoted and biassed) papers. Among front page examples from the *Mail* were 'Thatcher's warning: the Tyrants are waiting'; 'No questions please – I'm Kinnock'; and 'The Iceberg Manifesto', over a report which said:

> Labour's hard left have revealed their hand on the programme they want Neil Kinnock to adopt if they win the election. A manifesto sent out yesterday details a chilling list of demands for the virtual creation of a workers' state. It includes a threat to confront the bosses and the banks, repeal the public order laws, withdraw all troops from Ulster, the Falklands and Germany, pull out of the Common Market and open our doors to immigrants and refugees. The left want to impose punitive wealth taxes, abolish the monarchy and the Lords, and make the police, media and judges accountable to the working class.

Note in this 'report' the use of such code words as chilling, virtual, threat, confront and immigrants and remember that not one item mentioned was in the Labour manifesto.

At this level, however, it is Britain's biggest-selling paper, *The Sun*, with nearly 12 million readers a day, that is in a class of its own. Its election coverage was devoted much more to exposing the threat from Labour than the merits of the Tories: 72 per cent of its election coverage was devoted to the Labour Party. Saying that Page Three girls would be banned under Labour, it announced that 'The Loveliest Girls are in *The Sun* – but only under the Conservatives'. It also had 'Why I'm backing Kinnock – by Stalin.' All that was missing was why the late Doris Stokes, the spiritualist who in life was one of *The Sun*'s favourite characters, was backing Maggie from beyond.

On 29 May, *The Sun* devoted the length of its front page to a caricature Russian wielding a bomb with his boot on a cringing Kinnock. Armed only with a catapult, Kinnock was saying, 'One more step and I'll shoot.' On 5 June, *The Sun* asked: 'Do you want these men [Scargill of the miners and Todd of the transport workers] to run your life?' 'Notice the strangest chapter in the General Election story', it said. 'It is the total silence of the robber barons of the giant trade unions. How different it used to be!' On 8 June, it ran a special nightmare issue: 'Labour Wins! Wake up folks, this is just a bad dream. We felt we had to warn you about life under the Socialist jackboot. See pages 5, 6, 8, 9, and 13.' (It was a lengthy nightmare, which did not end for *The Sun* until the bright dawn of 12 June.) On election day, in its final pitch for 'Maggie', it ran a story on The Real Voice of Labour, showing pictures of five of the *Sun*'s anti-heroes, all standing that day: Pat Wall, Ken Livingstone, Valerie Veness, Bernie Grant and Neil Kinnock.

Against all this, the *Mirror* ran a lonely campaign for Labour. It started slowly – the manifesto was not even reported on the front page and got only 18 inches on page 2 compared with *The Sun* which attacked the manifesto across the front page and gave it 28 inches on page 2. The *Mirror* campaign, however, rose to a typical climax, even if it could never quite match the brutality or vulgarity of *The Sun* (it is perhaps the case that no Labour paper could live with itself if it did so). The *Mirror* went into top gear from 1 June, with an issue on Divided Britain, showing two ragamuffin children on a derelict building site and asking 'Whose Life, Whose future. She doesn't care about them. Do You?' On 5 June, it followed with a story about Mark Burgess, aged ten, who had been waiting a year for an operation to mend a hole in his heart:

> He should have had the operation on Monday. But only hours before he was due to be admitted to Guy's Hospital in London it was cancelled. Yesterday Mrs Thatcher was told of Mark's plight. 'Perhaps he will write to us and we will look at it' was her curt comment.

This was presented under the headline 'Dear Mrs Thatcher. When will they make me better?' On 8 June, the *Mirror* led on 'Shock report reveals grotesque life under Thatcher'. Under the banner headline 'That's rich', the page showed a bottle of champagne – sales up 72 per cent – and a Porsche – sales up 95 per cent. It added: 'Their bit: Burning it up and boozing on bubbly. Your lot: Broke, battered but not broken.' On 10 June, the message was

> Time to Choose. Privilege and Poverty. The Conservative Party exists to preserve its privileges. That is what it was created for. That is its historic role. The Labour Party was created to fight privilege, the degradation of poverty, the humiliation of unemployment, the misery of the slums. That is its historic duty.

On election day itself there were only seven words on the front page, around a picture of Kinnock: 'You know he's right – chuck her out.' This was a good campaign.

Today fought a lone but pugnacious battle for the Alliance with at least as much flair as the *Mirror* but attracted less attention – at 330,000, its circulation was a tenth of the *Mirror*'s and a fifth of the *Mail* or *Express*. It, too, published a placard front page on 11 June: 'Warning: Her government could

Table 10.3. *Public opinion of the extent of media coverage of the 1987 general election campaign*

Response	Newspapers %	Television %	Radio %
Much too much	30	49	12
A little too much	22	22	6
About the right amount	35	24	30
A little too little	2	2	3
Much too little	1	–	2
No opinion	9	3	46

Source: MORI

seriously damage your health. Vote for Change.' Alone among the nationals, *Today* advocated tactical voting. 'In 100 vital seats, the voters can do something', it urged:

> They can vote tactically and oust Mrs Thatcher. This could mean forswearing the habits of a lifetime, the pull of old family and party loyalties. But Mrs Thatcher has to be removed if Britain is to be made less divisive, if our society is to rid itself of the corrosive philosophy of devil take the hindmost. To do this brains must govern hearts. The Alliance will not let Labour in. The most likely outcome would be a Tory–Alliance coalition. But it would be without the scourge of Thatcherism, the random brutality of which is alien to traditional Conservatism. To secure the result, Labour must be supported in some seats, the Alliance in others.

The pure bias of the tabloid coverage raises the question of whether what appears in newspapers matters or makes any difference whatsoever to how readers vote. Newspapers certainly fared better than radio or television when voters were asked about coverage of the election (see table 10.3); 35 per cent thought that newspapers had about the right amount of coverage, compared with 24 per cent for television and 30 per cent for radio. The view that there was much too much coverage, moreover, was held by only 30 per cent of newspaper readers compared with 49 per cent of television viewers. At least, therefore, most newspaper readers were not bored by the newspapers' election coverage, were reading them thoroughly, and judging by the increased circulation of the serious papers were seeking elucidation of the issues from the papers and were therefore open to argument and persuasion. Unfortunately, however, few polls have yet asked voters whether they were influenced by their papers. Answers therefore depend on guesswork, hunch and instinct.

A comparison of two MORI polls, one of *The Sunday Times* panel during the election, the other on polling day, suggested that more readers 'voted' with their paper, certainly for the *Sun*, *Mirror* and *Express*, than ten days earlier (see table 10.4), suggesting that they had been 'converted' by their paper's

Table 10.4. *Mid-election and polling day voting intentions*

	Express % Con.	Sun % Con.	Mirror % Lab.
Pre-election	70	41	55
Election day	72	51	59
Difference	+2	+10	+4

Source: MORI.

Table 10.5. *Circlation, political content and political preference of national newspapers, and voting intentions of their readers, 1987 general election campaign*

Newspaper	Circulation (thousands)	Political preference	Readers			Bias	Political content of front page
			Con.	Lab.	All.		
Dailies							
Times	457	C	59	13	28	61(C)	42.7
Guardian	508	L	22	41	37	40(All)	41.1
Telegraph	1,175	C	69	10	21	85(C)	31.6
Independent	327	–	31	33	35	17(All)	39.7
Financial Times†	219*	C	78	14	8		16.4
Mail	1,771	C	55	11	34	75(C)	63.1
Express	1,666	C	72	10	18	86(C)	59.1
Today	318	All	41	21	33	14(All)	45.3
Sun	3,970	C	51	29	19	53(C)	29.7
Mirror	3,073	L	22	59	18	82(L)	26.8
Star	1,266	C	35	47	16	5(C)	22.2
Sundays							
Times	1,219	C	71	11	18	68(C)	50.6
Observer	786	–	32	28	38	23(L)	53.6
Telegraph	721	C	64	9	26	76(C)	46.2
Express	2,200	C	71	9	20	79(C)	32.8
Mail on Sunday	1,739	C	51	17	32	31(C)	36.5
News of the World	4,950	C	43	35	19	62(C)	26.1
People	2,765	L	42	38	18	31(L)	49.9
Mirror	2,941	L	28	47	25	65(L)	14.6
News on Sunday	350*	L	22	74	5	46(L)	

Based on two MORI polls, one during election, one on voting day.
* Estimates
† *Financial Times* circulation is for UK only.
Sources: ABC, MORI.

politics. Yet several other contradictory, conclusions can be drawn from the same two polls (see also table 10.5).

More than half the readers of *The Guardian, News of the World, Sunday Mirror* and the *People* voted *against* their paper's advice.

More readers of *The Sun* and *The Daily Mail*, two of the most propagandist papers, voted against their papers than with them.

The Star and *Today* were most out of tune with their readers. *The Star* endorsed the Tories, even though 47 per cent of its readers voted Labour. *Today* backed the Alliance, though 41 per cent of its readers were Tory.

The Independent was the paper with the most even spread of readers, with roughly a third for each of the parties.

The papers with the highest percentage of Alliance voters, in rank order, were *The Observer, The Guardian, The Independent, Daily Mail, Mail on Sunday* and *Today*.

The papers with the highest percentage of Conservative voters were, again in rank order, the *Financial Times, Daily Express, The Sunday Times* and *Sunday Express, The Daily Telegraph, Sunday Telegraph* and *The Times*.

At election times in particular, politicians get even more worried than usual about both the fairness and influence of the British press. The press of course has never been fair and although one could wish that it were otherwise it would be unrealistic. As for influence, what evidence there is points several ways – for some readers their newspaper either reinforces or converts them, others totally discount their paper's politics. Many readers, preferring not to be irritated by their paper, choose one that reflects their political outlook. Others deliberately choose a paper that offers a view different from their own or discount its political opinions because they like its other contents.

Common sense nevertheless dictates that all the relentless anti-Labour coverage – the emphasis on anti-hero personalities, the admiring profiles of the Iron Maiden and the emphasis on the patriotism and principle of David Owen, contrasted with the continual demolition of Neil Kinnock and the concentration on robber unions, loony lefties and black activists – in the mass-market tabloids *must* have some effect when the millions of undecided voters finally make their decisions.

That common-sense conclusion, based on hunch, now finds academic support. In *The Media in British Politics*[2] Martin Harrop strongly questions the thesis that the media are simply reinforcement agents. He shows that recent studies have demonstrated a clear relationship between media exposure and information gain, particularly among families that are uninterested in

Table 10.6. *Overlap in newspaper purchases, May–July 1987*

	May	June	July
% of *Times* buyers who also bought *Independent*	9	19	12
% of *Independent* buyers who also bought *Times*	10	17	12

Source: AGB Press Purchasing Monitor.

politics, where party loyalties are weak and when the issues are new. About three in four British adults read a national newspaper every day, as many as watch TV news, and they claim to spend longer with their paper than with news bulletins. 'Although television has become the main source of headline news, the quality papers still provide background information, while the tabloids continue to mix in prejudices all of their own,' Harrop argues. 'Undecided electors cannot be reinforced; they are much more likely to use the media positively to help them reach a decision.' He estimates that the effect of the press is worth a swing of about 1 per cent from Labour to Conservative between elections, worth approximately ten seats – as Harrop says, 'not to be sniffed at but hardly decisive either,' except in the case of a hung parliament.

Virtue was rewarded for some newspapers in at least one respect – their coverage of the election led to an increase in sales: of 28,000 for *The Guardian*, 18,000 for *The Times*, an important 16,000 for *The Independent*, 13,000 for *The Daily Telegraph* and 11,000 for *The Financial Times*. The only tabloid whose circulation increased, a tribute to its spirited Alliance campaign, was *Today*. At the serious end of the market, readers in search of elucidation also added to their buying of newspapers. According to the AGB Press Purchasing Monitor, there was a significant increase in the number of readers of both *The Times* and *The Independent* who bought the other paper in addition to their normal paper during the election (see table 10.6). Another indication, perhaps, that newspapers do matter. They mattered too, in one other profitable respect. More than £4,500,000 was spent by the three parties on advertisements, most of which went to newspapers. The spending was Conservative: £2,800,000 (62 per cent): Labour £1,500,000 (33 per cent), Alliance £210,000 (5 per cent). The Tories spent more than £2,000,000 in the four days leading up to the Tuesday before polling day, the biggest advertising blitz in British electoral history.

The polling booth is a very fine and private place and on 11 June 1987 it was the graveyard of Neil Kinnock's ambitions. Whether it was all that advertising, whether it was newspapers or television, all of them or none of them, that finally tilted the millions of private decisions that made for the

Tory victory, none of us know. But if newspapers don't matter, why are the politicians so obsessed with them?

Notes

1 M. Harrop, 'The Press', in D. Butler and D. Kavanagh (eds.), *The British General Election of 1987* (London: Macmillan, 1988).
2 M. Harrop, 'The Voters', in J. Seaton and B. Pimlott (eds.), *The Media in British Politics* (Aldershot: Avebury, 1987), pp. 45–63.

WILLIAM L. MILLER, DAVID BROUGHTON,
NIELS SONNTAG and DUNCAN MCLEAN

11 Political change in Britain during the 1987 campaign

Introduction: short-term change

When Butler and Stokes wrote their classic *Political Change in Britain* they used an ingenious analysis of contemporary opinion surveys as a basis for their discussion of the 'evolution of electoral choice' throughout almost a century of political history.[1] We are concerned with a mere four weeks, from Thursday, 14 May, to Thursday, 11 June 1987, and the first question we must ask is this: was there any political change in those four weeks? Undoubtedly there were major changes during what we might call the 'long campaign' – that is from the summer of 1986 to the summer of 1987. But was there any significant change in the last four weeks – during the 'short' or 'official' campaign?

In retrospect it is tempting to dismiss the 1987 campaign as a non-event – nothing of any political significance occurred, minds were already made up, and the public reaction to the campaign itself was to treat it as the yawn that it was. This interpretation is supported by the stability of the average trend in the published polls, even if individual polls varied widely, and sometimes wildly, from that average.

As a crude approximation to reality we would agree with that interpretation. It is certainly far more truthful than the alternative, which would portray the election as an exciting struggle between the parties, full of significant events, critical decisions, clever strategies, and important turning points. An absurd view, we may conclude in retrospect, yet not so absurd at the time – as the many accounts of 'Wobbly Thursday' and the adulation accorded Kinnock's TV spectacular bear witness. On balance, we think that the best crude approximation is the interpretation which suggests that nothing happened in the campaign of 1987.

However, that *is* a crude approximation. There were political trends during the campaign, though not of cataclysmic proportions. Moreover, a wealth of academic research suggests that the British electorate is now potentially volatile, characterised by weak and unstable party loyalties. So trends should be judged not only against the null model of 'no-change' but also against what might have happened – and indeed against what did happen during the 1983 campaign. When the circus performer succeeds in walking across the high wire and reaches the other side safely, we should not ask for our money back on the grounds that 'nothing dramatic happened'. Stability in a volatile world is an achievement.

It seems likely that only the Conservatives entered the campaign intent upon winning a majority in parliament. Labour and Alliance leaders had different objectives. Even Mrs Thatcher clearly had objectives other than a parliamentary majority, and enemies other than the Labour Party. Victory for Mrs Thatcher could have meant two different things – both of which she achieved. First, a parliamentary majority sufficient to allow the continuation of Conservative government. Second, a (much larger!) majority sufficient to quieten her critics within the party and allow the continuation of a Thatcher and Thatcher*ite* government. For Kinnock, there were three obvious groups of enemies. He was fighting the Conservatives with government the prize; fighting the Alliance with the status of opposition-leader as the prize; and fighting his critics within the party, with control of the Labour Party as the prize. Clearly, he lost one of those battles, but would seem to have won the other two. The question of objectives is important because the Labour campaign strategy can be faulted were its principal objective to unseat the Conservatives, but it made more sense were it to defeat the Alliance or its own dissidents.

Labour entered the campaign far behind the Conservatives. Its only hope of beating them was a high-risk dramatic-initiative strategy rather than the slickly presented 'safety-first' course that it adopted, designed to emphasise what the electorate already knew and believed. That strategy was, at best, likely only to solidify and confirm its existing support. However, if Labour's main enemy was the Alliance, and its main fear was collapse rather than mere defeat by the Conservatives – a rerun of 1983 – then the party was perhaps right to avoid dramatic new initiatives. It is a measure of the fundamental lack of truly dramatic initiatives that a ten-minute video of old news clips (Labour's famous 'Chariots of Fire'-style party election broadcast about Kinnock) attracted so much attention. At the same time, a Labour campaign focussed on its leader can have done no harm to the leadership in its continuing quest for mastery within the party.

The British Election Campaign Study (BECS) survey

The BECS survey at the University of Glasgow was a complex multi-wave survey, which interviewed respondents throughout Britain by telephone. Its

Table 11.1. *The BECS panel's voting choice*

	3-wave panel sample	Actual GB result	Panel sample error
Conservative	43.2	44.2	−1.0
Labour	31.7	32.2	−0.5
Alliance	25.1	23.6	+1.5
	100%	100%	
Conservative lead	11.5	12.0	−0.5

samples were drawn from respondents who had participated in either the 1983 British Election Study survey, or the 1986 British Social Attitudes survey, supplemented by a relatively few 'top-ups'. The BECS survey reinterviewed respondents once at the end of March 1987, twice during the four-week campaign, and once in the week after the election. Interviews were sequenced so as to provide approximately random subsamples on any one day of interviewing, and the two interviews during the four-week campaign were spaced so that each respondent was interviewed after an interval of about a fortnight. We asked about 200 questions in each wave of interviewing except the last.

This design allows a study of trends and turning points day by day through the campaign. Since we expect change in this short period to be small, the panel analyses presented here are restricted to the 1,176 respondents who voted Conservative, Labour or Alliance, and who (every one of them) told us about their voting intentions in the first fortnight and again in the second fortnight of the campaign. This is only a subset of the 1,567 that we interviewed in the week after the election, but even were this group of 1,176 not closely representative of the voters as a whole, they would still provide the best estimate of trends and change because they were the same 1,176 at each time point.

As it happens, once these voters were weighted to the proper interlocking class/age/sex/region quota they turn out to be very closely representative of the voters as a whole, as table 11.1 shows. On average the panel's votes were within 1 per cent of the actual figures, and the estimate of the Conservative lead was within half a per cent. We shall not adjust or 'correct' the panel's votes or voting intentions in any way.

Change in voting intentions

However, there is a danger that repeated interviewing encourages people to come to an early decision and then stick to it. In an effort to avoid this problem, we *never* asked our respondents to name the party they intended to

Table 11.2. *Overall change*

% who placed party top in first fortnight		% Eventual Voting Choice			
		Conservative	Labour	Alliance	Total (%)
Conservative top	44.2	89	2	9	100
Labour top	26.7	3	90	7	100
Alliance top	20.8	8	15	77	100
At least two equal top	8.4	18	44	38	100

vote for. Instead, for each of the three parties (four in Scotland and Wales), we asked respondents: give us a 'mark out of ten according to how inclined you are to vote for it'. We indicated that zero would imply the respondent was *certain that they would not* vote for it and ten would imply a *certainty that they would* vote for it. Our hope was that this style of question would reflect current attitudes without *crystallising* them.

The pattern of answers given to these voting inclination questions reveals a great deal about the amount of uncertainty and change during the 1987 campaign. First of all, we can categorise our 1,176 respondents' voting inclinations according to which party, *if any*, they gave the highest mark. During the first fortnight of the campaign 44 per cent were most inclined to vote Conservative, 27 per cent Labour, 21 per cent Alliance, and the remaining 8 per cent were equally inclined to vote for two (occasionally all three) parties. As a measure of the total amount of change and indecision in the panel we can ask: how many eventually voted for the party they were most inclined to vote for at the start of the campaign?

The answer is 79 per cent; 13 per cent voted for a different party, and 8 per cent did not have a preference for one party above all others when the campaign opened. So now we can answer the question posed at the start, about whether this was a campaign in which change was noticeably absent. Four-fifths of voters were unmoved by the campaign; one fifth were (see table 11.2).

Roughly 90 per cent of those who originally placed Labour or Conservative top, eventually voted for their original choice – but only 71 per cent of the panel originally put Labour or Conservative top. Those who originally opted for the Alliance were much more volatile; so too, by definition, were those who originally placed two or more parties jointly top.

Trends in voting intentions

When the campaign opened 8 per cent were exactly equally inclined to vote for two or more parties, but they were not spread evenly over all possible combinations of parties. Most were swithering between Labour and Alliance (5 per cent) or between Conservative and Alliance (2 per cent).

Table 11.3. *Trends in voting inclinations*

	First fortnight	Second fortnight	Vote
Conservative top	44.2	42.8	43.2
Labour top	26.7	29.8	31.7
Alliance top	20.8	19.6	25.1
Conservative/Alliance equal top	2.4	3.5	–
Labour/Alliance equal top	5.0	2.8	–
Conservative/Labour equal top	0.3	0.8	–
All three equal	0.7	0.8	–
Conservative lead over Labour	17.5	13.0	11.5

Towards the end of the campaign Conservative and Alliance support seemed to have eased marginally while Labour support was up 3 per cent. There were still 8 per cent undecided though now there were as many contemplating a Conservative/Alliance choice as a Labour/Alliance choice.

But when voting day came and decision could be postponed no longer it was the Alliance that gained most. All parties increased their support as indecision was resolved, but while the Conservatives gained half a per cent, and Labour 2 per cent, the Alliance gained almost 6 per cent (see table 11.3).

Within our panel, therefore, there is a pattern of early Labour gains followed by a considerable Alliance gain right at the end of the campaign. When we break down these figures even more precisely in terms of time, the results emphasise still more the lateness of the switch to the Alliance.

Battlegrounds: types of voting inclinations and a measure of uncertainty

There is another, more dynamic, way of categorising our respondents on the basis of their initial voting inclinations. That is to focus more on the parties that they *eliminated* from consideration, rather than the parties they were most inclined to vote for. Often, for example, their original first choice was *only marginally preferred* to their second, and switches between first and second choice were to be expected.

We define seven voter *types*. These correspond to the battlegrounds between the parties. Each type might well be responsive to different appeals. The first three types consist of respondents who originally placed one of the parties *behind both* the other two – the 'switherers' in table 11.4. Next, are three types which not only had a first-choice party but who rated the other two parties as second equal – the 'loyalists' in table 11.4. Last are the handful of panel respondents who rated all three parties equally.

Table 11.4. *Battlegrounds: voter types*

Voter type	Per cent in category at start of campaign
Switherers	
LA = Labour/Alliance switherers (i.e. put Conservative third)	34.7
CA = Conservative/Alliance switherers (i.e. put Labour third)	36.5
CL = Conservative/Labour switherers (i.e. put Alliance third)	8.7
Loyalists	
C = Conservative (i.e. put Labour and Alliance equal second)	11.2
L = Labour (i.e. put Conservative and Alliance equal second)	5.9
A = Alliance (i.e. put Conservative and Labour equal second)	2.3
Others	
CLA = Conservative/Labour/Alliance (i.e. rate all three equally)	0.7

Note: Our definition of the term 'loyalist' in this and subsequent tables is unusual, but empirically justified in the text.

The value of this typology is that it *effectively* distinguishes the party loyalists from those who were seriously considering two parties, since very few voters seriously considered as many as three parties. Roughly a third of the voters were open to Labour and Alliance appeals, and another third were open to Conservative and Alliance appeals. Relatively few voters (under 9 per cent) were open to both Conservative and Labour appeals.

The Conservatives had twice as many loyalists as Labour who, in turn, had almost three times as many as the Alliance, but on this definition there were remarkably few party loyalists amongst British voters in 1987 – a total of only 19 per cent! Four-fifths of voters were switherers, and almost three-quarters of all voters were either Conservative/Alliance switherers or Labour/Alliance switherers (see table 11.4).

It is by no means obvious that voters should rule their third choice completely out of consideration; nor is it obvious that those who rated two parties as equal second were unlikely to give serious consideration to either of these second choices. Nonetheless, that *is* the case, as we can show by looking at the ultimate voting behaviour of each voter type, or at the mean voting inclination scores that each type gave to the three parties (see table 11.5).

Those who were equally inclined to vote for all three parties were, more properly, equally *un*inclined. On average, they rated each of the parties at three out of ten! Those who had one first choice, but who rated the other two parties as second equal, typically gave both these second-choice parties a score of only one or two out of ten, while they gave their first choice nine out of ten, and over 90 per cent of them voted for their first choice party (see table 11.5).

The main political battleground consisted of those who had a first, second and third choice. They were numerous (80 per cent of all voters). They typically gave *very* low scores to their third choice. And *very* few of them

Table 11.5. *Voting inclinations and votes by voter type*

Voter type	Mean Inclination Scores (out of ten) given at the start of the campaign			Eventual vote (%)		
	Conservative	Labour	Alliance	Conservative	Labour	Alliance
LA switherers	1.4	7.5	6.6	2	68	30
CA switherers	7.8	2.1	6.1	69	1	30
CL switherers	7.7	5.7	3.1	74	21	5
C loyalists	9.1	1.9	1.9	92	0	8
L loyalists	0.8	9.4	0.8	5	93	2
A loyalists	1.2	1.2	8.4	9	4	87
CLA	3.0	3.0	3.0	26	34	40

Table 11.6. *Initial voting inclinations in selected voter types*

Voter type	First choice	Mean Inclination Scores (out of ten) given at the start of the campaign		
		Conservative	Labour	Alliance
LA switherers	Labour	1.2	8.8	5.7
LA switherers	Alliance	1.7	5.4	8.0
CA switherers	Conservative	8.6	1.9	5.5
CA switherers	Alliance	5.6	2.5	7.8
CL switherers	Conservative	8.3	5.3	3.2
CL switherers	Alliance	5.3	7.7	2.4

eventually voted for what had initially been their third choice. The main
contest therefore took place in three separate battlegrounds, in each case
involving only a pair of serious contenders. Within these essentially two-way
battlegrounds voters on average rated their first choice at eight out of ten;
their second choice at five and a half; their third at a mere two out of ten (see
table 11.6).

Different voting trends within different voter types

Insofar as any of the events of the campaign had an impact on the voters, we
should expect its impact to be different on the different voter types. That is
one reason why the overall impact of any event is limited. Certainly the trends
in voting inclinations appear different in the different voter types. Amongst
the Labour/Alliance switherers, Labour's lead increased sharply during the
campaign and held up on election day; amongst Conservative/Alliance
switherers, the Conservative lead held up during the campaign but fell

Table 11.7. *Trends in voting inclinations by voter type*

	Voting inclinations		
Amongst Labour/Alliance switherers			
	First fortnight	Second fortnight	Vote (change)
Labour	56	64	68
Undecided L/A	14	7	–
Alliance	30	26	30
Other	0	3	2
Labour lead over Alliance	26	38	38 (+12)
Amongst Conservative/Alliance switherers			
	First fortnight	Second fortnight	Vote (change)
Conservative	71	69	69
Undecided C/A	7	8	–
Alliance	22	20	30
Other	0	2	1
Conservative lead over Alliance	49	49	39 (−10)
Amongst Conservative/Labour switherers			
	First fortnight	Second fortnight	Vote (change)
Conservative	81	75	74
Undecided C/L	3	4	–
Labour	16	15	21
Other	0	6	5

sharply on election day; while amongst Conservative/Alliance switherers the Conservative lead fell steadily throughout (see table 11.7)

A campaign of scandals, images, agendas and credibility

We have described the changes in voting inclinations during the 1987 campaign. Now we seek to explain them. What happened in the campaign? Remember that we are concerned only with change within a four-week period. Thus, many of the things which, in a larger sense, affected the result, did so prior to the campaign itself. Well before the campaign, the public had got used to Labour's concern for the sick and the unemployed, its firm rejection of a nuclear defence strategy, its telegenic leader. Well before the campaign, they had developed a suspicion of Labour's capability on economic affairs. We cast our net widely when framing questions for the survey and many clear and striking patterns emerge – but few substantial last minute changes. Most of the strengths and weaknesses of each party were clearly visible by the time of our pre-election survey in March and changed little during the short campaign.

It need not necessarily have been so, but the parties chose to fight the

Table 11.8. *Political discussion and political interest*

	March	First fortnight	Second fortnight
% Discussed politics *often* during last week	20	33	37
% Find what's happening in politics at the moment *very* interesting	27	16	17

Note: This table is based on unweighted figures for the full cross-sectional samples at each time-point, not the three-wave panel.

campaign with strategies that avoided new initiatives. The voters themselves indicated that it was a dull campaign. Compared to our March survey, levels of political discussion went up sharply during the campaign, but levels of interest in political events went down equally sharply (see table 11.8). To be fair, our March survey coincided with Kinnock's trip to Washington and Thatcher's to Moscow but the fact remains that our respondents found the election campaign less interesting.

What was new and different during the campaign, if there were no events of major significance and no new policy initiatives? First, there were scandals, alleged or admitted, involving politicians of all major parties. Our survey shows that they were noticed, briefly, as they received publicity. Second, there was the attempt to enhance Kinnock's image by means of a spectacular film and a well-organised series of photogenic tours. Some of the published polls seemed to detect a substantial public response. We inquired closely into eleven different aspects of each leader's image and into four aspects of each party's image. We did not find great changes in leader images *during the campaign*, though Kinnock's image for 'decisiveness' was much better throughout the campaign than in that unfortunate week in March. He overhauled both Steel and Owen, but not Thatcher, on 'decisiveness' and went into top place on 'caring' (see table 11.9). Nonetheless a day-by-day breakdown of our figures shows little trend within the campaign itself, and the improvement in Kinnock's image was evident from the start of the campaign – that is, *before* the celebrated Kinnock party election broadcast. At best Labour's presentation of its leader *maintained* his image during the campaign, and offset some of his own gaffes on defence.

There was more change in whether the parties were seen as *united*. One effect of the Labour campaign's focus on Kinnock was not just to enhance his personal image but to show the Labour Party speaking with one single authoritative voice. By contrast the Alliance attempt to show leadership cooperation in action, in the persons of Steel and Owen, did not succeed during the campaign and was speedily abandoned after the result. In March,

Table 11.9. *Selected leader and party images*

		Average 'marks out of ten' score for applicability of adjective to person or party			Change since March	Change in campaign
		March	First fortnight	Second fortnight		
Kinnock:	Decisive	5.3	6.4	6.5	+1.2	+0.1
	Caring	6.4	7.1	7.1	+0.7	0
Thatcher:	Decisive	7.5	8.3	8.1	+0.6	−0.2
	Caring	4.6	5.2	5.0	+0.4	−0.2
Steel:	Decisive	6.7	6.3	6.1	−0.6	−0.2
	Caring	7.4	6.9	6.8	−0.6	−0.1
Owen:	Decisive	6.6	6.5	6.4	−0.2	−0.1
	Caring	7.1	6.6	6.5	−0.6	−0.1
Conservatives	United	7.5	8.0	7.9	+0.4	−0.1
Labour	United	5.1	6.2	6.7	+1.6	+0.5
Alliance	United	6.6	7.0	6.7	+0.1	−0.3

Note: This table is based on unweighted figures for the full cross-sectional samples at each time-point, not the three-wave panel.

Labour's score on being *united* was (on average) a full one-and-a-half marks out of ten lower than the Alliance score. In the first fortnight of the campaign it was about one mark out of ten lower. But by the second fortnight Labour had drawn level with the Alliance. Closer examination of the day-by-day subsamples suggests that Labour was well behind at the start of the campaign but advanced steadily and actually overtook the Alliance on unity towards the end of the campaign. Still, it was perhaps only a modest achievement for a single party to look as united as the alliance of the two Davids!

It has been suggested that the 1987 campaign was a *campaign of agendas* rather than issues. The parties had no major policy initiatives to present, but while Labour knew it enjoyed majority support on caring issues, the Conservatives knew they had majority support on military and defence issues. So each attempted to turn public attention to the issues where it had most support.

Between Labour and Conservative it may well have been a campaign of agendas. Between Labour and the Alliance it was more a *campaign over credibility*. The Alliance hoped to repeat their usual by-election feat of portraying Labour as a no-hoper and thus gaining from a surge of tactical (anti-Conservative) votes. Yet the growing perception of Labour as more united, and the Alliance as less united, must have damaged the Alliance attempt to present itself as the more credible alternative.

These were two areas – agendas and credibility – in which our survey did show very significant changes of perception (we stress *perception* rather than *opinion*) during the campaign. We shall examine their impact.

Table 11.10. *Perceptions and salience of the defence issue*

	First fortnight	Second fortnight
% perceiving Conservative Party stressing defence as its main issue	19	47
% of respondents saying defence was the main issue the parties *should* be talking about	6	11

The impact of the Conservatives' defence campaign

Some 'inside' accounts of the campaign suggest that Mrs Thatcher hoped originally to fight a clearly ideological campaign, a positive campaign for the extension of Thatcherism in all its aspects – notably privatisation of both industrial and social services. By these accounts, she was so frightened by the slickness of the Labour presentation that she switched quickly to less ideological themes – bashing Labour, first on defence policy, and then on its association with the 1978–9 Winter of Discontent.

That is certainly what our respondents perceived as happening. We asked: 'what seems to be the main issue being stressed by each of the parties at the moment?' Early in the campaign, our respondents were uncertain and divided about what issues the Conservatives were stressing. For example, on our fourth day of interviewing, Tuesday, 19 May, the most frequent response was *don't know* (29 per cent), followed by *privatisation* (14 per cent), *unemployment* (14 per cent), *inflation* (11 per cent) and *prosperity* (8 per cent). Defence was mentioned by only 5 per cent. But as the campaign advanced, our respondents perceived a growing Conservative emphasis on the defence issue (see table 11.10).

Between the first and second fortnights of the campaign the percentage of respondents perceiving defence as the Conservative Party's single main theme rose from 19 to 47. A closer look at the day-by-day subsamples shows that this perception of the Conservative stress on defence remained low until 21 May, rose sharply on 22 May, then stayed at the new higher level until 28 May when it shot up to a peak for three days before easing slightly towards the end of the campaign.

On 19 May a Conservative PEB emphasised the party's patriotism and on the 20th Mrs Thatcher attacked the Alliance for having a defence policy that would take Britain down 'the same disastrous road as the Labour Party towards a frightened and fellow-travelling Britain'. Dr Owen could not resist the temptation to respond and Mrs Thatcher then used his protests as the opportunity to expand on her theme. At her adoption meeting in Finchley on 21 May she launched a lengthy, detailed and well-publicised attack on the defence policies of both Labour and the Alliance, outlined the case for Polaris

Table 11.11. *Defence ratings by voter type (mean rating out of ten)*

Voter type	First fortnight		Second fortnight		Net Conservative gain
	Conservative Party	Labour Party	Conservative Party	Labour Party	
All panel respondents	6.7	4.8	7.1	4.6	+0.6
LA switherers	5.2	6.1	5.6	6.2	+0.3
CA switherers	7.6	3.8	8.1	3.3	+1.0
CL switherers	7.7	4.8	8.2	4.7	+0.6
Conservative	8.1	3.4	8.9	3.1	+1.1
Labour	5.0	7.2	5.1	7.0	+0.3
Alliance	6.0	4.6	6.3	4.1	+0.8

and Trident, and summed it all up in the words: 'the defence of Britain is safe only in Conservative hands'.

On 27 May another Conservative PEB touched on defence but, more importantly, President Reagan intervened to tell Labour that its defence policy was a 'grievous error'. His intervention received wide publicity. ITN's News at 5.45 devoted over a third of its programme to that one story. And the Conservatives used it to intensify the defence debate. That produced the second quantum leap in our panel's perceptions of the Conservative stress on defence.

However, in general our respondents did not agree with this emphasis on defence. While more and more perceived defence as the Conservatives' main campaign issue only a few more agreed that this was the issue that *should* be stressed. In our panel 6 per cent of respondents in the first fortnight, rising only to 11 per cent in the second fortnight, said that defence was the issue *they* wanted the parties to talk about. For two days after Reagan's intervention this figure rose to 18 per cent and 16 per cent respectively, but dropped back sharply again thereafter. Similarly, there was a sluggish response in terms of the numbers who said defence was *extremely important* in making up their mind how to vote. The numbers did increase, but not dramatically.

In short, the Conservative campaign had an enormous impact upon *perceptions of party agendas*, but a much smaller impact on the *voters' own agendas*. It had still less effect upon the voters' ratings of the parties on defence. We asked for 'marks out of ten' to indicate how much our respondents approved of each party on each of a number of issues. Between the first and second fortnights of the campaign, ratings of the Conservative Party on defence went up by 0.4 and Labour ratings went down by 0.2 – a net gain of only half a mark for the Conservatives. Moreover Conservative gains on the defence issue were greatest amongst C, A, and CA type voters – that is, amongst those who were likely to be Conservative or Alliance loyalists, or who

swithered between Conservative and Alliance choices. Labour and Labour/
Alliance switherers (i.e. L and LA type voters) were relatively unimpressed by
the hubbub over defence. So changing views on the issue had most impact on
those voter types who were very unlikely to vote Labour anyway (see table
11.11). Nonetheless, the issue damaged Labour slightly in all voter types.

We can investigate directly the impact of perceptions of the Conservative
Party's defence campaign on voting behaviour. By the time of our second
fortnight interviews, roughly half of our respondents who perceived a
Conservative stress on any issue at all, perceived the party as stressing defence.

The results of this analysis are ambiguous: amongst Conservative versus
Alliance switherers, perceptions on defence had little or no impact on voting
inclinations; amongst Labour/Alliance or Conservative/Labour switherers
there was no evidence of a defence impact during the campaign itself, but
right at the end – when the defence row had partially subsided – defence
perceptions seemed to hurt Labour amongst LA switherers yet help Labour
amongst CL switherers. The net effect of the defence row seems to have been
very small. Indeed, in the panel as a whole voting trends were totally
unaffected by perceptions of the Conservative emphasis on defence (see table
11.12).

We do not mean to imply that Labour's unpopular defence policy did not
damage its performance in the longer term. But its defence policy was clear
before the election and the attention given to the issue during the campaign
merely told people what they already knew, and had already taken into
account.

The impact of electoral credibility

Throughout the campaign we asked our panel whether they thought each
party had a *very good* chance, *some* chance, *very little* chance or *no chance* at all of
winning a majority in parliament. We also asked what they thought of each
party's chances of winning the election in their local constituency.

Throughout the campaign a majority thought the Conservatives had a *very
good* chance of winning a parliamentary majority while very few thought either
of the other parties had a *very good* chance. Nearly everyone thought the
Conservatives had at least *some* chance.

In our pre-election wave of interviews in March 1987 only 35 per cent
thought Labour had even *some* chance – considerably less than the 54 per cent
who thought the Alliance had at least *some* chance. Labour's credibility had
improved substantially by the time the campaign opened but on 14 May, the
very first day of our campaign interviews, there were still slightly more of our
panel who thought the Alliance had at least some chance (40 per cent) than
who thought Labour had at least some chance (34 per cent). On that day a
third of respondents said they had seen the Alliance second in the most recent

Table 11.12. *The impact of defence on voting trends by voter type*

Voter type	Perceived Conservative Party stress (in second fortnight)		Voting inclinations (changes)		
			First fortnight	Second fortnight	Vote
LA			% Labour lead over Alliance		
	On other issues		20	32 (+12)	35 (+ 3) (+15)
	On defence		33	45 (+12)	39 (− 6) (+ 6)
CA			% Conservative lead over Alliance		
	On other issues		45	48 (+ 3)	38 (−10) (− 7)
	On defence		52	52 (+ 0)	44 (− 8) (− 8)
CL			% Conservative lead over Labour		
	On other issues		65	61 (− 4)	55 (− 6) (−10)
	On defence		76	69 (− 7)	54 (−15) (−22)
All panel respondents			% for each part or combination		
	On other issues	Con.	47	45 (− 2)	45 (0) (− 2)
		Lab.	24	26 (+ 2)	29 (+ 3) (+ 5)
		All.	22	21 (− 1)	26 (+ 5) (+ 4)
		C/A	3	3 (+ 0)	
		L/A	4	3 (− 1)	
	On defence	Con.	44	43 (− 1)	43 (0) (− 1)
		Lab.	29	32 (+ 3)	33 (+ 1) (+ 4)
		All.	20	18 (− 2)	24 (+ 6) (+ 4)
		C/A	2	4 (+ 2)	
		L/A	5	3 (− 2)	

opinion polls, while half said Labour had been second. That morning Gallup in *The Daily Telegraph* had placed the Alliance second, while Marplan in *The Guardian* had placed it third, though only four per cent behind Labour.

But that was to prove the high point of the Alliance's electoral credibility. From then on it was downhill all the way. Even by the following day, our panel had decided by a five to one majority that the polls put Labour in second place and rather more (48 per cent) said Labour had at least some chance of a parliamentary majority than said so of the Alliance (37 per cent). Thereafter the gap widened rapidly as Labour's national credibility improved and the Alliance's declined. If the Labour campaign succeeded in nothing else it succeeded, with the help of the polls, in making Labour appear much more credible than the Alliance – at least in overall parliamentary terms.

These national trends had some influence on local perceptions but much less than might have been expected. Over the first three days of our interviews

Table 11.13. *National and local credibility trends*

	First fortnight	Second fortnight	Change
Nationally			
% perceiving Conservatives have chance*	98	98	0
% perceiving Labour have chance	52	62	+10
% perceiving Alliance have chance	29	17	−12
Locally			
% perceiving Conservatives have chance**	70	70	0
% perceiving Labour have chance	54	57	+ 3
% perceiving Alliance have chance	46	43	− 3

* 'very good' or 'some' chance of winning a parliamentary majority.
** 'very good' or 'some' chance of winning in the respondent's own constituency.

(14–18 May, because a weekend intervened) more people thought the Alliance had some chance locally than thought so of Labour, and even when Labour went ahead in local expectations it went ahead slowly and to a fairly limited extent.

Comparing perceptions in the first and second fortnights of the campaign, perceptions that Labour had a chance of a parliamentary majority went up from 52 per cent to 62 per cent, while perceptions of Alliance chances went down from 29 per cent to a mere 17 per cent. Locally, however, perceptions of Labour chances of winning the seat increased only from 54 per cent to 57 per cent, while perceptions of Alliance chances declined only from 46 per cent to a still very impressive 43 per cent (see table 11.13).

Of course, what is needed to define a tactical situation is not just an assessment of a single party's chances, but a combination of such assessments. We can construct a measure of tactical perceptions by noting which one, two, or three parties were perceived to have at least some chance of success. The possibilities are laid out in table 11.14 along with the percentages of panel respondents who perceived the tactical situation in each way.

Nationally, one third of respondents thought only the Conservative Party had some chance of a parliamentary victory. One third in the first fortnight, rising to half in the second fortnight, thought that electoral victory nationally lay between Labour and Conservative. The rest thought the Alliance had a chance.

Locally the pattern of expectations was much more varied, much more favourable to the Alliance, and much more stable through the campaign. Roughly one fifth thought their local contest fell into each of four categories – safe Labour, safe Conservative, Conservative versus Labour, and Conservative versus Alliance. One tenth perceived a Labour versus Alliance contest and another tenth thought it was a genuine three-way contest (see table 11.14).

Table 11.14. *Perceptions of the tactical situation nationally and locally*

Tactical perception of which parties have a chance	NATIONALLY		LOCALLY	
	First fortnight	Second fortnight	First fortnight	Second fortnight
Only Alliance	0	0	2	1
Only Labour	0	1	16	19
Both Labour and Alliance	1	0	12	10
Only Conservative	35	32	20	19
Both Conservative and Alliance	13	6	24	22
Both Conservative and Labour	35	50	17	19
All three have a chance	16	11	9	10

The impact of national credibility

We can assess the impact of both national and local tactical considerations by looking at how the trends in voting inclinations were affected by eventual (i.e. second fortnight) perceptions of the tactical situation.

First, the impact of *national* electoral credibility. As we saw in table 11.14, there were only two views held by substantial numbers of respondents in our panel: (i) that only the Conservatives had a chance and (ii) that Conservative and Labour both had a chance. Everyone was agreed that the Conservatives had a chance; so Conservatives should not have been encouraged by national tactical considerations to desert their chosen party. However, Labour and Alliance voters, and especially those who were swithering between Labour and the Alliance might possibly have been influenced by the relative national credibility of these two parties.

Within our panel, national tactical perceptions *did* influence voting. Trends amongst Labour/Alliance switherers did seem to depend somewhat upon national tactical perceptions. Those who thought Labour had no chance nationally swung ever so slightly away from Labour and towards the Alliance. Conversely, those who thought Labour did have a chance swung noticeably from Alliance to Labour (see table 11.15). In fact, they did so irrespective of whether they also thought that the Alliance had a chance nationally. The key factor was Labour's national credibility, irrespective of the Alliance's.

The impact of local credibility

Now let us look at the impact of *local* electoral credibility. Table 11.14 showed that about one fifth of our panel thought the local contest was a two-horse race between Conservative and Alliance candidates; another fifth thought it was a race between Conservative and Labour; while a tenth thought it was between Labour and the Alliance.

Table 11.15. *The impact of national credibility on Labour versus Alliance voting trends*

Perception of national tactical situation in second fortnight	Per cent Labour lead over Alliance			
	First fortnight	Second fortnight	Vote	Labour gain
Only Conservatives have chance	− 3	5	− 5	(− 2)
Both Conservative and Labour have chance	42	53	53	(+11)

Note: Table restricted to Labour/Alliance switherers.

In such places supporters of the third party would be under pressure to switch their voting inclinations. But they would only switch to a party they had some inclination to vote for anyway. The key groups of voters were the Labour/Alliance switherers and the Conservative/Alliance switherers. They were numerous, and frequently under pressure to defect. Ultimate voting choice should depend upon the interaction between voter-type and constituency-type, and indeed it did.

Labour/Alliance switherers moved towards the Alliance where they perceived Labour had no chance locally, and towards Labour where they perceived the Alliance had no chance.

Similarly, Conservative/Alliance switherers moved (very slightly) towards the Conservatives where they perceived the Alliance had no chance locally, and (very strongly) towards the Alliance where they perceived the Conservative candidate had no chance (see table 11.16).

The impact of *local* credibility on voting trends was much larger than the impact of *national* credibility. Most of the impact of local credibility seems to have occurred right at the *end of the campaign*. Amongst Labour/Alliance switherers, voting trends in contrasting local situations diverged only 11 per cent in the latter half of the campaign, but diverged by a staggering 47 per cent on election day. Similarly, amongst Conservative/Alliance switherers, voting trends in contrasting local situations diverged by only 7 per cent in the latter half of the campaign but diverged by 48 per cent on election day.

It seems that during the early days of the campaign, our respondents watched the opinion polls and rapidly came to the conclusion that the Alliance had no chance nationally. About a week later this seemed to transmit through into reduced perceptions of the Alliance's chances locally. The impact of tactical considerations on voting intentions was modest throughout most of the campaign but substantial on election day. When this end of the campaign effect occurred, it owed its force to perceptions of *local* rather than *national* credibility.

Table 11.16. *The impact of local credibility on voting trends*

Voter type	Perception of local tactical situation in second fortnight	Voting inclinations			
		First fortnight	Second fortnight	Vote	Change
		% Labour lead over Alliance			Labour gain
Labour/Alliance switherers	Con. + All. have chance	3	13	−12	(−15)
	Con. + Lab. have chance	43	64	75	(+32)
		% Conservative lead over Alliance			Conservative gain
Conservative/Alliance switherers	Lab. + All. have chance	57	49	12	(−45)
	Lab. + Con. have chance	71	70	74	(+ 3)

Paradoxically, the impact of local tactical considerations late in the campaign probably helped the Alliance most despite the fact that, as table 11.13 showed, fewer respondents thought the Alliance had a chance locally than thought so of Labour or the Conservatives. The paradox is explained by table 11.14. Half our respondents (51 per cent) felt they lived in places where, by the end of the campaign, only two parties had a chance. Of the 51 per cent, 32 felt that the local contest was between the Alliance and one of the other parties. In all these places the Alliance could expect to gain from the tactical pressures on either Labour or Conservative sympathisers. And of the 51 per cent, 29 felt that the local contest involved Labour and one of the other parties but that Labour could not expect to gain tactical votes in all these places for while many Alliance sympathisers might back Labour against the Conservatives, relatively few Conservatives would back Labour against the Alliance. A similar problem would afflict the Conservatives in their two-way fights. As always, tactical voting, if and when it occurs, is bound to help the centre party more than the parties of the left and right.

Notes

The authors would like to thank the ESRC, the IBA and the University of Glasgow for funding this research.
1 David Butler and Donald Stokes, *Political Change in Britain* (London: Macmillan, 1969).

12 Interviewing politicians

Ivor Crewe (Chairman)
I asked Sir Robin Day to talk to us about interviewing politicans for one simple reason. Although there are a large number of worthy academic research papers on all aspects of election campaigns, countless statistical analyses of party election broadcasts and the precise party bias of television news programmes, I know of no serious academic study, even in the more obscure journals, of the lengthy sustained interview of the senior politician. It goes undiscussed, a completely neglected topic of study. Yet if one thinks back to past elections interviews of politicians have been important campaign events. Most recently, in the 1987 election, the way Sir Robin Day forced David Owen into conceding that he could not imagine himself living within a Labour coalition but could in certain circumstances imagine an arrangement with the Conservatives was a significant moment of the campaign. I rather doubt that this could have happened in a forum other than the long interview, on which there is clearly no one better to talk than Sir Robin Day.

Sir Robin Day
I am a little nervous about the way you have introduced this talk because I have very few qualifications to take part in this conference. I am not a pollster. I am not a psephologist. I am not even one of the PhDs with which this room is peppered. I am not a party apparatchik and I am not a politician. So I speak to this audience with even more than my usual humility. I speak only as someone who has covered eight general elections as an interviewer. That doesn't give me any great qualification for talking about it, but it gives me a good standpoint from which to look at it.

All those elections have been since 1959 and may I remind you that David Butler started our conference this afternoon by pointing out that 1959 was a turning point in the history of the coverage of elections. 1959 was indeed a historic year in more ways than one: it was the year that Mrs Thatcher first succeeded in entering parliament and it was also the year that I failed to enter parliament! By such quirks of the popular will is the destiny of nations decided. And some of you who may be gifted with bad taste may be wondering what would have happened if it had been the other way around.

David Butler mentioned the fact which is familiar to all of you, or most of you, that the 1959 election was the first election which had anything like proper broadcast coverage. I would like to ram that point home if I may, because some of you may have forgotten the extraordinary circumstances which then existed. Until 1959 there was no coverage – even in a news bulletin on radio or television. Forget about current affairs and all these grand interviews and everything like that – there was no coverage *in the news* of a speech in the election. That was only a generation ago.

So that was the climate which existed until people like me started work in the mid 1950s. And what I want to emphasise today is that everything has got much freer; everything has got more relaxed. There is a much more liberal attitude between politics and television; much less tension than there was in those early days. And yet, paradoxically, this is the one point I am going to make in the course of my speech – you may disagree with it – paradoxically the interview, although it is now conducted in a much more liberal atmosphere than it used to be 25 years ago, has somehow ceased to function as it ought to. And I am going to suggest that the 'big interview' as you kindly called it is virtually a dead letter.

May I remind you what happened in 1964 and 1966. We didn't have any so-called 'big interviews' then. We had something called 'Election Forum' – an idea dreamed up by the great Mrs Wyndham-Goldie. It consisted of three journalists, competent fellows – Ian Trethowan, Kenneth Harris and myself – and then we went into a BBC room in Television Centre and we sorted out 11,000 cards which the viewers had sent in to Mr Heath and Mr Wilson and we selected cards to give us questions to ask. And we used to say, 'Mrs Higgins from Scunthorpe wants to know what you are going to do about unemployment' and then after a time we realised there was a way of putting supplementaries so we said 'Ah! yes, but . . . Mrs Morrison of Chorlton-cum-Hardy says you said that last time'. It was very dramatic. We couldn't really ask any questions ourselves; we could only just ask the questions on the cards, which we had selected. I remember vividly going along the corridors of the Television Centre past the dressing room where the interviewers were preparing to perform and hearing Kenneth Harris quite distinctly rehearsing the questions on his cards. 'Prime Minister' – 'Prime Minister' – in order to get the exact note of censoriousness into his voice. By the way, one little story about Election Forum. There were about 15,000 cards with questions on pensions, defence, unemployment. There was one tray with cards labelled 'rubbish' for which, of course, I made a beeline. I picked one out and read it and my eyes popped out, and I said, 'Phew! Ian, have you read this?' And Ian

Trethowan said, 'No, what is it?' It was in a young person's handwriting addressed to The Rt Hon. Edward Heath, Leader of the Conservative Party, c/o BBC, Election Forum – and it read as follows:

> Dear Daddy,
> When you get to No. 10, will you invite Mummy and me to tea?

I should explain that the process of sorting the cards into pensions and defence and atomic waste and so on, got a bit tedious. We needed some fun, so I said to Ian Trethowan, 'Do you think we could really suppress this? On the other hand, if we use it (in Disraeli's phrase about Palmerston) Ted Heath might sweep the country!' So Ian thought about it very carefully, and there was a Director-General even then in the making. He said 'Well, I think I know the answer, Robin, we'll use it in rehearsal.' So we used it as our rehearsal question and I read out 'Dear Daddy' and Mr Heath's shoulders shook with laughter! . . . but he never made any denial.

For the election *Panorama*s in 1979 we had two candidates either side of me – they were picked from the MPs of the old parliament. We decided to have a 'rough diamond' and a 'clever Dick' – Bryan Gould was the 'clever Dick' and the 'rough diamond' was Joe Ashton and between them, I remember, they made mincemeat of Francis Pym, the Tory spokesman, when he appeared. That was 1979. It all gradually developed and it became freer as it is today. And I, personally, haven't come across any tension or objections from politicians in the last election or the 1983 election. There was only one case where a protest was made in an interview in the 1987 election. That was when I was asking David Steel and David Owen about what they would do in a hung parliament and whether they would cooperate, with whom, and so on. David Steel said, 'Why don't you ask Mr Kinnock these questions? Why do you keep on at us?' and I said, according to the BBC transcript, 'I don't know whether you've interviewed Mr Kinnock' (this was to Mr Steel) 'but if you have you'll know that you don't always have time to get the questions in that you want to get in.' That struck me as a fairly inoffensive and courteous and factually correct statement, but within 30 seconds Patricia Hewitt was on the telephone to the producer of the programme demanding an apology. Slightly to my irritation I later discovered one was given. That was a very minor matter, but in general I haven't experienced any tension recently.

The point I want to get to is this. Although the whole atmosphere is freer and you have longer time, and you can cross-examine people at greater length, and argumentative questions are not objected to provided they are fair and relevant, nonetheless, the television interview is much less useful, much less effective than it used to be 20 years ago. Harold Macmillan, Alec Douglas-Home, Harold Wilson, Edward Heath – they answered questions in their own way, but at least they used to address the questions you asked them, and they used to deal with the point. Harold Wilson used to take me aside as we came down in the Lime Grove lift and he would say, 'Robin, you didn't ask me so and so, you should have asked me that, I wouldn't have been able to answer that question', and I'd say, 'Oh, what a lousy interviewer I am'. He treated it in a professional way, and so did all the other prime ministers. But current leaders (and I think Mr Kinnock and Mrs Thatcher are alike in this respect for different reasons of their own) decide to hell with the television interviewer, we are going to say what we want to say. Not that this worries my vanity or anything like that. I have always taken the view that television interviews are given an inflated importance, and I've always urged that parliament should be televised. I don't believe in unelected people like me having any spurious kind of power. But my point is that you don't have a dialogue with these political leaders. You don't really achieve anything very much. The television interview ought to be one of the voters' few defences against what David Butler would say was the advent of 'professionalism' in elections.

I'm not talking about putting the man on the spot, or anything like that, but about having dialogue and having questions answered in a reasonably direct way. I know the politicians are not on oath or anything like that, but they could answer in a more direct way. The advantage of that is that it is the viewers' one defence against the professional, the manipulation of the media. It's the defence against the image-maker, the ad-man, the tele-prompter, and everything like that. The viewer has a chance to see the political leader answering questions directly on the points raised at the time asked; not in prepared scripts, or in programmed answers. But nowadays they tend to come in with their manifestos all canned in their mind, all saying what they want to say. Now, I don't know what the answer is to this. Perhaps people like me have failed. I think that's probably the answer. Nigel Forman suggested this afternoon that we didn't give them enough time to answer. I do assure you that I have interviewed politicians for 50 minutes at length and still at the end of that they haven't answered the question in a reasonable way. At the last election after one 40 minute interview, my taxi-driver the next morning would say, 'Very interesting, last night! Yes. Did you understand a bloody word 'e said? Never answers the question does 'e?' I agree there is the problem of cutting people short and the producer saying, 'Go on to another subject', and all that. I don't think it applies to the major interviews, and sometimes I think the only solution to the problem is to start by saying 'Prime Minister, or Leader of the Opposition, what is your answer to my first question?' – and then come back 45 minutes later. It would certainly save a lot of problems.

I think the big interview has been hi-jacked by the politician. Now, there are certain exceptions to this. The *Election Call* format has been an interesting development, because the interviewer is merely there as an underliner of the viewer's or listener's point, who could get in genuine points which the politicians couldn't fob off so easily. That was the beauty of it. But the trouble with the 'Election Call' format is that only one or two viewers in any dozen or so whose questions get through ask really pointed or relevant questions; most just ask a familiar, predictable question and may not know how to follow it up. Not that the *Election Call* format is proof against the agile politician. The nurse asked a very awkward question of Mrs Thatcher. The PM said 'Where is your hospital?' and the nurse said, 'Mold in North Wales'. Mrs Thatcher said, 'Yes, I know. I was there the other day. You've got a very good hospital with five new dialysis machines, and fourteen this, that and the other . . .' and it was ammunition for her. Fair enough. *Election Call* doesn't crucify politicians, and it was not meant to. But it does help to get points across in a way that the ordinary formal interview can't.

So what I am saying is that although the whole atmosphere in which we work in television has become much more liberal and relaxed in the last 25 years, the 'big set-piece' television interview has ceased to be as effective as it should be to counteract the artificial professionalism of politics which David Butler so rightly mentioned at the beginning of the conference.

DISCUSSION

David Butler
Most of what I would like to say is really in support of Robin's general thesis – politicians do become uninterviewable. I have a glorious memory of the airport at Belfast in 1969 after an Assembly election, when I met Alastair Burnet who said he had had the ultimate comeuppance as an interviewer the previous night when Ian Paisley had failed to win the Bankside election which he had promised to win. When Alastair lent forward to him and said 'Why did you not do it?' – he said, 'What's that you say – let me smell your breath!' It was Jim Callaghan who used to answer, 'If I may say so, Sir Robin, you are asking me the wrong question.' Now, as Sir Robin says, people have got much more vulgar about it. They don't even bother to say 'you've asked me the wrong question'. They answer the question with the Central Office or whatever brief they have been given, and they have got their message and Robin is a kind of irrelevance.

Participant 1
How much is it a problem of the producer? Does the politician know that the producer will want to move you on to get through, say, four or five topics in the interview, and that you are actually only going to ask the question perhaps twice? Does the politician know that if you were to go on, and on, and on, on the same topic they would not be allowed to get away with it?

Robin Day
How does the producer move me on?

Participant 1
Well, isn't someone saying into your earpiece 'move on'?

Robin Day
Good God no! No – I've never had a 'deaf aid' in my ear during an interview, ever. I have one for a programme like Election Night Results. You have to have communication then so you can go to the result in wherever it is. But I never have it in an ordinary interview, although I believe some interviewers do, and some producers are foolish enough to try to run an interview by committee . . .

Participant 2
Why don't you ask the same question over and over again until the politician is really embarrassed?

Robin Day
Well, I don't know how many of my interviews you have seen in your relatively young life but I can show you some where I have asked the same question several times, a good many times. I remember asking Sir Alec Douglas-Home five times, I think, in the basement of the Imperial Hotel in 1964 whether he was going to run for the leadership of the Conservative Party, and he didn't answer the question each time, but he made it quite clear that he was. But that is just an incident which comes to my mind. You can't just indulge yourself. An interviewer isn't there just to pursue his own points. If there is an evasive or unsatisfactory answer, the interviewer has to decide whether to go on and ask again, or whether to say, 'you haven't answered my question', which I personally find a little offensive. You have to find another way of saying it, such as, 'May I give you an opportunity of making your position clearer on that', and you move on when you can. And you also have to decide whether it is important enough to go on, and on, and on. Very often the viewer picks up the fact that the politician hasn't answered the question without you underlining it!

Max Atkinson
I would just like to offer a possible solution to the question of why interviews get hi-jacked and then perhaps offer a way in which you might solve it.
  Since the last conference here one of the things I have learnt an awful lot about is that coaching in the interview technique is a booming industry in this country for both the businessman and the politician. And if you look at the central platform of most of the consultants who are coaching people in interview technique, the one thing they seem to go at is the idea that you should go into the interview with a clear idea of what you should say, and say

it irrespective of what the interviewer asks. And I think in a sense this is what you may be a victim of.

As to a solution it may be that one needs the same kind of approach. But before I develop that point, I think in some respects you should not worry about it too much because the fact that they are not answering the question is totally transparent to the viewer and it may be just as useful that viewers see politicians behaving in this way. As to a solution (I hope you don't regard this as disrespectful), if your interviewees are undergoing elaborate programmes of training then perhaps the solution might be that the interviewers themselves should also undergo similar programmes of training.

Robin Day
What would we be trained to do?

Max Atkinson
Well, there may be ways of analysing those interviews where people aren't answering the questions, just as there are techniques for avoiding your questions. Lots of research has been done into other kinds of question/answer sequences like police interrogation courses.

Robin Day
I have never acutally undergone a course like that, but if you will put me in touch with anybody I'll be very happy to undergo it to give my declining career a lift. I've often asked for advice on how to deal with this particular problem, mainly from people skilled in the forensic art. And contrary to the press who have traditionally regarded television interviews as an inquisition, members of the Bar and old judges regard television interviews as extremely wet in letting people off the hook all the time. And, indeed, one High Court judge said to me one day, 'By God, you let that rascal off the hook yesterday'. I said, 'Well, what am I supposed to do'. He was thinking that I should repeat the question, so he said, 'What you should say, is this – Mr X, did you hear my question?' 'Mr X, did you understand my question?' 'Mr X, will you now answer my question?' I decided to employ that in my last television interview. Then I remember asking another very senior practitioner of the forensic art. I said, 'I've got to interview the Prime Minister tonight'. He said 'Oh good, I'll watch that'. And I said, The trouble is, I know what policy questions to ask, but I can't just think of the best way of starting it. I want a good kick-off question, you see.' (I should explain that the Prime Minister concerned was not at the height of his reputation at that time.) And the old judge said, 'I know how you should start. Start by asking him this – "Does the word *shame* mean anything to you?"' I'm afraid I chickened out!

Linda Anderson

Was Michael Foot interviewable?

Robin Day

Oh yes, very much so. He loved it. He went on a long time, but he always had a dialogue, and he didn't mind how vigorous you were with him at all, providing you gave him a chance to answer the question. In fact, if you read his book about his disastrous election, he prints the whole of my Panorama interview with him in full, as an example of how fair an interview could be.

Glyn Mathias

I don't disagree with what Robin says about politicians hijacking interviews from him. I disagree slightly with him that it is just a recent phenomenon. I recall trying to interview Ted Heath in the latter days of his premiership and having a five-minute interview in which I got four lines in, one of which was thank you! And he didn't answer the question – he just came with a set-piece answer and he filled the time consciously with set-piece answers. I just don't think it is quite such a recent phenomenon as you suggest. I'd also quote the example of Enoch Powell, whom you have fenced with many times. I fenced with him rather fewer times. A most difficult man to interview who would never answer the question, and if he was really in a corner would quote to you in Latin! . . . and if he thought the interviewer was likely to understand he would quote in Greek!

Robin Day

I'm sorry you had a bad experience with Ted Heath. I interviewed Ted Heath many times and, of course, he could be very awkward, very tiresome; if it suited him just to give non-answers he did. But in general when he was interviewed in big interviews, such as after his counter-inflation policy, when he was a master of his subject and had lived with it, and slept with it, and eaten it and debated it in the House of Commons, pity the poor interviewer trying to ask him some questions about it! He would always address the questions. I never had any difficulty about that. I didn't necessarily get the answers everybody wanted, but you got the dialogue.

Now, on the question of Enoch Powell, I disagree with you entirely. He's absolutely fascinating to interview – I love interviewing Enoch Powell. He deals with every point you make, so much so that if you get your grammar wrong in your question, he picks you up on the grammar before he answers it. He certainly is not anxious to explain everything he doesn't want to explain, but he answers. He gives you very good intellectual exercise, I think.

Peter Riddell
I think you are in danger of underselling the big interview. I have thought that the most revealing insights into Mrs Thatcher over the last decade have come in the big interview. Whereas her speeches are so carefully worked over by Gordon Reece and Ronald Millar it is when she spurts out during the course of an interview (normally after the first half-hour) that she is revealing. Victorian values first came out in the course of a big interview; so did some of her views on the welfare state. I think they have been a totally revealing source, particularly with her, because she is away from some of the discipline of being at Number 10. And the second point: you come down to the Commons very often, Robin, to see Question Time and the big debates. Not many other interviewers do nowadays. What advantage do you think you gain from coming to the House?

Robin Day
Oh, enormous advantages, enormous! I've always – except when I was a travelling Panorama reporter, and was abroad a lot – ever since 1956 when I became ITN's parliamentary correspondent, I've always attended the Gallery of the House as often as I possibly could. Not only because it is general political background and you see the personalities, but also because it helps someone like me who doesn't, as it were, know anything about economics, and doesn't understand many of the issues in a technical sense. If I hear them debated by experts on both sides of the House it fixes some of the arguments in my mind more clearly when I do an interview than if I read a dull book or White Paper on it. And then I know where to look it up; I go back to the House of Commons, or Hansard, or the House of Lords, and look at the text of the debate.

But the main reason is not that. The main reason is that the interviewer, if he goes regularly to parliament, understands what parliamentarians regard as fair and honest questioning. I've never had a politician ever object to anything I asked him, because I always keep to what I regard as the rules and the standards which are used in parliament. And they can be very, very vigorous indeed. What the politicians object to is a trick question, and a rather shoddy question which isn't accurately based. I am sure I think it is very, very useful indeed, to attend parliament and I think more people should go regularly.

Ivor Gaber
I wonder if the situation that's developed with political interviews is similar to the development of ballistic missiles and anti-ballistic missiles, that Robin develops a style of interviewing which eventually draws forth the sophisticated preparation which creates the blocking or the headlines? It seems to me that one of the significant developments in 1983 and 1987 was and has been

the use of the public as interrogators; the Diana Gould confrontation with Mrs Thatcher; the soldier who put John Smith on the spot on Election Call . . .

[*Robin Day*: the alleged soldier]

. . . the alleged soldier, right, but who knows at the end of the microphone [*Robin Day*: Mr Warmington]

Maybe we've moved beyond the time of – I say this with great respect – the set-piece interview as being the most effective way of putting politicians through the mill. And because people are now much more familiar with television, and are no longer over-awed at the prospect of having a camera in front of them as they used to be 20 years ago, they've got the guts like Mrs Gould, and other people like her, to keep going and not feel intimidated. Maybe that's the way we should be looking forward, to broadening the number of interviewers, so to speak, and letting everybody have a go at the politicians.

Robin Day

Well, I think you're making a perfectly fair point there. Probably my time has come, but I think a lot of people do regard us as part of the Establishment, playing the Establishment game, offering a little Establishment sword play with the great men of our time, and everything like that. The ordinary person has the advantage over us in that respect. They talk a little more uncouthly and more freshly. On the other hand, I've got dozens of pieces of evidence of ordinary people and viewers who quite honestly don't see me as 'not on their side' – they regard me as on their side, and hardly a day passes without some person I meet saying they think of me as they think of an ordinary person angry about the unemployment, but they think of me as trying to help, as being on the viewer's side. Sometimes, anyway.

As to the two examples which you raised – I don't think they are parallel. I didn't think Mrs Gould was an ordinary person. She was put up as a lady who had made a study of the subject and no ordinary person has that knowledge of the way the Belgrano was going. I'm not talking about the merits of her question but she was not an ordinary questioner. On the other hand, this chap Warmington, whose brother was a lance-corporal who tipped him off about this, he had obviously thought about it, and he asked argumentative questions. But they weren't based on technical knowledge as Mrs Gould's were.

Mrs Gould's card came into the Nationwide Studio. It looked an interesting card amongst a lot of other cards about the Falklands. The researchers then spoke to all the people; Mrs Gould was told we were interested in her question and she went away and then made herself, in the two weeks she had, the world's expert on the Belgrano for that interview.

Ivor Gabor

I'm not saying that you're simply seen as the Establishment. I'm saying that the big interview is perceived as the gladiatorial contest – Sir Robin's taking on Mrs Thatcher, or whatever. Not that they are saying he is the lackey of Mrs Thatcher or Mr Kinnock, but it's perceived as an entertainment in itself, whereas, just to give another example, Wakeham was caught on Election Call by a very angry woman from up North – who again, didn't respect the sort of parameters that we set ourselves, who said, 'You don't know what you're talking about – it's a load of rubbish!'

Robin Day
But that's all right. That's an ordinary person; she hadn't had two weeks studying the problem she was going to raise with him, in a highly technical, nautical way. That's the point I'm making.

PART V

Television in the 1987 Campaign

13 Party political and election broadcasts, 1985–1987: their perceived attributes and impact upon viewers

Introduction

Television is widely thought of as the broadest channel whereby information and impressions about the political process reach the public. People believe television to be their principal source of national political information, and this testimony is accepted as valid by the political community, although good evidence suggests that a great deal of the information presented on screens is not retained by viewers.[1] Thus, the assumption that televised information and impressions have a particular potency remains at the root of arrangements designed to ensure that all plants in the political garden are equally fertilised.

Some of the structures for maintaining impartiality and balance on television have recently been examined by Boyle.[2] He describes the work of the Party Political Broadcasting Committee as the only 'forum' in which the broadcasting authorities and the parliamentary political parties transact decisions. The scope of the Committee is to allocate time for party political broadcasts and at election times for party election broadcasts. These broadcasts are messages made by or for the parties, and the broadcasting authorities are not responsible for the content of these messages but only for providing airtime, for which no charge is made.

There are at least two functions that party political – and election – broadcasts fulfil. One is to convey the party's case, explaining the policies and seeking support; the other function is implicit and symbolic, involving a demonstration (or so it is thought to be) of parity or of inequality of status as between parties. Thus, in the 1983 election the SDP/Liberal Alliance did not have as many PEBs as did either of the other national parties; but in 1987, on a basis of by-election performance as well as with evidence from opinion polls that the public felt that more time should have been allocated to Alliance PEBs, equal numbers were allocated to the three major parties.[3] This gave the Alliance one way of arguing that it was (as well as seeing itself as) a party on parity with its two major rivals. At the other extreme, the Ecology Party had no PEBs and this made its existence, in broadcasting and political terms, much less visible.

The explicit functions of party political and election broadcasts have been explored in a number of studies. In 1974 there were two general elections and at the first of them a study sought to relate the percentage voting turnout in each of twelve regions in the Independent Television system, to measures of viewing of PEBs, of current affairs and of overall television viewing.[4] Partial correlations, holding the overall amount of viewing constant, suggested a tendency for heavier viewing of PEBs to be associated with lower turnout figures.

Five years later a special survey found that viewers were willing to see comedy deal with the election but preferred straight explanation to dramatic or comic vignettes in PEBs.[5] The replies suggested that policies had been more effectively conveyed for the Labour than for the Conservative case, which had tended to emphasise personalities, an inference being that such affective aspects may have been important in influencing some voting.

Those who reported seeing more Labour and Conservative PEBs were more likely to say that TV helped them to understand each party's policy, but the same relationship did not pertain for the Liberal case. The inference was that the extent of grasp of the Liberal case was low, and had not been aided either by the (smaller number of) Liberal PEBs seen, or by general TV coverage of the Liberal position.

Following this a joint national survey done by the IBA and BBC asked people about their knowledge of politics, relating this to experience of PPBs.[6] There was a limited indication that even when other attributes which are linked to viewing and to knowledge were partialled out (such as age, interest in political programming and involvement in political activity) those who watched more PPBs tended also to know more about politics.

In the 1983 election Grant reported that Labour's PEBs' brief was 'to avoid the slickness [of the Conservatives' PEBs] while developing the fundamental Keynesian point of Labour's economic policy'.[7] The party leader had been portrayed (by newspaper cartoons and certain images on television) as aged and weak, and the PEBs did nothing to alter such an image. Grant reported that Labour had appointed a production company to give continuity to PPBs from 1985 onwards; and the 1987 PEBs for Labour were conspicuous for their attention to the party leader. One of the PEBs which focussed on the party leader was, indeed, simply reshown. Press discussion suggested that Labour's PEBs were not only well made, but successful in strengthening support for the party, in contrast to Conservative PEBs which seemed less remarkable.

Two possibilities with regard to Labour's PEBs present themselves in the light of the actual election result. One is that the fortifying role of building regard for Labour's leader was very successful in beating off an Alliance challenge to become the main opposition party; the other is that in spite of its acclaim, the Labour campaign – with PEBs as an important feature – did little or nothing to overhaul the Conservative lead.

Although it is difficult to prove that some features of television's content bring about some expected effect in real life, the indications are sufficiently strong to keep the topic alive both as a political opportunity and as a research problem. This study explores the explicit purposes of PPBs and PEBs, through a fund of data that was set up to provide parties with piecemeal assessments of their broadcasts shortly after each one's transmission. The analysis that follows can not go further than is inherent in the nature of the data, but its presentation may well add to an understanding of the process of political communication in the mid-1980s.

Method

The Broadcasters' Audience Research Board (BARB) contracts with the BBC's Broadcasting Research Department to issue diaries each week to a large nationwide sample of individuals. These diarists endorse each programme of which they have seen enough to form an opinion with a mark to show the degree of their appreciation. There is a facility in the questionnaire for users of the survey to ask additional questions about selected programmes. In this case the same set of additional questions has been used for every PPB and PEB for several years. These questions start with two items on whether the viewer supports the party's point of view, and continue with seven rating scales. In each of these, the PPB viewer is asked to say how much he or she agrees or disagrees with a (leading) statement about that PPB. The items, and the abbreviated titles used for them in this study, are as follows:

Important	:	the subject matter was important
Informative	:	the broadcast was informative
Provoking	:	the broadcast was thought-provoking
Interesting	:	the subject matter was interesting
Helpful	:	the broadcast was helpful to me
Presented	:	the party's point of view was well presented
Easy	:	I found it easy to understand the party's point of view

The scores of 5 (for strongly agree) down to 1 (for strongly disagree) are transformed to a mean position for the group on a 100-point scale and are tabulated for the whole sample as well as those of each sex, six different age bands and four separate social class groups. For the 1987 set of PPBs and PEBs the smallest sample of viewers supplying these evaluations numbered 272 and the largest 643.

Since early in 1986 the sample reached by these questionnaires has been a panel. Over 2,000 in the leanest weeks and well over 3,000 in the fuller weeks have returned completed diaries and additional questionnaires. During 1985 and for the early part of 1986 the diary was placed with a 'rolling' sample recruited on a five-day cycle. At that time it was not possible to find a core sample for longitudinal analysis. Nor is it practicable, even now, in spite of the large overall sample size, to make longitudinal analyses for 'programmes' such as PEBs which in themselves have moderate or small audiences.

After the evaluative ratings just described, respondents were asked, 'How much of the broadcast did you see?' They were required to reply either 'all of it', or 'part of it'. The percentage who claimed to have watched all of it is taken here as an overall measure of attention to the broadcast.

All these descriptive ratings, as well as the attention measure and a 'measure' of party (scoring 3 for Labour, 2 for Alliance and 1 for Conservative) have been used in a multiple regression analysis procedure to relate them to the dependent variable which is called Swing. Swing has been calculated from the first two questions in the set, which are as follows: '*Before* the broadcast did you expect to agree with its point of view?' (Yes, No and Not Sure); and, '*After* the broadcast, did you agree with its point of view?' The percentage who agreed (minus those who disagreed) gives the measure of support acknowledged for the time before seeing the PPB; likewise, the difference between agreement and disagreement after seeing the PPB is the level of support presumed as the outcome of the PPB. The difference between these two support levels is the Swing. An example can illustrate the procedure: before one particular PPB, supporters numbered 19 per cent compared with 32 per cent who did not support the point of view – a 13 per cent disadvantage; after the same PPB the same people included 37 per cent who said they now supported the point of view, against 33 per cent who did not – a four per cent advantage. Overall, the transformation of a 13 per cent disadvantage to a 4 per cent advantage constitutes a swing of 17 per cent.

The information has been assembled in two time bands. The first runs throughout 1985 and 1986 and assembles data on 31 PPBs, eleven for Labour and ten each for the Alliance and Conservative parties. In 1987 there were 18 PEBs but five of these were scheduled too soon to have been listed in the diaries and for the more complex analyses of the links between attributes the number is perilously small. Since it is (statistically) desirable to include more cases, earlier PPBs during the year were added in to the analysis, except for Budget broadcasts which are different in character. In effect, the 1987 array is largely of PEBs though the prior PPBs came increasingly to have the nature of a preparation for the election to come.

Table 13.1. *Ratings of characteristics of party political and election broadcasts*

					Rating Scales			
		Important	Interesting	Easy	Well presented	Thought-provoking	Informative	Helpful
Labour (11)*	1985–6	77	67	63	61	59	58	46
(8)	1987	74	63	65	63	53	60	45
		−3	−4	+2	+2	−6	+2	−1
Alliance (10)	1985–6	72	60	63	63	59	60	44
(8)	1987	71	60	64	63	54	60	45
		−1	0	+1	0	−5	0	+1
Conservative (10)	1985–6	67	54	58	56	51	52	37
(7)	1987	74	63	69	65	57	61	49
		+7	+9	+11	+9	+6	+9	+12

* numbers of broadcasts rated

Scores from 5 (for strongly agree) down to 1 (for strongly disagree) have been transformed to a mean on a 100-point scale.

Results

The first step is to examine the scores on the descriptive scales, looking at these for each party's broadcasts, and in the two periods that have been defined, namely 1985 and 1986 which constitute a mid-term stage and 1987 which saw the run-up to and the election campaign itself.

Although caution is needed in interpreting small differences between mean scores as reliable, the samples are sufficiently large as to allow two firm points to arise from the results. One is that scores are certainly different as between attributes – importance and simplicity are to the fore, and informativeness and helpfulness are much less strongly felt. The second matter is that for Alliance broadcasts there is a marked similarity in results in each of the two periods.

For the Labour broadcasts the mid-term results were probably better than the pre-election ones on importance, interest and thought-provokingness; on the other hand, the pre-election ratings may perhaps be regarded as an improvement over the mid-term ones, as regards each of comprehension, presentation and informativeness.

The Conservative Party's broadcasts, for all their lower acclaim in the press, had better results on all the rating scales during the pre-election period in comparision with the mid-term years. Thus, whereas the Conservative ratings in mid-term broadcasts were poorer than Labour's on all the scales, for the pre-election period the gap had been closed in terms of importance,

Table 13.2. *Attention to party broadcasts, and support for party opinions (%)*

			Support for views expressed						
		Atten-tion	Pre-broadcast support Pro	Anti	DK	Post-broadcast support Pro	Anti	DK	Net swing
Labour	1985–6	84	22	47	31	41	41	18	26
	1987	89	23	43	34	35	42	23	14
Alliance	1985–6	83	18	36	46	41	38	21	21
	1987	86	20	35	45	36	37	27	13
Conservative	1985–6	84	23	45	32	33	50	17	5
	1987	89	34	37	29	45	37	18	11

interest, presentation and informativeness; the Conservative broadcasts were better rated than Labour ones as more helpful, more thought-provoking, and easier to understand, in the pre-election period.

From these viewers' evaluations of party political and election broadcasts it becomes easier to understand the other evidence of the campaign, which consisted of a stable Conservative lead in several dozen opinion polls and a majority of over 100 seats at the electoral poll.

What were the other results on attention, and stated support for the parties' positions? These questions are answered in table 13.2

The measure of attention shows little variation from broadcast to broadcast, but it does appear that anticipated agreement with parties' broadcasts was slightly greater during the election year by comparison with the mid-term period.

People were less likely to say they did not know whether they agreed with a party's view after seeing its broadcasts. The amount of uncertainty acknowledged about Alliance points of view was clearly greater than that for the other two parties, especially before the broadcasts; even after they had seen an Alliance election broadcast more people said they were uncertain about the Alliance viewpoint than was the case for the two other parties.

Labour's mid-term efforts produced a large net swing, mainly by making inroads into the uncommitted. In contrast Conservative broadcasts in the mid-term ended with only a small net swing. Alliance broadcasts in the mid-term brought swings closer on average to the large one for Labour than to the modest Conservative gain.

Swings were lower in the pre-election phase and also within the PEB sequence itself. Taking the last twelve PEBs, four for each party, the average swing across the first three of these was 16 points, dropping to 13 and then 11 points for the penultimate and the final PEBs. There was, nevertheless, considerable variation in the swing within each party's PEBs. The Conservatives' largest swing, of 18 points, occurred for the broadcast drawing attention to left-wing extremists. Labour's item, the next day (on the Health Service), had a 19-point swing while the Alliance PEB featuring the two leaders produced an 18-point swing.

The measure used here of whether the viewer supports the party's viewpoint probably goes no further than a judgement of the particular policies dealt with in a specific broadcast. Thus, neither support for the views in the broadcast nor the swing after the broadcast measures voting intention, though either may influence it. The rest of the campaign, in the press and on television, has to be acknowledged as having a major influence on voting; but what has been shown here is that party broadcasts do have some short-term role in affecting opinions, since pro-party swings are reported for the great majority of these broadcasts (though not for all of them, as two items in the pre-election series each have net swings of −1 per cent).

It remains now to show whether the degree of swing can be associated with any of the perceived characteristics of the broadcasts. The procedure here is to calculate a multiple regression equation for each of the two time periods that have been defined. For technical reasons it was advisable to include a few PPBs from earlier in 1987 with the PEBs and also to reduce the number of perceived characteristics of the broadcasts used to predict swing.[8]

The results showed that for the mid-term PPBs the perceived importance of the content was negatively associated with swing. That is, greater swing occurred on occasions when the subject matter was felt to be of less importance. This result, at first sight possibly surprising, is more easily understood if it is taken to indicate that the acknowledged change of opinion is a relatively superficial phenomenon, more easily accomplished with matters that are not 'core' beliefs for the individual.

Three other measures had some claim to be regarded as significantly linked with swing; these are interestingness, thought-provokingness and, at a marginal level, the extent of attention that was generated. The attributes of ease of understanding and quality of presentation were not associated with the degree of swing, nor was the extent to which viewers said each broadcast was informative.

Although several measures were independently associated with the extent of swing in mid-term broadcasts, the analyses of the broadcasts during the election year suggest that swing does not link in any significant way with any of these characteristics.

Conclusions

Party Political Broadcasts have been shown to produce substantial amounts of swing in terms of viewers' readiness to say that they had come to agree more with a party's point of view. These swings have tended to apply more to opposition parties' broadcasts and to be linked with perceptions that the issues dealt with were *not* particularly important, but that the broadcasts were interesting and thought-provoking. However, these characteristics could be shown to link with the degree of swing only in the 1985–6 broadcasts. No link could be demonstrated in broadcasts closer to the election, which in any case produced smaller swings.

Viewers of Alliance broadcasts were most likely to say they did not know whether they supported its point of view. If the communication system has a goal of producing similar and thorough knowledge of all the main parties' policies, then this was not achieved for the Alliance.

Party election broadcasts seem to be less important in terms of informing and persuading viewers than mid-term party political broadcasts. To report that PEBs are likely only to have had a limited effect, if any, upon voting intentions or turnout is not to deny that they may have had other indirect effects. Thus, a PEB which gains critical acclaim may enhance the morale of party workers and politicians, leading to better performance in news and current affairs interviews and on the streets facing the voters. However, it would be extremely difficult to demonstrate such effects, let alone to quantify them.

Notes

1 Barrie Gunter, *Poor Reception: Misunderstanding and Forgetting of Broadcast News* (Hillsdale, New Jersey: Lawrence Erlbaum, 1987).

2 A. E. Boyle, 'Politics and broadcasting: the SDP case', *Media Law and Practice* (April 1987), 6–10.

3 Mallory Wober, Michael Svennevig and Barrie Gunter, 'The television audience and the 1983 general election', in Ivor Crewe and Martin Harrop (eds.), *Political Communications: The General Election Campaign of 1983* (Cambridge: Cambridge University Press, 1986), pp. 95–103.

4 Mallory Wober, *Television Coverage and the First 1974 British General Election* (London: Independent Broadcasting Authority, Research Department Report, 1974).

5 Mallory Wober, *The May 1979 General Election – Viewers' Attitudes Towards Television Coverage* (London: Independent Broadcasting Authority, Audience Research Department, Special Report, June 1979).

6 Mallory Wober and Michael Svennevig, *Party Political Broadcasts and their Use for the Viewing Public* (London: Independent Broadcasting Authority, Audience Research Department, Special Report, October 1981).

7 Nick Grant, 'A comment on Labour's campaign', in Crewe and Harrop (eds.), *Political Communications: The General Election Campaign of 1983*, pp. 82–7.

8 Mallory Wober, *Party Political and Election Broadcasts* (London: Independent Broadcasting Authority, Audience Research Department, Special Report, October 1987).

14 Indecent exposure? Three-party politics in television news during the 1987 general election

Introduction: decent exposure?

The Alliance parties gained a notable victory in preparing for the general election. They won 'parity' in the allocation of party election broadcasts, and saw this extended to the general coverage of the election on television. In granting parity the broadcasters acknowledged the position of the Alliance as a substantial third force in British politics. More than this, they seemed to be rehearsing the ground rules for coverage of a more robust and permanent form of three-party politics which might obtain after the election, and may be said to have anticipated signal changes in British politics and the British constitution. The Conservative and Labour parties at first protested, but then acquiesced in this minor revolution in election broadcasting.

The broadcasters proceeded to stopwatch their way through the election, timing every item, attempting to weigh the general tendency, favourable or unfavourable, and adjust the balance. Under the newly established 'rule of three', every item about one party was followed by items about the other two, and in the early part of the campaign at least, every studio discussion required three talking heads, even if one of them was not actually in the studio. Needless to say it was all too good, or perhaps too bad, to last. Channel 4 News was the first to break ranks. In the third week of the campaign they abandoned the seeming artificiality of the three-way debate in favour of a format in which one party's views on an issue was followed by a studio discussion between representatives of the other two.

Context

The broadcasters had entirely decent intentions, with the consequence that coverage of the election was sober, bland and rather self-consciously respectable. For the broadcasters were on their best behaviour, anxious, especially in the BBC, to be seen as worthy guardians of the long traditions of public service broadcasting. Events had made them unusually sensitive to the constraints of that tradition and the concomitant obligation to political balance. First, the comfortable monopoly of BBC and ITV was threatened by rapid changes in communications technology and by the government's free market ideology. Second, for the BBC, the election followed closely on Norman Tebbit's accusations of bias in the reporting of certain news stories, notably the US raid on Libya, and the Alliance's crusade for 'proportionality' in news coverage. (This had culminated in an out-of-court settlement in the previous autumn.) Longer term complaints about election news coverage have emphasised the extent to which the medium has underplayed substantive issues in favour of personalities and the trivial pursuit of 'good' pictures. Programme makers were obviously sensitive to the hostile background against which their election coverage would be assessed, and at least some of their decisions about the structure and content of news programmes (including BBC1's decision to extend its flagship *Nine O'clock News* to fifty minutes), were designed to anticipate and thus to defuse an adverse reaction.

Indecent exposure?

Despite the best of intentions the broadcasters were guilty of what might be called indecent exposure. In one sense this may be understood simply as showing too much of a good thing. Comparison with a study of television news conducted in 1986[1] reveals the scale and density of election news coverage. In the earlier study, an eight-week period of research yielded 841 political items from 399 broadcasts of national and regional news. During the election, the five-week period of study, monitoring only 160 national news broadcasts, yielded 926 political items. Election items accounted for 91 per cent of all political news, as defined in the study.[2] This saturation coverage took its toll. On 31 May *The Sunday Telegraph* asked, 'is anyone still watching out there?' The answer seems to be that people did continue to watch 'live' television (as opposed to programmes recorded on video), but that some news programmes, indeed election coverage in general, were deserted by a substantial proportion of viewers. It was not always possible to escape. On Thursday, 28 May, there was a point when Labour's defence policy was being discussed simultaneously on BBC1 (*Campaign Question Time*), BBC2 (*Newsnight*), and ITV (*Campaign 87*). Over the campaign as a whole viewing figures for the BBC's extended *News and Election '87* fell by nearly 3 million, and *News at Ten* ratings were down by half a million on the previous month. (There are some seasonal factors which account for part of this drop.) By comparison, on this measure, *Channel 4 News* at seven o'clock had a better election. By the third week of the campaign proper its hour-long programme had improved its ratings by about 20 per cent.

In the event such extensive coverage and painstaking commitment to parity amounted to over-exposure for some of the protagonists, notably the Alliance parties, for all that it had been one of their main goals. The reason was that parity as worked for by the broadcasters (procedural parity), the fruit of their honest labours and decent intent, turned out to yield less than parity in outcome (substantive parity). This was so because in the end broadcasters cannot control perceptions, or determine political reality; the strong two-party tendencies of the British political culture and the British constitution were beyond the reach of the broadcasters' sustained attempt to weight the parties equally.

For the broadcasters the challenge of the election undoubtedly turned on the question of parity and on the related question of agenda setting. According equal status to the Alliance put extra pressure on programme makers and imposed a harsh discipline especially in terms of time-keeping. They aimed at and largely achieved what one executive called a 'running balance' between the parties. This was in face of continuing complaints from all the contenders, but especially from the Labour Party, aimed at 'improving' their image in news and current affairs programmes. This balance is best understood as a kind of procedural parity whereby in the coverage of the election, the main protagonists are treated in an evenhanded fashion in terms of time devoted to them, their placement in the running order, the number and style of leader profiles and so on, right down to the reporting of gaffes made while on the stump. The news programmes were able to deliver a procedural balance which is uncanny in its consistency. Almost any breakdown of the figures produces the same sort of profile. For example:

Table 14.1. *Mention of party by weekday news programmes as a percentage of all mentions of parties in each programme (Conservative, Labour and Alliance only)*

News programme	Conservative	Labour	Alliance
ITN 5.45	24.2	37.2	26.0
ITN 10.00	28.7	34.1	26.9
BBC 6.00	30.0	35.1	25.2
BBC 9.00	29.9	35.0	27.7
C4 7.00	29.9	35.0	27.1

Alternatively:

Table 14.2. *Mention of party by selected news items as a percentage of all party mentions in that item category, all broadcasts (Conservative, Labour and Alliance only).*

Item	Conservative	Labour	Alliance
Manifesto	26.0	30.1	25.5
Polls	30.8	32.4	31.5
Campaign strategies	27.2	33.8	29.9
Leader/party profiles	16.2	34.8	44.1
Constituency profiles	31.8	32.3	27.5
Banana skins/own goals	35.2	33.6	28.0

Similar profiles emerge from a calculation of the placement of the parties in news item running order, so that the Conservatives achieve 28 per cent of mentions in lead items, the Labour Party 37 per cent, and the Alliance 28 per cent. Only the leader/party profile category is heavily skewed, and even there the Labour Party receives more coverage than any other party, a finding which holds up across the board.

Procedural parity included being equally nice and equally nasty about the party leaders and campaign styles. Early, quite benevolent profiles of the leaders gave ample scope for public relations and were scarcely distinguishable from a better quality party political broadcast. For example, the *News at Ten* profile of Mrs Thatcher on 13 May featured not only Denis Thatcher, but a dog and a small child for good measure. More barbed commentary was also on offer, exemplified by Michael Crick's series of leader profiles on *Channel 4 News* in the last two weeks of the campaign. These 'Private Eye' style profiles were full of innuendo, clever editing and the occasional petulant gibe at the politician's lack of sensitivity to the trials of a working journalist. These profiles are characteristic of a more rebellious, or at least irreverent, style of broadcasting. Clips of eminent people, including party leaders being refused entry to naval bases (David Owen), or looking glum while eating cheese (Mrs Thatcher), were fairly evenly distributed among the contestants.

Thus procedural parity was achieved by the broadcasters. Some of this was the result of simply reporting the activities of politicians, even collaborating with campaign managers in the production of news which showed the contestants in a favourable light. Photo-opportunities were no longer the politician's dream they had been in 1979, and to some extent in 1983, and a good deal of footage showing leaders going about their business tinged with a roseate hue was left on the cutting room floor. Hugo Young (*The Listener*, 16 July 1987), suggests that the requirement for balance between the parties tends to hand over the treatment of issues to the politicians. While there is some truth in this, it is also true that television cast a somewhat more critical eye on the antics of the party leader. Some of this was just pure luck – Young himself mentions Mrs Thatcher's unfortunate reference to those who 'drivel and drool' about caring as a good example of an unrehearsed exposé. But some of the more negative coverage was due to a deliberate attempt by broadcasters to distance themselves from the process of electioneering, and to do more than just react to 'news' which was manufactured for them by the parties. This is hardly surprising. As early as 18 May, BBC *Nine O'Clock News* had announced that 'Television will rule the campaign'. Self-respecting broadcasters were duty bound to seek ways to combat the inevitable attempts by the parties to hijack the election agenda on television.

Parity and the Labour Party

Procedural parity of the sort indicated above does not always work, and probably can never work, to the advantage of all the parties. The Labour Party, which enjoyed a slight 'advantage' of mentions in all news programmes (table 14.1), might with hindsight claim that in their case more did mean worse. This was especially so in the sensitive agenda items of defence which peaked in the week beginning 25 May, and taxation which became a central issue in the penultimate week of the campaign. Undoubtedly the party's 'professional' campaign came across well on television, with plenty of warm and emotional footage of the leader and his wife and some carefully managed photo-opportunities. In general the Tories fared less well in the coverage of their 'road show', partly because the Prime Minister was caught up in a security cocoon. Compared with the Labour tour her efforts seemed stilted and formal. The advantage Labour gained through sympathetic treament of a slickly run campaign was offset by the reporting of the major gaffes by Kinnock (Dad's Army), and Healey (private health care), their inability to control the news agenda on defence, the economy or taxation, and the niggling charges about the 'lethal' or 'loony' left which kept cropping up throughout the campaign. In these areas the broadcasters were often unwilling to set aside their judgement about what constituted a 'good' story in the interests of strict procedural parity. As judged by the criteria of 'news value', Labour's backs to the wall posture on defence, and the tendency for some of its leading personnel to self-destruct on camera, were well nigh irresistible.

Parity and the Alliance

The Alliance went through the election with a quite remarkable absence of disadvantage in access to television. But equal time turned out to be disastrous in a rather insidious fashion. At one level it sustained the illusion of a three-party contest. On the screen the Alliance leaders matched their rivals

Table 14.3. *The presidential campaign: mention of political personality as a percentage of all mentions of political personalities in election items.*

M. Thatcher	17.4
N. Kinnock	17.6
D. Owen	8.5
D. Steel	6.2
Owen + Steel	5.9
Government spokesperson	10.1
Conservative spokesperson	3.4
Labour spokesperson	9.3
Alliance spokesperson	4.8
MPs (sitting until dissolution)	3.7
Candidates (where not 'sitting MPs')	2.1
Campaign organisers	4.1
Others (minor party etc)	6.8

photo opportunity for photo opportunity, and rally for rally; to all appearances they were serious contenders. On another level procedural parity killed the Alliance with kindness. For one thing there was the inescapable fact – for the most part, carefully reported in analysis of poll data – that they (and Labour of course), were always coming from a long way behind. Every day of the campaign the near-impossibility of their task was demonstrated. For another, the dual leadership of the Alliance was not impressive in a campaign covered as though it was a presidential contest (Table 14.3). The 'two Davids', apart from caricaturing their own collegiate/federal approach to leadership (Steel's quip about Tweedledum and Tweedledee was widely covered) were unable to reassure a public distrustful of coalition politics, and still wedded to the idea that leading men and women ought not to share the spotlight with another pretender to the throne.

According to the BBC/Gallup Election Survey, almost one quarter of voters seriously considered voting for the Alliance, but did not do so. Over one third of these did not do so because 'it was obvious that they could not win'. Parity gave altogether too much exposure to the Alliance, and triggered the third-party squeeze. This occurred in two ways. First, as shown above, procedural parity carried a lethal charge for the Alliance, and a less damaging one for Labour. Paradoxically, the Alliance in particular needed procedural equality to sustain it, since the broadcasters were unable to deliver substantive equality, that is a treatment of the parties as equal contenders, as being of equal substance. In part this failure (if it is a 'failure'), arises from the very nature of the protagonists themselves, and the firmness of their identity (or lack of it), in the culture of British politics. In part it results from the reluctance of broadcasters to break the mould of election broadcasting. They did not do so because, as Hugo Young says, television is itself a suppliant,

Table 14.4. *The agenda of the campaign on television: major issues as a percentage of all political items.*

Major issues	Percentage of all items
Defence	20
Employment	14
Education	13
Economy	12
Health	11
Taxation	8

Table 14.5. *The flow of the campaign: mention of selected items per week of campaign as a percentage of all items in that category*

Item	week 1	week 2	week 3	week 4	week 5
Defence	17.4	22.9	42.6	10.1	6.8
Education	3.4	49.4	30.1	11.1	5.8
Health	15.1	13.5	23.9	38.2	9.1
Economy	10.4	19.3	24.7	32.0	13.5
Employment	17.6	19.2	23.4	33.7	6.7
Taxation	22.2	13.2	13.2	31.2	20.1
Constitutional reform	44.1	24.4	26.7	1.1	3.4
Campaign strategies	27.5	21.8	25.0	15.6	9.8
Polls	10.4	13.8	28.2	29.3	18.0

eager for the largesse which politicians dispense simply by agreeing to appear on a news or current affairs programme,[3] and because their conception of politics has been shaped to the contours of two-party politics – metropolitan in focus, adversarial in style and leader dominated.

Setting the agenda

Whether programme makers did in fact hanker after the good, dead days of the swingometer, as Maggie Brown suggested in *The Independent*, is not clear, but what is evident is the making of a substantive agenda pretty much in the image of the conflict between the Conservative and Labour parties. The issues which dominated the election on television are shown in table 14.4.

No other issue was covered in more than six per cent of items. But more interesting still is the flow of agenda items across the whole campaign as shown in table 14.5. Defence, the most widely covered issue in television news, peaked in week 3 of the campaign, when the Labour Party was struggling to ride out the deleterious effects of Neil Kinnock's remarks to David Frost about 'making [a Russian] occupation totally untenable', while trying to keep its own agenda item, at this time health, in the public eye. Health peaked to the advantage of Labour in week 4, fuelled by coverage of hole in the heart boy Mark Burgess, but by this time the Conservatives were making inroads with the increased coverage of the economy, employment and taxation. With the exception of defence, which was always going to prove debilitating for Labour, those items most likely to favour the Tories received most coverage from the mid-point of the campaign. For Labour, education peaked too soon and with too little effect, while health proved a mixed blessing, and in the end became obscured by the vituperation and sensationalism which surrounded Healey's angry scene with Anne Diamond on TV-am over his wife's private hip operation. The Labour Party would no doubt claim that they were 'worked over' by the Tory tabloid press, in this and the defence issue, and there is more than a grain of truth in this. Television treatment, however, was generally calmer, while still feeding off or taking its cue from press reaction.

For the Alliance the agenda proved almost impossible to manage. Nothing demonstrates this more clearly than the decay of their 'blue riband' agenda item, constitutional reform. After substantial early coverage, it had all but disappeared in the last two crucial weeks of the campaign. In the early weeks there was little competition for this rather cerebral item, and the Alliance made the running, especially in the 'phoney campaign' from 11 to 17 May. Thereafter the distinctiveness of their policies proved to be 'unteachable' in a medium more used to the black and white verities of adverarial, two-party politics. Adversarial politics, even adversarial policies, are perhaps easier to package than the politics of moderation. These have little in the way of news value to recommend them to broadcasters accustomed to reporting two-party contests, red in tooth and claw, and all the more saleable for that. With its agenda items gone, the Alliance survived on the diet provided by coverage of its leaders' frenetic campaign trail. On policy matters which were not about electoral or constitutional reform they were reduced to a subaltern role, responding to but seldom initiating issues. Outside the confines of their peripheral agenda items and their unusual (and for many electors, unnatural) style of leadership, the Alliance enjoyed no clear identity. Thus they were easily dominated by the more 'authentic' voices of mainstream British politics with respect to most areas of policy. For example, on Friday, 15 May the launch of the Alliance housing policy, and in particular the 'rent-a-room' scheme, was overwhelmed on television by the first campaign speeches by Kinnock and Thatcher, and curiously by the competing interest in David Owen's air travels and remarks on the 'loony left'.

The Alliance faced further difficulties about being accepted as an equal competitor. Its minority position in parliament, and more seriously, in the polls, made Labour the main contender. The Alliance leaders seemed to accept this position and so opened themselves up to questions about a hung parliament, and a possible coalition or partnership. The media interest in this was legitimate and not unacceptable to the Alliance. But this raised the awkward question about which party would be the favoured partner, a choice which revealed differences between the Alliance leaders. Long before the end there was no avoiding the fact that the Alliance was not only not going to form a government, but could not be fitted into any foreseeable scenario of government.

Conclusion

There are clearly powerful constraints on the achievement of substantive parity. However it must be said that the broadcasters (with their decent intent), went some way towards establishing it:

1 For all that the election agenda was in effect determined by the contest between Conservatives and Labour, neither party could be entirely satisfied with its coverage under certain issues, and neither party was able to completely exclude issues which were damaging to it, although the Conservatives were more successful at damage limitation than their main rivals. The defence question was contested on Conservative terms, the issue of health rather more on terms laid down by the Labour Party. The Tories could not exclude health issues, but were rescued by the gleeful attention paid by the tabloid press to Denis Healey's verbal scrimmage with Anne Diamond on Breakfast television, a contretemps reported with some restraint by television news.

2 Normally government dominates the news,[4] but this was not so for the period of the election. Notably, the Conservative Party in the guise of the government did not score quite the publicity triumph it expected from Mrs Thatcher's brief visit to the Venice Summit. This received modest coverage – 3.3 per cent, more than privatisation or local government, less than pensions or even constitutional reform. The Summit was treated as an election item rather than an act of government or diplomacy, and the most striking television images are not those of the Prime Minister's triumphal progress, but those showing opponents giving full rein to their poetic abilities ('only time for a sandwich and a sermon' – Neil Kinnock; 'one cornetto' – David Owen; 'the Grand Banal' – Denis Healey). The killing of the Summit is the most clear-cut evidence of the highly self-conscious nature of the campaign, in which the more ambitious marketing projects were deflated by forewarned sceptics given ample scope to express their scepticism by the broadcasters.

These are not inconsiderable gains, but they are not the pure milk of substantive parity. This would have required that the three major parties were portrayed as equal competitors – different appearances, different track record, but similar and well-matched runners in a race. The risk for the Labour Party was always that it would be portrayed as, or at least might look like, an opposition party, characteristically not the government; on the other hand the Conservatives would be portrayed as, or might look like, the Government, established and powerful. Both parties were allotted well-known parts in the British political drama. By contrast the Alliance had no clearly defined role. The media coverage to some extent both reflected and reinforced the plot, underlining the strength and invulnerability of the governing party, and casting the others as aspiring contenders, evidently of unequal measure, in pursuit of a hopeless cause. There is no deliberate bias here; indeed the broadcasters were aware of the difficulties and consistently attempted to offset any advantages enjoyed by the governing party. But the inequalities are built in and cannot be dispelled by procedural parity. The effect of procedural parity was to promote the Alliance into a league in which it could not flourish. This was so not just because the broadcasters took their cues from the two major parties, or saw little news value in the politics of moderation, but because parity could not change the prevailing climate of opinion, much less the British political culture and constitution. There is little room in either for a third party, especially one tagged with the non-identity of the centre, the no-man's land of modern British politics. What third parties have to do is to transform themselves into a second party. This Cinderella-into-Princess transformation will be a difficult process, in which the medium of television will play a part, even if only to bear witness to it. In the summer of 1987 however, the broadcasters' anticipation of a three-party system cast them in the unwitting and unwanted role of reinforcing the two-party model.

Notes

This study is based on a monitoring exercise which covered national, evening news programmes. A total of 160 broadcasts were monitored, from Monday, 11 May (when the election was announced), through to the 10.pm ITN bulletin on 12 June. The news programmes monitored were:

ITN News at 5.45 and 10.pm

BBC News at 6.pm and 9.pm

Channel 4 News at 7.pm

All weekend variants of the above.

1 Barrie Axford and Peter Madgwick, *The Coverage of the Party System in Television News* (September 1986), report prepared for the Liberal–SDP Alliance.

2 Here 'political' was taken to mean any item about the government and politics of the United Kingdom, in whatever context.

3 Hugo Young, 'Broadcasting and politics: the unanswered questions', *The Listener*, 16 July 1987, p. 6.

4 Axford and Madgwick, *The Coverage of the Party System in Television News*. During the period of the study, the Government (as analytically distinct from the Conservative Party), secured 35 per cent of all political references, while named parties achieved only 25 per cent. During the election this balance was reversed in dramatic fashion, the Government taking 19 per cent of all mentions, and parties 63 per cent.

JAY G. BLUMLER, MICHAEL GUREVITCH and
T. J. NOSSITER

15 The earnest versus the determined: election newsmaking at the BBC, 1987

Election communication for television is a subtly composite product that emerges from the mutually adaptive efforts of journalists and politicians in pursuit of overlapping yet distinct goals. In 1987 there were signs that their different purposes had crystallised into sharply opposed models of campaign message projection. From a BBC vantage point at least, earnest newscasters, applying a social responsibility view of their role, confronted partisan forces, each determined that, if they could not control the campaign agenda, nobody else would. To the former, communication was a tool of public enlightenment; to the latter, a weapon in a two-way power struggle – against rival parties *and* professional journalists.

The authors became aware of this conflict while observing, for the third election in a row, production of the *Nine O'Clock News* at the BBC on intermittent days during the 1987 campaign.[1] As previously, access was essentially open and free, except to editorial conferences whose participants we could interview afterwards. Communication systems are not indissoluble, and by returning to the scene of previous observations we hoped to form some sense of how changes over time might be refashioning election communication in a major mass medium.

Emergence of the models, 1983–7

Broadcasters

'The BBC treated the event with due seriousness.' This was how a senior executive interpreted the Corporation's decision to inject massive resources from the current affairs group into *Nine O'Clock News* coverage of the 1987 campaign. That step was remarkable, even heroic, given the disasters that had attended a similar attempt to strengthen the analytical component of election news in 1983. Universally condemned as a failure, the 1983 attempt had had no unified objective or line of command. The leading presenter from current affairs had felt like Prince Charles over the water, under-supported on alien turf. Opposed camps (news versus current affairs) had formed and struggled continually for ascendancy, differing over philosophy, running order priorities, the nature of the campaign and their appropriate roles in it. Unsurprisingly, like the team, the programme had rarely knitted together. It had been a 'searing experience', from which the participants emerged 'battle scarred' (as 1987 informants recalled). Consequently, the news division recommended at the time that at the next election sole coverage responsibility should revert to it.[2]

Why, then, did the BBC venture an even bolder combined operation to present the 1987 campaign? Essentially it was because momentum for the closer integration of news and current affairs had accelerated irreversibly over the intervening four years. By 1987 both the editor of television news, Ron Neil, and the head of the current affairs group, Peter Pagnamenta, were true believers. BBC2's *Newsnight* was widely regarded as a shining model of such a fusion. Another praised example, the *Six O'Clock News*, designed specifically to blend news and analysis, was scheduled on BBC1 from 1985. Moreover, the furtherance of this trend was guaranteed when, shortly before the election was called, John Birt, a noted critic of conventional television journalism for its 'bias against understanding', was appointed Deputy Director General of the BBC.

The parties

Nevertheless, BBC relations with the parties had gone through a bad patch, including several vociferous complaints of bias. Contending that its 1983 electoral support justified more extensive news coverage than it was getting, the Alliance applied for a judicial review in July 1986 (dropped after previously confidential BBC records on party appearances in programmes were released). There were also heavily publicised Conservative accusations of bias in BBC reporting of the American bombing of Libya from bases in Britain. Although no equally prominent complaint emanated from Labour, the Corporation presumed it could expect similar vigilance from a party for which retention of official Opposition status was a sheer survival matter. In the background, there was also anxiety over the BBC's institutional future. New communication technologies and a free market ideology had given the government opportunity and incentive to restructure British broadcasting in ways that might eventually imperil BBC funding and status. It could therefore be worrying if anything happened during the campaign to exacerbate anti-BBC sentiments among national politicians.

Moreover, BBC officials sensed that for all parties the name of the modern election game had become deliberate agenda setting: 'Everybody is making a determined attempt at agenda-setting now; at a general election every party hopes to conduct debate on the issues advantageous to itself'. Apparently, it had been 'suggested quite heavily that the broadcasters would have to follow the issues laid down by the parties'. One party had 'said that they will only make their spokespersons available to speak on issues which they have decided are the proper ones', even implying 'that the Representation of the People Act would support this view'. Of course, campaign conflict with the parties over priority issues is not new,[3] and nobody expected such demands to be taken to their literal extremes. Nevertheless, many in the BBC felt that attempts to set the television news agenda had become a more central, considered and concerted element in the strategies of all three parties than at any previous election.

The programme concept

Instead of pulling in its horns, the BBC resolved to pursue the 1983 path towards its more ambitious conclusion. The *Nine O'Clock News* would be doubled in length from 25 to 50 minutes (exceeding even the generous 40-minute ration of 1983). Of this, up to 35 minutes might normally be devoted to campaign materials, including news of the parties' activities; analytical commentary; regular reporting of opinion poll developments; up to six three-party debates (each preceded by a filmed 'set-up' giving background on the issue to be discussed); interviews with leading politicians; and up to eight film reports on key issues and how the campaign was being received by voters in the country. For these purposes, a generous near-£2 million budget was set aside, and an unprecedented migration from current affairs was arranged. Compared with the transfer in 1983 of only two presenters and two producers, in 1987, in addition to David Dimbleby (presenter), John Cole (political editor) and Peter Snow (poll reporter), the *Nine O'Clock* newsroom would be filled with 'doctoral fire power' – a veritable army of current affairs producers stripped from *Breakfast Time*, *Panorama*, *This Week/Next Week* and specially *Newsnight*. Five reporter-producer and camera teams would also be brought over to make longer films under its own assignment editor. The Institute for Fiscal Studies was commissioned to prepare a factual guide to economic and financial issues that might feature in the campaign, and an Institute expert would be regularly on hand for back-up information and advice. A similar briefing on how to interpret opinion polls, their methods, uses and limitations, was also distributed to the team.

According to pre-campaign interviews with the planners, four considerations shaped this far-reaching approach. First, focussing analysis on prime news points and giving news an explanatory surround was the way that journalism was moving in the BBC anyhow:

It is true that this is a one-off exercise for this election; but it is also bound to be seen as a pilot to determine how these systems might interrelate with each other in the future.

Second, a news and current affairs merger did not have to be like a shot-gun wedding; with proper planning and ample resources it could work well. Third, executives aimed to redress the imbalance in pre-planning priorities, whereby at previous elections great attention had been given to the results programme but 'very little proportionately to how the campaign coverage, which could help determine the ultimate outcome on Polling Day, would be presented'. Fourth, there was a strongly asserted public service principle, holding that at election time more of what *Newsnight* usually offered a minority audience on BBC2 should be made available to the mass audience on BBC1:

> In the past, campaign debates were often on at times and in channels where only 'the chattering classes' would be likely to view them. Now they will go out at a peak time when the masses are available to be reached.
> In 1983 far too much good material was hidden away on *Newsnight* . . . it was on the air late and reached only a limited audience. We had to ensure that the mass audience on BBC1 had the civic benefit of exposure to more substantial coverage of the campaign, even if this had to be gained at the expense of *Newsnight*.

But would that audience stay the solid course plotted for it? We were struck by the planners' unanimous refusal to be deflected by fears of 'election overkill':

> When people complain that there is too much of something, they are perhaps best interpreted as saying that what they are getting is not on the right lines for them.
> The privilege of democracy obtains in only 39 countries, of which we are one. We are bloody lucky to have carried into our living rooms a large amount of material showing what politicians are saying and prioritising when competing for votes.

How, then, would the 1987 operation overcome the weaknesses of its 1983 predecessor?

First, there would be more lead time to plan in light of anticipated problems. Thus, the programme's editor and deputy editor were designated as early as autumn 1986, charged to think through questions of staffing, equipment and editorial policy. There would also be advance dry runs and pilots, leaving as little as possible to chance. Second, steps to ensure smooth teamwork were taken. 'Ecumenical figures' were appointed as editor (Tony Hall) and deputy editor (Paul Norris), each having previously worked in both the news and current affairs departments. They brought relatively youthful producers and reporters into the team, less likely to be wedded to separatist philosophies of news or current affairs. A clearly defined editorial structure was established, giving the editor responsibility for all *Nine O'Clock News* output. A more unified programming style without an election 'ghetto' was envisaged. There was to be 'a common thread in the coverage, not jumping from one thing to another', and 'the campaign coverage should have its own feel, through the nature of the titles, the graphics, the nature of the set, the voice of the presenter, a style that would run throughout the campaign'. Third, the entire team was dedicated to exclusive *Nine O'Clock News* use, in contrast to 1983 when many individuals also worked for the lunch-time and early evening bulletins.

Past experience considered, such a concept seemed brave and imaginative. In face of the 1983 failure, the BBC could have concluded that the potential for conflict and difficulty was inherent in news and current affairs differences; instead it met head-on the challenge of showing that they could be harnessed effectively for campaign coverage. In face of the more threatening political climate of the mid-1980s, the BBC could have kept a low profile; instead it entrusted the operation to a 'young Turk', not an experienced political hand. The Corporation was also risking much financially by putting so many of its coverage eggs in the *Nine O'Clock News* basket. To do so, it drastically narrowed the role of *Newsnight*, which was instructed to eschew campaign reporting and to limit itself to presentation of a series of longer inter-party debates.

Execution

How did these intentions fare in the heat of the actual campaign?

Plan and performance

On the whole, the team accomplished what it set out to do, deviating little from the original plan. The aim of giving a high and guaranteed priority to election coverage was adhered to throughout the three-and-a-half weeks. Typically, the programme opened with election news (only rarely leading on some other national or international story), and 35 minutes were spent on campaign material. Even when it was learned that the audience had fallen sharply in the first week,[4] the team stood its ground.

It is true that there was some learning on the job, but most of the resulting adjustments were minor. First, the notion of the programme as a 'seamless web' had to be abandoned in the first week as unacceptably top heavy. Yielding 35 minutes of unrelieved election coverage, it was decided to break this up into a tripartite pattern, signposting for viewers what kind of material was coming next. Thereafter, part I was largely devoted to 'the essential election news of the day', part II to main *non*-election news and part III (about 22 minutes nightly) to items of campaign news 'development, discussion, reflection and analysis', including debates and interviews, longer films, and opinion poll reports. When, rarely, a major non-election story topped the bulletin, the programme was split into four parts. Second, a way of treating part I election news more analytically evolved during the campaign. This fell to John Cole, who occasionally delivered a short essay, weaving together party press conference or hustings material to identify a key contrast between the parties. Third, in the event, two of the eight pre-commissioned films on which much thought and production effort had been expended – on 'Inner Cities' and 'Divided Britain' – were not screened.

Team working

The determination to run a smooth election coverage ship was fully realised. Most team members showed enthusiasm for the new approach, and no 1983–like storms erupted:

> The programme is much better organised than last time, that's for sure. The great thing is not having the institutional rows between news and current affairs that dogged us last time. This gives us all more time and energy properly to think through what we ought to be doing each day.

Factors favouring such harmony may have included recruitment (bringing in likely sympathisers); more time for pre-campaign planning and trial; the editor's firm but unabrasive leadership style; and a more congenial working space than the cramped 'bunker' of 1983, including (a 1987 innovation) personal recourse for every team member to a battery of word processors, strung along six bench-like desks in the main election newsroom. This last feature gave everybody instant access to the current state of play on running orders, assignments and scripts and allowed last-minute changes to be made quickly and conveniently. A potential downside, however, was that in 1987 'the machine' sometimes seemed to have taken over functions that in 1983 depended more on human zip, and we suspected that if the flow of information had increased, the amount of cross-team discussion and inter-action had diminished.

Election roles of television journalists

From our 1983 observation and interviews, four different notions emerged of the roles that television journalists should play when covering a campaign:

Prudential	Reflecting a concern to ensure that television journalism was, and would appear to be, politically beyond reproach – perhaps even politically innocuous;

Reactive
: Looking predominantly to party publicity initiatives (press conferences, walkabouts, evening speeches), which TV news was presumed to have a *duty* to report;

Conventionally journalistic
: Reflecting concern to filter election developments through predominantly professional criteria, looking for events to report that would be strongly laced with elements of drama, conflict, novelty, movement and anomaly;

Analytical
: Based on a sense of duty to strive for coherence in reporting, teasing out the essential arguments and issues and helping viewers to compare one party with another for their stands on the issues.

We also reported in 1983 that of these perspectives, the analytical role had proved 'most difficult to sustain effectively', while the 'coverage mode' of the conventional journalists 'seemed more dominant than in any previous British campaign'.[5]

Considered in these terms, the 1987 approach was very different – predominantly *Reactive plus Analytical*, pursued more or less back to back. Thus, we were struck by the much reduced influence of the 'conventionally journalistic' mentality on the making of the programme. Compared with 1983, there was much less headline chasing, less seeking after the sensational, less dismissal of overly sober political material, less drive to fasten onto what was 'new' and what might be the 'bull point' for the top story of the day.

This is not to imply that fulfilment of the analytical brief was entirely straightforward. Even for the most dedicated analysts, it was sometimes difficult not to be swamped by the torrent of daily events that demanded attention from early morning to late evening. It was not easy to get an intelligent grip on all the available material, and although the team was rich with political minds, the possibility that somebody could serve as overall political editor was somewhat vitiated by the fact that on most days all the key individuals were tied down by specific time-consuming tasks.

Nevertheless, we were impressed with the strenuous efforts made to ensure that the debates and interviews of part III secured constructive contributions from the participating politicians. Typically, David Dimbleby spent 4–5 hours daily just preparing this segment of the programme. He was plied with a great deal of background information on the issue to be discussed, including details of party stands. Formulations of probing questions were offered, hashed over and revised. Even dummy runs, with producers role-playing the politicians, were conducted. In addition, a filmed 'set-up' was carefully prepared to precede most exchanges. As explained, its aim

was to dispense in the preamble with the factual ground of an issue, so as to enable the discussion to concentrate on the real questions that belonged to it. So much time can be wasted when all the politicians do is trade their pet versions of appropriate figures, slanted to their own sides of an issue . . . So the main purpose is to clear the ground before getting down to the nitty gritty of the issues at stake in an area of debate.

The debates themselves were often organised more as a series of three separate one-on-one interviews (Dimbleby to the Conservative, to the Labour spokesperson, to the Alliance representative) than as a discussion, because in a more free exchange (it was feared), somebody might try to hog the available time or one or more participants might wander off the point.

In 1987 we also became aware of yet another view of the television journalist's campaign role, one we had not previously noticed, although it is quite widely held by American political correspondents.[6] On this view, now that the bulk of election news is carefully pre-packaged for the cameras, those who relay such events are under an obligation to open viewers' eyes to the manipulation underlying the message. In a BBC reporter's words:

Thinking of the campaign as it is organised by the political parties, all we can do is point out that things do not happen by accident. It is not a mere whim for Kinnock to have chosen a red rose as the party's symbol, to have selected a certain passage of Brahms for repetition . . . What we should do in this context is to point·out the degree to which deliberate campaign management goes on and what the principal managers hope that viewers will see and will not see.

And when we asked why television journalists should try to expose such practices, he replied:

Television is such a passive medium that people might often just sit before it and let the way in which the election is presented wash over them . . . but we can see behind that and are in a position to show how that has got where it is. It is important to show that the campaign is being fought in a way that campaign managers want it to be fought, which may not be in the interest of viewers and voters.

Thus, the tendency of American reporters to 'disdain' the very news they are presenting could be increasing in this country as well. In both systems, the practice seems to rest on: 1) an assumption of viewer gullibility in the face of party propaganda in television news; 2) a belief that workers in television are well placed to see how campaign management is conducted and have a responsibility to convey that understanding to the viewing public; and 3) a fear that if they do not expose such campaign machinations, they will become merely passive purveyors of party propaganda instead of independent journalists. The recent growth of such attitudes here presumably reflects an impression that the British state of the art of professionalised electioneering for television is now approximating its more pervasive and thorough-going entrenchment in the United States.

One consequence of the predominantly Reactive-Analytical formula of 1987 was that access to the audience was almost monopolised by politicians and journalists, particularly since so much of part III was devoted to debates and interviews. Although such concentration is natural, it can shut out the concerns of other interests, unless they happen to be voiced by either of the more 'authorised' election communicators. Apparently this problem was raised in a news and current affairs meeting early in the campaign, when it was suggested that programmes from departments other than current affairs – an arts programme, a science programme or a religious programme – might occasionally step into the gap, looking at the election from the standpoint of other interests at stake. The objections were revealing. One was the difficulty of achieving a proper balance of contributors (say, between left-wing and right-wing doctors). The other concerned the BBC's control machinery for ensuring that politically sensitive programmes are made by people used to assessing the judgements involved, which would not apply to producers in other departments who might veer dangerously off course. According to the participant, the conclusion was that, 'In an election period it should only be the politicians who regularly get on the air'.

The 'awkward parties'

So what were the producers' relations with their predominant campaign sources like? How did this affect their own work on the expanded election news?

External relations

In one respect, BBC–politician relations were not so troubled as expected. The more threatening climate of the mid-1980s was *not* a prelude to a campaign of attempted intimidation and blazing rows.[7] Anticipating difficulties, the BBC had set up a special Election Advisory Unit at Broadcasting House under the director for news and current affairs to give guidance on coverage problems, act as a reference point for campaign producers needing advice and deal with party complaints and resulting conflicts. In the event, the Unit had little to do, for (in a member's words), 'I had fully expected a lot of bloodshed, lots of blood and guts all over the corridors, but nothing like that happened.'

Nevertheless, the producers we observed often seemed as if surrounded by 'awkward parties', whose sensitivities and reactions made their jobs more difficult and less pleasant than they might have been. Party forces were rather like a set of heavy clouds, hovering in unrelieved grey over the Television Centre, that rarely erupted into actual storms. Producers understood the reasons for this:

> For the parties it's a matter of life and death; hence the constant horse trading over who will appear and on what terms . . . They are also more aware of the tricks of our trade now – for example, over how interviews are edited – and that how they are exercised could put them at a disadvantage.

Broadcaster perspectives on campaigning politicians seemed to be shaped by three dominant perceptions. First, they regarded the parties as determined would-be agenda setters. As a newsreader put it, 'The really extraordinary and different thing about this campaign is how persistent the efforts of the parties have been to set the news agenda in their own terms.' At one point we listed the strategies of attempted party agenda control that had been drawn to our attention as follows:

> Coordinating a leader's activities to reiterate a chosen theme or issue throughout the day – centring the morning press conference on it, symbolising it in an afternoon walkabout and addressing a party rally in the evening about it.
>
> Putting only one or two leading speakers on the hustings on a given night to limit the cameras' ability to go to somebody who would not be voicing the chosen message of the day.
>
> Declining interviews on subjects off the party's preferred agenda or making them particularly difficult to arrange.
>
> Holding more than one press conference on the same theme on a given day, addressing it from different angles or through different spokespersons.
>
> Attempting to put a rival party on the defensive by raising a series of questions about an issue unfavourable to it for journalists to press on it.
>
> Systematic complaining along the lines of: Why are you proposing to deal with so and so when such and such is so much more important? Why have you been leading with our opponents' favoured issues more often than ours?

Second, the parties were regarded as ever-vigilant monitors of broadcasters' news choices and angles. When we asked a reporter assigned to a party entourage what was most noteworthy about his role, for example, to our surprise he replied,

> the public scrutiny of what we do. As journalists we make certain judgements, but the pressures on us can be enormous. This is especially the case now after two to three years of ever-growing party scrutiny of BBC affairs. Everything you say and do you know is quite intently being monitored by the Labour and Conservative parties. This does not distract me from doing what I think I should do, but we are very conscious of it.

Third, the parties were perceived as moaners, continually commenting negatively on broadcasters' intentions and output:

> Questioning of our political judgements by the political parties is par for the course. When visiting — Party headquarters the other day, I was told that we had been

leading on the — Party's position and issues more often than theirs. Clearly this was designed to keep me on my toes – and I suspect with deliberate intent.

I start conversations with them on the assumption that anything I say may later be held against me.

Internal restraints

Campaign coverage is also circumscribed by various internally accepted limits. For one thing, the broadcasters were ambivalent over their own agenda-setting role. If to some degree inevitable, it should be secondary to party agendas, transcending them only in clearly justifiable circumstances. For another, pains were taken to ensure something of a party balance in top-of-news story choices. Again the outlook was ambivalent:

> We would want to be driven by journalistic imperatives – so that if an issue developed a strong element of charge and counter-charge or had elements of ambiguity or lack of frankness – then we would want to follow that. On the other hand, you have got this constraint of being seen to be fair, and that has to do not only with the amount of time that is allotted to presentations by speakers from all the parties but also with what they want to get onto centre stage.

Yet another example concerned use of the term, 'tactical voting'. Realising that TV '87 was a 'get-the-Tories-out' campaign, the head of the Election Advisory Unit instructed programme editors not to introduce the notion of 'tactical voting', unless it emerged from the players themselves.

A focus of particularly close attention concerned presentation of opinion poll findings. Well in advance of the election this was noted by policy makers as a 'booby-trapped' area. Because 1983 experience showed that the parties could seek to generate campaign momentum from interpretations of opinion poll findings, it was decided that care should be taken to ensure that nothing the BBC did could be unduly exploited for such a purpose. Consequently an elaborate policy was evolved, including the following elements:

> Full and regular reporting of published opinion poll results, avoiding sporadic coverage that might inadvertently favour one or another party.
>
> Attempts to inform the audience throughout the campaign about polling methods, such as sample sizes, fieldwork dates, error margins, etc.
>
> No BBC commissioning of national voting intentions polls. Given the large number of polls already available, 'If our result told the same story it would be redundant; but if it told a different story, it could be a worry to us.'
>
> BBC polls to be commissioned only to gain specific journalistically interesting information not otherwise available – as in a poll of young voters or by inserting questions into a Gallup survey to elicit electoral responses to certain issues and personalities. And after some hesitation, a *Newsnight* proposal to conduct a panel survey of 60 selected marginal seats was accepted on the understanding that, while

tracking trends in such constituencies, it could not be extrapolated to the national scene.

This last decision, however, was responsible for the most difficult internal controversy of the election, including much argument and revision of scripts. The problem arose because in the third week of the campaign the *Newsnight* panel produced a result that seemed to foreshadow a 'hung parliament' if generalised to the country at large. Whereas those responsible for presenting the result in the *Nine O'Clock News* and *Newsnight* wished to underline this prospect, senior management insisted on adherence to the original understanding that the poll could not serve as a national projection. In the end, the latter prevailed, and the former had to resort to tortuous verbal circumlocutions when presenting the story.

In fact, the *Newsnight* poll was inaccurate as a national guide, apparently validating management caution over its presentation. In hindsight, however, the policy of damage limitation in advance was probably misconceived, causing the BBC to fall between a journalistic and a counter-journalistic stool. If a news organisation undertakes a survey, it can only do its best to get the methodology right, after which it should be prepared to publish the results for whatever they are worth. A lesson could be that an attempt to stamp health warnings on seemingly exciting evidence is futile in heated campaign conditions.

Philosophically intriguing was the case of those two non-screened film reports on 'Inner Cities' and 'Divided Britain'. Because they had not made it into the early coverage, they could not, we were told, have been shown later in the campaign:

> This would appear to be bringing to the top of the agenda an issue that would not have been justified by the events of the day. It would have been easier to justify such a film – showing the BBC standing back and setting an issue in a context that had only been touched on by the politicians – early in the campaign. Sensitivity increases the later you get into the campaign. It could have been interpreted as an Opposition issue had it been screened in the last week.

The explanation illustrates how the meaning of what reporters do or say changes, not because of the actions or words themselves, but due to the context, the timing and the surrounding political atmosphere. What could be seen as political analysis at one moment or in one situation is seen as a political statement at another.

The consequences

It should not be concluded from the above that the programme makers merely handed the television campaign over to the politicians to shape to their own images. There were a number of ways in which the *Nine O'Clock News* sought to be more than a party platform:

> The forum function regularly performed by part III, particularly the care taken in preparing for the interviews and debates that featured so centrally in it, including the preceding 'set-ups'.
>
> The scope given to John Cole to fashion think-piece essays, drawing on material from party events, not to reproduce them so much as to use them to underscore some fundamental contrast of party approach.
>
> A decision to limit party walkabout material largely to the prefatory parts of correspondents' packages, which instead would focus chiefly on evening rallies and speeches.
>
> The overall aim of situating party statements and events within thematic and explanatory contexts.

But there was also a risk that such a pile-up of external scrutiny and internal inhibition would make the campaign coverage task seem:

More worrying	I would always refer upwards to protect my back.
	Many people are worried and looking over their shoulders.
Less fun	Now more things seem to be governed by rules, and producers have mainly to think about how to organise things so that what they have done fits some notion of the rules that are supposed to apply . . . All this makes the process less interesting, both for us and probably for viewers as well.
More delicate	It means that everything has to be watertight.
Less meaningful	There is this tendency where we react to the parties and feed off them, and they react to us or feed off us. It is rather like my son's hamster in a cage. With advanced technology . . . it is as if the hamster's wheel can now spin faster . . . and is in a transparent ball . . . through which he can see the world. Yet the hamster's horizons are still confined to the same limited diameters as before.

Was it worth it?

Television and democracy

For a quarter of a century television has exerted a formative influence on British public debate. Keen to reach its mass audience, politicians and pressure groups have adapted their message-making ways to the medium's cameras, interviewers and brisk rhetorical conventions. Although the pending era of multi-channel broadcasting, break-up of the BBC–ITV duopoly and audience fragmentation may eventually reduce its role, in 1987 this was still pivotal. It accordingly remains appropriate to consider the criteria by which the campaign contributions of television to democracy may be evaluated.

First, since 'Election campaigns, for all their faults, may be the major learning experience of democratic polities',[8] television coverage should be designed to inform and enlighten those following it. By this standard, the makers of the 1987 *Nine O'Clock News* passed with flying colours. They succumbed neither to cynicism about viewers' interest levels nor to perceptions of television as essentially an entertainment medium. Compared with the American networks' days at the election horse races,[9] their unflagging commitment to the provision of a substantive diet was impressive.

Second, election television should serve as a forum for a national dialogue about the future of society and be designed to constrain politicians to address the public in as illuminating terms as possible. Here too the *Nine O'Clock News* earns high marks for the numerous debates and interviews screened in part III. Although politicians often complain that the mass media tend to ignore their more serious contributions to public debate, in this case the news team took the initiative to seek them out.

Third, journalists should aim to perform an accountability function, framing and putting the questions for which politicians should be answerable to voters in light of their records, promises and campaign statements. Our observation suggests that the thorough back-up and preparation behind the part III debates and interviews were designed with precisely this end in mind, seeking suitable questions for David Dimbleby to ask and strategies to oblige the politicians to answer them.

Judged by such democratic criteria, then, it is difficult to fault the programme, which treated the 1987 campaign not as a parade of events or an elaborate game but as a 'process of critical choice for the nation'.[10]

Internal criticism

Most of those associated with the venture or in sympathy with its original objectives were proud of its achievements. An editor sounded this note:

> This was far and away the best BBC election programme with a fusion of news and current affairs that the Corporation has ever put on . . . This time we tried to think things through in terms of one programme, to put on a properly integrated programme. Of course one could improve upon this model, perhaps by tightening up the material in parts I and II, but we got the basic approach right.

Most ideas for future improvement from this circle were modest and marginal: to shorten the programme by about five minutes (a widely-voiced suggestion);

proportionately more reporter power and less producer power; more reports from the campaign in the country; and off-beat 'side-bar' items.

More fundamental criticisms were mainly voiced by those journalists whose election work had been sidelined or compressed due to the high priority accorded the *Nine O'Clock News*. For their part, some *Newsnight* producers felt that the *Nine O'Clock* programme had been saddled with an unattainably comprehensive remit:

> We simply do not think that any single programme can do everything and cope with all of it. There are a number of distinct roles that can be achieved that are best handled by broadcasting a number of separate attractive vehicles for them.

The conclusion was that *Newsnight* should have been allowed to be more true to itself, offering studio analysis and 'interesting and thoughtful background reporting from the field on what the issues *are*' in keeping with its tradition and style. One reporter even argued that the *Nine O'Clock* project violated a natural division in the public itself:

> The *Nine O'Clock News* and *Newsnight* serve totally different audiences. The former is a mass tabloid audience in direct competition with *News at Ten*. It should not be apologetic about addressing a *Daily Mail/Daily Express* audience. They should have left the more substantial coverage to an expanded *Newsnight* . . . You can offer the mass audience a degree of election analysis, but if the mass audience turns off, then the objective negates itself.

Some news division members took a similar line from their opposite vantage point. One, for example, criticised the guiding objective as misconceived:

> Of course the whole thing is unsatisfactory. The pace of the campaign process is so hectic, and although a lot is said about the desirability of giving the viewer a certain amount of analysis, this cannot be done in any significant way; and if it was, it would lower the audience.

Another castigated the programme on the basis of what he had seeen:

> It's boring. They haven't taken the trouble to make it interesting; and if they fail in that, they will lose viewers hand over fist.

The audience verdict

Did that happen? The answer is, 'Yes, to a not insignificant degree'.[11] Whereas in the four weeks before the campaign, the average *Nine O'Clock News* audience was 7.6 million nightly, for the four weeks of the campaign, it fell by a quarter to an average of 5.7 million. Details for separate time segments suggest that much of the loss reflected the fact that fewer viewers than before the campaign watched the news from the outset; that there was a certain amount of switching off or over in the first half-hour of the programme; and that a further slight decline took place in the last 20 minutes. Moreover, although the *Newsnight* audience fell to a similar degree, ratings for the BBC's daytime news programmes (*Breakfast Time, One O'Clock News* and *Six O'Clock News*) all held steady.

Caution is necessary in ascribing responsibility for these results specifically to the *Nine O'Clock News* model. As summer approaches, people tend to watch less television; ITV scheduled highly competitive programming from 9–10 pm during the campaign; and on many evenings the *Nine O'Clock News* followed a party election broadcast. Of these factors, the last could have been most significant, but its influence is impossible to calculate exactly, and the most plausible interpretation is that an appreciable number of usual *Nine O'Clock News* viewers decided not to watch it. That conclusion is somewhat mitigated by the fact that ITV's *News at Ten*, which was extended by only five minutes during the campaign, also suffered audience erosion though not to the same degree. From a four-week pre-campaign average of 6.2 million, it fell by 11 per cent to a 5.6 million campaign-period average.

In assessing this record of audience response, four considerations should be borne in mind.

First, the success or failure of an ambitious effort of this kind should not be evaluated by audience ratings alone. The net contribution to public enlightenment of a more popular programme with different content might have been appreciably less than the *Nine O'Clock News* achieved in 1987.

Second, even when judged in audience exposure terms, the daily rating should not be the only criterion, since many viewers were probably exposed from time to time to the programme's more analytical style. Despite lower average ratings, its cumulative reach over the full campaign period could have been quite substantial. Moreover, those who stayed with it were apparently not just current affairs buffs. A breakdown of the programme's audience for the pre-campaign and campaign weeks shows no significant change in age, sex or social class terms.

Third, the fall in the *News at Ten* audience suggests that some viewers at least were not rejecting the BBC format specifically but whatever they found unsatisfactory and unpalatable about the campaign on television at large.

After all these considerations have been allowed for, however, it must be asked, fourthly, whether the audience decline could have been checked and more done to sustain viewers' interest. A BBC executive told us as early as January 1987 that the programme makers should 'think back from the viewer and not go about things simply from the standpoint of organisational dispositions', but while with the team ourselves, we were exposed to few signs of people saying to themselves or others, how can we make this relevant and meaningful to the average viewer?

This has nothing to do with elitism. Rather, the viewer as a point of reference for producers becomes remote because during a hectic campaign so many other pressing and immediate preoccupations block him or her from sight. Although much of this is inevitable, in 1987 the resulting distractions may have been compounded by the political climate of the time, including all the external pressures on the producers to watch their steps and the internal concerns to avoid booby traps. Although such an influence cannot be measured, it cannot have been beneficial in the sense of encouraging and helping broadcasters to 'think back from the viewer'. After all, it still holds true that, 'whether viewers feel that an election has been interesting and informative to follow will depend in great part on the enterprise and imagination that producers have been able to give to its coverage.'[12]

Notes

1 We are enormously grateful to the many BBC executives, editors, presenters, producers and reporters who responded to our presence and questions so courteously and informatively. The results of our 1979 and 1983 observations appeared, respectively, in: Michael Gurevitch and Jay G. Blumler, 'The construction of election news: an observation study at the BBC', in James S. Ettema and D. Charles Whitney (eds.), *Individuals in Mass Media Organizations: Creativity and Constraint* (Beverly Hills and London: Sage, 1982), pp. 179–204; and Jay G. Blumler, Michael Gurevitch and T. J. Nossiter, 'Setting the television news agenda: campaign observation at the BBC', in Ivor Crewe and Martin Harrop (eds.), *Political Communications: The General Election Campaign of 1983* (Cambridge: Cambridge University Press, 1986), pp. 104–24.

2 Blumler *et al.*, 'Setting the television news agenda'), p. 121.

3 See, for the 1966 general election, Jay G. Blumler, 'Producers' Attitudes Towards Television Coverage of an Election Campaign: A Case Study', in Paul Halmos (ed.), *The Sociology of Mass Media Communicators* (Keele: *The Sociological Review Monograph 13*, 1969), pp. 85–115.

4 See pp. 171–72 below for details.

5 Blumler *et al.* 'Setting the television news agenda', pp. 115–18.

6 Jay G. Blumler and Michael Gurevitch, 'The election agenda-setting roles of television journalists: comparative observation at the BBC and NBC', paper presented to 36th Annual Conference of the International Communication Association, Chicago, May 22–26, 1986.

7 Even the much publicised angry telephone call by Norman Tebbit to the chairman of the BBC over the cancellation of Cecil Parkinson's invitation to appear in an edition of Breakfast Time was resolved with due propriety. The chairman did not intervene in a management matter by contacting the editor directly but simply notified the director of programmes about the complaint; and the Conservative Party chairman subsequently apologised in writing for his impulsiveness – though it may be symptomatic that more sinister versions of the incident did circulate through BBC corridors and for a while were given credence by some.

8 Elihu Katz, 'Platforms and windows: reflections on the role of broadcasting in election campaigns', *Journalism Quarterly*, 48, 2 (1974), 304–14.

9 Thomas E. Patterson, *The Mass Media Election: How Americans Choose Their President* (New York: Praeger, 1980).

10 Blumler *et al.*, 'Setting the television news agenda', p. 119.

11 The data presented here appear in a BBC Broadcasting Research Department paper, *The General Election, June 11th 1987*, September 1987.

12 Jay G. Blumler, Michael Gurevitch and Julian Ives, *The Challenge of Election Broadcasting* (Leeds: Leeds University Press, 1978).

ROBIN McGREGOR, MICHAEL SVENNEVIG
and CHRIS LEDGER

16 Television and the 1987 general election campaign

Coverage of the 1987 general election campaign by broadcasters, particularly on television, was extensive, and preceeded by a long period of speculation before a date for polling was finally announced. Certainly during the four weeks preceding polling day, viewers encountered extended news programmes, special editions of current affairs programmes, daily campaign round-ups and special series of election issue coverage on all four channels on a more or less daily basis.

Given the weight and intensity of coverage, together with the cumulative evidence from previous campaigns pointing to television's increasingly dominant role in informing the electorate, the BBC and IBA jointly mounted a large-scale research project, as in previous elections, to monitor public opinion on election coverage. Under the terms of the BBC's Charter and the Broadcasting Act by which the IBA is bound, a central requirement of political coverage is impartiality, and this was a central element of the research. However, broadcasters' responsibilities do not simply stop at achieving an equitable balance, but also aim to inform voters about issues and policies, preferably in ways which hold viewers' interest and attention.

In order to establish a baseline of opinion towards the beginning of the campaign and monitor any changes in opinion over the election period, three quota samples of around 1,500 people representative of the population of Britain were interviewed. Interviews took place two weeks before (26/27 May), 1–2 days before (9/10 June) and 5–6 days after (16/17 June) polling day itself (11 June):

Wave 1 – 26/27th May
Wave 2 – 9/10th June
Wave 3 – 16th/17th June

By using larger sample sizes than in previous election surveys in 1983 and 1979, it was possible to analyse differences in public opinion between

Scotland, Wales and the South, Midlands and North of England, as well as to take a separate look at public opinion of media coverage within marginal constituencies.

In addition, attitudes towards broadcast coverage of the general election were also monitored, for the first time, in Northern Ireland, although on a smaller scale than for the main survey. Interviewing did not take place during Wave 1 in Northern Ireland, but during Waves 2 and 3 samples of around 200 people, representative of the population of Northern Ireland, were interviewed. In addition, special analyses of BARB (Broadcasters' Audience Research Board) data were conducted.

Opinions of the amount of television coverage

An increasingly large majority of people throughout the election period felt that too much time was being devoted to the general election on television; 65 per cent of viewers in Wave 1 rising to 72 per cent at Wave 2. However, as we shall see, although the great majority of viewers felt there was too much election coverage they did not actually turn off or over in significant numbers.

The level of stated dissatisfaction, roughly equivalent in all regions of the United Kingdom, was significantly higher than in 1983, where less than six in ten viewers said there was too much campaign coverage. While it must be noted that the questions are not exactly comparable, the differences in perceptions are large enough to signal a real change in public opinion. This rebuke from viewers might lead one to expect that people would have radically changed their viewing behaviour. However, BARB data do not support such an expectation. Compared with the same four-week period in 1986, the average total hours of viewing fell only slightly, and where viewing patterns changed they tended to move away from the main channels (BBC1 and ITV) towards the smaller ones (BBC2 and C4).

Quality of Coverage

Viewers' perceptions of the quality of election coverage can be divided into three areas:

1) Perceptions of the most interesting and informative media coverage;
2) Opinions about the balance of time devoted to personalities, policies and polls;
3) Perceptions of impartiality of the coverage.

Perceptions of the most interesting and informative coverage

In all three waves of surveys people were asked to choose, from a number of different media sources, which they thought had given the most interesting coverage, the most informative coverage and which the best coverage of local issues.

Table 16.1. *Perceptions in Wave 2 of the most interesting and informative coverage and best coverage of local issues (percentages by row)*

Wave 2	BBC-TV	ITV/C4	Radio	Press
Gave *most informative* coverage of general election	31	17	8	9
Gave *most interesting* coverage	25	18	7	8
Gave *best coverage of local issues*	11	22	11	12

The results illustrate the continued dominance of television in the public view as the primary source of information during an election (see table 16.1). Between 4 and 5 in 10 thought that television, and primarily BBC-TV, had provided the most informative and interesting coverage; just over a quarter said they did not know and the choice of the remaining 1 in 5 was more or less equally divided between radio and newspapers. BBC-TV was seen to have performed best, relative to ITV, in the North and South of England, while ITV's best performance was in Scotland, where it was chosen as the most informative and interesting media source very nearly as often as BBC-TV. This distribution remained fairly constant across the three waves of interviewing. The higher social grades (ABC1), people who had been, or were, in higher education, and readers of the quality press were more likely than others to choose BBC-TV than ITV as both the most informative and interesting, all of which reflects the known viewing preferences of the general public.

One third (33 per cent) of those questioned thought that television, and this time primarily ITV, had provided the best coverage of local issues; ITV was seen to perform particularly well in Scotland and Northern Ireland, while BBC-TV's best performance relative to ITV was in Wales and the South of England. Of particular note was the 1 in 5 who said that *none* of the media sources were best – an indicator of a strong undercurrent of dissatisfaction with local coverage during election time. Even 44 per cent of those people who said that too much time had been devoted to election coverage on TV thought that television had provided the most interesting coverage, and about half (48 per cent) thought TV had given the most informative coverage.

Opinions of the balance of time devoted to personalities, policies and polls

In the post-election wave of the research respondents who had seen some election coverage were asked whether they thought that the amount of time devoted to politicians' personalities, policies and polls, by each channel, was too much, about right or too little.

Table 16.2. *Balance of time on television devoted to policies, personalities and polls*

Wave 3	Party policies			Politician's personalities			Opinion polls		
	BBC-TV %	ITV %	C4 %	BBC-TV %	ITV %	C4 %	BBC-TV %	ITV %	C4 %
Too much	34	33	12	65	64	31	73	71	45
About right	42	43	47	25	24	35	19	20	22
Too little	19	18	16	3	3	8	1	2	3
Don't know	4	6	26	7	9	27	6	7	30

Base (those viewers who had seen something about the election on the particular channel) as follows: BBC-TV, 1043; ITV, 950; C4, 142.

A large majority (between 6 and 7 in 10) of viewers considered that both BBC and ITV spent too much time covering politicians' personalities and polls,[1] while, markedly fewer (3 and 4 in 10) thought the same of C4 Television (see table 16.2). This similarity of views about BBC and ITV coverage is an important finding considering that the BBC, in the opinion of most media commentators, did in *actuality* devote more time to election coverage than ITV. Clearly it was coverage of personalities and opinion poll results that a large number of viewers said they felt satiated with, for in comparison, a much smaller number of viewers, only around a third, felt that too much time had been given over to discussion of party policies on BBC and ITV. Indeed, nearly 20 per cent felt that *too little* time had been spent covering party policies. Again, in contrast, viewers' opinions about C4 were most favourable, 5 out of 10 of its viewers feeling that the amount of time devoted to party policies was about right, compared to just over 4 out of 10 who felt the same about BBC and ITV. Unfortunately, we have no content analysis data with which to compare these perceptions. Even so, it is clear that large sections of the audience felt that too much time was devoted to opinion polls and politicians' personalities. This presents potential problems for the broadcasters, for while an opinion poll is readily identifiable, 'politicians' personalities', as the questionnaire stated, are rather more difficult to tease apart from the rest of the coverage. In addition, this aspect of coverage is highly dependent upon how much politicians themselves want to push certain characteristics to the fore to the detriment of political issues.

Perceptions of impartiality of election coverage

In line with previous surveys (e.g. *Attitudes to Broadcasting*, IBA, 1986), conducted outside of an election period, a large majority (between 6 and 8 in 10) in the present surveys considered that television coverage had treated all parties fairly.

Table 16.3. *Level of perceived bias – BBC/ITV/C4*

	BBC			ITV			C4		
	Wave 1 %	Wave 2 %	Wave 3 %	Wave 1 %	Wave 2 %	Wave 3 %	Wave 1 %	Wave 2 %	Wave 3 %
Favoured some parties over others	18	22	27	15	16	17	11	10	4
Don't know	11	10	11	14	13	14	20	12	17
Treated all parties fairly	71	68	62	71	72	69	68	78	79

Base for BBC: Wave 1 = 969, Wave 2 = 1,099, Wave 3 = 1,043; base for ITV: Wave 1 = 883, Wave 2 = 1,038, Wave 3 = 950; base for C4: Wave 1 = 149, Wave 2 = 189, Wave 3 = 142.

The proportion of viewers who thought ITV was biassed remained fairly constant over the election period at around 16 per cent, but an increasing number of viewers felt BBC coverage to be partisan as time progressed. Two weeks before the election 18 per cent of viewers said the BBC's coverage was biassed (not many more than thought the same about ITV at that stage) but after the event over one quarter of viewers thought BBC coverage of the election campaign had favoured some parties over others, many more than retrospectively felt the same about ITV coverage. There was also a corresponding decrease in the proportion of people who considered the BBC to have treated all parties fairly (see table 16.3). Viewers in Scotland and the North of England were more likely than viewers in the rest of the United Kingdom to think BBC coverage biassed.

Comparatively few viewers (around 1 in 10) claimed to have seen anything about the general election on Channel 4, and of those who did a relatively larger proportion seemed to have no particular opinion about the fairness of its coverage. Nevertheless, among its viewers who expressed an opinion, C4's coverage was seen to be the fairest of all. By the end of the campaign, and after the election, more than three-quarters of viewers thought C4's coverage had been fair to all parties, a significantly greater proportion than for BBC or ITV.

Labour voters were more likely to feel that BBC and ITV coverage was biassed than either Conservative or Alliance voters. Such was also the case during the 1983 general election. Now, as then, Labour voters were significantly more likely to perceive bias in television coverage after the election rather than before. During the 1987 election the proportion of Labour voters claiming bias on BBC increased from 29 per cent to 38 per cent between the second and third waves while the respective figures for ITV were 18 per cent and 28 per cent.

Table 16.4. *Parties given too much coverage by BBC-TV/ITV*

	BBC-TV			ITV		
	Wave 1 %	Wave 2 %	Wave 3 %	Wave 1 %	Wave 2 %	Wave 3 %
Conservative	62	49	47	49	45	57
Labour	24	32	22	27	29	24
Alliance	11	10	7	15	11	3
Other parties	2	1	1	*	*	2
None of the above	13	18	27	17	20	18
Don't know	4	7	6	5	6	7

Based on respondents who thought BBC-TV/ITV showed some favour. Respondents: could name more than one party. Base and (percentage of base for table 16.3): as for BBC: Wave 1 = 177 (18%), Wave 2 = 244 (22%), Wave 3 = 280 (27%); for ITV: Wave 1 = 131 (15%), Wave 2 = 153 (16%), Wave 3 = 165 (17%).
* less than 1 per cent.

Perceived direction of bias

Although a significantly greater proportion of viewers felt BBC, rather than ITV, coverage to be biassed, the perceived direction of that bias on both services was very similar. Of those people at the end of the campaign who felt BBC–TV or ITV coverage to have been biassed, the greatest proportion felt that there had been too much coverage of the Conservative Party, and that the tone and approach had been too favourable towards the Conservative Party. Between 2 and 3 in 10 felt either that coverage of the Labour Party had been too much or too favourable; but less than 1 in 10 felt the same about coverage of the Alliance (see table 16.4). At the same time, very few viewers (less than 1 in 10) felt that either the Conservative Party or the Labour Party had been given *too little* coverage on BBC and ITV.

Overall, therefore, it is clear that most people (two-thirds or more) thought that television treated all parties fairly. Among those who felt that the broadcasting media showed some favour, the Conservative party was felt to be the most favoured party, and the Alliance least favoured (see table 16.5). This parallels viewer opinions of coverage of the 1983 election campaign.

Learning during the election

People were asked, both in 1983 and in 1987, whether they felt they already 'know enough about most of the general election issues' or wanted to 'know more about most of the general election issues'. In 1983, two weeks before the election, just over half of those sampled (55 per cent) felt they knew enough and just under a third (31 per cent) said they wanted to know more. In 1987,

Table 16.5. *Parties given too favourable coverage by BBC-TV/ITV*

	BBC-TV				ITV		
	Wave 1 %	Wave 2 %	Wave 3 %		Wave 1 %	Wave 2 %	Wave 3 %
Conservative	60	57	57		49	53	63
Labour	19	29	28		32	27	21
Alliance	7	6	3		10	6	2
Other parties	2	*	*		*	1	1
None of the above	17	11	12		14	15	13
Don't know	4	5	4		4	6	6

Base here as for table 16.4
* less than 1 per cent.

again a fortnight before the poll, nearly 7 in 10 (68 per cent) felt they knew enough and just under a quarter wanted to know more. It is clear that a significantly greater proportion felt sufficiently informed at an earlier stage in 1987 than in 1983. One might speculate that this was the result of a long 'unofficial' election campaign which some commentators said began with the party conferences in 1986, and may well have contributed to the feelings of saturation noted earlier.

On the eve of the election in 1987 a little under 8 in 10 (77 per cent) felt they already knew enough, a marginally higher proportion than in 1983 (70 per cent). The decrease in the proportion who wanted to know more (from 24 per cent to 16 per cent) was relatively small compared with 1983 (from 31 per cent to 18 per cent). Clearly, if the *desire* to learn more is anything to go by, the last two weeks of the campaign had less of an effect in 1987 than in 1983. This is particularly notable amongst young voters (18–24-year-olds); two weeks before the election 4 in 10 (40 per cent) young people felt they wanted to learn more; two weeks later this proportion had only dropped to a third (33 per cent).

Perceptions of the amount and source of learning

Respondents were asked how much they *felt* they had learned about the points of view of the parties from six different sources of information during the election.

More people felt they had learned from television (excluding PEBs) than any other media source. Between 5 and 6 out of 10 (56 per cent) said they had learned 'a great deal' or 'a fair amount' from television, compared to around 4 out of 10 (41 per cent) from newspapers, and a little under a quarter (23 per cent) from radio (see table 16.6). Whereas in 1983 the value of television and newspapers, in the public eye, was very nearly equivalent, television was seen

Table 16.6. *Amount of Perceived Learning*

	Degree of perceived learning from each medium			
	A great deal	A fair amount	Not very much	Nothing
TV (excl. PEBs)	13	43	24	14
Newspapers	11	30	27	23
Radio	4	19	31	29
Talking to people	6	18	32	33
Information provided by parties	3	21	31	36
PEBs	9	35	28	17

Based on all respondents (1,544) in Wave 2

to have performed much better than newspapers this time around.

Other sources of political information also have a role to play. While around a quarter (24 per cent) said they had learned 'a great deal' or 'a fair amount' from posters and leaflets at Wave 2 (incidentally a rise of 15 per cent over two weeks) more than 4 in 10 (44 per cent) said the same about PEBs. This is a greater proportion than those who said they learned from newspapers and not far below the proportion of those who said the same about television in general. Additionally, among people who claimed to have seen at least 3 PEBs, 6 in 10 said they had learned 'a great deal' or 'a fair amount'. Clearly PEBs are seen to be an important information source during election campaigns.

Amount of actual learning

Claims of learning are not the same by any means as actual learning of party platforms and policies, so further questions were asked in order to assess 'true' learning. Ten fairly straightforward, unambiguous party policies were chosen and respondents were asked to state whether each was the policy of either the Conservative Party, Labour Party or the Alliance. Each of these policies was detailed in one of the party manifestos.

The results indicate that two weeks before the election 42 per cent of people were able to correctly associate 7 or more of the 10 policies with the appropriate party, while at the other extreme 20 per cent could only get 3 policies or less 'right' (see table 16.7). As a rough approximation at this stage the 'average' person could correctly associate around 6 out of 10 policies with the appropriate party.

Such a question was not asked in the 1983 survey and therefore a historical point of comparison is not available; nevertheless, the results indicate a high level of public knowledge of at least the *outline* of party policies at this stage in the campaign.

Table 16.7. *Knowledge of 10 party policies*

	Wave 1	Wave 2	Wave 3
Number of policies associated with correct party	%	%	%
7 or more	42	47	44
4–6	38	35	37
3 or less	20	18	19

Base for Wave 1, 1,536; for Wave 2, 1,544; for Wave 3, 1,571.

Looking at changes in knowledge as the campaign progressed we can see that the level of awareness increased only marginally over the final two weeks of the campaign (from 42 per cent to 47 per cent correctly associating 7 or more out of 10) and slightly declined after polling day (to 44 per cent) close to the levels a fortnight before polling day.

All in all, this supports evidence presented above that the public both felt, and indeed were, well-informed at an early stage of the campaign, but this level hardly changed as the campaign progressed.

There is some evidence also that claimed viewing of television coverage was associated with and even aided learning. Questioned a day or two before the election around half (52 per cent) of those people who had seen any coverage of the election on television could correctly associate 7 or more policies with the appropriate party. In contrast, only 2 out 10 (22 per cent) of the minority of people who said they had not viewed any coverage could do so. Or to put it the other way round it appears as if the well-informed and the interested were drawn towards the coverage while the less well-informed and uninterested were not so attracted.

Party election broadcasts

In 1983 there was some controversy over the PEB allocations to the three major parties, with Conservative:Labour:Liberal/SDP Alliance being allocated 5:5:4 PEBs respectively. For the 1987 election the allocations were 5:5:5, and public opinion was quite different from 1983; in 1987, 85 per cent felt 5:5:5 was a fair allocation, whereas in 1983 only 42 per cent felt 5:5:4 had been fair.

This satisfaction did not extend to Wales and Scotland, however, where viewers tended to feel that Plaid Cymru and the SNP respectively had been unfairly treated. In Wales, 30 per cent of viewers felt the PEB allocation had been unfair, and in Scotland 45 per cent felt the same way. Since the 1987 study extended to Northern Ireland, the opportunity was taken to question viewers about the unique PEB/party access system operating there. The full quota of major parties' PEBs are shown in Northern Ireland, as in the rest of the UK, despite the fact that none of the PEB-allocated parties stand for election in any Ulster seats. Instead, and in addition to these PEBs, the various Northern Ireland parties get either small 'mini-PEBs' or extended interview slots in regional news and current affairs output. Half of the viewers interviewed in Northern Ireland just before polling day felt that the BBC and ITV airtime given to the various NI parties was fair, while large minorities (around 40 per cent) had no opinion. Less than one in ten felt that BBC or ITV had been unfair to any NI parties. On the issue of Conservative, Labour and Alliance broadcasts shown throughout Northern Ireland, over six in ten (63 per cent) felt there were too many; a clear indication of dissatisfaction with this somewhat anomalous situation.

Summary and conclusions

While a majority of those surveyed thought there was too much coverage of the election on television public viewing behaviour was little different from the comparable period in 1986. Television, primarily BBC-TV, was chosen above all media as providing the most interesting, and most informative coverage of the election, and this time primarily ITV, as giving the best coverage of local issues.

Overall a large majority thought BBC-TV and ITV (although not C4) devoted too much time to polls and 'politicians' personalities', while many fewer said the same about party policies.

Between 6 and 8 in 10 over all three survey waves considered that television had treated all parties fairly. However, while the proportion who considered ITV to be partisan remained constant, the proportion who thought the same of the BBC increased quite markedly during and immediately after the campaign. The direction of any bias perceived on either ITV or BBC was consistently seen as leaning towards the Conservative Party above all others.

Many more people felt they knew enough about the issues two weeks before the election in 1987 than in a comparable survey in 1983. This must have made the broadcasters' job more difficult and may have contributed to the criticisms of the amount of coverage noted earlier – more people thought they knew enough early in the campaign. Having said this the desire to know more was particularly prevalent amongst the young where 4 in 10 first time voters wanted to know more.

In 1987, compared with 1983, television moved clear of newspapers as the medium most people said they had learned 'a great deal' or 'a fair amount' from during the election (TV 56 per cent, newspapers 41 per cent). The proportion who said they had learned from radio coverage and 'talking to people' was roughly equal (radio 23 per cent, talking 24 per cent). The survey also highlights the importance of PEBs as well as information provided by the parties themselves (e.g. leaflets), with 44 per cent and 24 per cent respectively saying they had learned a great deal or a fair amount from these sources.

Two weeks before the election 42 per cent of those questioned could match seven or more out of ten manifesto statements with the correct party, compared with 20 per cent who could only get three or less policies 'right'. Although this absolute level of knowledge increased only marginally as the campaign progressed, overall knowledge of policies was much higher amongst those who said they had watched television coverage of the election than amongst those who said they had not.

Note

1 It is important to note that opinions about polls are solely concerned with the amount of *time* spent analysing the results of opinion polls, not with feelings that opinion polling itself is inappropriate during election time. In a separate question roughly equal proportions of all respondents, around one quarter, said they felt that the publication of opinion polls during elections was helpful or harmful; around a half felt that opinion polling was neither helpful nor harmful.

PART VI

The role of the local media in the 1987 campaign

17 Two sides to the border: reporting the campaign in Scotland

Once the results were known, it was clear that Scotland was different. The Conservatives had lost more than half their seats, dropping to 10, while Labour had won 50 out of the 72. In the following weeks 'The Scottish Question', as *The Times* called it, became a popular topic in the national newspapers and on network television. But why not during the campaign? Why were newspaper readers and network viewers in England given so little advance warning? Within Scotland itself the press and broadcasters had made the prospect plain.

Blind eyes in the South

The first firm evidence came midway through the campaign. For months before there had been talk in Scotland of the 'Doomsday Scenario', by which Labour's hold would be strengthened north of the Border but nullified by Conservative success in England. On Thursday afternoon, 28 May, the results of a System 3 poll were delivered to Scottish Television (Sc. TV hereafter) and to *The Glasgow Herald.* It showed that the Edinburgh South constituency, previously held by a Scottish Office Minister, Michael Ancram, was likely to be won by Labour with a comfortable majority.

The effect in Sc. TV's newsroom was electric. Half the items prepared for the early evening Scottish news were scrapped, and the election package was extended to take twenty of the programme's twenty-five minutes. Of that, the System 3 poll was to occupy the first eight or nine minutes. Bill Miller, Professor of Politics at Glasgow University, was called in to comment. Live on the programme, he said that polls in Central Scotland were not a guide to what might happen in the Highlands or the North-East. But he went on to offer a cautious projection of about 50 seats for Labour and 11 for the Conservatives. (We also now know, through the diary of a Scots politician published after the election, that on hearing of the Edinburgh South figures through his car telephone, Malcolm Rifkind was 'stunned' and 'knocked back in a way I have never seen before'.[1]

BBC Scotland – having decided before the election not to take part in constituency polls – nevertheless got in on the act. It heard of the poll by chance because Labour's leader in Scotland, Donald Dewar, arrived in an ebullient mood having already been asked by Sc.TV for his reaction. That day the BBC's Scottish news was going out half an hour after its rival's, so it picked up the detailed figures from the transmission. Its lawyers advised that copyright could no longer apply once the figures had been broadcast. But BBC Sc. still rated the sacking of Celtic football club's manager as bigger news than the Edinburgh South poll. (The Scottish early evening news programmes are, of course, transmitted only in Scotland and are not seen in England.)

Next morning *The Glasgow Herald* and *The Scotsman* both gave the story prominence. No London-based newspaper carried any report until the following week, apart from a small note in the *Financial Times*, nor was there any mention in the BBC's nine-o'clock network news or ITN's News at Ten, the two premier UK news programmes. The 'Doomsday Scenario', however, cropped up briefly in Sir Robin Day's *Campaign Question Time*, recorded in Glasgow on the evening of 28 May; and *The Guardian's* television commentary (Saturday, 30 May) rightly remarked that here was a topic so far not aired in England.

Further evidence came a few days later in three more System 3 polls. On Monday, 1 June a survey in the Stirling constituency showed Labour overtaking the sitting Conservative, and on Wednesday, 3 June a poll covering nearly all of Scotland brought confirmation of a probable 50 seats for Labour and at best 10 for the Conservatives. This news coincided with Mrs Thatcher's only visit to Scotland during the campaign – although she had been at the Scottish Conservative conference in Perth just beforehand – and her presence brought the first real hint to readers and viewers in England that her party was in trouble in the North.

Even then, these were muted warnings. While the broadcasters and newspapers within Scotland were giving extensive cover to the latest System 3 polls – showing Labour likely to win 50 seats, the Conservatives possibly down to single figures, and an apparently strong demand from Scots voters for devolution through a Scottish Assembly[2] – little of this was being reported in England. The clearest picture on UK network television came in a C4 election special, *The View from Scotland*, in peak time on Wednesday, 3 June. It was made for C4 by Sc.TV and included detail of the System 3 polls and a lively studio discussion of their validity. It was seen throughout the United Kingdom.

Mrs Thatcher's visit to Scotland was, of course, widely reported. The heavies among the network and newspaper journalists came with her. Their reports were less than illuminating. The BBC's John Simpson – distinguished in the international field – had either not consulted his Scottish colleagues or decided to disregard their advice. He provided a straight report of Mrs Thatcher's 'set-piece speech' in Edinburgh (his term), attacking trade union domination of Labour policy. Of the threat to Conservative seats in Scotland there was not a word in the main 9 o'clock news. On ITN an hour later, the report from Edinburgh at least opened by saying that in Scotland 'opinion polls are running against the Conservatives', but there was no further enlightenment. As with the BBC, Kevin Dunn for ITN concentrated on the Prime Minister's attack on trade union influence. Next day, when Mrs Thatcher faced sharp questioning from Scottish journalists in Glasgow, not a word was relayed by the BBC or ITN in the main evening news. The local programmes in Scotland covered the exchanges well (see 'editorial decision-making' below). The English audiences were left in the dark.

By this time, however, the English-based newspapers were beginning to fill in some of the background. Until then reporting had been spasmodic, although *The Daily Telegraph*, *The Guardian*, *The Independent*, and *The Times* had all found generous space for colourful features from the Western Isles. (*The Times* had also published a historical piece about devolution, suggesting that now the Alliance and SNP were 'weak', the Tories had less to worry about.) *The Financial Times*, more perceptively, had given the essentials of the System 3 poll on Saturday, 30 May.

With Mrs Thatcher's visit to Scotland the travelling London journalists provided substantial extracts from her assault in Edinburgh on trade union influence and on the hard left. In addition, *The Daily Telegraph* on Wednesday, 3 June carried a feature under a five-column headline 'Tories the Unpopular Party in Scotland'. Written by Norman Stone, Professor of Modern History at Oxford, it plugged some previous gaps. *The Times* that day briefly reported the System 3 polls of earlier days, and *The Independent* also caught up briefly next day. *The Guardian* that Wednesday published the only extensive report of what it called 'half an hour of vigorous and almost entirely hostile questions' at Mrs Thatcher's Glasgow press conference – and on her insistence that the Conservative campaign was not faltering in Scotland. On Friday, 5 June it followed up with a feature across six columns, 'Scottish Office Ministers face local difficulty', in which the Edinburgh constituencies in particular were analysed. *The Times* alone found no significant space for the Conservative crisis.

Among the popular papers, only *The Daily Record* and *The Daily Express* gave any substantial cover to the campaign in Scotland. Maxwell's *Record*, published in Glasgow, has daily sales of around 775,000 – thus reaching one household in three in its circulation area, the highest figure of any UK newspaper. It reserved its most strident salvos until the last fortnight of the campaign, when it fired six on its front page in twelve days. They were polemics rather than reporting. The last began, 'Mrs Thatcher has a blind spot . . . It's called Scotland'. *The Daily Express* in its Scottish editions (with sales just under 200,000) was notably less partisan than its parent in the South, and its constituency reports still bear reading long after the election. But it refrained from providing any overall indication of the perilous plight of the Conservatives in Scotland, and it did not report Mrs Thatcher's rough ride during her visit to Scotland. Two days before polling it gave the Secretary of State, Malcolm Rifkind, a half page to put the Conservative case; the other parties enjoyed no such generosity. *The Sun*, with sales above 250,000 in Scotland, carried next to nothing about the campaign north of the Border although it was blistering in its cover of Labour and the Alliance nationally, with splash headlines such as 'When the Red Rose turns Yellow' on Labour's defence policy. Since the election *The Sun* has started to carry extra pages for Scottish news in its Scottish editions, but politics are low in its priorities.

Editorial decision-making

During the campaign most politicians appeared to assume that television mattered more than newspapers. They were probably correct – we shall know more clearly when the joint BBC–IBA studies are ready[3] – although for detail or discussion of the issues newspapers carried greater information and closer analysis.

Contrary to their own anxieties, both *Scotland Today* (Sc.TV) and *Reporting Scotland* (BBC) held their audiences throughout the campaign, although late May and early June normally bring a seasonal decline. Grampian's *North Today* also maintained its figures. *Scotland Today* held at around 30 to 35 per cent of households in Central Scotland, helped perhaps by having *Take the High Road* soon afterwards on two evenings a week. (The latter is a popular Scottish soap, usually with over 40 per cent, the highest figures for any regular programme in Scotland: Wogan enjoys no such popularity north of the Border.) Grampian's *North Today* also held at 30 per cent or more. *Reporting Scotland*'s figures were lower, but still with a respectable 22–25 per cent of households – which puts it consistently among the top three of BBC regional news programmes, with Manchester and Plymouth as its rivals. It reached a 27 per cent peak in the last few days of the campaign.

If there is an overall criticism to be made of television reporting in the election, it is that analytical studies of the issues were absent. On both sides of the Border, analysis was more readily found in the 'heavy' newspapers. Thus, for example, between 28 May and 8 June *The Scotsman* carried articles on defence, devolution, education policy, unemployment, 'the Scargill factor', law and order, public finance and social security. *The Glasgow Herald* in that period dealt with devolution (twice), foreign relations, unemployment and the Scottish Universities. *The Scotsman*'s devolution article was headed 'The fuse that burns slowly' and the *Herald*'s second article was headed 'The issue which refuses to lie down'. Television in Scotland initiated no such analysis of issues, apart from some mini-commentaries on BBC Sc.'s *Campaign Trail*, broadcast around midnight. There was, however, one outstanding programme – the BBC's *Scottish Question Time* of Friday, 5 June – and two notable new series mounted by Scottish Television in their *Scottish Assembly* and their *Scottish Questions*. These will be discussed later, in 'Hustings on the box' below.

Day by day in the two television newsrooms in Glasgow, much the same preoccupations were evident:

1 How to avoid being boring, with election news and other news competing for time;
2 Political fairness and balance, as required by the Representation of the People Act (RPA) and by the healthy conventions of British broadcasting;
3 Treatment of 'near-political' events that were not part of the campaign but presumably were timed to influence it (examples: civil service and teacher's rallies, and reports on inner-city poverty);
4 Where to send crews, how to get the most out of limited resources;
5 What the mandarins upstairs and down in London are saying (a serious preoccupation at BBC Sc., but not at Sc.TV).

As already noted, both the early evening news programmes in Central Scotland and Grampian's in the North did well in holding their audiences – evidence enough that they were not boring. And all three respected the requirements of fairness and balance. There were of course complaints about particular items, but to an outside observer none that stood examination.

Decision-making followed its normal swift pattern, as required by deadlines, but with one apparent advantage at Sc.TV. There, the 'producer of the day' decided news priorities, whether connected with the election or not. At the BBC a separate election unit produced a package, which in practice meant that there was less flexibility in each evening's running order. Thus when Mrs Thatcher was in Scotland, *Scotland Today* went straight in with her press conferences and her claim that few people were really interested in devolution. *Reporting Scotland* relegated the election package to second place, rather than sacrifice the first eight or nine minutes to solid politics, and led instead with progress by a Glasgow medical team on development of a vaccine against Aids. The greater flexibility of Sc.TV was also illustrated by its treatment of the System 3 polls – particularly the first, with its dramatic (and ultimately correct) forecast that Mr Michael Ancram would lose his seat in Edinburgh South. The producer of the day did not hesitate about that, nor would he hesitate, he said later, about ditching almost all the election material were the general news exceptionally strong.

As to maintaining balance, just how meticulous the BBC's daily monitoring was may be seen from *Reporting Scotland*'s final figures:

Conservatives, 36 mins 20 secs; Labour 36 mins 12 secs;
Alliance, 36 mins 0 secs; SNP, 35 mins 27 secs;
Greens (11 candidates only), 5 mins 39 secs;
Communists (5 candidates), 5 mins 15 secs.

Even at Cowcaddens (Sc.TV), however, there was grumbling in the ranks. As one reporter said, it was irksome if you had two stories in the day – one a Labour launch with Robbie Coltrane and Donald Dewar and the other a dreary SNP piece – and then had to balance the time. 'You cut one to one minute so that it barely makes sense and you have to stretch the other to make a minute, which isn't what you want.' In practice Sc.TV was more ready to take risks, letting the balance be corrected over a few days. As producers in both newsrooms said, for the parties themselves the images would probably have been better if they had received more time on some days and less on others. And, as they also said, the numerical balance is a crude test anyway.

Again, as an outside observer it seemed to me that the journalists were often torn between their genuine wish to be fair and accurate – with attitudes far removed from those of the popular tabloid newspapers – and their sense of frustration at having to keep within strict guidelines. They all knew that, apart from the two or three political specialists in Sc.TV and BBC Sc., they must avoid comment. Yet some felt that they ought to have more freedom to point to half-truths from politicians or to choose their own topics. Day after day, the political parties were allowed to set the agenda. 'We ought to have decided what topics *we* wanted each day and invited the politicians who were relevant', one said. 'We shouldn't just take the politicians we're given.' 'Scotland is far too nice and cosy', another said. 'A bit more aggression might be no bad thing.'

The one notable exception came during the Prime Minister's visit. 'Photo opportunities' such as went with her and other leaders in England were rare in Scotland, but on the evening of her arrival she was seen driving a fork-lift tractor while her entourage struggled to keep up and then seen with Denis drinking beer at a brewery. During that sequence on *Scotland Today* she was also seen turning to answer a shouted question about adverse polls in Scotland and replying, 'No, we're steadily going up.' Bravado or inadequate briefing? That remains unknown.

At the Glasgow press conference next morning and in her two television interviews afterwards, she was persistently questioned about the Conservatives' unpopularity in Scotland and about devolution, unemployment, and the Ravenscraig steel plant. On unpopularity she said that the party had not yet 'got across' in Scotland the scale of its achievements. On devolution she said that only the media asked questions about it, whereas 'ordinary folk' were not interested. On unemployment she said that jobs came from successful business, and on Ravenscraig that everyone was working hard to get more orders. The replies were stonewalling, but the questions had been put. They were ones she did not want to answer.

Only a little of the exchanges was carried on network television news at midday, and nothing outside Scotland in the evening. As already noted, *Scotland Today* led with their interview, edited down from nearly seven minutes to just over three; *Reporting Scotland* gave its interview in full (just short of eight minutes), but not as the lead. Both programmes had problems over the editing because in each interview she had given one long (two minutes) general reply, speaking so fast that it could not be cut. Sc.TV therefore dropped the whole of that answer, while BBC Sc. decided to leave it in. These were decisions taken only after consultation with senior editors. Normally, both at BBC Sc. and at Sc.TV reporters edited their items themselves. The choice of which passage to include from a speech or exchange was left to them. The producer or editor of the day would usually preview the item before transmission, unless time was too short, or if one of the specialists wanted advice the producer would sit in on the first stages of the editing. In both newsrooms the supervision was by quick conversation. Formal direction was something we never saw. The system worked by mutual understanding.

Apart from the Prime Minister's visit, the only notable 'photo opportunities' were when Glenys Kinnock toured Edinburgh schools, saying little but looking sympathetic, and near the end of the campaign when Labour staged a symbolic display of the unemployed in a Glasgow park – which told nobody anything but was pleasing to watch from cameras mounted on a high crane. Those apart – and excluding some blatantly bogus events that were ditched – the programme producers tended to complain that there were too few attractive pictures. One or two of them, indeed, believed that the best opportunities were ones they had created for themselves through the scenic elements in constituency reports (even in industrial Lanarkshire and North Cunninghame) and in light relief from such places as the islands of Mull, Oronsay (population of four registered voters, one supporting each party, and wonderful seascapes), Islay and Arran.

Hustings on the box

The evidence summarised so far suggests that, within the limited air time available, the two television newsrooms in Central Scotland did a competent, professional job in covering the campaign. They reported the day's events, filled in at least a little of the background, maintained the balance of time and treatment between the parties, and, unlike their colleagues in the South, they were alert to the changing political scene in Scotland. Among their journalists there was some frustration with the extent to which the political parties were allowed to set the agenda, and a feeling that there ought to be more enterprise if not aggression in political reporting. But some recompense came from the election 'specials' which supplemented the early evening Scottish news.

Of the 'specials' there were 14 on Scottish Television, each lasting an hour or more, and three on BBC Scotland. These gave voters their chance to speak, to question politicians, and to set their own agendas. For its specials, BBC Scotland invited organisations – political and non-political – to nominate members of the audience and propose questions, from which a choice was made by the producer and presenter. For Sc.TV's *Assembly*, the MORI polling organisation provided 1,000 names grouped to provide an exact cross-section of all Scotland by age, sex, occupation and social class, and from these 100 were invited with their travel and overnight expenses paid. Both systems produced some sharp questions and supplementaries. Kirsty Wark for the BBC and Malcolm Wilson for Sc.TV proved well able to control their audiences and to bring politicians back to the point.

The *Scottish Question Time* of the Friday before polling covered only four topics, although seven had been planned. They included a fast ball from a Glasgow Stock Exchange man on the jobs likely to be lost because of defence policies, a prickly inquiry from an academic economist on how to rebuild Scotland's destroyed industrial base, and a medical man's call for explanation of how the health services could cope with increasingly costly technology. With the exchange on each topic lasting 12 to 14 minutes, this was the nearest we saw to serious analysis. It was also lively. Starting at 10.37 pm with a 12 per cent audience, it succeeded in holding and slightly increasing the numbers in the next 45 minutes – no mean achievement at that time of night. More programmes of that quality would be welcome.

Sc.TV's massive effort with its *Assembly* and its *Questions* derived from the appointment some months earlier of the company's director of programmes, Gus Macdonald, who had run the *Granada* 500 series in four previous elections. Soon after his return to Scotland he set up a monthly programme in which a representative audience took part in a discussion of current issues. It was a successful dry run for the election series. The aim of the *Assembly*, its producer said, was 'to get the flavour of what Scotland is thinking'. Its first two election programmes explored attitudes, with discussion among the audiences and no politicians present. It came up, among other findings, with 45 of the 100 ready to go in for tactical voting, with only 37 believing that tax cuts could stimulate the Scottish economy, while 79 (on a separate question) were prepared to see higher taxation to provide for increased public spending. Of the 100, 71 thought proportional representation more fair than the present system and 63 wanted a Scottish Assembly (a real one, not just on television) within the UK. These findings were before the System 3 polls were published; and the longer each debate went on the higher its quality became. The audience figures, however, were erratic – from only 3 per cent on a Sunday afternoon (on devolution) to 21 per cent for the final one, with the four Scottish party leaders, in peak time two days before polling.[4] Each of the later programmes brought politicians face to face with the representative 100, and the exchanges were sensible and good tempered. As short, clear expositions of the issues in Scotland these programmes must also rank high.

One other Sc.TV 'special' deserves mention – the *View from Scotland*, commissioned by C4. It not only carried to England the message of the System 3 polls but also included a short studio discussion of devolution. It maintained pace in a way likely to hold audiences, and it gave essential information not previously given to audiences in the South. It was castigated by a media reviewer in *The Times* (a Scot) for its 'heavily loaded reporting' of the Conservatives' troubles in the North. His previous article, on a *Times* centre page, had condemned television journalists for failing to report realities.

A Scots hiccup and a BBC worry

This observation of journalists at work in Scotland would be incomplete if it omitted to mention two misfortunes. The first and less lasting was that Sc.TV's election night programme had to be cancelled. That followed from disagreements between the local NUJ and the company over extra payments. The management view was that the NUJ had signed an agreement under which up to £300 in bonus was available to journalists working that night, whereas the journalists believed – incorrectly, according to the management – that much larger sums were to be paid to technicians. A deadlock led to cancellation, to everyone's disappointment. BBC Scotland's journalists, with no more than £125 extra on offer, worked hard that night – and won a vastly larger audience in Scotland than the results programme improvised by ITN in the absence of Sc.TV (although ITN gave many of the Scottish results first).

The other misfortune afflicted the BBC and was more lasting. To someone once employed by the corporation, it was painfully evident that some of its most experienced journalists in Scotland felt insecure and unable to rely on support from above. As one said, rightly or wrongly, 'the management is running scared and the Governors just don't want to provoke Maggie'. Analysis of policies, in his view, was impossible without drawing attention to the flaws in party statements. 'That's too dangerous for the BBC in this election'. He was not alone in his view. A dozen specific complaints came up, although none in itself so compelling as the general atmosphere. Among them:

> It was on advice from London that BBC Scotland turned down the offer of a share in the System 3 polls;
> A directive from London said that BBC staff should not initiate discussion of tactical voting, although in Scotland it was seen as a relevant factor in some constituencies;
> BBC Sc. was given no opportunity to provide a network programme such as Sc.TV's for C4;

'Dull' programmes resulted, it was thought, because tough questioning was seen as too risky.

And so on. The deep worry, however, lay in the suspicion that the higher authorities in London would condemn any controversial initiative in Scotland.

Midway through the election the new Director General, Michael Checkland, made his first visit to Glasgow since his appointment. While there he crushed rumours of impending change in the top management in Scotland, and he appeared to give a reassuring impression to those who heard him. At the same time, although the detail was not known until later, the audience figures were a counter to the fear of 'dull' programmes.

The malaise was there, nevertheless. By the next election, it must be hoped that nothing of the kind remains. That will depend on the new management in London and on an absence of Government interference. Unless the malaise is remedied, it will be damaging not only to all British broadcasting but to British democracy.

Notes

This paper was prepared with the help of research assistants Claire Dean and Alison Driver, University of Stirling.

1 Brian Meek, 'On the road with Rifkind', *Glasgow Herald*, 20 June 1987.

2 The three further *System 3* polls were these.

(a) *1 June* for Sc. TV and *The Glasgow Herald*, in the Stirling constituency. It gave Labour 39 per cent (+11 per cent over the 1983 election), Conservative 29 (−11 per cent), Alliance 18 (−6 per cent) and SNP 13 (−2 per cent). Excluded were 20 per cent undecided or refusing to answer. It also gave details of respondents' readiness to go in for tactical voting. (In the event, the Conservative held the seat.)

(b) *3 June*, for *The Glasgow Herald* in 40 Scottish constituencies. This showed Labour at 45 per cent (+10 per cent over 1983), Conservatives 19 (−9 per cent), Alliance 18 (−6 per cent) and SNP 17 (+4 per cent). Excluded were 21 per cent, undecided or not answering. This, *The Glasgow Herald* said, would put 15 of the 21 Conservative seats at risk, possibly giving nine to Labour (= 50), five to the SNP (= 7) and one to the Alliance (= 9). In the result the SNP lost its two existing seats but won three others.

(c) *3 June*, for C4. This incorporated the figures above and asked further questions. On 'what do you want for Scotland?', 25 per cent said total independence (a figure not reflected in the SNP's own final vote, which totalled only 14 per cent); 51 per cent wanted a Scottish Assembly within the UK, 18 per cent no change and 5 per cent 'don't know'. The poll further asked 'how important' respondents thought it was to have a Scottish Assembly, to which 32 per cent said 'very important', 30 per cent 'important' and 25 per cent 'not important'. Within the overall figures of those supporting the Conservatives 10 per cent wanted independence, 38 per cent a Scottish Assembly, 49 per cent no change and 3 per cent 'don't know'.

Towards the end of the campaign, *System 3*, through *The Glasgow Herald* and Sc. TV, provided another three polls with similar findings.

3 The joint BBC–IBA study of the 1983 election, by Barrie Gunter, Michael Svennevig and Mallory Wober, showed 43 per cent of people gaining much of their information about political parties from television, 37 per cent from newspapers, 15 per cent from radio and 18 per cent from other people. (The figures are not mutually exclusive.) That study also showed a majority (69 per cent) saying that television coverage was excessive, although in practice audiences increased during the campaign instead of going into a seasonal decline. (The 1987 figures are in chapter 16 of this volume.)

4 Although 21 per cent looks good for an election special, that programme was preceded by *Take the High Road* at 39 per cent and followed by *Taggart* at 33 per cent, which tells us more about popular priorities.

18 The media, the polls and the general election campaign in Wales

A general election campaign in Wales is part of the wider United Kingdom national campaign, yet retains an identity of its own. It is at once both self-contained yet subsumed within the broader national trend. This creates a perspective on politics that has been termed 'bifocal'.[1] This dual perspective pervades all aspects of the election, from the parties' planning to the electorate's reaction. Most marked of all, however, is how this dualism is reflected in the media. In recent years Wales has developed a lively and forceful media, especially in television, but at an election it is inevitably secondary to British-wide reporting. Its focus and emphasis is firmly on the Welsh dimension of politics, creating a forum for political communications of a character and nature quite different from that of the national campaign. This can make for lively political interchange, none more so in 1987 than that involving the media's use of opinion polling.

In order to understand and appreciate the part played by opinion polls in the 1987 election campaign in Wales, it is necessary to briefly review their growth. Various incidents over the years have given polling a notoriety and created mistrust between political professionals and the media. For many, polling represents an unwelcome intrusion into the electoral process.

The emergence of Welsh politics

There was little polling of all-Wales samples before the late 1960s. The pattern of Welsh politics, combining, as it did, the Labour heartland of the South Wales coalfield with the lingering Liberalism of the Celtic Fringe, was remarkably stable between 1945 and 1966. As such, it can be argued that polls were largely redundant in the face of such Labour hegemony. The subsequent frequency of such polls mirrors the ebb and flow of Welsh politics. When Wales featured in British national politics in the aftermath of the Carmarthen by-election, for example, there followed a spate of polling.

Otherwise, pundits and commentators were required to extrapolate Welsh trends from British samples.

Beneath the surface, however, a more distinct 'Welsh politics' was emerging. Pressure to create a Minister for Welsh Affairs had finally been acknowledged. The Labour Party committed itself to the creation of a cabinet post for Wales, a pledge it redeemed in 1964 with the creation of the Welsh Office. The long-standing agitation for measures to stem the decline of the traditional Welsh language and culture took on a new momentum with the creation of Cymdeithas Yr Iaith Gymraeg, the Welsh Language Society. The remarkable victory of Plaid Cymru at the Carmarthen by-election in July 1966 encapsulated the political transition in Wales – from the traditional pattern to the radical unknown. Wales was suddenly news.

As a product of the same forces of social change, there were now regional media to record these events and, in turn, to help define a Welsh politics. The 1960s saw the full establishment of daily news and current affairs coverage on both BBC and Independent Television, thus creating all-Wales broadcasting to supplement the rather regionalised daily press. The coming together of this new media market with the emergent newsworthiness of Wales created the opportunity and demand for opinion research.

Opinion polling in Wales

Political opinion polling did not become commonplace in Wales until the run-up to the Referendum on Devolution in 1979. The debate over devolution created an issue well suited to periodic polling. Once implementation of the Wales Act became dependent upon a referendum, however, estimates of the state of opinion became even more newsworthy and frequent polling occurred. The polls accurately tracked the gradual erosion of support for a Welsh Assembly and emerged creditably from the campaign. With the public voting four to one against devolution, it would have been difficult, perhaps, for the polls to get it wrong.

Flushed with this success, the media planned their coverage of the 1979 general election with a significant news input from opinion polling. In particular, a series of specific constituency polls were commissioned, both on television and in the press, which subsequently proved to be of very mixed accuracy. Much of the present discontent with opinion polling in Wales stems from the poor record of the polls at the 1979 election.

The new salience of Wales as a distinct region also provided an impetus for market and opinion research companies to set up in Wales. Although all the major London companies maintained fieldworkers in Wales, it was widely felt that they lacked sufficient staff to conduct a poll in, for example, a remote rural constituency, or to generate an all-Wales sample. Given, too, the new assertiveness and self-confidence of Welsh business and institutions, there was a clear propensity to commission polls locally. The rivalry between the various media outlets also encouraged a tendency to contract with one agency alone, whereas in reality the potential Welsh market could probably not fully support more than one commercial agency. Correspondingly, mistakes were made, false economies were sought in order to appear competitive and these failings were aided and abetted by inexperienced commissioning staff within the media.

There was widespread disquiet within the political community in Wales about the poor record of the polls in 1979. The main parties, however, after a momentary complaint, continued about their routine business. For Plaid Cymru, though, Gwynfor Evans' loss of Carmarthen was attributable solely to the 'inaccuracies' of a constituency poll commisssioned by the BBC. An extremely ill-tempered response was forthcoming from the Nationalist Party and relations between the party and the media were strained for some time. In the relatively closed world of public affairs in Wales, relations between politicians and journalists are, to mutual advantage, close. Plaid Cymru's apportionment of blame for Gwynfor Evans' defeat severely strained this relationship and left a nagging prejudice that could only too easily be rekindled.

The 1987 election

Pre-campaign polling

Opinion polling in Wales has remained irregular, although it is now more frequent than hitherto. Most polls were commissioned for 'one-off' specific purposes rather than as part of a regular series. It was thus a considerable innovation when Beaufort Research of Cardiff initiated their quarterly Welsh omnibus surveys in June 1986. HTV, which had achieved a notable *coup* with Beaufort at the time of the Brecon and Radnor by-election in 1985, became a client for the voting intention questions of these studies. The data gathered, however, were treated as background research material rather than a 'top of the bulletin' news story. Thus, although polling was occurring there was little public discussion of the results. Media interest was muted by their unexceptional nature, the slightly dated nature of the data, and their limited news value outside an imminent election.

A combination of competition and rivalry resulted in HTV commissioning their next study from Research and Marketing, also of Cardiff, rather than Beaufort which had conducted most of their recent work. This study focussed upon the current state of the Welsh Language, but was based upon an all-Wales representative sample and included a voting intention question. The poll was primarily for a programme to mark the 25th anniversary, in

February 1987, of Saunders Lewis' famous lecture on the language struggle within Wales. For artistic and editorial reasons, the documentary film that HTV produced did not use the data on current language usage, attitudes to education, linguistic policy, etc. Although the material gathered on linguistic issues appeared perfectly consistent with accepted trends, the data on voting intention showed a division of opinion which greatly inflated Plaid Cymru's normal level of support in such polls. There is good reason to believe that the principal subject of the survey – the Welsh language – led to some biassed selection of respondents in the fieldwork. This may have prejudiced the political complexion of the sample. Together with certain problems during the analysis stage, this meant that HTV did not even carry the political data from the survey as a news item. In the small world of Welsh politics, this information quickly leaked to Plaid Cymru and the press and suddenly HTV was accused of suppressing the poll to damage the prospects of the Nationalists.

The pre-election period was also notable for a polling innovation in the production by the Press Association (PA) of a national poll with a sufficiently large sample to allow regional breakdowns. Two PA polls were published, in November 1986 and April 1987. The second breakdown for Wales showed the Labour Party to be trailing the Conservatives by three per cent (37 per cent to 34 per cent), a situation that seemed so unlikely to be true that the veracity of the whole PA exercise was thrown into doubt.

Meanwhile, on the other channel, the BBC had launched a new weekly current affairs programme, Public Account, scheduled in a Welsh regional opt-out from BBC2. The programme was presented by one of Wales' most senior broadcasters, Vincent Kane. Partly in order to ensure a high profile launch of this programme, the BBC commissioned, from Beaufort, a series of five polls in marginal, or politically sensitive, constiuencies at a time when discussion of the likely election date was becoming widespread. The broad climate of opinion is important here, for although the election campaign had not formally begun, an election was now imminent. The general public might not have yet acquired the heightened consciousness of an election campaign, but for the party professionals and candidates the 'phoney war' of mid-term was over and the coming electoral contest was beginning to assume clearer proportions, especially in the marginal constituencies. Two of the constituencies chosen by the BBC, Ynys Mon and Carmarthen, were the objects of particular Plaid Cymru ambitions, thus conflict was once more likely to break out between the party and the media over opinion polls.

The Beaufort/BBC poll in Ynys Mon (Anglesey), taken between 19 and 21 February, gave the Conservatives 38 per cent, Labour 30 per cent, Plaid Cymru 20 per cent, and the Alliance 11 per cent (table 18.1). This was in a seat where Plaid Cymru had run second in 1983 and felt poised to consolidate the anti-government vote in a highly Welsh, rural constituency. The Nationalists

Table 18.1. *Beaufort/BBC pre-campaign polls*

Constituency	Last fieldwork	Number polled	Conservative	Labour	PlC	Alliance
Pembroke	3 Jan.	542	41%	37%	2%	19%
Ynys Mon	21 Feb.	769	38%	30%	20%	11%
Brecon & R.	12 Mar.	753	30%	31%	2%	36%
Clwyd SW	16 Apr.	775	29%	36%	7%	27%
Carmarthen	9 May	1,000	29%	32%	16%	22%

were predictably furious and attempted to discredit both the poll and the research company in the press and on television. Carmarthen, the other constituency of special interest to Plaid Cymru, was not polled until early May, by which time an announcement of the election date appeared inevitable. Indeed, transmission of the programme carrying the poll results was only possible because it took place between the announcement of the election and the dissolution of parliament. Although disappointed with the results of the Beaufort/BBC poll in Carmarthen, Plaid Cymru's complaints were temporarily overtaken by events.

Campaign Polls

Once the election had been called, differing editorial strategies emerged amongst the media in Wales. The BBC in Wales chose to forgo any polling during the campaign, some would say for reasons of economy, but formally this decision was based on a statement from Mr Ron Neil that 'we should not open ourselves to the charge of telling the voters what to do'. Subsequently in the campaign much would be made of this rationale. HTV had devised a strategy for their election coverage with polls linked to particular pro-grammes; a combination presenting both an all-Wales perspective and individual constituency profiles in marginal and interesting seats. HTV were also servicing two separate markets: producing their own news and current affairs programmes, in English, as part of their normal ITV output within their franchise area, and also producing the current affairs output, under contract, to Sianel Pedwar Cymru (S4C), the Welsh-medium fourth channel in Wales. This latter responsibility brought the company into much more likely confrontation with Plaid Cymru. For whilst the Nationalists remain fairly marginal in an all-Wales context, they are considerably more significant politically in the context of the audience of S4C.

HTV's first election poll was of the Welsh marginals, commissioned for an election review of Wales made for C4 (but not shown in Wales). Sections of this review, including the poll material, were then re-edited and repeated on their own English current affairs programme, *Wales This Week*. Constituency studies were commissioned of Ynys Mon, Carmarthen and one of the Cardiff constituencies. An all-Wales poll was also commissioned, to be presented on a programme in which the leaders of the parties in Wales answered questions from a live studio audience. The field contracts for this research were divided between Beaufort Research and Research Marketing, both of Cardiff. The justification for this division was the desire to maintain links with both companies rather than be committed to one. The results of these polls are shown in table 18.2 on p. 207.

The first poll in this series was the survey of Ynys Mon, conducted by Research and Marketing. Given the furore over the previous Ynys Mon poll by Beaufort, Research and Marketing seemed to be the logical contractor for the job. Ynys Mon remained highly marginal with Nationalist ambitions given even greater credence following the resignation of the sitting Conservative member, Keith Best. Furthermore, the Labour candidate, Colin Parry, was Glenys Kinnock's brother and it was expected that the Labour leader would visit and take part in the local campaign. All these ingredients combined to make Ynys Mon an irresistible location for television election journalism. Given the previous problems on Anglesey, great care was taken in preparation of the survey. Also of note is that relations between the parties and the broadcasters are subtly transformed during the electoral period. The conventions regarding balance under which election coverage is broadcast give, *de facto*, great power to the parties and candidates in their dealings with television and radio. To ensure future participation and cooperation of the parties with other election programmes, HTV were, perhaps, overly solicitous of the parties in securing their endorsement of the Ynys Mon poll. Technical details of the sample were not discussed, but there was a dialogue concerning some questions, especially the need to use candidates' names and show cards in assessing voting intention rather than mere party labels.

The effective power of the parties and candidates during the campaign itself is too often overlooked. Neither need this potential power be linked solely to one broadcast or to an item on one constituency, as various appearances can be linked in such a way that a party retains an effective veto over a whole range of election journalism. Any programme that requires participation from party leaders, spokesmen or candidates is subject to such a veto. Of course, the party must weigh up the consequences of such action and calculate whether the loss of television exposure is acceptable. Even this calculation is made easier, however, for such action simultaneously denies media time to its opponents. In addition, the mainstream, national UK electoral coverage of the national, UK campaign will continue uninterrupted from London and be recieved in virtually every home in Wales. As Plaid Cymru already feels discriminated against in the media, especially in the London-based media, they would perhaps suffer disproportionate loss should threats to veto election coverage be carried through.

Although Plaid Cymru was the most vociferous protester about opinion polling, it should be noted that the only occasion in the campaign in Wales when a party forced a change in broadcasting policy was through the refusal of the sitting Conservative MP for Cardiff Central, Ian Grist, to participate in a programme, which would have included a poll, based upon his constituency. This programme was then redesigned to feature another Cardiff constituency, Cardiff South and Penarth, formerly the seat of James Callaghan which, whilst perhaps more 'telegenic' than Cardiff Central, was not as valid a political story. Of course, editorial freedom was not being absolutely curtailed in that a Cardiff Central poll could still have been commisssioned and broadcast – the parties could not prevent it. The parties can, however, affect how a poll, or any election story, is delivered through the broadcast media by refusing to cooperate. Self-interest will determine the party's, or candidate's decision and as such, pure news value is not always allowed to determine the broadcaster's policy.

Back in the field on Ynys Mon, however, the best laid plans 'go aft a-gley'. It came to light that Research and Marketing were employing some young, inexperienced and ineligible interviewers. This breach of the standard code of practice had become widely known amongst the parties on the island. Even before completion, the poll had been effectively discredited. HTV cancelled their contract immediately, before any results of the survey were known. The agency completed the job, analysed the results and even weighted to remove the data submitted by the suspect interviewers in an effort to redeem its position. HTV continued to refuse to receive, let alone publish, any data from Research and Marketing, and cut all links with the agency. The further polling contracts that Research and Marketing would have fulfilled for HTV were transferred to NOP, the well-known London agency.

Once again, in the small world of Welsh politics, the results of the poll quickly became known and were published by competing media, only too happy to embarrass a rival. The findings confirmed the close battle between the Conservatives and Plaid Cymru and so, once more, HTV was accused of suppressing a poll favourable to the Nationalists. Plaid Cymru went even further and used these findings to substantiate its rejection of the earlier BBC/Beaufort poll. All this helped to sustain Plaid Cymru's underdog, victimised, self-image. Even in the absence of a poll, the filmed profile of the election in Ynys Mon was broadcast, with a studio audience of local electors. The candidates could not be included because the programme was transmitted after the dissolution of parliament but before nominations for the election closed. This is a rarely noticed vacuum period during which little constituency material can effectively be broadcast.

The all-Wales polls, by comparison, were collected, analysed and broadcast without incident. Both indicated the prevailing trends in Wales but, in the context of political discussion, were invariably set against national polls

Table 18.2. *HTV campaign polls*

Constituency	Last fieldwork	Number polled	Conservative	Labour	PlC	Alliance
Welsh marginals	16 May	1,043	35 %	35 %	6 %	24 %
General election result			34.9%	39.6%	6.6%	18.9%
Cardiff South	29 May	1,008	34 %	51 %	2 %	13 %
General election result			36.5%	46.7%	1.3%	15.4%
All Wales	5 June	1,001	28 %	50 %	6 %	16 %
General election result			29.5%	45.1%	7.3%	17.9%
Ynys Mon	7 June	1,020	34 %	23 %	34 %	9 %
General election result			33.2%	16.9%	43.2%	6.7%
Carmarthen	7 June	1,017	26 %	43 %	16 %	14 %
General election result			27.4%	35.4%	23.0%	13.3%

indicating a Conservative victory. As such, all-Wales polls, at election times, have limited value as, when it suits them, politicians will defer to broader British trends or ignore such to emphasise the Welsh position. In the 1987 election both main parties could draw comfort from one or other source of data. All-Wales polls have an inherent interest for those whose universe is defined by Wales: the media, specialist academics and, of course, Plaid Cymru. For the rest, the result in Wales is of little real consequence, unless genuinely critical to the outcome at Westminster. The election is a British contest, No. 10 is the goal. Although there is a distinct Welsh politics, it remains, as yet, peripheral.

Further polls in Wales were commissioned from Marplan by the *South Wales Echo*, a Cardiff-based evening daily paper, for the constituencies of Newport West, Cardiff Central, Cardiff West, Cardiff South and Penarth, and for Bridgend. These seats were all marginal and the *Echo* commissioned two surveys in each, the first in the second week of the campaign, the second immediately before polling day. For those concerned about tactical voting, especially in Cardiff where the Alliance had a considerable local presence, the *Echo* policy was tailor-made. There was consequently some disquiet from the Alliance candidate in Cardiff Central, when shown to be running in third place in the first poll. Technical reservations and criticism were expressed concerning sample sizes and fieldwork procedures but, as usual, the politicans' main objections were to results that they did not find helpful. Successful tactical voting depends on knowledge of the standing of the parties, such as that offered by constituency polls, but far from being the automatic beneficiaries, the Alliance, in several of these constituencies, actually lost support between the two waves of the survey as the election polarised between the two main parties. When compared with the actual election results, the *Echo* series appears to have been quite successful (see table 18.3).

Granada Television, based in Manchester, has an extensive audience in

Table 18.3. *South Wales Echo* constituency polls (in percentages)

Constituency	1st wave	2nd wave	General election result
Cardiff Central			
Conservative	33	36	37.1
Labour	39	35	32.3
Alliance	26	26	29.4
Plaid Cymru	2	1	1.3
Other	2	2	
Cardiff West			
Labour	34	40	45.5
Conservative	35	39	36.5
Alliance	25	17	16.3
Plaid Cymru	3	4	1.6
Other	3	3	
Cardiff South and Penarth			
Labour	37	49	46.7
Conservative	37	37	36.5
Alliance	23	12	15.4
Plaid Cymru	2	2	1.3
Other	1	1	
Bridgend			
Labour	32	43	47.5
Conservative	41	40	38.0
Alliance	22	15	12.1
Plaid Cymru	3	1	2.3
Other	1	1	
Newport West			
Labour	44	44	46.1
Conservative	39	40	40.1
Alliance	16	14	13.0
Plaid Cymru	1	1	0.8
Other	1	1	

North-East Wales and selected Clwyd South West as one of their special constituency studies. A poll conducted by MORI confirmed the earlier Beaufort/BBC suggestion of a possible Labour gain, as indeed it proved to be on 11th June. Such survey information was vitally important to both the Labour Party and to potential tactical voters, because if Labour were to win Clwyd South West they would be doing so after coming third in 1983. To have any prospect of securing office, many such seats throughout Britain would have to be won from third place and evidence that this was possible became an important element in the battle between Labour and the Alliance. In the event, Labour achieved such a reversal only in Clwyd South West and again, constituency polling may have worked against the Alliance by more accurately quantifying the relative challenge to the sitting member.

In the last week of the campaign, HTV Wales published their remaining constituency polls, now commissioned from NOP. At last a rigorous, methodologically sound, study was produced of Ynys Mon, even if the results largely confirmed those of the abandoned Research and Marketing poll. For once, unsurprisingly, publication of the poll attracted no criticism from Plaid Cymru. The Alliance candidate, however, was moved to telephone NOP in London to remind them that two candidates shared the surname Evans, and to enquire whether they were sure they had not got them mixed up! This poll was now carried as a news item, rather than as a constituency special, on both HTV and S4C.

The more elaborate, outside-broadcast presentation, with the candidates and a local audience, was reserved for Carmarthen, with transmission on the Tuesday evening before polling day. Those involved were, perhaps, slightly apprehensive about this broadcast because of the special place of Carmarthen in recent Welsh political history, its symbolic importance for Plaid Cymru and its significance in polling mythology. Had not a poll in 1979 been responsible for the fall of Gwynfor Evans? Although Plaid Cymru consented to appear on the programmes, before the results were known, thus enabling the full panel of candidates to be interviewed, they had again tried throughout the fieldwork period to discredit the poll. They attempted to demonstrate that respondents had been interviewed outside the constituency boundary and they reputedly had sworn affidavits from respondents who claimed not to have been offered the required show cards. All this culminated in a solicitor's letter sent to NOP requesting that no evidence be destroyed pending forthcoming legal action of an unspecified nature. The NOP findings forecast a clear majority for Labour and showed Plaid Cymru to be running a poor third place. The Plaid Cymru candidate in Carmarthen, Hywel Teifi Edwards, gave a robust and lively performance during the programme. On polling day, however, he came in behind Labour and the Conservative, but with a higher share of the poll than forecast by NOP.

Although the main political parties complain and bicker about polls they find unhelpful, at the end of the day they accept the legitimate place of opinion surveys in electoral journalism. Most politicians are aware of the benefits, as well as the disadvantages, of polling, and besides, the serious business of politics must continue. From Plaid Cymru, however, no such detachment is assured and the battles of the election need not end on polling day.

Conclusion

Recriminations over the media's use of opinion polls continued in Wales for some weeks after the election. Although no formal legal action was ever initiated by Plaid Cymru against NOP, an extensive press and media campaign kept the issue alive and in the public eye. The specific targets were the commissioning agencies, especially BBC Wales and HTV Wales, and Beaufort Research Limited. Plaid Cymru was able to press its dissatisfaction with HTV even further by requesting a meeting to discuss future broadcast-ing policy regarding opinion polling. This request coincided with reports of a grass-roots mood vaguely threatening to make HTV transmissions from the 1987 National Eisteddfod from Portmadoc in August 'difficult'. Such a threat of direct action was not, of course, endorsed by the party officially. It does serve to illustrate, however, the peculiar interaction between the political and cultural spheres of life in contemporary Wales. For many, political activity is not restricted to participation in elections and a long tradition of unorthodox political behaviour runs through Welsh politics. Such pressure is, of course, resisted but it can rarely be ignored.

Plaid Cymru was granted its meeting with HTV where it advocated a ban on all opinion polling for the duration of an election campaign. This is a viewpoint also held by others, not least by the South Wales Labour MP, Ray Powell. HTV sought to convince Plaid Cymru of its impartial journalistic objectives, its commitment to employing the highest professional standards in polling, having learnt from their past experience. HTV remained adamant about its editorial freedom to cover the election as it saw fit. Polls remain one method available to electoral journalism. Thus no policy implications flowed from this meeting, other than Plaid Cymru again emphasising its ability to make trouble and, perhaps, increasing the pressure on any future programme maker wishing to commission a poll. From such a process of attrition little is gained, but for Plaid Cymru the post-electoral inquest on polling goes beyond the usual loser's sour grapes. Within Welsh politics, for over two decades, Plaid Cymru has been the prime mover, setting the political agenda and generally acting as the catalyst to reform. Such a presence is way in excess of its electoral support and the enjoyment of such stature is clearly undermined by the perennial reaffirmation of its numerical inferiority invariably given in opinion polls.

Thus far from being an unfair intrusion into the electoral process, polls remind us that elections themselves are but one aspect of political life. The substance of Welsh politics is not wholly determined by electoral outcomes, neither are electoral outcomes determined by the media's use, or abuse, of polls. The use of poll data may never become such a common element in Welsh politics as it is for Britain. But the media, the parties and the electorate all need to become more familiar with polling so that its advantages become more clearly apparent, whilst its occasional fallibilities are more easily understood.

Note

1. P.J. Madgwick *et al.*, *The Politics of Rural Wales* (London: Hutchinson, 1971), p. 228.

19 Local parties, local media and the constituency campaign

Little is known about how political communication is organised at the constituency level or how political parties try to present their policy alternatives through local media in the constituency campaign. Studies of local electioneering are few[1] and have tended to focus on the impact of expenditure on electoral outcomes;[2] case studies of particular campaigns by academics[3] or individual (usually successful) protagonists;[4] the local campaign in other democratic polities;[5] a particular party's approach to the constituency campaign;[6] or the analysis of issues promoted by candidates in their election addresses.[7] The overall conclusion of this handful of studies is that the constituency campaign is largely irrelevant to the outcome of a general election, since 'local electioneering has been overtaken by the nationalisation of the campaign and the growth of the mass media'.[8] What is missing here is any consideration of local parties' perceptions of the possibilities for exploiting local media for constituency electioneering purposes. This academic neglect is particularly curious when trends in electoral and local media systems suggest that local campaigning might be growing in importance. The emergence of a new political grouping, the absence of uniform national swings, partisan dealignment, the expansion of free newspapers and the development of local radio and regional television, in aggregate signal enhanced possibilities for the constituency campaigns; as Ivor Crewe suggested, locally there might simply be 'more up for grabs'.[9]

To explore local parties' contacts with local media during the general election, extensive post-election interviews were conducted with election agents for the three major political groupings in ten West Yorkshire constituencies: Batley and Spen, Bradford North, Bradford South, Colne Valley, Halifax, Leeds East, Leeds North, Leeds West, Pudsey, and Wakefield. The selection of constituencies was guided by the political criteria of marginality of the contest, incumbency status of candidates, party affiliation of incumbent candidates, and the seniority or 'celebrity' status of politicians; it was hypothesised that these factors might be influential in determining media interest in the constituency. Editors and journalists on local newspapers, as well as broadcasters with responsibility for election output at BBC Leeds and Yorkshire Television, were also interviewed.

West Yorkshire offers a particularly suitable site for such research. In media terms it boasts a diverse range of local newspapers, including almost 50 weekly and free papers, three alternative newspapers and five dailies, which express a variety of political commitments in their editorial stances. The region is also served by BBC and Yorkshire Television and three local radio stations. West Yorkshire politicians offer an equivalent diversity. There are 23 constituencies in the region and before the 1987 election Labour held ten seats, Conservative eleven and the Liberals two. The various MPs and prospective parliamentary candidates (PPCs), moreover, represented a wide range of background so far as incumbency and political seniority were concerned.

Four factors structured local parties' assessments of the utility of local media to the constituency campaign. First, the geographical 'fit' (or lack of it) of media circulation (broadcasting) areas with political constituency boundaries; second, party dissatisfaction with media reporting of political, especially electoral, affairs; third, the differential media coverage of candidates reflecting certain characteristics such as incumbency status; and finally, election agents' attitudes towards local media.

Geographical congruence of media and political boundaries

The number and range of media outlets within a constituency boundary, and the extent of competition between them were critical to parties' judgements of their campaign importance. This was particularly true for newspapers where any one of four possible circumstances of media/constituency fit might exist.

First, in constituencies where a single newspaper, especially a daily newspaper, enjoys a monopoly of distribution, parties believe that strategically the paper cannot be ignored. 'In Halifax', an election agent observed, 'the press is absolutely critical . . . the *Courier* circulates about 40,000 and 25,000 of those will be read in Halifax City itself . . . two to three people read each paper, so with an electorate of 70-odd thousand that's how important it is.'

Second, *The Yorkshire Post* and *The Yorkshire Evening Post* illustrate a different, almost completely opposite, circumstance where a single newspaper reports the campaign to a large number of constituencies, with the consequent competition for access by political parties. Even though *The Yorkshire Post* is

Leeds-centred in its reporting, election agents in these constituencies felt the possibilities for coverage would be very slight.

Third, in some constituencies there is simply no local daily newspaper for parties to target. Batley and Spen, for example, borders the Bradford *Telegraph and Argus* and the *Halifax Courier* circulation areas and only two weeklies, the *Batley News* and *Spenborough Guardian*, circulate within its constituency boundaries. This sets strict limits on local parties' press campaigns. Realistically, their best hope is for one story in each edition of these papers, which dictates a ceiling of five or six press releases throughout the entire campaign.

Fourth, where a newspaper reports more than one constituency, it may try to balance coverage of the parties across two or three constituencies. The Conservative candidate in constituency A may be reported with the Labour candidate in constituency B and the Alliance candidate in C. Consequently, Conservative candidates must compete for coverage not only with their rivals in other parties, but with Conservative colleagues in other constituencies in the newspaper's circulation area.

Parties perceive similar problems with local radio. Local stations broadcast over a large area embracing a number of constituencies, creating fierce competition for the limited air time. Some constituencies, moreover, are on the edge of a station's catchment area. In West Yorkshire, Radio Pennine tends to focus upon Bradford while Radio Aire and Radio Leeds concentrate upon Leeds. An agent in the Colne Valley complained 'nobody has a specific brief to deal with our area. They're all based somewhere else . . . I'm not convinced they care. We seem to be peripheral.'

Yorkshire Television and BBC Leeds are likewise regional and broadcast to over 70 constituencies. Consequently, few agents or candidates expected television coverage and they were rarely disappointed. So far as media personnel were concerned, they had to decide which constituencies or candidates to select for coverage from this very large pool. An interesting difference between BBC-TV and Yorkshire Television emerged. The former claimed that geographical spread round the region would be an important criterion guiding selection, while Yorkshire Television claimed marginality would be critical, 'the key', as one producer expressed it.

Party dissatisfaction with press reporting of the constituency campaign

Local parties were highly knowledgeable about the law regulating their access to television and conceded that generally television coverage had been fair. Most agents, moreover, alleged that local radio had largely ignored the campaign and, consequently, this section deals exclusively with the local press.

Parties expressed almost universal dissatisfaction with local press reporting of the local campaign; only one of the 30 agents did not complain. This was surprising because interviews with journalists and editors had revealed their commitment to equality of coverage, at least in quantitative terms, for each party. An editor affirmed:

> We have very strict rules about the coverage of local and general elections. We are in touch with the political agents before the start of the actual campaign and we outline to them what we propose to do by way of coverage. The three major parties will get the same coverage, and that means the same number of photographs of the same size, the same number of meeting reports, and exactly the same amount of press coverage, and we go to the point of measuring it literally in column inches.

Despite this resolution, serious complaints about local press coverage were repeatedly voiced. First, widespread dissatisfaction was prompted by simple omission in the reporting of candidates. Agents suggested that press coverage in the period six months to a year prior to the election was important to establish a candidate's identity in the constituency. One agent had issued weekly press releases over the three years since her candidate's selection but, 'nothing ever got published', despite visits to the newspaper to discuss the matter with the editor. Failure to report candidates in this pre-election period was regarded as a matter for complaint by many agents, even when coverage during the three weeks of the campaign itself had been scrupulously fair.

A second objection focussed upon newspapers' use of various layout and editing techniques. Agents complained that reports of their candidates were poorly positioned and always 'tucked away at the back', others objected to misrepresentative headlines, while others were aggrieved by the alleged manipulation of the letters page to partisan advantage.

Third, some agents were concerned by inaccuracies in the reporting of candidates. The wrong name, party, or constituency was attributed to candidates and on occasion, candidates' names were missed from the list of speakers at a meeting. There was a commonly-expressed suspicion that such mistakes were too frequent to be mere 'errors'.

Fourth, it was alleged that the press reported some candidates in an unfavourable way. In a Bradford constituency, for example, the agent complained that throughout the campaign his candidate had been described as a member of the 'hard left' or 'the loony left' and that such references were electorally disadvantageous.

Fifth, dissatisfaction was evident when agents judged that the local press was giving excessive, and more favourable, coverage to an opposition candidate or candidates. A Labour agent complained that 'on the final Thursday, on election day itself, when the local paper came out I don't think they had a picture of our candidate in . . . whereas the Conservative candidate had three or four photos . . . including one on the front page'.

Finally, agents occasionally denounced local papers for their out and out partisanship. One local weekly published a front page editorial urging readers 'to vote for the positive next move forward with . . . the Conservative Party' and dismissing the Alliance which, 'as far as this constituency is concerned can be written off'. Such partisan editorialising is, of course, accepted as legitimate and indeed lauded as a press tradition within the framework of a 'pluralist' theory of the press. But, it is important to note the absence of pro-Labour editorials.

There was, then, substantial local party dissatisfaction with local press reporting of the constituency campaign. Two important points, however, should be noted. First, concern with local newspaper coverage was not confined to a single party. This is illustrated by the case of a Leeds constituency, where all agents expressed suspicion of partisan reporting by the *Yorkshire Evening Post*; each agent, however, held a different view about the direction of that partisanship. The Liberal agent claimed the newspaper was pro-Labour and was, as he put it, 'in the pocket of the Labour Party'. The Conservative agent denounced the *Yorkshire Post* as a Liberal newspaper, alleging that the Liberal candidate had friends who worked there, 'which ensures his stuff gets in'. Finally, the Labour agent alleged that the *Yorkshire Post* is, by disposition, a Conservative newspaper, but because the constituency is unwinnable for the Conservatives the newspaper backed the Liberal candidate as its second choice, to exclude the Labour Party. This example illustrates neatly the cross-party character of local politicians' dissatisfaction with the local press.

Second, parties responded to these difficulties in quite contrary ways. Some parties quite simply gave up. 'We didn't send anything in any more', an agent confessed, 'it became a complete waste of time.' Other agents persisted and indeed worked harder since they had no other positive media strategy; 'We simply felt we had to plod on and see what happened.' An obvious strategy for parties was to complain to the editor, but a number of agents warned that complaints could make matters worse. 'How can I put it?,' an agent speculated, 'You're trying to limit damage. You know what to expect from the paper and you don't want to make it any worse. In the end our paper gave us as bad as we'd expected.' Five agents reported complaining to editors with little or no effect. The Conservative Party in Halifax, where the incumbent lost his seat, alleged unfair coverage and complained to the *Evening Courier*. The paper responded by inviting the ex-editor of the *Birmingham Post and Mail* to undertake a thorough investigation. Whatever the outcome of that investigation, however, it is clearly too late by the time the inquiry reports to undo any potentially harmful effects of the initial reporting.

Party perceptions of media interest in candidates

Parties considered that some of the difficulties inherent in constituency level political communication could be ameliorated if their candidates possessed certain characteristics such as incumbency or a national reputation. 'The press will undoubtedly take more notice', an agent confirmed, 'if you can stick the magic words MP after someone's name.'

BBC Leeds and Yorkshire Television both signalled a preference for incumbents above PPCs as participants in their electoral programmes. The reluctance to use a PPC was more than a concern not to offend electoral law by offering potential advantage to a candidate. At the BBC it reflected a concern to get an accomplished performer, 'people who are TV capable'. Yorkshire Television was unequivocal. It was a matter of 'basic programme philosophy. Without an MP the programme is out. A PPC is of no interest.'

The seniority of candidates within the party or their national 'celebrity' status, was also judged to generate a number of media advantages. Agents in all three parties reported that it was relatively easy to get coverage in both local and national media with a national celebrity. The agent for a well-known Labour politician in Leeds confessed, 'I've had too simple a task. He's so well known. There's this great thing about him, his eyebrows. If anyone just drew two eyebrows on a piece of white paper and asked anyone who it was they could tell you.'

Such celebrity candidates, of course, tend to appear in the media not as candidates for constituency X, Y or Z, but as spokespersons for their party. This can have disadvantageous effects on lesser known opponents in the constituency contest. In the West Yorkshire region, Denis Healey, Giles Shaw and Michael Meadowcroft were making statements in the media on issues about which their opponents undoubtedly held views, but editors seemed to prefer to balance a national spokesperson with a figure of equivalent status from an opposition party. In this battle of the giants, the lesser known PPCs tend to get squeezed out and suffer 'a relative media deprivation'.

Agents implied, however, that without regard to the merits of particular candidates, media displayed a preference for certain types of story. Serious or sustained discussions of policy matters generally came a poor second to more whimsical, 'quirky' stories. Accordingly a Liberal agent capitalised on the discovery of someone called Michael Meadowcroft who was invited to meet Michael Meadowcroft MP for a press photo opportunity. The Conservative agent in a Leeds constituency arranged for the *Yorkshire Post* to publish photographs of his candidate jogging in the local park. The agent confided that Sir Keith Joseph, the previous candidate, had never been successful in securing local coverage, although the national media maintained a considerable interest in him:

> One of Keith's pastimes is rowing so I said let's get you in a boat in the middle of Roundhay Lake and we'll get some photographers there, but he just wouldn't have it

. . . so whenever I called a press conference Keith would stand there and lecture the assembled journalists on the merits of the monetary system and of course they didn't give a twopenny damn and nothing ever got publicity.

This suggests that the amount of coverage candidates received is influenced as much by their willingness to comply with the demands of local media for certain sorts of stories as by their standing as a celebrity.

Election agents' orientations to local media

The factors outlined above establish the context within which local parties' media strategies are formulated, but agents' attitudes towards media proved especially important in structuring the constituency campaign. Two antithetical appraisals of the significance of local media emerged which, for convenience' sake, may be termed 'traditionalist' and 'modernist'.

Traditionalists considered local media were not important to the outcome of the campaign and knew little about the structure and organisation of local media, media audiences, or media effects. They judged local media to be largely beyond their control and preferred direct communication strategies such as leafleting and canvassing where they were able to determine the content. This attitude towards the media had clear implications for the structure of the campaign team and strategy. Where traditionalist attitudes prevailed, it was commonplace for no-one to be given a specific brief as press officer, the task usually being left to the candidate or worse, the election agent. No contact was made with media personnel prior to the campaign to discuss plans for coverage. In brief, 'traditionalist' agents gave media a low priority within the overall campaigning strategy.

Traditionalists were not confined to any political party or associated with any particular type of candidate, although they seemed to predominate among older agents. Quotations from two agents, both of whom had winning candidates in highly marginal seats, the first a Conservative incumbent, the second a Labour PPC, will help to illustrate traditionalist attitudes. A Conservative traditionalist said, 'I don't think local media helped our campaign at all . . . As far as I'm concerned if we'd had no newspaper coverage, no television coverage, we wouldn't have missed it.' A Labour traditionalist, in a different constituency drew similar conclusions:

> I must confess I'm sceptical, extremely sceptical, about how much influence media have. The *Yorkshire Evening Post* isn't that widely read and those people who read it read it often for sport, small ads. and to find out what's on television.

Modernists made a quite contrary assessment of local media. They considered media were extremely important to the outcome of the campaign, were usually very knowledgeable about media and often possessed experience of working as a journalist or in public relations. They believed that media content could be influenced by the local party, and tended to see newspaper reporting of politics as the consequence of negotiation between political and media personnel.

Not surprisingly, it was commonplace in campaigns where modernist attitudes prevailed for the campaign team to include a press officer who was often an ex-journalist or someone with public relations experience. A systematic media strategy was planned in advance of the election campaign which, in some constituencies, involved quite detailed market research to identify issues of key concern to voters for later use in election publicity. Regular contacts had been established with press, television and radio and prior consultation with media had been undertaken to discuss plans for coverage.

In between the two extremes were a range of other positions. A group which might be termed 'reluctant modernists' were not necessarily convinced of the effectiveness of media, but were compelled to try to exploit them because they lacked the human and financial resources to mount a more traditionally based campaign. 'Local media were very important', an agent confided, 'because we were so short of bodies. We made a decision early on to try and get as much information as possible out through the media.'

The reverse, of course, was also true. A group which could be called 'reluctant traditionalists' were keen about the possibilities of exploiting local media coverage to their electoral advantage, but lacked the necessary skills. This lack of media skill was often apparent when party members were generally inexperienced, where membership was low and in constituencies where parties enjoyed little chance of winning the seat. 'Media-wise we were inexperienced', an agent confessed. 'We asked during the campaign if someone would look after the area but no-one was forthcoming. It's a matter of regret to me and it showed up throughout the entire campaign.'

Conclusions

Local parties perceived local political communications to be an extremely difficult task in which a number of obstacles must be confronted. Their assessments of the potential effectiveness of local media in the constituency campaign depend upon a range of factors including the status of their candidate, their appraisal of the impartiality of the local press and their judgements concerning the opportunities to gain access to media. Party agents of a traditionalist disposition, however, may simply judge that the game is not worth the candle and ignore local media without regard to the possibilities or constraints of the party's media situation.

Local politicians' dissatisfaction with local media, moreover, are not party specific. This is not a Manichean battle between the Labour Party and the

Tory press, but a situation in which all political parties expressed dissatisfaction with the entire local press; on one occasion cited above, each party alleged partisanship against the same newspaper. In certain circumstances, the difficulties of local political communication may be partially ameliorated, perhaps by a candidate who enjoys a national reputation, but such circumstances are untypical. Where they prevail, moreover, candidates often make a greater contribution to the national rather than the local campaign.

Two interesting differences between national and local political communication systems are worth stressing. First, in the local context, a perception prevails that if a party receives bad coverage there is little to be done. Complaints, at best, have no effect, at worst they exacerbate poor coverage. Nationally, however, politicians complain persistently and forcefully when they consider reporting has been unfair. They expect national media to hear, and act upon, their grievances.

Second, the relationship between politicians and journalists which Blumler and Gurevitch characterise as 'mutual adaptation'[10] seems less well developed in the local context. Local politicians seem relatively unwilling to adapt their publicity messages to meet perceived media needs while for their part, local media appear less interested than their national counterparts in gaining access to local politicians for interviews, news and the inside information about the general election. The explanation of why mutual adaptation between political and media personnel is not so well developed must, in large part, derive from the presence of traditionalist attitudes at the local level.

The general feeling that emerged in interviews was that local media could be included in an overall campaigning strategy as a supplement to more traditional techniques. Judgements about campaigning at the local level suggest that, not withstanding the increase of new technology, computerised canvass returns, and local media, it remains an art and not a science. Consequently there is uncertainty about which campaigning techniques are most effective and the mood which prevails is that 'you need to do a little bit of everything'. Overwhelmingly there was a belief that locally a party's best or worst efforts affected the outcome of the election only marginally. 'It's how well the national party does on the box which counts', was a commonplace analysis. If the campaign does not take off nationally all the local party can do is 'hold back the flood tide'. Enlivened by a good national campaign, the local party, perhaps by using local media, can 'put 5 per cent on top.'

Notes

1 Dennis Kavanagh, *Constituency Electioneering in Britain* (London: Longman, 1970).
2 Ronald Johnston, *Money and Votes: Constituency Campaign Spending and Election Results* (London: Croom Helm, 1987), especially chapter 5.
3 Robert Holt and John Turner, *Political Parties in Action: The Battle of Barons Court* (London: Collier-Macmillan, 1968).

220   *Bob Franklin*

4 Austin Mitchell MP, 'The local campaign, 1977–9', in Robert Worcester and Martin Harrop (eds.), *Political Communication: The General Election Campaign of 1979* (London: George Allen and Unwin Ltd., 1982), pp. 36–43.
5 Edie Goldenberg and Michael Traugott, *Campaigning for Congress* (Washington DC: Congress Quarterly Press, 1984).
6 Edward Janosik, *Constituency Labour Parties in Britain* (London: Pall Mall Press, 1968), pp. 62–85.
7 David Butler and Dennis Kavanagh, *The British General Election of 1983* (London: Macmillan, 1984), pp. 255–64. And David Butler and Dennis Kavanagh, *The British General Election of 1979* (London: Macmillan, 1981), pp. 290–3.
8 Butler and Kavanagh, *The British General Election of 1979*, p. 292.
9 Ivor Crewe, 'The campaign confusion', *New Society*, 8 May 1987, p. 11.
10 Jay G. Blumler and Michael Gurevitch, 'Politicians and the Press: An Essay on Role Relationships', in Dan Nimmo and Keith Saunders (eds.), *Handbook of Political Communication* (London and Beverly Hills: Sage, 1981), pp. 467–97.

PART VII

Opinion polls in the 1987 campaign

PIPPA NORRIS

20 The emergence of polls of marginals in the 1987 election: their role and record

One striking development in the 1987 campaign was the increased focus on marginal polls. In the previous general election the only marginal polls were produced by Harris for *Weekend World*, attracting little attention in the media.[1] In contrast, in the months leading up to the 1987 campaign there were marginal polls by MORI for *The Times* and by Gallup for *Newsnight* which attracted considerable coverage in the press. During the 1987 campaign there were 20 marginal polls by the major companies, the equivalent of one published every other day of the campaign. The series included polls by NOP for *The Independent*, Marplan for *The Daily Express*, Gallup for *The Daily* and *Sunday Telegraph*, MORI for *The Times*, Harris for *Weekend World*, and BBC *Newsnight*. The results often proved controversial, generating headline news.

Given this expansion we need to examine the role and record of the marginal polls in the light of three central questions. What generated the interest in these polls? What distinctive problems were raised by their methods, especially in the selection of marginal seats? How accurately did they reflect the results? It will be suggested that the marginal polls were innovative attempts to cope with the complexities of voting behaviour but they faced serious problems of method. We need to compare the magnitude of the national polls' deviation from the actual national vote in Britain with that of the marginal polls' deviation from the actual vote in the marginal seats. Judged by this criterion the national polls out-performed all the marginal surveys in the 1987 election. There is therefore a case for the research community re-considering the methodological problems raised by these surveys.

Why the expansion in marginal polls?

From the start of the 1987 election, the outcome seemed in little doubt, if one assumed a uniform national swing. The national opinion polls consistently

Table 20.1. *National campaign polls, 1987 (in percentages)*

Week	No. of polls	Con.	Lab.	LSDP	Con. lead over Lab.
11–17 May	5	42	31	25	11
18–24 May	8	42	34	22	8
25–31 May	9	43	34	21	9
1–7 June	9	43	34	21.5	9
8–11 June	8	42	34	22	8
Result		43.3	31.5	23.1	11.8

showed a Conservative lead throughout the campaign, the only matter of controversy being the exact size of the estimated parliamentary majority. According to almost 40 national polls published during the campaign (counting only one in four of Harris' daily 'rolling-sample' polls for TV-AM) there was minimal net change in voting intentions (see table 20.1).[2] Some results from the major national polls were out of line with each other. In particular, the MORI panel for *The Sunday Times* gave a higher estimate of the Conservative lead than polls by Gallup and Harris with similar fieldwork dates. But a seven-day average of the polls suggests a remarkably steady pattern of party support.[3]

Given this consistency, a comfortable Conservative parliamentary majority seemed in no doubt but there were grounds to question whether in this election the national polls could provide accurate seat projections. Firstly, there was evidence of significant *regional* swings. In particular, the increased North–South divide was apparent in large-scale polls which allowed for the analysis of regional sub-samples, such as Marplan's poll for the Press Association conducted on 8–10 April among over 9,000 electors. In this widely publicised poll Marplan found that the Conservatives had improved on their 1983 performance in certain areas with a high number of key marginals, including Greater London, and the East and West Midlands. Marplan suggested that Labour had increased their support in certain heartland areas where there were fewer Conservative seats to be gained, such as the North-East, although Labour had also improved in the regions where they might expect to win seats including the North-West, Yorkshire, Humberside and Scotland. During the campaign there was evidence that these regional trends were continuing but the national polls could not provide a precise estimate of regional variations given the size of their samples. There were regional and constituency polls that pointed to the Scottish dimension although these were given minimal coverage in the British national press.[4] Regional swings added an edge of uncertainty to national seat projections.

Secondly, many believed that, given tactical voting, patterns of party support might differ in certain types of *marginal* seats. Throughout most of

1986, following the Westland affair and the American bombing of Libya, the government experienced a period of unpopularity during which Labour felt confident of achieving an overall majority in the next election. But in the autumn, following the Liberal defence debacle at the Eastbourne conference, the government started to recover support in the national polls and by early spring they had re-established their lead. Observing the omens, many on the Centre-Left felt that the only way to provide an effective electoral challenge to the government was to consider tactical voting, supporting whichever party provided the stronger opposition in Conservative seats. Tactical voting was not new: there is evidence from differential constituency results that it has been present in British elections since the late fifties. But developments in the run up to the campaign gave tactical voting new emphasis. Dramatic shifts during the Greenwich by-election in late February acted as the catalyst for an extensive debate about the impact of tactical voting. This led to the founding of Tactical Voting '87 (TV87) associated with Colin Crouch, Andy Shaw, Paul Eakins and Jeremy Seabrook. Support for the practice of tactical voting generated publications by Michael Young of the Institute of Community Studies, Eric Hobsbawm in *Marxism Today*, Stuart Weir in *New Socialist*, Hugo Young in *The Guardian* and Alan Watkins in *The Observer*. Tactical voting in key marginal seats, if it materialised, might also undermine conventional seat projections.[5]

Speculation increased during the run-up to the general election, when a series of polls suggested that voters in marginal seats might vote differently from the rest of the country. In December 1986 the Gallup 9,000 poll broadcast on *Newsnight* suggested that the Conservatives were doing better in their marginals than nationally. In February, polls by Harris for *Weekend World*, Gallup for *Newsnight* and MORI for *The Times* found that Conservative support was stronger in the marginals than across all seats.[6] The implications were dramatic. For example, the MORI poll in February suggested that the Conservatives might be returned with a comfortable 94-seat majority based on their performance in the marginals, while at the time the national polls estimated that the Conservatives might not achieve an overall majority. Yet not all the evidence pointed in the same direction; for example, in April MORI found that trends in the marginals were in line with national polls, although by the start of the campaign MORI again suggested the Conservatives were performing more strongly in their target seats.

The increased interest by journalists in target seats generated a series of marginal polls by all the major companies (see Table 20.2). It seemed to make sense to take polls in the election battleground where seats were most likely to change hands and decide the result. The polls were widely publicised as they added an element of uncertainty to the campaign, allowing commentators to speculate that the results might not be wholly predictable, despite the consistent picture presented by the national polls. Tactical voting in key seats

Table 20.2. *Marginal polls in the 1987 campaign*

Company	Date of publication	Published in	Date of field work	Seat sampling points	Total sample size	Type of sample
WEEK 1:						
MORI	15/5	*Times*	11–13 May	73	1,424	Quota
Harris	17/5	*Wkend Wld*	13–15 May	100	3,164	Panel
Newsnight	18/5	BBC	14–17 May	60	2,410	Panel
NOP	21/5	*Independent*	19 May	52	1,976	Quota
Gallup	21/5	*D.Telegraph*	19–20 May	72	1,397	Quota
WEEK 2:						
Harris	24/5	*Wkend Wld*	20–22 May	68	1,386	Panel
Gallup	28/5	*D.Telegraph*	26–27 May	72	1,329	Quota
NOP	28/5	*Independent*	26 May	52	1,978	Quota
WEEK 3:						
Harris	31/5	*Wkend Wld*	27–28 May	67	1,168	Panel
Marplan	31/5	*S.Express*	29 May	50	1,302	Quota
MORI	1/6	*Times*	29–30 May	73	1,420	Quota
Newsnight	2/6	BBC	29 May–1 June	60	2,116	Panel
NOP	4/6	*Independent*	2 June	52	1,989	Quota
Gallup	4/6	*D.Telegraph*	2–3 June	72	1,328	Quota
WEEK 4:						
Harris	7/6	*Wkend Wld*	3–5 June	66	1,169	Panel
Marplan	7/6	*S.Express*	5 June	50	1,300	Quota
MORI	8/6	*Times*	5–6 June	73	1,443	Quota
Newsnight	9/6	BBC	7–8 June	60	2,023	Panel
Gallup	10/6	*D.Telegraph*	8–9 June	72		Quota
NOP	11/6	*Independent*	10 June	52	1,668	Panel
Mean				66	1,596	

was seen as the dark horse which just might upset the best-laid plans of party strategists and campaign managers. But in developing specialist surveys to meet this demand – polls of marginals, local areas and individual constituencies – the research community faced a range of problems.

Problems of method

In theory, polls which focus on a sample of marginal constituencies should provide a more accurate indication of which seats will change hands than polls which sample the whole country, *ceteris paribus*. It is the 'weather-vane' seats which determine the outcome in a close race, the Halifaxs, Darlingtons and Baths, not the Solihulls and Rhonddas. But in practice the marginal polls faced distinctive methodological problems. Firstly, there are no agreed definitions of a 'marginal' seat. There are no established criteria for selection.

Each polling company was therefore drawing its sample from a different universe which led to confusion in the comparison of the results. Secondly, within any definition of marginality there were difficulties with categorising types of seat. Thirdly, in moving away from a nationally-based sample there are problems in obtaining accurate information to establish representative quotas. Lastly, there are fundamental problems in translating polls which only include certain types of marginal constituencies into national seat projections.

For national polls there is a clearly defined universe (i.e. all British constituencies) with established procedures for selecting a sample of seats. Constituencies are commonly stratified by region, urbanisation and percentage (Labour/Conservative) vote, then selected at a standard interval from a random starting point. Companies employ slightly different survey techniques, for example in the phrasing and ordering of the voting intention question, the design of quota controls and fieldwork procedures. Nevertheless, we can compare the results of one national poll with another because there is a common universe. This is not the case with marginal polls. 'Marginal seats' are conventionally understood as those which might change from one party to another during an election. The criteria used to define the universe of marginal seats necessarily include questions of judgement. The most straightforward operational measure is the seat's majority (i.e. the difference in the percentage share of the vote held by the first and second parties in the previous general election). But is a marginal seat one with a majority of 5 per cent, 10 per cent or 20 per cent? Do we take into account the share of the vote held by third and fourth parties? Do we restrict the analysis to Conservative seats, or do we include seats held by Labour and the Alliance which they might lose? Should the analysis include the existing tactical vote in 1983? Do we exclude seats with 'special circumstances'? Do we take into account region, incumbency, intervening by-elections or candidates? Do we include only seats which are listed as official party targets? What is the rationale for selecting one universe rather than another?

The criteria used for defining marginal seats are clearly a matter for continuing debate. The most straightforward procedure is a random selection of seats stratified by *majority*, below a specified level. But the appropriate level is not self-evident; it is a matter of judgement. In the last election Marplan included in their poll 50 Conservative and Labour seats with the lowest majority (less than 4 per cent) in the previous general election (see table 20.3). Although straightforward, this criterion tells us little. The opposition could have won all 23 Conservative marginals without changing the balance of power in parliament. The results of the poll could say nothing about Conservative seats with higher majorities which Labour eventually gained, such as Newcastle Central and Halifax.

In their marginal surveys Gallup included the 72 Conservative seats with the lowest majority, since the loss of this number of seats would deprive the government of their parliamentary majority. All the Gallup seats had majorities of less than 10 per cent. Other companies selected constituencies with a higher level of majority, up to 16 per cent (NOP) 20 per cent (Harris, MORI) and 24 per cent (*Newsnight*), as Labour needed to win such seats if it was to hope to form a government. We can dispute which criterion is preferable. The important point is that as a consequence the results of the marginal polls were not strictly comparable. It is misleading to contrast the direct share of the vote in polls by NOP, MORI or Harris as each company uses different seats based on its own criteria of marginality.

Marginal polls differed in other important respects. Most polling organisations confined their fieldwork to pre-selected marginal constituencies. In contrast Gallup carried out a normal national survey of over 2,500 voters with respondents subsequently subdivided according to whether they lived in Conservative marginals or other seats. This process may increase sampling error. In addition it should be stressed that MORI, NOP and Marplan used conventional cross-sectional samples while the Harris and *Newsnight* surveys involved panels of voters who were repeatedly interviewed. Panel surveys have many advantages in measuring individual change within the period of the campaign, including the flux as well as the flow of the vote.[7] In theory, given a high response rate, successive waves of panel surveys should provide a more accurate estimate of changes over time than separate cross-sectional samples. Nevertheless, in practice panel designs suffer from well-known difficulties. If the original sample is biassed in ways which are not apparent, for example if the first wave of the *Newsnight* panel appeared demographically accurate yet included slightly too many Labour voters, this bias could be repeated in subsequent waves without opportunity for correction. The *Newsnight* and Harris polls each depended on one sample for their series of polls. In addition, panel surveys become 'corrupted' over time. The process of repeated interviews may make respondents atypical, as they become more aware of the campaign than the general electorate. After repeated interviews panel respondents may be reluctant to admit to change in their voting intentions. Despite their theoretical advantage panel surveys may therefore prove problematic, although there is no evidence that the method introduces any inherent, systematic, partisan bias.

Polls also differed in how far the majority in a seat was taken as the defining characteristic of a marginal, to the exclusion of other factors. An analysis of the 1979 and 1983 election results suggests that region and urbanisation were independently correlated with two-party swing and therefore needed to be included in selecting constituencies. The significance of regional balance, particulatly for the Labour vote, was recognised by NOP, Harris and *Newsnight* in their selection. Other factors which may affect marginality were more controversial, especially the influence of incumbency, the 'squeeza-

Table 20.3. *The selection of marginal constituencies*

Company	Type of seat	Highest majority (%)	Number of seats in universe	Number of seats in sample	Total selected
NOP	Con.–Lab.	15	80	20 ⎫	
	Lab.–Con.	5	30	10 ⎬	52
	Con.–LSDP	16	38	22 ⎭	
Harris	Con.–Lab.	20	93	60 ⎫	
	Con.–LSDP	20	60	40 ⎭	100
MORI	Con.–Lab.	20	100	50 ⎫	
	Con.–LSDP	10	44	22 ⎭	72
Newsnight	Con.–Lab.	22	82	27 ⎫	
	Con.–LSDP	22	94	20 ⎬	60
	3-Way	24	54	13 ⎭	
Gallup	Con.–Lab.	9	51	51 ⎫	
	Con.–LSDP	10	44	17 ⎬	72
	Con.–Nat.	8	4	4 ⎭	
Marplan	Con.–Lab.	4	16	16 ⎫	
	Con.–LSDP	3	6	6	
	Con.Nat.	2	1	1 ⎬	50
	Lab.–Con.	3	17	17	
	Lab.–LSDP	3	2	2 ⎭	

bility' of the third party vote or the presence of tactical voting in 1983. Curtice and Steed estimate that in the average marginal constituency in 1987 the MP's personal support may have been worth 1 per cent of the vote. They suggest that there were at least six marginals where the Conservative incumbent might have lost in 1987 without the effect of the personal vote, including Hyndburn, Bury North and Batley and Spen.[8] The personal vote which an incumbent MP can build up through local constituency work is particularly important for Alliance MPs. There are also 'special cases' in which the 1983 result may be unrepresentative for reasons such as an incumbent Labour MP who defected to the SDP (Hayes and Harlington), an intervening by-election (Brecon and Radnor, Ryedale) or seats where the sitting MP had local problems (Billericay, Ynys Mon). Selecting marginals solely on the basis of majority assumes that the 1983 election represents the 'normal' vote for a constituency, without questioning whether this is the case.

There were also problems associated with categorising sub-samples of marginals. Most companies classified their selected seats into two basic types: the Conservative–Labour (Con.-Lab.) and the Conservative–Alliance (Con.–LSDP) marginals. There were some variations to this; for example, NOP presented results for the 'Labour battleground', which included ten

Labour–Conservative marginals as well as twenty Conservative–Labour seats. There was also confusion about the classification of some individual seats, with Croydon North West and Bradford North identified as Labour or Alliance targets by different companies. Some Conservative–Nationalist constituencies were included in the samples selected by Gallup and Marplan.

BBC *Newsnight's* selection was distinctive in adopting a category of 'three-way' marginals, which others defined as Conservative marginals – Renfrew West, for example, which was split three ways between the Conservatives (32.7 per cent), Liberal/SDP Alliance (29.5 per cent and Labour (29 per cent), with the SNP vote (8.7 per cent) adding a further element of uncertainty. In other seats such as Strathkelvin and Bearsden, Conservatives (36.5 per cent) had a stronger lead over the Alliance (28.7 per cent) and Labour (25.6 per cent). Yet the difference between the parties in second and third place is so small that it is unclear whether this should be identified as an Alliance or Labour target. In the *Newsnight* classification this was placed in the 'three-way' category (defined as those with a Conservative majority of less than 24 per cent where the difference between the second and third party was less than 5 per cent in 1983). Polling companies have tended to include some of the three-way seats in their list of Alliance targets because of the second place showing last time. But it can be argued that most are Conservative–Labour marginals in which, for various reasons, the Alliance did well in 1983. In some cases this was because there was a sitting MP who defected (Hayes and Harlington, Mitcham and Morden, Renfrew West).

Given the majority in these seats (less than 24 per cent) they might not always be considered marginals. But it was expected that if tactical voting were to develop on any scale it was in this sort of constituency that the most surprising results might occur; there was considerable potential for Labour to squeeze the Alliance, or vice versa. The distinctive pattern of the 'three-way' marginals was confirmed by the eventual results. Both Renfrew West and Strathkelvin and Bearsden were eventually gained by Labour from a third place position in 1983. Labour improved its share of the vote by 6.3 per cent in the 'three-way' seats analysed by *Newsnight*, compared with 3.2 per cent nationally, although regional variations also contributed to this difference. Companies which included 'three-way' seats in their list of Con–LSDP targets may have under-estimated Alliance strength.

Within a given selection of seats there are problems in obtaining accurate demographic information necessary for quota controls. By the 1987 census, material available at the constituency level was six years old. Central government departments provide information on national and regional demographic trends since 1981, for example on housing tenure, employment status and migration patterns, but often not at the constituency level. Demographic data are provided by local authorities but the information is not standardised, it takes time to be collected and access depends largely on the efficiency and goodwill of local departments. While invaluable for constituency and by-election surveys, it would be impractical to use local sources for marginal polls.

Lastly, serious reservations have to be expressed about presenting the results in terms of national seat projections. The point of the marginal polls was to focus on particular types of seat which might behave differently from the national pattern. The NOP and Marplan polls, which included Labour and Conservative-held marginals, provided the best basis for a national seat projection although the number of seats in each sub-sample was relatively small. The other polls were restricted to Conservative marginals. An accurate national projection of seats requires a sample of marginal constituencies held by all parties, including those which the opposition parties might lose (such as Walthamstow, Battersea and Stockton South), or others which might switch hands (such as Labour's gain of Glasgow Hillhead from the Alliance and Dundee East from the SNP). To state a point which was often overlooked in the newspaper presentation, marginal polls of Conservative seats tell us about Conservative marginal seats. National polls tell us about national trends.

Accuracy of the results

The essential point of marginal polls was to identify any significant variations from the national trends. The polls could be justified if they could analyse whether the parties were doing significantly better, or worse, in the marginals than across the whole country. Did they prove accurate in this respect? Given the different universe of seats selected by companies we need considerable care to compare like with like. The results of the polls should be judged on the basis of the difference between the actual and the estimated share of the vote in each company's list of selected seats.

In judging the accuracy of the polls we can use three alternative measures. The first is the criterion common to journalists, politicians and members of the public: did they 'get the story right'? Did the polls correctly identify the *direction* of any variation between the marginals and national trends? Did they accurately estimate whether the Conservatives were doing better or worse (by whatever margin) in these seats than in the country as a whole? This provides only a rough and ready guideline because a poll might be accurate within the accepted standards of error and yet still estimate the wrong direction of change. This therefore needs to be supplemented by a second measure: the average error per party, i.e. the mean of the difference between the predicted percentage and the actual vote percentage, ignoring the sign. This gives the size of the error but conceals any direction of bias. The 'average error' is the standard measure which is most often used to assess the accuracy of polls.[9] Thirdly, we need also to measure *systematic error*, which takes account of biases by comparing the mean error of the predicted versus actual vote, taking account of the sign. There are two main sources of error. The first arises from the selection of particular constituency sampling points, as these may prove unrepresentative of all marginal seats within the defined universe. For example, too many Con.–Lab. marginals in Scotland could provide a misleading picture for Con.–Lab. marginals across the country. The second source of error arises from the actual poll, as the estimated voting intentions may prove unrepresentative of the actual 1987 result in the selected seats.

The record of the marginal polls needs to be set in the context of the results of the national polls. In the last election the final national polls by the major companies proved to be accurate to within the accepted standards of sampling error, with an average error ranging from 0.5 to 1.5 percentage points. But there was evidence of systematic error: five of the seven final polls (Harris/ TVAM, Marplan/*Guardian*, ASL/*Sun*, Gallup/*Telegraph* and Gallup/BBC) over-estimated the Labour vote by 2 per cent to 3 per cent.

It has not been clearly established whether this was due to a last-minute shift in support or to differential turnout at the ballot box.[10] For a number of reasons we would expect the marginal polls to have a higher average error. Strictly speaking, four of the six final marginal polls were not predictive, as only Gallup and NOP carried out fieldwork in the last two days. The size of the sub-samples in Conservative–Labour and Conservative–Alliance marginals was considerably lower than those used in the final national polls. Due to sampling error we could at best expect surveys to be accurate to within + or − 4 per cent or 5 per cent on an average random sample of about 600–900 at the accepted 95 per cent confidence level. Clustering could be expected to increase sampling error even further. Given these qualifications, what was the record of the marginal polls?

Results in Conservative–Labour marginals

What the marginal polls should have identified in the Conservative–Labour seats was that compared with 1983 the percentage point change in both the Labour and Conservative shares of the vote was more favourable in marginal seats than in the country as a whole (see table 20.4). Nationally, the Conservative share of the vote declined by 0.2 per cent but in the selected marginals its vote improved (from + 0.4 per cent to + 2.4 per cent). Across Britain, Labour increased its support by 3.2 per cent but in the marginals (up by + 3.4 per cent to + 5 per cent) it performed even more strongly. In the Conservative–Labour marginals, the polls should have detected that the third-place Alliance would be squeezed.[11] This suggests that there was some tactical voting, but the impact on seats was limited because Alliance deserters did not switch in a uniform anti-government direction. Examination of the polls in the Conservative–Labour marginals suggests that they got the story

Table 20.4. *Results of Conservative–Labour marginal polls, 1987*

Company	Published in	Start of fieldwork	Sample size	Con. %	83–87	Lab. %	83–87	LSDP %	83–87
Actual 1983 vote in selected seats									
Harris				43		33		22	
MORI				42		33		23	
Newsnight				43		35		21	
Gallup				41		37		21	
NOP				40		36		21	
Mean				42		34		22	
Week 1									
MORI	*Times*	11 May	1,094	41	(−1)	33	(0)	24	(+1)
Harris	*Wk.Wld*	13 May	1,674	40	(−3)	38	(+5)	21	(−1)
Newsnight	BBC	14 May	871	39	(−4)	41	(+6)	18	(−2)
NOP	*Independent*	19 May	1,276	39	(−1)	38	(+2)	20	(−1)
Gallup	*D.Telegraph*	19 May		44	(+3)	35	(−1)	20	(−1)
Week 2									
Harris	*Wk.Wld*	20 May	714	39	(−4)	41	(+8)	19	(−4)
NOP	*Independent*	26 May		40	(0)	40	(+4)	19	(−2)
Gallup	*D.Telegraph*	26 May		42	(+1)	39	(+2)	19	(−2)
Week 3									
Harris	*Wk.Wld*	27 May	674	40	(−3)	41	(+8)	19	(−4)
MORI	*Times*	29 May		42	(0)	34	(+1)	23	(0)
Newsnight	BBC	30 May	896	40	(−3)	43	(+8)	16	(−5)
NOP	*Independent*	2 June	1,289	41	(+1)	40	(+4)	17	(−2)
Gallup	*D.Telegraph*	2 June		42	(+1)	40	(+4)	17	(−4)
Week 4									
Harris	*Wk.Wld*	3 June	626	39	(−4)	39	(+6)	22	(−1)
MORI	*Times*	5 June	1,109	40	(−2)	39	(+6)	18	(−5)
Newsnight	BBC	7 June	871	40	(−4)	45	(+10)	15	(−6)
Gallup	*D.Telegraph*	8 June	938	41	(0)	39	(+3)	18	(−3)
NOP	*Independent*	10 June		40	(−1)	42	(+6)	17	(−5)
Mean Con.–Lab.				40	(−2)	41	(+7)	18	(−4)
Actual 1987 vote in selected seats									
Harris		11 June		44	(+1)	38	(+5)	16	(−6)
MORI		11 June		43	(+1)	38	(+5)	17	(−6)
Newsnight		11 June		44	(+1)	39	(+4)	16	(−5)
Gallup		11 June		43	(+2)	40	(+4)	16	(−5)
NOP		11 June		40	(0)	41	(+5)	18	(−4)
Mean Con.–Lab.		11 June		43	(+1)	39	(+4)	17	(−5)
Mean Great Britain				43.3	(−0.2)	31.5	(+3.2)	23.1	(−2.9)

Note: Figures in parenthesis represent change in the share of the vote in the selected marginal seats since the 1983 general election. The Marplan poll is excluded because their results were not disaggregated for the Con.–Lab., Con.–Alliance and the Con.–Nat. marginal seats. Total percentages may not sum to 100 per cent due to rounding error. For some polls the number of respondents in each sub-sample of Con.–Lab. and Con.–Alliance seats was not published.

Table 20.5. *Error of final Conservative–Labour marginal polls*

Poll	Publication	Fieldwork date	Con.	Lab.	LSDP	Average error
Harris	*Wkend Wld*	3 June	−4.9	+1.2	+4.7	3.6
MORI	*Times*	5 June	−3.6	+1.6	−0.1	1.8
Newsnight	BBC	7 June	−4.7	+5.6	−0.9	3.7
Gallup	*D.Telegraph*	8 June	−2.1	−0.6	+2.0	1.6
NOP	*Independent*	10 June	−0.7	+2.6	+1.7	1.7
Systematic error			−3.2	+2.1	+1.5	2.5

Note: Error is measured as the difference between the actual change in the vote and the predicted change in the vote for the major parties in the seats selected by each company.

wrong. They failed to identify the rise in support for *both* major parties and under-estimated the squeeze on the Alliance.

The polls published in the final week correctly identified that in these seats Labour support had increased since 1983 although estimates varied about the extent of the change. On election day Labour performed more strongly in the seats selected by Harris, MORI, *Newsnight* and NOP, which the polls detected, than in the marginal seats selected by Gallup and Marplan. In terms of systematic error all of the final polls except Gallup tended to underestimate Conservative support by between 1 and 5 per cent. In addition, the Harris, MORI, *Newsnight* and NOP polls failed to identify the direction of change in Conservative support, suggesting a slight decline in the Conservative vote while on the day their vote slightly increased. The consistency with which most of the final marginal and national polls tended slightly to over-estimate the Labour vote lends additional support to the idea of a last-minute swing or differential turnout.

Given the smaller size of the sample and the earlier date of the fieldwork it was only to be expected that the marginal polls would prove less accurate than the national polls, and indeed this proved to be the case. As shown by table 20.5 the average error of the final marginal polls in the Conservative–Labour seats ranged from 1.6 to 3.7 percentage points. It should be stressed that the difference between each company's estimate of party support was not large, given standard sampling error for this size of sample, but it was sufficient to produce substantially different seat projections.

Results in Conservative–Alliance marginals

In the Conservative–Alliance marginals there were two different stories for the polls to get right. In the final result in the seats selected by Harris and *Newsnight* there was evidence of limited tactical voting towards the Alliance (see table 20.6). In these marginals the Conservatives and Labour performed

Table 20.6. *Results of Conservative–Alliance marginal polls, 1987*

Company	Published in	Start of fieldwork		Con. %	83–87	Lab. %	83–87	LSDP %	83–87
Actual 1983 vote in selected seats									
Harris				48		14		36	
MORI				43		18		37	
Newsnight				48		16		35	
Gallup				54		15		30	
NOP				45		18		35	
Mean				48		16		35	
Week 1									
MORI	*Times*	11 May	659	42	(0)	25	(+7)	30	(−7)
Harris	*Wk.Wld*	13 May	1,490	44	(−4)	21	(+7)	33	(−3)
Newsnight	BBC	14 May	620	44	(−4)	19	(+3)	35	(+1)
NOP	*Independent*	19 May	997	44	(−1)	25	(+7)	30	(−5)
Gallup	*D.Telegraph*	19 May		51	(−3)	21	(+6)	27	(−3)
Week 2									
Harris	*Wk.Wld*	20 May	672	45	(−3)	22	(+8)	32	(−4)
NOP	*Independent*	26 May	997	43	(−2)	28	(+10)	27	(−8)
Gallup	*D.Telegraph*	26 May		54	(0)	25	(+10)	21	(−9)
Week 3									
Harris	*Wk.Wld*	27 May	594	45	(−3)	23	(+9)	32	(−4)
MORI	*Times*	29 May		43	(−1)	25	(+7)	29	(−8)
Newsnight	BBC	30 May	634	42	(−5)	20	(+4)	36	(+1)
NOP	*Independent*	2 June	1,017	45	(0)	26	(+8)	27	(−8)
Gallup	*D.Telegraph*	2 June		50	(−4)	24	(+9)	25	(−5)
Week 4									
Harris	*Wk.Wld*	3 June	629	45	(−3)	22	(+8)	32	(−4)
MORI	*Times*	5 June	664	40	(−2)	27	(+9)	30	(−7)
Newsnight	BBC	7 June	620	42	(−6)	19	(+3)	37	(+3)
Gallup	*D.Telegraph*	8 June	311	47	(−7)	21	(+6)	31	(+1)
NOP	*Independent*	10 June		45	(−2)	18	(+7)	33	(−5)
Mean Con.–LSDP				44	(−4)	21	(+5)	33	(−2)
Actual 1987 vote in selected seats									
Harris				47	(−1)	15	(+1)	35	(−1)
MORI				43	(0)	22	(+4)	34	(−3)
Newsnight				47	(−1)	18	(+2)	34	(−1)
Gallup				54	(0)	19	(+4)	27	(−3)
NOP		1		45	(0)	21	(+3)	32	(−3)
Mean Con.–LSDP				47	(0)	19	(+3)	32	(−2)
Mean Great Britain				43.3	(−0.3)	31.5	(+3.2)	23.1	(−2.9)

Note: See note to table 20.4.

Table 20.7. *Error of final Conservative–Alliance marginal polls*

Poll	Publication	Fieldwork date	Con.	Lab.	LSDP	Average error
Harris	*Wkend Wld*	3 June	−2.2	+6.7	−3.5	4.1
MORI	*Times*	5 June	−2.9	+4.9	−3.6	3.8
Newsnight	BBC	7 June	−5.5	+1.6	+3.5	3.5
Gallup	*D.Telegraph*	8 June	−2.6	+5.1	−2.5	3.4
NOP	*Independent*	10 June	−2.2	+3.9	−2.1	2.7
Systematic error			−3.1	+4.4	−1.6	3.5

slightly worse than across the country as a whole. By contrast, in the Conservative–LSDP seats selected by MORI and Gallup, Labour but not the Alliance performed slightly better than average. Therefore, in identifying significant variations from the national trends the polls in Conservative-marginals could accurately point in alternative directions.

The contrast in the actual results can be explained by the different selection of seats by companies, especially the classification of 'three-way' constituencies as Alliance targets. The *Newsnight* and Harris polls selected Alliance targets where the Alliance performed better than average because they took into account a variety of local factors as well as the 1983 majority in the seat. Alliance targets are difficult to identify because their support depends in large part on political factors specific to particular constituencies, such as individual candidates, strength in local government, party organisation, by-election successes and the position of third and fourth parties. Excluding these factors from the selection process may lead to an underestimate of Alliance strength.

If we compare the predicted with the actual share of the vote, all the marginal polls proved to be less accurate in the Conservative–Alliance targets, with an average error of 3.5 per cent (see table 20.7). In particular, Harris, NOP and MORI seriously over-estimated Labour strength in these constituencies, while Gallup and *Newsnight* under-estimated the Conservative vote. The most successful poll was by NOP, with the latest fieldwork, which lends further support to the idea of a limited last-minute shift from Labour to the Alliance in these seats.

Conclusion

The marginal polls were developed to deal with the complexities of voting behaviour. If the polls could accurately identify variations from the national trends, they could provide a useful supplement to national polls. If tactical voting had developed on a significant scale, undermining the concept of a uniform national swing, the polls could well have proved invaluable. But in the end the marginal polls failed to tell us much that was not already available in the national polls. A straightforward seat projection based on the conventional assumption of a uniform mean national swing could predict the number of Conservatives returned to parliament to within five seats. There was evidence of limited tactical voting in the marginals, but the shift was not in a consistent anti-government direction, so few seats changed hands as a result. The polls in the Conservative–Labour seats failed to identify the main story which was the slight rise in support for *both* major parties at the expense of the Alliance.

The results from the marginal polls needed to be treated with care and the way they were presented in many newspapers may have generated more confusion than enlightenment. The size of the Conservative–Labour and Conservative–Alliance sub-samples needed to be larger to minimise sampling error. There are serious conceptual and methodological problems which need to be resolved by the research community to establish standard procedures in the area. Lastly, judged by the acid test, all the final national polls proved to be more accurate than all the final marginal polls. There will probably continue to be a media demand for the occasional marginal poll. They should not necessarily be abandoned, but there is a strong case for reconsidering the value of such polls.

Notes

The author would like to acknowledge the invaluable contributions of John Curtice, Michael Steed and Vincent Hanna to the ideas presented in this paper. The author would also like to thank Ivor Crewe, Robert Wybrow and Robert Waller for commenting on an earlier version of this paper, Nick Moon (NOP) and Peter Hutton (MORI) for providing information about their marginal polls and all colleagues who collaborated on the BBC *Newsnight* marginal surveys.

1 In the 1983 election there were polls of 44 marginal seats by Harris published by *Weekend World* on 15 May, 22 May, and 29 May 1983. These were widely misreported in the press as though they were national samples. See David Butler and Dennis Kavanagh *The British General Election of 1983* (London: Macmillan, 1985), p. 129. The idea of polling marginal seats was not new in itself: Gallup sampled a group of marginals in the 1959 general election.

2 This includes polls with national samples published during the campaign by the major companies, excluding surveys of individual constituencies, marginal seats and telephone polls. The analysis includes the mean share of the vote for each party in polls with fieldwork carried out during each week of the campaign. The analysis takes Monday, 11 May as the starting date for the 1987 campaign.

3 According to the national polls from early May to June Conservative support stayed steady at about 42 per cent to 43 per cent of the electorate. In the first week of the campaign Labour made slight gains at the expense of the Alliance, moving from 31 per cent to 34 per cent. Other than a short-term blip in Labour support after the Hudson/Kinnock party political broadcast, the national polls suggest that there was little subsequent movement in party support until the final days. On 11 June there may have been a last-minute shift in support as five out of the final seven polls over-estimated the Labour vote by 2 or 3 per cent, although this may have been due to differential turnout.

4 See Alastair Hetherington, chapter 17 of this volume.

5 See Andrew Shaw and Nina Fishman, chapter 24 of this volume.

6 See David Butler, 'Complex message from voters as poll confirms Conservatives' lead', *The Times*, 7 April 1987.

7 See Pippa Norris, 'Four weeks of sound and fury . . . The 1987 British Election Campaign', *Parliamentary Affairs*, 40 (1987), 458–67.

8 For a detailed analysis of the complex pattern of tactical voting see John Curtice and Michael Steed, 'An Analysis of the Voting', in David Butler and Dennis Kavanagh (eds.), *The British General Election of 1987* (London: Macmillan, 1988), pp. 316–62, esp. pp. 335–41.

9 It should be noted that although average error provides the standard measure, an alternative estimate of error can be derived from a comparison of the party lead.

10 The Harris/ITN exit poll suggests that Labour may have under-polled due to differential turnout. In particular, only 17 per cent of their random sample of voters leaving polling stations were local authority tenants, compared with 26.7 per cent in Britain as a whole (Housing and Construction Statistics, DoE, December 1986). As a result, quota samples which controlled for housing status may have overestimated the Labour vote.

11 Individual constituency polls in Conservative–Alliance marginals provide further evidence that the Labour vote was squeezed at the last minute. See Robert Waller, chapter 21 of this volume.

21 Constituency polling in the 1987 election

Very many polls, and many different kinds of poll, were conducted during the 1987 British general election. There were 'standard' national polls, regional polls, the largest exit poll ever undertaken in Britain, and polls in groups of marginal constituencies. Some of them were generally judged successful, some were the object of calumny and vilification. There were also a large number of polls in individual constituencies – without doubt, the largest number ever conducted in a British election. I consider here 78 polls, in 52 different constituencies, conducted by at least 15 different research suppliers – and such was the flood that I am by no means confident that all the constituency polls that were undertaken have come to my attention. Details of these polls are presented in table 21.1.

What might be the justification for all this constituency polling? To some extent it is the same as that for surveying groups of marginal seats. The national voting intention pattern, even if correctly identified in the standard polls appearing during an election campaign, can be misleading if the mood is not uniform across the country. The plurality or first-past-the-post electoral system is not proportional, and if different types of seat and different individual seats behave in different ways, the national polls alone will not reveal the eventual make-up of the House of Commons. Individual seats can guide us as to what is happening in the various types of contest in the various regions, and in places where various social and economic groups are concentrated. If the marginals do behave differently from the norm, they demand the lion's share of attention, for they alone, by definition, can change hands.

The idea of the 'bellwether' seat, that 'typical' place which will fall to whichever party wins the election, is an attractive one to media clients, enabling them to focus attention on a manageable and individual locality. They also provide a way for the local or regional media to provide a home-based slant to their election coverage and potentially to attract national media attention.

Table 21.1. *List of constituency polls during 1987 general election campaign (11 June results underlined)*

Constituency	Research organisation	Media outlet	Field-work	Sample size	Con. %	Lab. %	Lib/SDP %	Others %
Bath	Marplan	*Today*	27–29 May	763	36.0	23.0	40.0	1.0
					45.4	10.6	42.7	1.3
Birmingham Erdington	Marplan	*Birmingham Evening Mail*		1,009	39.0	46.0	14.0	
					39.2	44.9	12.4	
Birmingham Hall Green	Marplan	*Today*	27–29 May	765	39.0	29.0	31.0	
					44.9	28.2	27.0	
Birmingham Yardley	Marplan	*Birmingham Evening Mail*	5 June	1,035	44.0	35.0	21.0	
					42.6	36.6	20.8	
Bolton NE	*Scantel	*Manchester Evening News*	11 May	1,000	46.0	37.0	17.0	
	MORI	*Granada TV*	22 May–1 June	804	44.0	41.0	15.0	
					44.4	42.6	13.0	
Brent E	Harris	*London Daily News*	4 June	529	34.0	53.0	10.0	3.0
					38.4	42.6	14.5	4.4
Bury N	MORI	*Granada TV*	22 May–2 June	814	48.0	37.0	14.0	
					50.1	37.8	12.1	
Calder Valley	Harris	*C4 News*	20–21 May	648	36.0	40.0	24.0	
	Harris	*C4 News*	27–28 May	646	30.0	45.0	24.0	
	Harris	*C4 News*	4 June	621	34.0	40.0	26.0	
	Harris	*C4News*	9 June	642	35.0	42.0	23.0	
					43.5	33.4	23.1	
Cambridge	Harris	*Spectator*	30 April–3 May	715	36.0	31.0	32.0	1.0
	Harris	*Spectator*	23–25 May	811	35.0	35.0	28.0	1.0
	Marplan	*Today*	27–29 May	705	39.0	29.0	31.0	1.0
	Harris	*Spectator*	30 May–1 June	832	40.0	34.0	26.0	
	Cambridge CAT	*Anglia TV*	4–7 June	573	28.5	35.0	33.0	3.0
					40.0	28.3	30.6	1.1
Cardiff Central	Marplan	*S. Wales Echo*	29 May	506	33.0	39.0	26.0	2.0
					37.1	32.3	28.4	1.3

Constituency	Research organisation	Media outlet	Field-work	Sample size	Con. %	Lab. %	Lib/SDP %	Others %
Cardiff South & Penarth	Beaufort	HTV	26–29 May	1,008	34.0	51.0	13.0	2.0
					36.5	46.7	15.4	1.5
Carmarthen	Beaufort	BBC	7–9 May	1,000	29.0	32.0	22.0	16.0
	NOP	Harlech TV	3–7 June	1,017	26.0	43.0	14.0	17.0
					27.4	35.4	13.3	23.0
Cheltenham	Harris	C4 News	17–19 May	648	47.0	17.0	36.0	
	Harris	C4 News	24–26 May	648	44.0	20.0	35.0	
	Harris	C4 News	31 May–2 June	648	53.0	11.0	36.0	1.0
	Harris	C4 News	8–9 June	648	41.0	14.0	45.0	
					50.2	7.5	42.3	
City of Durham	*Audience selection	Tyne-Tees TV	31 May–3 June	737	25.0	52.0	23.0	
					21.9	44.9	33.2	
Clwyd S.W.	*MORI	Granada TV	23 May–3 June	819 (366 tel.)	34.0	39.0	20.0	7.0
					33.2	35.4	22.3	8.5
Copeland	*MORI	Granada TV	22–31 May	830 (184 tel.)	41.0	50.0	9.0	0.7
					43.0	47.2	9.1	1.0
Coventry S.W.	BBC	BBC *Newsnight*	8–9 May	738	44.0	34.0	22.0	
					43.3	37.0	19.7	1.0
Dudley W.	Harris	C4 News	15–17 May	648	43.0	39.0	17.0	
	Harris	C4 News	23–24 May	648	47.0	36.0	17.0	
	Harris	C4 News	30–31 May	648	50.0	38.0	12.0	
	Keele University	*Wolverhampton Express and Star*	30 May	689	44.9	40.1	14.8	
	Harris	C4 News	8–9 June	649	44.0	36.0	21.0	1.0
					49.8	34.0	16.2	
Dulwich	Harris	LWT	8–12 May	643	40.0	40.0	19.0	
					42.4	42.0	14.5	1.1
Edinburgh S.	*POR System 3	*Daily Star*	12 May	445	31.0	38.0	25.0	6.0
		Glasgow Herald/STV	26 May	990	27.0	38.0	24.0	11.0
	*POR	*Daily Star*	7–8 June	997	31.0	40.0	23.0	6.0
					33.8	37.7	22.5	6.0
Exeter	Marplan	*Today*	30 May–2 June	746	45.0	22.0	32.0	
					44.4	22.5	31.8	
Finchley	Harris	*London Daily News*	4 June	594	49.0	37.0	13.0	2.0
					53.9	31.7	13.9	0.4

Table 21.1. (cont.)

Constituency	Research organisation	Media outlet	Field-work	Sample size	Con. %	Lab. %	Lib/SDP %	Others %
Halifax	BBC	BBC Newsnight	8–9 May	800	36.0	42.0	21.0	1.0
					41.3	43.4	15.4	
Hazel Grove	MORI	Granada TV	21 May–1 June	789	46.0	19.0	35.0	
					45.5	11.8	42.0	
Hertfordshire N.	Harris	LWT	8–12 May	609	48.0	20.0	32.0	
					49.7	18.5	31.8	
Hyndburn	MORI	Granada TV	23 May–4 June	806	40.0	44.0	16.0	
					44.4	39.8	15.2	0.6
Islington S. and Finsbury	Harris	LWT	8–12 May	609	30.0	44.0	23.0	2.0
	Marplan	Today	27–29 May	767	25.0	36.0	36.0	3.0
					20.6	40.1	38.1	1.2
Leicester S.	*POR	Daily Star	12 May	468	46.0	29.0	24.0	1.0
	*POR	Daily Star	7–8 June	862	48.0	33.0	18.0	1.0
					40.8	44.2	13.8	1.2
Littleborough & Saddleworth	MORI	Granada TV	22 May–4 June	799	44.0	31.0	25.0	
					43.1	26.0	30.9	
Liverpool Broadgreen	MORI	Granada TV	20–27 May	826	21.0	48.0	30.0	1.0
					15.5	48.6	35.9	
Luton S.	Luton College of HE	Anglia TV	20–22 May	644	48.0	33.0	18.0	1.0
					46.2	36.7	17.1	
Manchester Withington	MORI	Granada TV	21–28 May	805	31.0	46.0	22.0	1.0
					36.2	42.9	19.8	1.1
Newcastle Central	*Audience Selection	Tyne-Tees TV	31 May	722	34.0	44.0	21.0	1.0
					38.8	44.2	15.8	
Newport W.	Marplan	S. Wales Echo	22 May	518	39.0	44.0	16.0	1.0
					40.1	46.1	13.0	0.8
Norfolk NW.	Norfolk CFE	Anglia TV	20–22 May	668	48.0	19.0	33.0	
					50.6	17.5	31.9	
Norwich S.	E. Anglia University	Eastern Daily Press	3–5 June	630	32.0	41.0	25.0	2.0
					37.3	37.9	24.9	
Nottingham S.	NOP	Central TV	30–31 May	750	46.0	36.0	17.0	1.0
					45.0	40.8	14.1	
Oxford W. and Abingdon	Marplan	Today	27–29 May	713	44.0	21.0	33.0	2.0
					46.4	14.9	37.4	1.0
St Ives	Marplan	Today	27–29 May	683	42.0	21.0	33.0	
					48.2	17.8	22.8	3.0

Constituency	Research organisation	Media outlet	Field-work	Sample size	Con. %	Lab. %	Lib/SDP %	Others %
Staffs. S. E.	*POR	*Daily Star*	?	?	48.0	22.0	29.0	
					46.6	25.7	27.7	13.0
Stirling	System 3	*Glasgow Herald/STV*	29–31 May	951	29.0	39.0	18.0	
					38.3	36.2	14.8	10.7
Stockport	*Scantel	*Manchester Evening News*	11 May	1,000	43.0	30.0	26.0	1.0
					39.0	38.0	21.0	
Stockton S.	*Scantel	*Manchester Evening News*	5–6 June	1,110	39.0	38.0	21.0	1.0
	Marplan	*Today*	27–29 May	733	41.4	35.3	22.1	1.1
	*Audience Selection	*Tyne-Tees TV*	31 May–3 June	714	34.0	28.0	36.0	
					34.0	35.0	30.0	
					35.0	31.3	33.7	1.1
Strathkelvin and Bearsden	System 3	*Glasgow Herald/STV*	3–5 June	1,103	31.0	37.0	24.0	9.0
					33.4	38.1	21.4	7.1
Tottenham	Harris	*London Daily News*	4 June	587	23.0	57.0	18.0	2.0
					35.4	43.6	17.9	3.2
Twickenham	Marplan	*Today*	27–29 May	769	36.0	23.0	36.0	
					51.9	8.4	38.3	1.4
Walsall S.	Keele University	*Wolverhampton Express and Star*	June	665	43.3	43.9	12.7	
					42.7	44.9	12.4	
Welwyn Hatfield	*POR	*Star*	12 May	475	52.0	19.0	29.0	
	*POR	*Star*	7–8 June	909	53.0	20.0	26.0	1.0
					45.6	26.4	27.3	0.7
West Bromwich E.	Keele University	*Wolverhampton Express and Star*	23 May	633	36.5	46.8	16.5	
	NOP	*Central TV*	30 May–2 June	742	41.0	43.0	36.0	
					40.3	42.6	17.1	
Winchester	Marplan	*Financial Times*	27–29 May	726	47.0	12.0	40.0	
					52.3	6.5	40.2	
Wolverhampton NE.	Keele University	*Wolverhampton Express and Star*	16 May	663	37.7	42.5	19.0	0.8
					42.1	41.7	16.2	
York	*POR	*Daily Star*	12 May	455	44.0	35.0	21.0	1.0
	*POR	*Daily Star*	7–8 June	923	42.0	42.0	15.0	1.0
	?	*York. Evening Post*	?	?	45.0	35.0	20.0	
					41.6	41.4	15.9	1.0

* Poll conducted entirely or partially by telephone. All polls were sampled by quota rather than random method.

? accurate information not available.

The thinking behind the three C4 News 'Battleground' constituencies which Harris polled frequently in the run-up to the election and during the campaign, was that the vital issues could be covered within one Conservative–Labour marginal (Dudley West), one Conservative–Alliance marginal (Cheltenham) and one three-way marginal where all the main parties had a chance (Calder Valley).

Indeed in the end Calder Valley did produce the result closest of any seat to the British picture as a whole: 43 per cent Conservative, 33 per cent Labour, 23 per cent Alliance. If only the polls there had got it right!

One other reason can be offered for commissioning constituency polls: the lure of personality for the media. All the seats polled could reasonably be described as marginals, with the exception of those involving famous or controversial 'names': Bernie Grant in Tottenham, Ken Livingstone in Brent East, and Margaret Thatcher herself in Finchley. *The Spectator*'s choice of the much-polled Cambridge as the one seat to follow may also have had something to do with the presence of Shirley Williams as SDP candidate, as well as the nature of that weekly's readership.

So, in theory constituency polls are a good idea, one which can focus media attention on a recognisable and comprehensible unit (and familiar faces). Yet it would be very hard to claim that many of the constituency polls were fully satisfactory, and some very clearly went wrong. It is of course impossible ever to prove that a poll taken in advance of an election result is inaccurate, for a late swing is always possible, and pollsters usually say that they make no predictions. However, the media and other commissioning agencies undoubtedly do see polls as having predictive functions, the public tend to judge them according to this criterion, and there is little evidence of a significant and consistent swing during the 1987 campaign.

Bearing all this in mind, it might be pointed out that 13 of the 78 polls considered here 'named' the 'wrong winner' (see table 21.2).

Twenty-four of the polls gave figures for two or more parties which were each over 5 per cent away from their eventual actual percentage of the vote (see table 21.3).

Once again it must be reiterated that this variation could be accounted for by subsequent changes of preference, and that the polls might conceivably have been accurate at the time they were taken; this obviously applies more strongly the earlier the polls were conducted. However, given the lack of 'swing' during the campaign, it is an acceptable working hypothesis that mistakes were made too, when the margin of error was greater than that which is mathematically inevitable and which is acceptable. I would certainly admit this as far as my own polling company is concerned, the Harris Research Centre, which conducted more constituency polls than any other organization during the 1987 campaign.

Overall, we were disappointed with our constituency surveys. The final

Table 21.2. *'Wrong winners'*

	Named	Actual
MORI/Hyndburn	Labour	Conservative
Marplan/Cardiff C.	Labour	Conservative
Marplan/Stockton S.	Alliance	Conservative
Audience Selection/Stockton S.	Labour	Conservative
Keele U/Wolverhampton NE.	Labour	Conservative
Harris/Calder Valley (4 times)	Labour	Conservative
Harris/Cheltenham	Alliance	Conservative
POR/Leicester S. (twice)	Conservative	Labour
Marplan/Bath	Alliance	Conservative
Cambridge CFE/Cambridge	Labour	Conservative

Total = 14

Table 21.3. *Polls over 5 per cent out – two or more parties*

Poll	Seat	Plus	Minus
Harris	Tottenham	Lab	C
Harris	Cheltenham 2	Lab	C and A
Harris	Cheltenham 4	Lab	C
* POR	Welwyn 1	C	Lab
* POR	Welwyn 2	C	Lab
Cambridge CFE	Cambridge	Lab	C
* POR	Leicester S 1	A	Lab
* POR	Leicester S 2	C	Lab
Marplan	Bath	Lab	C
* POR	Halifax	A	C
Harris	Calder Valley 1	Lab	C
Harris	Calder Valley 2	Lab	C
Harris	Calder Valley 3	Lab	C
Harris	Calder Valley 4	Lab	C
MORI	Hazel Grove	Lab	A
Marplan	Cardiff S	A	Lab
MORI	Liv'pool Broadgreen	C	A
Marplan	Bridgend	A	Lab
* Audience Selection	City of Durham	Lab	A
Harris	Islington S	C	A
Marplan	Winchester	Lab	C
Marplan	Twickenham	Lab	C
NOP	Carmarthen	Lab	PC
NOP	Ynys Mon	Lab	PC

Total Polls = 24
Labour overestimated   15 times, underestimated 6 times
Conservative overestimated 5 times, underestimated 12 times
Alliance overestimated   4 times, underestimated 5 times
Total overestimates =   24, total underestimates = 23

* Polls conducted by telephone.
Number after some seats indicates 1st, 2nd etc of a series of polls.

Table 21.4. *Notably good polls (all parties within 3 per cent of final result)*

Poll	Seat
Marplan	Cambridge
BBC	Coventry SW.
Harris	N. Herts
Marplan	Newport W.
System 3	Strathkelvin & Bearsden
Marplan	Birmingham Yardley
NOP	West Bromwich E
MORI	Copeland
MORI	Bury N.
Harris	Dudley W. (no. 2)
MORI	Bolton NE.
MORI	Stockport
* POR	York (no. 2)
Marplan	Birmingham Erdington
Keele U	Walsall S.
Marplan	Exeter
Norfolk CAT	Norfolk NW.
Total = 17	

* Poll conducted by telephone.

polls in the C4 news 'Battleground' series, broadcast the day before the election nominated the 'wrong winner' in two out of the three seats. In Cheltenham a freak poll put the Liberals ahead of the Conservative incumbent who held on to his seat the next day. In Calder Valley, as in all five previous Calder Valley polls we had done since autumn 1986, we placed Labour comfortably ahead. The Conservatives actually retained the seat with a 10 per cent majority. Harris also undertook polls about a week before the election in three London constituencies for the late *London Daily News*, all of which very substantially overestimated the Labour vote and underestimated Conservative support.

It is true, too, that a number of very accurate constituency polls were published during the campaign. Table 21.4 lists the 17 that I have found in which all parties' shares of the vote were within 3 per cent of the eventual results. Nevertheless, Harris at least feel that it is clearly necessary to draw lessons from our failures and to re-think our methods. What are the special difficulties involved in individual constituency polls, and why did 1987 produce such a mixed set of results?

1   National polls can as a matter of regularity and routine be quota-sampled according to the established variables of class, age and sex, for which information is available from the latest census and other, more up-to-date, sources such as the National Readership Survey. All major pollsters are experienced in employing a standard set of sampling points which may be

used monthly or even weekly. For individual constituency polls, however, and for surveys of groups of marginals, special quotas and sampling points have to be devised. Current demographic, social and economic information is not always available on a constituency basis: the occupational information contained in the census is not always in the most convenient form, and like other indicators such as housing tenure and racial group it is already six years out of date. The chances of securing accurate information are patchy; sometimes Housing Departments of local councils are helpful and reliable, sometimes not.

What is more, considerable local knowledge and special investigation is required to ensure that the sampling points chosen actually reflect the geographical spread of the constituency. All in all a poll in one constituency is considerably harder to organize than a survey of the nation as a whole.

2   This point is hard to make to clients: why, they tend to ask, should they pay as much for a survey designed to elicit the views of a unit of 65,000 people as for the whole electorate of over 40 million? Why should the sample size approach 1,000 when little more than that is sufficient (we tell them) for a national survey? As a result, it is hard to sell constituency polls at the same rate as a national poll, and a commercial squeeze can be placed on sample sizes and other cost elements. Very few (6) of the constituency polls conducted during the 1987 election campaign had sample sizes of over 1,000 and several slipped to as little as 400–600. The average sample size was approximately 700–750 and this modest sample was divided between a limited number of sampling points. None of this, however, lowered the expectations of the media and public of their accuracy.

3   Since more constituency polls than ever before were attempted in 1987, economic pressure was placed on the resources of some of the research companies involved. Harris, for example, undertook polls in Calder Valley, Dudley West, Cheltenham and Cambridge each week during the campaign, and attempted simultaneous polling in the first three on 8–9 June to be broadcast on C4 news on 10 June, the eve of the election. Harris also undertook three constituency polls in London for the *London Daily News* on 3–4 June – all this in addition to national polls, private polls, a panel in 100 marginals, and our daily 'rolling poll'. It is clearly difficult to assemble a score or so of interviewers in a single constituency at any one time; in a national poll one interviewer is sufficient to look after each sampling point in which interviewing is taking place. This can lead to the necessity of sub-contracting some work outside the company's own field-force, and also to a pressure to rush the job. This in turn can produce various kinds of inefficient practice.

4   In order to get jobs done in time for media deadlines and to free interviewers for all the other work piling up during the election, there is a tendency to allow interviewing to be conducted in the street rather than in-

home. Even with quota controls, this can produce an odd sample, as well as making it very difficult to establish a fair residential spread of respondents around the constituency. Certain types of people are more likely to be found on the streets and may be more approachable.

The problems of possible interviewer bias are well known, and interviewing in the street gives an even greater level of choice to interviewers (within their quotas) than other forms of non-random sampling. Normally it is assumed that interviewers tend to be middle-aged, middle-class females; in Harris' case, there is a much wider range of interviewers, and a considerable proportion of interviewers in London at least are non-white, part of our 70–80 strong 'ethnic field force'. It is conceivable that this may have led to a pro-Labour bias in our polls in the capital, perhaps because of the type of respondent who might agree to an interview with a non-white interviewer.

5   Hastily-conducted surveys by quota can lead to excessive geographical 'clustering' of interviews, as the interviewers rush to complete their allocation. Whether working in-home or on-street, interviewers have considerable freedom in their choice of respondents. It is rare that they will visit villages, outlying communities, or individual farmhouses, which leads to incomplete coverage of the rural parts of a mixed constituency. It is quite likely that Harris's consistent failure to place the Conservatives in the lead in Calder Valley was partially due to an inability to reach the isolated farms and communities on the moors. This is not a new phenomenon in semi-rural constituencies; other research companies found difficulties in polling during the Brecon and Radnor by-election in 1985.

6   Intriguingly, evidence from Harris' national exit poll for ITN on election-day itself casts doubt on the basis of the quotas used in many constituency polls. Such polls are often dependent on housing tenure information, updated since the 1981 census if possible. Interviewers are set quotas to find the appropriate proportion of respondents who are owner occupiers, council tenants or private renters in a constituency. Yet the Harris/ITN exit poll, randomly conducted and interviewing in detail over 4,500 respondents in fifty constituencies, found only 17 per cent who said they lived in council houses.[1] Despite new private housebuilding and the sale of council houses, we believe that over 20 per cent and probably nearer 25 per cent of British voters still live in the local authority rented sector. This suggests a differential turnout – council tenants were simply less likely to come out to vote than owner-occupiers. Since council tenants voted Labour by over 2 to 1 on 11 June, any 'over-representation' of this sector in quota surveys would lead to a pro-Labour bias – the very problem that many 1987 campaign polls in marginals suffered from. This would apply to individual seats and to groups of marginals – anything quota-sampled by tenure. This effect is, of course, measurable and can be tested by retrospective weighting: it certainly

did not account for the whole of the inaccuracy perpetrated during the campaign. It is also true that the registration and turnout of Afro-Caribbean voters appears to have been significantly lower than that of whites and Asians. Once again, if a survey were quota-sampled according to the percentage of Afro-Caribbeans in the electorate, this differential turnout would lead to a pro-Labour bias in the poll, given the overwhelming support for Labour usually shown among black voters.

It is perhaps not coincidental that Harris' very inaccurate poll in Tottenham a week before the general election was quotad by tenure and race. Yet it is clearly dangerous for a research organisation to take the responsibility of guessing about the different turnout levels of various social and economic groups, and it cannot be very wrong in theory to quota by the correct proportions of those groups within the electorate. We must leave suggestions for improvement in this regard to the final section of the paper. It is notable that the most common single form of inaccuracy in the constituency polls of the 1987 election was to overestimate Labour support and underestimate the Conservatives' share of the vote.

Comparing the inaccurate campaign polls listed in table 21.3 with the final results in the constituencies, the Labour share was more often overestimated (15 times) than underestimated (6 times). This phenomenon is made even more clear if we eliminate polls conducted entirely by telephone (a technique traditionally held to increase the Conservative percentage). Face to face polls erred in favour of Labour 13 times and in favour of the Conservatives twice. Similarly, the Conservative vote was underestimated by face to face polls 12 times while the Labour vote was underestimated only twice (both times by Marplan in South Wales).

I believe these systematic discrepancies are accounted for by two sets of causes. Pollsters can do nothing about the first. Labour was probably 'squeezed' tactically during the campaign in those seats in which it finished third, where the main contest was clearly between Conservatives and the Alliance: Cheltenham, Twickenham, Bath, Hazel Grove, and Winchester come into this category. Secondly, there were probably genuine errors at the time of taking the polls, caused by the factors mentioned above: quotas by tenure and ethnic group, over-clustering in town centres and urban areas, and on-street interviewing.

We should devote some attention to the *content* of the 1987 campaign constituency polls. In general, pollsters and their clients confined themselves to similar questions to those posed in other types of survey, such as those national polls, panels, and polls of marginals.

Some of these questions produced responses which varied interestingly between constituencies: for example, when Harris polled three seats in the capital for the *London Daily News*, a plurality of voters in Labour Brent East and Tottenham felt that they were personally worse off than they had been five years ago, whereas in Conservative Finchley more electors felt that they were now better off than worse off.

A number of polls attempted to relate local issues to the campaigns and standings of the parties in the constituencies surveyed. Harris asked whether the record of the 'left-wing' Brent Council made respondents more or less likely to vote Labour in Brent East on 11 June (the answer was: less likely 39 per cent, more likely 21 per cent, no difference 29 per cent and 11 per cent offering no opinion). Questions were also asked about the level of recognition for individual candidates and their relative attractions. Shirley Williams remained the best-known candidate in Cambridge throughout the campaign, although her main rivals 'closed the gap' in name recognition as election day approached. Ken Livingstone's record on Ireland and gay/lesbian rights made 39 per cent of his Brent East electorate say they were less likely to vote for him, and only 16 per cent of them more likely. On the other hand, more approved (39 per cent) of Mr Livingstone's record on representing London than disapproved (31 per cent).

However, an attempt was then made to assess the importance of local issues and local candidates. In the final Harris 'Battleground' surveys conducted over the weekend before the election only three to five per cent of respondents named local issues or local candidates as the single most important factor in deciding which way to vote. Only three to four per cent said that local issues caused most worry to the respondent and their family. None of this suggests that we should revise the conventional wisdom that in a general election campaign national issues predominate; and constituency polls must still mainly be seen as accessible local indicators of the state of national opinion.

What effects do constituency polls have, whether accurate or inaccurate? During parliamentary by-elections, polls have undoubted had a decided effect in assisting voters to cast their ballots 'tactically' should they so wish. Both at Bermondsey in early 1983 and at Greenwich in early 1987 the Liberal–SDP Alliance candidate was certainly helped by polls which showed them in second place by the middle of the campaign, suggesting that they were in the best position to defeat a left-wing Labour candidate. In places such as Fulham in 1986 it was perhaps made clear that the Alliance campaign was failing to make a substantial impact, thus helping to unite the anti-Tory vote behind Labour's Nick Raynsford.

However, it is much more doubtful that constituency polls can affect the result during a general election, when a national campaign led by national figures is taking place primarily on TV; when a government is being chosen, not simply the selection of a candidate as MP in the middle of a parliamentary term. This did not prevent a certain degree of passion being stimulated among the political parties and the candidates by various published polls. A few examples may suffice. On 8 June *The Glasgow Herald* carried a System Three poll in the marginal seat of Strathkelvin and Bearsden which showed Labour's Sam Galbraith ahead with 37 per cent of the vote, the defending Conservative MP Michael Hirst second with 31 per cent and the Liberal Jim Bannerman third with 24 per cent. Mr Bannerman responded by saying 'our recent canvassing showed us clearly ahead of the Tories. I would also question the validity of the poll.' Mr Hirst 'also questioned the accuracy of the System Three poll'.[2] In the election itself the poll was vindicated: Labour did win with 38 per cent, the Conservatives were second with 33 per cent and the Liberals were third with 21 per cent.

However, it must also be said that parties, politicians and others could justifiably complain at the media's treatment of various constituency polls. 'Socialists to win seat – poll', blared *The Wolverhampton Express and Star* on 21 May, nearly three weeks before the election, reporting a Keele University poll showing a Labour lead in Wolverhampton NE of less than 5 per cent on a sample of 663 – well within sampling error. The Conservative candidate, Maureen Hicks, who gained the seat in the general election, described this as 'not a true reflection'.[3] The Conservative Michael Forsyth compared a System Three poll in Stirling for *The Glasgow Herald*, which showed him 10 per cent behind Labour to Brecon and Radnor, pointing out the difficulties of surveying large, semi-rural seats. He retained Stirling on 11 June.

After the election Chris Davies, the Liberal Alliance candidate in Littleborough and Saddleworth, wrote to Granada TV to complain about a MORI poll conducted between 22 May and 4 June which had placed Labour in second place, not himself (he was the eventual runner up):

> Now that the dust has settled and passions have calmed, I feel it necessary to make a formal complaint about the poll. Opinion polls are supposed to have a 3 per cent margin of error and the actual result suggests this was well exceeded. But the opinion poll helped shape the final result and it's my belief the real error at the time the results were broadcast was very much greater.
>
> A week before the election our canvass figures gave the Alliance 37 per cent of the vote with Labour well down in third place. The arguments for tactical voting were proving very successful from our point of view. The poll completely changed this by suggesting that the Labour Party had a stronger chance than, in fact, proved the case. Frankly after all this, I think it astonishing that the Alliance managed to hold on to its second place position by such a convincing margin. The poll may not have been the only factor in securing the re-election of the Tory MP, Geoffrey Dickens, but it certainly did a great deal to divide the opposition vote and provide him with a 6,000 majority.[4]

The Daily Star twice used Programmes Opinion Research to poll four seats which they somewhat rashly described as 'the big four marginals' – 'they reflect the entire range of 117 seats Labour must win to grab an overall majority'.[5] *The Daily Mirror* ironically drew attention to the Programmes Opinion Research poll in SE Staffordshire whose Alliance candidate was none other than Elizabeth Gluck, director of Programmes Opinion Research.[6] It could also be pointed out, however, that the voting intention found in that SE Staffordshire poll proved accurate within 4 per cent polling error.

There is no real evidence that the fact that some constituencies – the C4 'Battlegrounds' and Cambridge, for example – were heavily polled, affected the result. There may have been a late squeeze on the Labour vote in Cheltenham, and this could well have happened at Bath too, and other Alliance–Conservative marginals. The size of the lead indicated for Bernie Grant at Tottenham may just have been alarming enough to help to disprove the message of that Harris/ *London Daily News* poll. But all in all, *pace* Mr Davies of Littleborough and Saddleworth, individual constituency polls were probably largely lost in the welter of information during the general election campaign, and it was, ironically, the candidates and the parties themselves who paid most attention to the polls and the media coverage thereof.

However, since the performance of constituency polls during the 1987 general election campaign does raise some doubts about their methodology and accuracy, it is worth suggesting some conclusions that we might draw from the campaign. The Harris Research Centre, at least, certainly feels that there is room for improvement and that lessons should be learnt. These could be applied to the by-election polls of the next parliament, polls which definitely have a chance of being influential in themselves.

(a) The pressure from media clients to produce cut-rate and hasty polls should be resisted. Given the various special difficulties they face, good constituency polls need as large a sample as national polls, 1,000 if possible.

(b) Fieldwork should be spread to allow interviewers to avoid clustering. It is notable that the relatively successful series of MORI polls for Granada TV was conducted over lengthy periods, reaching as much as 13 fieldwork days and never less than 8 days. However, it is unlikely that this luxury will be afforded to research companies in a by-election campaign but this is the direction in which national polling may also be travelling, so experimental effort would be well worthwhile.[7]

(c) Questions about likelihood of voting may help to catch the problem of turnout among council tenants, Afro-Caribbeans and other affected groups.

(d) Polling organizations should resist the blandishments of the media to overstretch their resources which may lead to subcontracting, street interviewing and other undesirable practices.

(e) Where possible, random sampling should replace quota sampling. Given the constraints of time and money this may well lead to renewed experiments with telephone polling, which would also remove the danger of clustering and enable outlying communities and households to be reached in semi-rural and rural areas. Of course techniques of weighting to compensate for non-telephone owners will have to be developed.

(f) If random or telephone sampling is not adopted, a maximisation of the number of sampling points in which interviewers have to work should be ensured by the use of census EDs (enumeration districts).

(g) To compensate for differential turnout, more use of the 'certainty to vote' question might be made: in the case of each of Harris's final week polls, the opinion of those who said they were 'certain to vote' on 11 June was closer to the final result than the opinion of all respondents who stated any preference.

As a fresh series of mid-term parliamentary by-elections approaches, it is incumbent on those who commission and carry out the polls to respond to the responsibility created by any influence they might have. The overall record of individual constituency polls must improve when they become the sole source of polling information in a campaign. Otherwise they may, with some justice, come to be accused of worse iniquities than helping to re-elect Mr Geoffrey Dickens of Littleborough and Saddleworth!

Notes

1 See Robert Waller, 'The ITN–Harris exit poll 1987', *Journal of the Market Research Society*, 29 (1987), 419–28.
2 *Glasgow Herald*, 8 June 1987.
3 *Wolverhampton Express and Star*, 21 May 1987.
4 *Manchester Evening News*, 23 July 1987.
5 *Daily Star*, 10 June 1987.
6 *Daily Mirror*, 14 May 1987.
7 MORI conducted their polls in Clwyd SW and Copeland for Granada partially by telephone, with satisfactory results.

DISCUSSION

Ivor Crewe

Two points about Robert Waller's paper. My first relates to the consistent and extraordinary underestimate of the Alliance vote and the overestimate of the Labour vote in Conservative–Alliance marginal seats. The kind of explanation you've given for this, Robert, does not actually hold water. It cannot be to do with the slight inaccuracy of information about the social composition of these constituencies because census and other data on these constituencies is not so much out of date that it could possibly explain 9 or 10 per cent underestimates for the vote for the Alliance – or similar overestimates for the Labour vote. Nor can it be explained by last-minute tactical voting from Labour supporters to the Alliance because we do not see anything like that switch in the Conservative–Alliance marginal surveys which Pippa has listed. Pippa's paper suggests that there might have been a very small swing to the Alliance from Labour in the last two or three days – but certainly not to the extent that could explain the underestimate of one and the overestimate of the other in these constituency polls.

Might I suggest another explanation? Most constituency polls do not check whether the people they interview in that constituency necessarily live there or are registered in that constituency. They may ask whether they live in the constituency, but have no good way of checking whether they are registered there.

Robert Waller

I certainly remember spending many hours looking through lists of respondents' addresses. If I can take as an example the constituency poll of what was an Alliance target, Cheltenham, I rather doubt whether Labour supporters were swarming in from rural Gloucester to swell the numbers that we found in Cheltenham. I do think that there is something in the tactical voting squeeze idea. In Cheltenham a very interesting thing happened. At one point we decided to switch from asking about parties without names of candidates. When nominations closed we could put the names of the candidates on the list, and around about that time – *not* because people's minds were jogged by what they would see on the ballot paper – and also because the campaign concentrates people's minds about what is going on in their constituency, the Labour vote suddenly halved, from about 20 per cent down to 10 or 11 per cent. What probably happens in constituency polls in the early stage of the campaign is that one finds out how people are identifying nationally, rather than how they are actually going to vote in that constituency. Another example is Islington South and Finsbury, a controversial poll which showed far more Conservatives and fewer Alliance supporters than found by a later Marplan poll taken in the campaign itself. In the early polls and before nominations close people think 'Am I basically Labour? Whom do I want to be in government?' As the campaign goes on, people become aware of tactical considerations. I think the predictable squeeze on the Labour vote in places like Bath and Cheltenham, which was not always caught by the constituency polls, might have been if these polls had been conducted at the last minute.

Ivor Crewe

Am I allowed to raise the second point, very quickly? You say that some means should be found of measuring differential turnout. It's awfully difficult – Cathy Marsh did a very interesting study based on Cambridge, which was published in *Political Studies*, showing that people's prediction of their certainty of voting bore very little relation to whether or not they actually voted, when checked against the electoral register.

Pippa Norris

Could I just support Ivor's point: I do think turnout is one of the most difficult things to estimate, and all the polls got it wrong. Perry in the United States, who is in charge of Gallup over there, has done some very useful work. He basically suggested that one needs about three different indicators added together in a fairly complicated way, to predict turnout. One measure is the likelihood of voting, but another is interest in the campaign. You really need to split your sample and try and use some of these measures and see if, in the British context, they would work. This is one thing we could experiment with very usefully.

Brian Gosschalk
I really have to disagree quite strongly with a number of points which have been made. Firstly, the certainty-to-vote figure which we get in polls is a remarkably good predictor of actual turnout, and that goes back for a decade.

Robert Waller
This is overall levels of turnout as opposed to checking the individual voting behaviour.

Brian Gosschalk
Absolutely, not checking individuals. It seems to me that both Pippa and Robert have got a fundamental problem. You are talking about predictive polls. I am dismayed to see Robert citing polls on 18 April, before the election had even been called, in the table of polls used to gauge how accurate constituency polls are. In fact, of the 76 you refer to, I count only seven where fieldwork was in the last week. If you are going to gauge the accuracy of constituency polls by their 'prediction of the share of the vote', you should ignore anything done more than seven days before polling day.

Robert Waller
These constituency polls will be judged by clients and by the public according to actual electoral results, and I do feel that in Calder Valley, for example, it's no use me saying, 'Well, we may have been right at the time. You can never disprove this.' I think we were probably wrong at the time, and therefore I think you can take evidence from these 70 or 80 polls, rather than confining it to the last six or seven polls.

Paul McKee
There is one sentence in Pippa Norris' paper which I think is totally wrong, namely that marginal polls cannot provide a legitimate basis for national seat projections. The converse is the case: they provide the *only* legitimate basis for national seat projection. Polling in marginals started to do exactly that and the classic test of this was October 1974 where, in order to make on-the-night projections based on exit polls, two halves of the same organisation conducted exit polls. One half of the organisation, i.e. Harris for the BBC, did a projection for the BBC based upon a national constituency sample, of all constituencies, and left Bob McKenzie in the position of projecting a Labour landslide, with a majority in excess of 140. ITN, with ORC, the other half of

the Harris organisation, did a similarly conducted poll, in marginal constituencies – different groups of marginals, Conservative–Labour, Labour–
Conservative, a strong third party, SNP etc. It was the first largish, major exit
poll, and that predicted a small Labour majority, and caused a little bit of
concern in both places until it was decided which engine looked to be on the
right track. That is why marginal polls are the *only* legitimate basis for doing
seat projections.

What's gone wrong is that the write-up in most of the papers and the
discussions on television, are incomprehensible. It doesn't matter about the
definition of what is a marginal, and percentages do not matter. The change in
share of vote matters. One of the things that you both neglect is that the
nature of marginals has changed radically over the last two decades,
influenced, I think, heavily by the boundary changes that came into operation
in 1983. What has also happened is that the internal demography of
marginals has changed. Whatever group of marginals you take, the seats are
no longer homogeneous which is part of the reason why you get some of the
peculiar variations up and down the country. I could construct a sampling
point which looked absolutely identical – I could give you two sets of
sampling points which by all measures look identical – and I would guarantee
to produce fundamentally different results from each of those two sets of
sampling points. I wouldn't touch a constituency poll now that isn't done on a
random basis.

Peter Hutton

I concur with what Paul was saying. The point that the *Newsnight* poll was, in
fact, a panel, doesn't seem to come out from Pippa Norris's paper, and that
seems to be rather crucial. With a panel there is a danger that on recall you
will get a differential response from people of different voting persuasions,
and I would be interested to know how, if at all, this was really taken into
account. It also has a very major advantage in this context: if you have a bias
built in at the beginning and if you can identify that bias, you know that it is
also very likely to be there at the end. One thing that stands out from the
figures for the Conservative–Labour marginals is that the *Newsnight* poll does
seem to have a bit of a Labour bias compared with the other marginal polls.
My question to Pippa is, 'Did this stand out to her, having looked not only at
week 1, but also week 3, week 4? Was this information passed on to those who
were presenting the information?' In the television presentation we were
given a whole list of caveat: in the sense of, 'Here are the caveats and, by the
way, we accept all the caveats, but this is the best poll that's been done with
the best methodology and we don't believe the others.' Yet the evidence is
there to suggest that maybe there was a reason for saying that there is perhaps
a two-point bias to Labour in our sample and we would be in danger of
misleading the public about the likely result if we don't point this out.

Pippa Norris
You mentioned the question of the Labour bias at the start of the *Newsnight* poll and how it seemed to continue. This seemed to characterise many of the panels; certainly Martin Collins suggests that the *Newsnight* panel, the MORI panel in *The Sunday Times*, and the Gallup panel *all* found a swing towards Labour during the campaign, which the single national polls did not find, so maybe it has something to do with the panel design.

Peter Hutton
But that doesn't actually address the question. Were you conscious, having seen one or two weeks of this, that you had a bias, and did you do anything about it? Was it taken into account?

Pippa Norris
Whether we had a bias depends on the question of comparability. You can look at the other marginal polls: when ours were published we'd just had the *Weekend World* ones for Harris and, of course, ours were closest to those, and so when we were comparing ours with Harris we felt we weren't that different. We were obviously different to the NOP and the MORI polls, but since they used a different selection of seats – different criteria and levels of marginality – we didn't feel that necessarily one or the other could be tested until the night. On the night we'd know which was right and which was wrong. The fact that two polls show one thing and three polls show the other doesn't really help in the middle of a campaign.

David Butler
I want to make one point about the *Newsnight* poll which is no criticism actually of John Curtice or Pippa Norris; and that is the total absence of control about early leaks. I know that MORI and Harris were very, very cautious about letting people know. I was in contact with them during the day, I didn't ask them, they didn't tell me or volunteer information about the polls yet one went to the press conferences in the morning and all the journalists said 'Have you heard what *Newsnight*'s going to say tonight?' It really leaked out on a grand scale, and the BBC said it was just the people of the Newsroom phoning their friends but you can control these. The pollsters have shown they can control it, and *Newsnight* got itself, I think, some of its bad reputation and some of its extra hype through just this journalistic leaking of things, which was nothing to do with Pippa Norris – or with conducting polls.

A last point, just a constructive suggestion: it would be useful if Pippa Norris did what may be a rather tiresome, statistical operation, of working out what the outcome was in the universe from which the sample of marginals was taken, because that would give an indication of how far you were unlucky in your sample.

Bob Worcester
I remember before the election began (I believe it was in February) when we were doing a national poll in *The Sunday Times*, and *Weekend World* was about to put out one of Harris' marginals. I turned on, I think it was the 8.30, ITN News and saw to my horror two sets of figures, one the national figures from the marginal, showing maybe a 3 per cent Conservative lead, and my own from *The Sunday Times* showing a 9 per cent lead, and the commentary was how the polls were all over the place. When you adjusted for marginality, bang, they were spot on, right together. Being a helpful sort of chap I tried to get through to the BBC newsroom – the duty officer said they were busy preparing the news – and I tried to warn them off, but sure enough, at 9.15 or whatever that Saturday night, the BBC compounded it by making the same false comparison.

PART VIII

Pressure group communication in the 1987 campaign

22 Mobilisation and distance: the role of trade unions in the 1987 election campaign

In this chapter I explore two interconnected processes – the attempt by trade unions to mobilise support for the Labour Party and the handling by the Labour Party of trade union-related issues during its campaign. In particular, I focus on the management of 'distance' in the relationship.

The legacy of 1983

The 1983 general election was a disaster for the Labour movement – that much was widely agreed within the unions and the Labour Party. But behind the defeat it was possible to discern some positive and improving aspects of the trade union campaign.[1] The unions were in the process of changing some long-established attitudes towards communication and campaigning and beginning to organise their contribution to political mobilisation in novel ways.

In this sense, the 1983 campaign marked a significant advance for them, although it was an advance from a very low level of activity shaped by many years of complacency and neglect. Their improvement was limited and constrained by the powerful pro-government political current, and hidden by the abysmal performance of the Labour Party – including its organisational and communicational incompetence.

Two sets of consequences flowed from the 1983 election. Support for the Labour Party amongst trade unionists having been reduced to 39 per cent, there was a new vulnerability to the unions' financial and political support for the Labour Party. Aware of this vulnerability, the new Conservative government pressed ahead with legislation which required a union's political fund to be authorised in a ballot held in 1985–6 and every ten years thereafter. Thus the unions' ability to involve themselves in political mobilisation was legally challenged for the first time since 1913.

Secondly, although it was widely recognised that Labour's defeat in 1983 had been primarily a political defeat, it was also clear tht the Labour Party's central administration, its communicational capacity and its campaigning organisation were in need of a drastic overhaul. This reconstruction, heralded in a speech by Neil Kinnock on 12 September 1983, was carried through with enough vigour and flair for the Labour Party to be able to seize the initiative during the first week of the 1987 general election campaign, thus rescuing the party from a dangerous political position and, ultimately, forcing the Alliance into political crisis.

The political fund ballots

The performance of the unions in these ballots came as a shock to many union critics and a welcome surprise to many supporters. When the ballots were imposed, a common view was that the Labour Party would be beset by a fundamental crisis due to the reduction in finance and affiliation as a result of losses in the ballots.[2] In practice, every affiliated union voted to retain its funds, eight other unions voted to establish a fund, one union – the broadcasting union, BETA – later voted to affiliate to the Labour Party, and several other unions now have ballots for funds or affiliation in the pipeline.

The scale of the 'yes' vote raises questions about union organisation and the political attitudes of trade unionists too numerous and too complex to enter into here. But for our purposes it is important to note:

1. The case for unions having a political fund was a strong case irrespective of the electoral responses of trade unionists to Labour. The government's legislative change in the definition of 'political' made the case stronger. This issue, *not* affiliation to the Labour Party, was the central question posed by the legislation.
2. Over-confident of the incapacity of the unions and inhibited by the naked partisanship of the legislation, the Conservative Party refrained from an organised political campaign within the unions.
3. The unions created and took control over the coordinating organisation – the Trade Union Coordinating Committee. Although unions varied in their expressions of commitment to the Labour Party, the TUCC kept up an image of distance between the unions and the party – an image which was utilised in many unions.
4. The unions were much better organised to participate in these ballots than their critics believed. The campaigns were cleverly staged and staggered, and based on a workplace 'campaign contact' network created specifically for the purpose. Campaigning material was of a high standard and geared heavily to relevant industrial issues which required 'a political voice'. The final task of mobilising the 'yes' vote was carried through with impressive efficiency.

These successes in the Political Fund ballots stimulated a renewed campaigning confidence in the unions at a time when the defeat of the miners had reduced their industrial strength. A new organisation called Trade Unionists for Labour (TUFL) was created out of a fusion of the Trade Unions for a Labour Victory (TULV) and the Trade Union Coordinating Committee. It aimed to take the best practices of both organisations and, in the aftermath of the political fund successes, it was able to draw in the engineers and the mineworkers, both of whom had been alienated from, and heavily critical of, TULV. TUFL defined its purpose of maximum assistance to the Labour Party primarily in terms of electoral mobilisation and eschewed any involvement in Labour Party policymaking.

A TUFL campaign unit of three (later four) people was set up on a permanent basis – a unique development. An executive committee of senior union officials was created and there were additional committees covering finance and an election victory fund. The executive committee was shadowed by a committee of union political officers. At regional level, TUFL, in effect, took over the existing TULV/TUCC structures.

Coordination with the Labour Party was facilitated by party representation on TUFL committees. TUFL also replaced TULV in terms of representation on the party's Campaign Strategy Committee. And within Labour Party headquarters, a Trade Union Liaison Officer was appointed – a political innovation to fill one of the strangest gaps in politics.

As in the past, these interconnections were not without territorial and personal tensions. Further, the potential of the new organisation was held back by a range of difficulties including considerable variations in the commitment of individual unions; a similar point can be made about operations within the various regions of TUFL. Nationally, as always, financial obligations were carried out with varying degrees of enthusiasm. Eventually, 30 of the 35 affiliates paid their 3p per political levy-paying member towards the upkeep of the unit – an income of £162,000.[3]

Alongside this organisational legacy there was no immediately obvious electoral benefit to Labour from the political fund ballots. Neither public opinion polls, nor the by-elections in the period of the ballots, showed any sharp shift of trade unionists to Labour. The party's own private polls conducted by MORI show some remarkable consistencies over the period from Kinnock's election to the winter of 1986–7.[4] In the first three quarters of 1986, Labour support amongst trade unionists averaged 48 per cent – exactly the same as in the first three quarters after Kinnock's election. However, these figures did hide a degree of change in the composition of the trade union vote which had been changing to Labour's disadvantage (from blue collar to white collar) for several years. Retaining support – for whatever reason – probably indicated a small advance amongst members of affiliated unions.

Greenwich mean time and into the election

Then came 26 February 1987 and Greenwich where the SDP won its first by-election from Labour. In this result, there were signs of major disaffect-ation by traditional working-class voters. Further, the by-election was followed by a sudden sharpening of focus on Labour's internal problems with the London Left and on the latter's 'oppressed groups' strategy.[5] A short, sharp burst of well-publicised internal conflict followed. These events taken together appear to have acted as a catalyst with the trade union vote which appears to have fallen, if anything, more rapidly than the party's overall level of support. One private poll is understood to have touched as low as 36 per cent amongst trade unionists at this time.

Subsequently a recovery did take place but Labour never regained its steady upper-forties support in this sector. The unions, like the party, went into the 1987 general election at a psychological and political disadvantage that few thought conceivable in 1986.

From March to May, party and union morale sagged in tune with the opinion polls and with the widely critical reactions to Kinnock's trip to Washington. This situation, plus a sense of *déjà vu*, may well account for the fact that in some unions there was a noticeable lack of *élan*. Even in NALGO, where in January 1986 an attempt was made in the Make People Matter campaign to replicate the resourceful Put People First campaign of 1983, it took nearly four months to get the campaign under way and it failed conspicuously to ignite.

Once under way, it was challenged by Conservative NALGO members who contended that the expenditure was contrary to the 1983 Representation Act (Section 75) and the 1913 Trade Union Act (Section 3). The Court declared it unlawful under the 1913 Act on the grounds that as the union did not possess a political fund, it could not attempt to persuade someone to exercise his or her vote one way or another.[6]

Although there were a lot of 'do-your-own-things' going on in the individual unions, no one union mounted a campaign with the flair of the Telecom union's campaign in 1983. And there was no People's March or similar. The impetus to this kind of mobilising venture had run out in 1983 and no-one had thought of an adequate replacement. The party leadership did not want any resources syphoning off and the TUC, which had had an unhappy experience of supervising the March of 1983, was quite happy to see all political initiatives being left to the party leader. The collective political mobilisation of trade unionists was left to TUFL. The TUC General Council did pass a resolution of support for the Labour Party which pulled in a surprising number of 'neutral' unions, but no action was expected and none followed.

The TUFL campaign

For the period of the general election campaign, a separate Trade Union Unit was set up in Labour Party headquarters with a staff of seven (four from TUFL, two from the Trade Union Liaison Office, and one from the research department of the union TASS). It had a wide-ranging role in relation to mobilising the trade union vote and assisting the party with union resources. It monitored the coordinators, it ensured that the coverage of target seats was actually taking place, it provided trade union speakers, it distributed TUFL literature and it liaised with the party over finance.

The establishment of TUFL as a distinct full-time organisation had meant that a wide and detailed range of preparation had taken place by the time the unit was formed. Not all of it was successful. The election Victory Fund fell short of its target. The sum raised was £3,732,000; the target based on *pro rata* of affiliated membership had been just short of £5 million.[7] The 'day's pay' and 'hour's pay' voluntary appeals produced disappointing results.[8] Training packs had been produced in consultation with the unions and training courses were held in some regions, but the overall amount of detailed training had been limited. However, the main priority and the biggest improvement on 1983 was the early establishment of the campaign organisation in the field.

The TULV regional organisation, which had been created in 1982–3, then passed almost intact to TUCC in 1984, was by now a much smoother and better staffed operation. Target Seat Coordinators, covering over 140 offensive and some defensive seats, were in place in many cases up to eight months before the election began. In some seats, the Target Seat Coordinators had a team of union helpers. Altogether, some 1,300 names were in place by June, formally linked to the constituency parties either through a Trade Union Liaison Officer of the constituency or its secretary or agent.

Region by region, the pattern varied, with the North and North-Western areas and the South-West considered 'good' in terms of their union contribution. The London area was an improvement on 1983 but still not very satisfactory and the West Midlands the worst and very difficult to put together – an extraordinary change from the post-war pattern. Some regions were handicapped by union conflicts over the coordination and operation. Wales had an inter-union dispute between two of the largest unions. Scotland, as usual, had its own distinctive linkage to the Scottish TUC.

Although union by union the input into the campaign was higher than in 1983, the AEU was still the union most complained about in terms of contribution. According to reports from coordinators, the T&GWU and NUPE were the most involved numerically although close observers noted a big improvement in the performance of the GMB and USDAW. Amongst the middle-sized unions, COHSE and TASS were particularly active.

The major organisational improvement on 1983 was still accompanied by a range of weaknesses. TUFL's central organisation reported later that there was a widespread view that the field structure was still set up too late, that in a large percentage of target seats the coordinators did not begin campaigning until well into 1987 and some not until the election was called. Although there was evidence of a big improvement in this coordination at local level compared with the past, the union contribution was still marred by examples of intra-union chauvinism, by a variable union involvement and by the tendency for union business to suddenly intrude – even though commitments had been given for time away from the union. In nearly a third of seats, it was reported to TUFL later, there had been little coordination and planning between the unions.[9]

The TUFL contribution before and during the campaign was serviced by a range of well-produced literature which was far superior to that produced in 1983. The material published in advance of the general election included artwork for leaflets and posters (which unions could adopt or adapt). In the general election campaign, TUFL produced, free of charge to unions, a range of cards, booklets, leaflets, training packs and notes. Each item was cleared with the party before printing – a process which produced some 'creative tensions'. The fact that many unions produced their own, often high quality, material, in addition to that by TUFL, meant that in some cases coordinators were inundated with too much material from too many different sources – and often too late.

The coordination of material into union journals did not work very well in the pre-election period. Front bench speeches were sent to the unions via the PLP Secretariat but it was not always timely, and was patchily used. A Union News Service was launched from the Trade Union Liaison Office just prior to the general election and sent to all affiliates. This was considered to be 'very useful' and was fed into union journals which took up the Labour Party's case in the election period. Most unions ran a special edition urging a vote for the Labour Party.

A first attempt at the stimulation of target mailing to individual trade unionists was only a partial success. Many unions lack up-to-date membership address lists and consequently target mailing took on a wide range of definitions – including personal leafleting. Nevertheless, several unions did begin to take this seriously and as the unions become more capable of locating members, so the technique is likely to grow.

Strategic diversion

The distinctiveness of TUFL lay as much in its strategic focus as in its organisation. The success of the Political Fund ballots had been based on 'campaign contacts' creating a 'two-step-flow' of communication to rank-and-file trade union members at the place of work. TUFL's main electoral concern – at least in the minds of its national officials – was to build upon this process, and move away from the traditional notion that the job of the unions in an election campaign was simply to provide resources. The value of these resources was widely recognised but it was also acknowledged that election work was not the special expertise of union officials and that a more important job of work needed to be done – persuading union members at the place of work to vote Labour.

Thus, TUFL nationally sought to encourage the general election equivalent of the 'campaign contacts'. Unions were asked to appoint a person in every workplace who would be responsible for carrying Labour's message. TUFL's material, including 850,000 copies of 'Briefing to Win', was aimed at these contacts. In practice, there was always uncertainty about this strategic focus amongst the affiliated unions. Many of them, including the most adventurous such as the GMB and USDAW, simply did not feel equipped to tackle the task as prioritised by TUFL officials, and they made the provision of resources their major effort. Each region of TUFL tended to have its own agenda and its own definition of the strategy. And at local level the strategy was also reshaped. In only 22 per cent of the target seats was the mobilisation of trade unionists the main purpose. [10]

There were many reasons for this redefinition of TUFL strategy. The first was simply tradition – unions had for years seen resource assistance as their main electoral function and often simply moved into the old routines. In this, they were reinforced by many of the local parties who had come to expect that a good union contribution was visible in material terms. As TUFL's own report after the election lamented:

> Our general impression at national level was that the Party still sees the unions as the source of cash, cars and canvassers above all else. We were seen to have 'failed' if we did not deliver these in quantity, but scant attention was paid to the need to target trade union members as potential voters. [11]

As for the unions at the grass roots, their willingness to accommodate a TUFL Target Seat Coordinator often fell short of giving him or her full access to information about the location of members – this was true even in places where the union was otherwise playing an involved role in TUFL. The problem of involving the lay membership was compounded by the fact that in many unions the 'campaign contact' system tended to wither once the political fund ballots had been won. And once political activity was seen as party-political activity, there was a diffidence by many shop stewards about their role and there was renewed resistance by members to being pulled into a party campaign. Thus, TUFL, though better linked to the workplace than in 1983, was still essentially 'an organisation of organisers'.

Resistance to politics in the workplace was also encouraged and reinforced by some employers who were now in an industrially stronger position to deny access to union political meetings and other election facilities. In addition, a range of new work development inhibited this direct mobilisation. These days, workplace breaks are shorter, work times are more flexible, and workers increasingly use forms of transport which take them quickly past the workplace gates. The wider travel-to-work area also means that coordination from workplace to political constituency is much more difficult.

Party strategy and the management of 'distance'

Alongside these differences of strategy between unions, national and local, there were tensions between the TUFL approach and the party's own national strategy. TUFL was created at a time when the party's campaigning strategy was moving closer towards influencing 'national opinion formers' and the national media. TUFL's focus on local union opinion formers and local mobilisation was not well integrated into this approach – a position which caused some prickliness at national level and post-election union complaints that at local level the party was not 'seen' to be campaigning.

More complex and more deeply rooted was the tension between TUFL's strategy, based on persuading rank-and-file union members at the place of work that party policy was relevant to them, and the party's management of 'distance' in its relationship with the unions.

The creation of a practical 'space' in the union–party relationship is as old as the relationship itself. The institutions are surrounded by a culture of rule-governed, role-playing behaviour which is concerned to allow each set of institutions – party and unions – to establish a functional autonomy and to keep the confidence of their distinctive constituencies. At different times and in different dimensions of the relationship there are movements towards greater integration and movements towards creating space. The latter are often mistaken (sometimes mischievously, sometimes hopefully) for the primary stages of separation. In fact, the periodic creation of space is part of the subtle flexibility which allows the Labour movement to survive. Since Kinnock's election, but particularly since his triumph at the 1985 Labour Party Conference, there has been a much greater assertion of the autonomy of the party.

Something of the subtlety of the relationship comes across when we consider that alongside a renewed creation of policymaking space in the relationship in the pre-election period, was both a greater campaigning integration *and* a stronger presentation of 'distance' in the relationship.

The integration was quite striking. There had never been an organisation to rival TUFL in its breadth and coordination of union support for the Labour Party, both at national and local level. During the campaign, the Trade Union Unit was more integrated as a functional unit into head office campaigning and feedback processes than any previous trade union effort. Personnel from the unions were also more integrated. A range of union officials were formally seconded to positions in the party's national campaign aiding Walworth Road, the front bench and the party's leader in a much more systematic way than previously. At a more symbolic level, the Leader's Campaign Committee included five union leaders – an effective point of influence had this committee played the role expected of it.

But alongside this new integration was a change in the handling of the unions and union-related issues by the party's communicational management. It was shaped by three major considerations. There was first the need for the party to make a broader appeal than to its union base, given that the numbers were declining in that base. There was, second, the belief that Kinnock must be seen as strong and 'presidential' and therefore supreme in his relations with the unions. Finally, there was the awareness that the party must, if possible, avoid associations with examples or reminders of unacceptable and unpopular industrial styles – particularly those involving picket-line violence and illegality. One key example of such a reminder which the party leader never forgot was the intervention of Arthur Scargill just prior to voting in the Brecon and Radnor by-election, held by some to have cost the party the by-election.

Thus, the general election strategy of the party involved publicly distancing itself from the most electorally damaging associations of the trade union connection. It was not, and in a sense could not be, a distancing from the unions as such. Given the nature of the relationship – particularly the new integration – that would have been (as one union leader put it later) 'like distancing yourself from your left leg'.[12] What this involved in practice was the rejection of any implication of subservience to the TUC and union leaders: it meant encouraging a low party profile for trade union leaders. And it also involved avoiding evocations of potentially harmful associations with some past experiences including 'the winter of discontent' and the Miners' strike – even to some extent 'the old corporatism'. When pressed on such issues as secondary action, mass picketing and the closed shop, the Labour leadership responded to criticism with a clear defence of trade union rights, but these were not issues which the leadership themselves sought to highlight.

This handling of 'distance' was both well understood and, in principle, well received within the TUC where it was seen as a concomitant of autonomy and politically necessary given the unions' own diminished political prestige. The sympathy of the TUC was reinforced by the *realpolitik* of its political situation. The need for a Labour victory produced a remarkable new pre-election loyalism. Kinnock was able to tread and win in areas where no Labour Opposition Leader had dared venture before – union ballots being the most striking example. In the final phases of policymaking, Kinnock's personal ascendancy on crucial issues extended not only to particular policies but also to the mode of policymaking. And it was characteristic of the relationship between the front bench and the TUC that the TUC's threatened boycott of the Job Training Scheme should be postponed because of Labour Party worries that it might be electorally counter-productive.

Even so, the failure of the expected pro-Labour surge to materialise, the tensions raised by a number of internally sensitive issues, and the feeling of being taken for granted, led to some brooding, and muttering, and the occasional digging-in of heels amongst union leaders. In the dark days after Greenwich, their anxieties about the party's trajectory occasionally surfaced in public comments.

There were two general worries from March to May. There was an immediate concern that the party's priorities were not shaping up to the need to win back the working-class vote – indeed, that in some ways the party was getting lost in media-led trivia 'because the press wants to talk about side issues . . . or because some idiot attacks the party leader. The call was 'back to basics".[13]

And there was a more general concern that the manual working-class trade unionists were being sidelined by two alternative strategies for broadening the party's electoral appeal. One from the party leadership appeared to be aimed at a key middle section of white collar workers who were concerned with 'quality of life' issues; the other, from a section of the left, appeared to prioritise 'oppressed groups' – particularly gays, blacks and women (with gays and blacks receiving the most publicity).

In practice, the election campaign did focus on traditional Labour supporters, and trade unionists (with youth and women) were a specially targeted group on the Campaign Committee. And once the campaign began, the anxieties and irritations of trade union leaders were put to one side and replaced in great measure by a new enthusiasm. It was a campaign, handled with skill and organisational efficiency, which appeared light years ahead of 1983. Neil Kinnock himself rose above the adversity of the Spring in a way which excited many erstwhile party critics and sceptics. The 'thousand generations of Kinnocks' speech was a brilliant evocation of working-class roots and of talents unrealised – a reminder both to the traditional working class and to the upwardly mobile. It went down especially well with working-class viewers.[14] The campaign as a whole relied heavily on issues with a strong working-class appeal – particularly on the basic issues of unemployment and the welfare state.

And yet there remained a strategic tension, niggling away. Although one of the innovations of the Kinnock leadership had been the definition of Labour as 'the party of production', issues relating to the place of work were not central to the campaign. The unions found themselves attempting to mobilise at the place of work but alongside a party which appeared to be steering clear of that area in its emphasis. There was always a covert disagreement on this balance – a disagreement which has since come more to the surface. It focusses particularly on the failure of the party to give more prominence to rights at work, to health and safety and to low pay. At a very late stage in the campaign, the Campaign Management Team had sought to redress the balance but by this point, neither the party nor the unions were properly geared up for it.

Nevertheless, during the campaign, union leaders in the main accepted their self-effacing role, saw it as part of a sharing of responsibilities and accepted that in policy terms this was the party's show. Some problems did emerge with the non-affiliated unions. Neither the civil service unions nor the teachers' unions were responsive to appeals from the party to moderate their industrial militancy during the election period. Even amongst affiliated unions, there were some grumbling outbursts. The NUPE leadership's public defence of 'the winter of discontent' at its annual conference was not well received in the party leadership. But, overall, the discipline of the movement held to a remarkable degree.

It would be easy to overstate the extent of the sidelining of trade union leaders in this election. In general, since the early 1950s, union leaders have not played a high profile role in Labour's election campaigns and you have to go back to the special circumstances and special stature of Jack Jones in 1974 to see a union leader playing up front at meetings alongside the politicians. In 1987, union leaders were not much in evidence at press conferences but they did appear on a range of party platforms including the leader's own meetings. That their speeches were barely reported may have been a product of timing – when the TV lights were off – but it was also a reflection of the fact that union leaders and union issues were not generally considered very big news in this election.

This declining interest in industrial relations issues was also reflected in the Trade Union Unit, where requests from within the Labour Party for trade union speakers were estimated to be well down on previous elections. Union leaders were, however, slotted into a variety of regional and local speaking engagements. Some offers to speak were not taken up. Some union leaders jockeyed for position at key regional rallies. Some misunderstandings caused a little bad feeling. But there was no central mechanism of prohibition. Rather, there was a more subtle atmosphere in which 'the word was around' about what was needed, what was not needed and what role trade union leaders were expected to play. As always, some feelings were hurt but the sufferings were generally endured quietly. Arthur Scargill's later public complaints of 'pressure' to prevent him speaking were highly unusual and relate apparently to two incidents, one of which involved a rejection from a marginal seat in an area which had already caused him considerable problems – Nottinghamshire.[15]

Appraisal

In this election, the trade union mobilisation on behalf of the Labour Party continued a development evident since 1979 towards a more coordinated campaign. It built on the organisation and experience of the 1983 general election and the Political Fund ballots, and was more thoroughly integrated into Labour's campaign organisation than in the past. In their final report, the TUFL organisers made the judgement that

> The general impression of almost everyone concerned, including the Labour Party, was that trade union input at all levels was better organised than in previous elections.[16]

It seems to me a fair judgement, especially when placed against TUFL's own frank assessment of shortcomings. In particular, it was conceded that there was still 'too little too late'[17] and that the attempt at a fundamental reorientation of trade union tactical objectives from resource provision to mobilisation at the place of work was a disappointment when compared with the Political Fund ballot experience.

There were many factors at work here reshaping the strategy within individual unions and at local level, including the traditions and expectations of the local parties. Employment and work conditions mediated against the new strategy as did some old-established union prejudices and weaknesses. One deeply-rooted difficulty was the resistance to party-political campaigns at the place of work when compared with the union political campaigns which were more distanced from the party in 1984.

That trade unionism was not as big an issue in the 1987 general election as it had been since the general election of 1970, reflected both the declining industrial power of the unions at the hands of the Conservative government and the management of the issue by Labour's leadership. During the campaign, Conservative and Alliance leaders tried to raise the bogey of the violent picket and of 'trade union bosses in Downing Street' but with little effect. The image handicap of 'extremism' appears to have been a party rather than a union phenomenon. The issue of 'strikes' virtually disappeared.[18] 'Trade unions' came low down in public explanations of Labour failure.[19]

On the other hand, the TUFL strategy of aiming at trade unionists at the place of work – a strategy which has long-term benefits – suffered some handicap in that the Labour Party laid no special emphasis on the kind of work-related issues that trade unionists feel happiest and most authoritative at handling. However, it is doubtful whether this weakness was fundamental when compared with a range of other economic, sociological, political and image factors which reduced Labour's support amongst trade unionists. In particular, as TUFL officials noted, a continuing problem was shown in the feedback over the party's economic credibility, and over taxation policy as it affected trade unionists in the West Midlands and the South.[20]

It must also be noted that for all the effort involved, the evidence indicates that the campaign after the first week did not appear to have been very influential in changing party support.[21] Those first few days, however, may well have been crucial in shaping the future pattern of Opposition politics and there were some indications in the party's private polls that defecting trade unionists were present in greater measure than others in the returners of that period.

Be that as it may, the final result was, as Labour's General Secretary put it, 'disappointing'[22] – particularly when compared with the level of support amongst trade unionists in 1986. As compared with the disastrous performance of 1983, Labour's vote amongst trade unionists rose by only 3 per cent to 42 per cent and amongst manual worker trade unionists by 5 per cent.[23] Amongst this latter group, from which Labour's affiliates are heavily drawn, the party did regain the psychological important level of 51 per cent support. The Conservatives dropped back by 1 per cent to 30 per cent and the Alliance by 4 per cent to 26 per cent.[24] In this sense, the Labour movement had been strengthened, as in 1985.

Notes

1 See Lewis Minkin, 'Against the tide: trade unions, political communication and the 1983 general election', in Ivor Crewe and Martin Harrop (eds.), *Political Communications: The General Election Campaign of 1983* (Cambridge: Cambridge University Press, 1986), pp. 190–206.

2 A typical forecast was 'Union levy poll spells disaster for Labour', *Guardian*, 2 March 1985. In contrast, see Lewin Minkin, 'Polls apart: the union battle to stay in politics', *New Socialist*, 22 (December 1984).

3 Information in this chapter relating to the work and internal politics of Trade Unionists for Labour is derived from interviews with TUFL officials, party officials including the Trade Union Liaison Officer, officials of individual trade unions and local party and union activists. In addition, I have drawn from the report of the TUFL National Coordinator to the TUFL Executive Committee dated July 1987.

4 Private information.

5 Much attention was focussed on a private letter from Neil Kinnock's press secretary, Patricia Hewitt, which was leaked to the press. In it, Hewitt warned that the 'gays and lesbians issue is costing us dear'.

6 'Nalgo's political campaign broke union law', Law Report, *Independent*, 4 June 1987 and Keith Ewing, 'Out of court', *Guardian*, 5 June 1987.

7 TUFL Report, 'Finance Report', part I, p. 1.

8 TUFL Report, 'Finance Report', part I, p. 7.

9 TUFL Report, 'General election questionnaire', p. 1.

10 TUFL Report, 'General election questionnaire', p. 8.

11 TUFL Report, 'The general election', p. 6.

12 John Edmunds, GMB General Secretary, speaking to the *Tribune* Rally, Brighton, 30 September 1987. Author's notes.
13 John Edmunds speaking to the Scottish TUC, quoted in *Labour Weekly*, 24 April 1987.
14 Bob Worcester, 'Trying the food on the dog', *New Statesman*, 24 July 1987, p. 12.
15 'Scargill: I was gagged by Kinnock', *Sunday Times*, 14 June 1987. The main tension is understood to have concerned the Mansfield seat.
16 TUFL Report, 'The general election', p. 1.
17 Minutes of Meeting of TUFL Regional Coordinates and TUFL national union officials, 18 August 1987.
18 Ivor Crewe, 'Tories prosper from a paradox', *Guardian*, 16 June 1987.
19 Gallup Political Index, July 1987, table 72.
20 TUFL Report, 'The general election', p. 11.
21 Crewe, 'Tories prosper from a paradox', *Guardian*, 16 June 1987.
22 Labour Party National Executive Committee Report, 1987, p. 4.
23 MORI/*Sunday Times*, 13 June 1987.
24 MORI/*Sunday Times*, 13 June 1987.

23 Black Sheep?
Race in the 1987 election campaign

The context

'Race' and immigration were not issues in the 1987 general election campaign. Yet their influence may have been greater than at any time since the infamous Smethwick campaign in 1964.[1] And it was in this context that four black[2] candidates finally laid the ghost of Dr David (now Lord) Pitt's defeat in Clapham in 1970.[3]

The influence of race and immigration derived less from specific party political initiatives during the campaign itself than from three developments between 1983 and 1987 which rendered such initiatives largely unnecessary.

The 1983 results finally punctured the myth of 'the Black Vote', which for nearly ten years had had the parties competing for black electoral support.[4] The underlying assumptions that black voters only voted Labour because no other party had made overtures to them and that they voted as an organised group were shattered. Although all parties had made more efforts to woo them than at any previous general election, there was little attrition in black voters' support for the Labour Party; and it was apparent that this attrition was not organised nor was it necessarily racially motivated.[5]

Secondly, the 1985 riots had had an inhibiting effect on the extent to which the parties were prepared to be seen to be courting black people – for electoral or any other purpose. The Government's response to the 1981 riots had been calculated to deflect potentially hostile public reaction on the implicit promise that a recurrrence could be prevented. Once that gamble had not paid off (and, this time, lives were lost) the public was not so easily to be appeased. There was a more marked government disposition squarely to blame the rioters rather than their circumstances. This time, constructive (as distinct from condemnatory or punitive) responses needed to be made with extreme caution and presented in a low key: none should be open to interpretation as 'rewards to the rioters' and – given that the rioters were identified as black – still less should there be any hint of special measures in favour of black people .

Meanwhile, the battle between central and local government had become ever more intense and embittered. Its party political character made it likely that voters in the general election would perceive the Conservatives as the party of central government and Labour as the party of local government. This was especially true of younger voters for whom a Labour government was part of political folklore, beyond the scope of personal recall. Together, the media and Labour's opponents had very effectively replaced this spectre of Labour in government with a more up-to-date bogeyman (or, perhaps, bogeyperson) – that of the 'Looney Left' Labour local authority.

Among the excesses routinely ascribed to such authorities were initiatives associated with their race equality policies. Publicity surrounding the McGoldrick affair in the London Borough of Brent had already been a cause of considerable concern to the Labour leadership.[6] And, in the local election campaign only weeks before the general election, the London Borough of Islington went to court for an injunction against the SDP. The latter were intending, in a party political broadcast, to allege that a small white boy in an Islington nursery school had been reprimanded for singing the nursery rhymes 'Baa Baa Black Sheep' which council policy, the SDP claimed, held to be racist. In the event, the reference was dropped from the catalogue of ridicule presented by John Cleese, but the majority of the remaining references concerned other supposed excesses in the name of racial equality.

Of the three main parties entering the 1987 general election campaign, then, the Labour Party was faced with the starkest dilemmas on issues of race and immigration. Already, from the GLC abolition campaign, from the increasing resentment of CLPs and local authorities in its regional heartlands against 'the London effect' and from the results of the Greenwich by-election,[7] it had become obvious to party managers that it was electorally vulnerable for being too closely identified with unpopular 'minority' causes. It was also evident that the other parties were aware of this and could be expected to exploit it. Further, Labour was at its most vulnerable in the many key marginal seats which stood to be won or lost on white votes. Yet it could not afford to jeopardise its support among black voters. And, apparently set to make history with the election of the first black MPs since the main black immigration to Britain,[8] nor could it afford a poor showing on their part.

Black Sections

Since 1983, moreover, the new Labour leadership's determined pursuit of party unity and discipline had been beset by the campaign for Black Sections – a demand which first appeared on the Conference agenda that year and became an acrimonious annual fixture from then on. Initial attempts to head off trouble by establishing a working party to look at ways of improving black involvement proved counter-productive. Supporters of Black Sections were strongly represented on the working party and its majority report recommended constitutional change to meet their demands. This the NEC opposed and the virulent public denunciations of racism in the Labour Party – and among the party leadership in particular – escalated.

The Black Sections movement was primarily London-based and rapidly attracted support from the left of the party (with the exception of Militant supporters), especially in the capital. There were skirmishes with custodians of the party constitution at both regional and national level over the involvement of Black Section 'delegates' in the selection of MPs – most notably the choice of Russell Profitt in Lewisham East. The best-known black political figures in the Labour Party, including the six likely MPs, all had London bases and were all publicly identified with the campaign.[9] In September 1986, the movement threw in its lot with the newly formed 'hard left' umbrella group, the Campaign Forum.

In popular perception, then, (including that of traditional white Labour Party supporters) the Black Sections movement and those associated with it stood for the London far left 'extremists', with all that already connoted, plus the additional ingredient of politically formalised Black Power. In the usual chicken-and-egg fashion, this perception dovetailed with and was reinforced by media allegations that Neil Kinnock – despite his high-profile onslaught on Militant – was still a prisoner of the left. As *The Daily Express* put it on 9th April 1987, 'Months after the head of the Militant body was cut off, it seems to have sprung up again in the form of defiant black extremists'. Two days later, *The Sun*, forgoing any such palliative allusions to classical mythology, predicted:

> Drowning Neil Kinnock has six months to live as Labour leader ... The Left is already looking for someone to lead a party which will contain more hard-liners, sexual deviants, black extremists and Marxist revolutionaries than ever before.

Following the Greenwich debacle, and faced with the danger of a re-run in the forthcoming local and anticipated national elections, the party leadership appears to have decided that drastic action was called for. In April, Birmingham Labour MPs led by the party deputy leader, Roy Hattersley, publicly wrote to the organisers of a meeting the Black Sections movement intended to hold in the city, to tell them they were not welcome. The thrust of the letter was that, as members of London local authorities, they should have their work cut out sorting out the mess they had got themselves into; Birmingham, by contrast, was doing quite nicely without their advice.[10]

The meeting, however, went ahead and afforded the leadership a further opportunity to take a strong, public, last-ditch stand against the Black Sections movement (and, thereby, all they had come to represent). Sharon

Atkin, the black Labour candidate in Nottingham East, used the occasion – admittedly in particularly strident terms[11] – once again to call the Labour Party racist. By this time there was an increasing rift within the Black Sections movement between Sharon Atkin and Linda Bellos on the one hand and leading members (who included the other main parliamentary candidates) on the other. Indeed, the four candidates standing in winnable seats had already made a public declaration of their support for the leadership only weeks previously. Having by now abandoned hope of winning Nottingham East (and knowing also that the most effective sources of possible protest were neutralised), the NEC decided to debar Sharon Atkin as a candidate and to impose a local Asian councillor (opposed to Black Sections) in her place.

Predictably, the main voice of publicised protest was a solo from Linda Bellos, leader of Lambeth council and herself one of the media's choicest black folk devils. Immediately and very deliberately, she challenged the NEC by repeating the charge of racism against them. But their bluff was not to be called: they were not going to crown the Black Sections movement with martyrdom and they declined to take further action against Linda Bellos. So the Labour Party entered the campaign with the Black Sections issue not so much resolved as in stalemate, in the wake of a burst of publicity which can only have been damaging to its 'image'.

The campaign

Against this background, the campaign proper inevitably saw the parties taking fewer initiatives to woo black voters than in 1983. There was certainly nothing comparable with the Alliance's '7-point Policy Package for the Ethnic Communities' nor the Conservatives' advertisement 'Labour says he's Black – Tories say he's British'. The Labour Party was by now fairly well locked into a tradition of campaigning in black areas and its recently appointed full-time Black and Asian Adviser[12] was responsible, for example, for finding a range of articulate black party supporters to appear on platforms as representative of the multi-racial nature (and appeal) of the party. But such initiatives stopped well short of high profile, race-specific bids to consolidate its black support.

The party manifestos variously reflected the changed climate since 1983 and, in particular, the revived preoccupation with immigration control. This had, predictably, surfaced as part of the public response to the riots but had also been boosted politically by scares about Labour's immigration policy raised during Neil Kinnock's visit to India in May 1986 and by the publicity surrounding the introduction of visas for visitors from black Commonwealth countries and Pakistan in September of the same year.[13] Labour was again branded publicly as 'soft' on immigration, with the Alliance in danger of being found guilty by association.

In their 1983 manifesto, the Conservatives had committed themselves to immigration policies which were 'strict but fair', but implied that no major changes were called for now that their Nationality Act had 'created a secure system of rights and a sound basis for control in the future.' More importantly, this commitment was made in the context of their 'utter opposition to racial discrimination' and their 'determination to see that there is real equality of opportunity.' To the forefront in 1987, however, was the commitment to 'tighten the existing law to ensure that the control over settlement becomes even more effective'. And the government's record of tough action against bogus visitors, illegal immigrants and fraudulent refugees was invoked before any reference was made into the party's aim of ensuring that black people have equal opportunities as citizens – an aim which now included 'accepting their full share of responsibility'. The manifesto referred to racial discrimination as an injustice and expressed particular concern over racial attacks. But it went on to stress that 'Reverse discrimination is itself an injustice' and to warn that ethnic minorities 'will suffer permanent disadvantage if they remain in linguistic and cultural ghettos'.

The Alliance's proposals remained much as they were in the 1983 manifesto, with an additional reference to the question of racial harassment. However, where in 1983 sex and race equality had been treated in parallel, the emphasis in 1987 was squarely on sex equality. And, as with the Conservatives, in 1987 their commitments in the area of racial equality were prefaced by a reference to immigration – specifically 'the Alliance accepts the need for immigration controls', underlined.

The Labour Party in 1987 similarly placed equality for women first among its commitments on 'Enhancing Rights, Increasing Freedom', with a number of specific promises including a Ministry for Women. Next came trade union rights (under the somewhat coy heading 'Democracy in the Workplace') and only then 'Equality for Ethnic Minorities'. Again, the one new commitment was to 'firm action' against racial attacks, and the party's promises were summed up in the manifesto's marginal notes as two-fold: 'Promote racial equality' and 'Firm and fair immigration control'.

Perhaps in an attempt to clarify the distinction between the Labour formulation and the Conservative commitment to immigration control which was 'firm *but* fair', some publicity was given at the beginning of June to a letter from the Home Secretary to Piers Merchant, the Conservative candidate for Newcastle Central.[14] This provided details of the ways in which a new Conservative government would legislate further to curtail rights of entry and to abolish certain immigrants' rights of appeal against removal which were allegedly being 'abused'.

At national level, no further such explicit hint was given of 'the race card' being played. And any temptation to do so might readily have been resisted; for any gains to be made in this area could more effectively be made at the very potent level of party 'image' by specific reference to party policy. Here the die was well and truly cast before the campaign began and the images projected in election broadcasts did no more than reinforce those already prevalent.

Labour's election broadcasts were, of course, dominated by the repeated Kinnock spectacular, whose implicit emphasis on gender equality in the context of 'normal' family life economically reinforced the party's appeal to women while distancing it from the 'Loony Left' association with homosexuality. Through its more routine broadcasts, however, Labour easily retained the record for consistently depicting Britain as a multi-racial society (even if it over-egged the pudding in linking this with images intended to reinforce its position on gender equality). Its education broadcast was the most notable in this respect. Included were shots of Asian girls working in a science class and West Indian boys taking home economics, along with an interview with a black mother complaining about the Conservatives' attitude towards state education.

Black people had a lower profile in the Alliance broadcasts and their function was more ambiguous; the Alliance too interviewed an anonymous black member of the public – a young man who appeared implicitly to threaten further rioting. Under the Conservatives, he said, people saw no future:

> And they're bloody right, basically. It's not a game any more and if somebody doesn't get it right, there won't be any political system: people will do their own thing . . .

The Conservatives' images of black people were markedly different again, and of particular interest. In stock shots, crowd scenes and walkabouts there was little hint – if any – of Britain as a multi-racial society and the black hands shaken by Mrs Thatcher seem exclusively to have belonged to international statesmen. Black people cropped up in Conservative broadcasts, however, with greater frequency than they did in those of the Alliance. But they did so, for the most part, in conjunction with references to the Labour Party. The most remarkable in this respect began with a series of shots of Neil Kinnock (overlaid with Brahms), one of which had isolated from a group scene the image of the Labour leader hand in hand with a young black, their arms raised in triumph. It then cut to John Moore saying 'You have just seen the new Labour Party of Neil Kinnock'. Behind Labour's glossy facade, the argument went, and despite Neil Kinnock's vaunted toughness with Militant, he had endorsed extremists as parliamentary candidates. Five were singled out for special mention of whom two (Bernie Grant and Dianne Abbott) were black; and these were followed by a list of 101 runners-up (as originally selected by the Alliance) which included the remaining black Labour hopefuls. Moving on to demonstrate what difference it would make if Labour got into power,

Moore cited its record in local government, illustrated by an ILEA-suggested reading list for schools which included 'Black Lesbian in White America'. And the broadcast ended with the caption 'Help the Conservatives Stop the Left.'

Whether or how the race card was played locally has not been systematically researched and may never be. In any case, it would be impossible with hindsight to document the way the campaign was waged on the doorsteps. What is certain is that canvassers will have met prejudice against the Labour Party because of its 'image' on race and immigration. But the likelihood of Labour's opponents refusing to exploit this can only be a matter of conjecture.

Black candidates

In 1987 there were 27 black candidates standing for the main political parties – an increase of nine from 1983. The main focus of attention, however, was on the handful of Labour candidates who stood a chance of being elected, although there was the occasional glance in the direction of Conservative candidates John Taylor in Birmingham Perry Barr and Nirj Deva in Hammersmith, both of whom were fighting marginal seats held by Labour.[15]

Ever since their selection, Bernie Grant, Dianne Abbott, Paul Boateng and Russell Profitt in particular had been regularly profiled in the national press. References to them (and to Sharon Atkin and Keith Vaz) consistently dwelt on their 'extremism', their connections with 'Loony Left' London authorities and their support for Black Sections. Thus *The Daily Telegraph* of 1 October 1986 ran the headline 'Why the First Black Woman MP will be Trouble for Labour'. After stating that Dianne Abbott was 'at pains to tell you that she is on the "hard left" of the party', it went on to say that she was press officer for Lambeth Council and

> among the looniest of the left-wing boroughs and a spokesman [sic] for the anti-imperialist, anti-white thoughts of its lesbian feminist, black leader, Linda Bellos. She is a hard line feminist.

In the case of Bernie Grant and Dianne Abbott, the press were further able to point to the fact that they had been selected as a result of '*coups*' against sitting Labour MPs who were themselves already far to the left of the party. And Bernie Grant's notoriety for his remarks during the Tottenham riots of September 1985 had already cast him as Number One Political Hate Figure.

So persistent and potentially damaging was the national publicity they received that the four main London candidates (all of them Afro-Caribbean) approached the Labour Party in mid-April with a statement of their loyalty to the leadership which they wanted issued by party headquarters. This was, in fact, granted and even made the main BBC news on 13 April, but only after the leadership had siezed the initiative for negotiating conditions with them over the future conduct of their candidacy.

Yet the publicity continued in the same vein throughout the campaign itself, with very personal as well as political slurs added in the case of Bernie Grant. In *The Daily Mail* of 6 June, a double page spread was headed 'The Dogs Who Don't Bark' over an article which began:

> Ann Leslie investigates the curious case of some militant Labour candidates who are behaving as if they were standing for a village cricket committee instead of a Labour government . . . She concludes that their silence is definitely temporary.

The main story was illustrated by a photo of Bernie Grant playing cricket, surrounded by black fielders; and Grant was the exemplary 'militant Labour candidate' on whom the article focussed. At least for the duration of the campaign, such candidates were being kept on a tight rein by Walworth Road:

> The 'close watcher' in his [Grant's] case is his ever-protective girl-friend Cllr. Sharon Lawrence . . . a tall, close-lipped blonde with a taste for interesting earrings.

In passing references, the candidates were issued with their 'tags' even where these had no relevance. Thus, a seven-line story about an attack on the Labour Party offices in Hackney North, included:

> An attack on the campaign headquarters of a hard-Left candidate . . . in Hackney North . . . where Black Sections activist Dianne Abbott is a candidate.[16]

Locally, some of the campaigns appear to have been characterised by heightened personal antagonisms between the main black candidates and their chief opponents, with race (explicitly or implicitly) as a factor. Keith Vaz, in Leicester East, seems to have been stung by the imputation that the ethnic composition of the constituency was what had attracted him to it. Russell Profitt obtained a High Court injunction to prevent his Conservative rival issuing a leaflet and newsletter claiming that he was in favour of uncontrolled immigration. Dianne Abbott issued a writ against her Conservative opponent and claimed that the Alliance candidate was running a racist campaign against her. And Bernie Grant's Conservative opposite number caused a furore at an election meeting in Haringey's Indian Culture Centre when he claimed that 'The biggest group who are discriminated against over the right to buy [their council homes] are West Indian women whose men have left them', a reference which had personal as well as racial implications.

Most, however, would not claim that the main thrust of the campaign against them was racist. 'Extremism' was the common theme, with the addition in Bernie Grant's case of the gays and lesbians issue which, in Haringey, was the subject of a well-organised parents' campaign and threatened his popularity with sections of the black communities. Indeed, a leading Conservative in one of the constituencies in question confided to me:

> Actually, I feel rather sorry for X. You see, as a person I quite like him . . . and his politics aren't nearly as extreme as I'm telling people on the doorsteps they are.

In the circumstances, it was hardly surprising that many of the Labour black candidates (and Dianne Abbott and Bernie Grant in particular) suffered swings against them (see tables 23.1 and 23.2). The degree to which these may be attributed to a racist backlash against them personally, or to the inordinate hostile publicity they had received, or to their 'extremism', is impossible to tell. But it is worth noting that other Labour candidates occasionally yielded equally bad results for which their colour could not offer a ready-made 'explanation'. Thus, while Labour's share of the vote in Brent South dropped by 1.4 per cent, in Brent East – where Ken Livingstone had ousted the sitting MP Reg Freeson – it dropped by 4.4 per cent. And Dianne Abbott's result, which was 3.3 per cent down on Labour's vote in 1983, almost exactly matched the drop for Mildred Gordon in neighbouring Bow and Poplar.

Outside London, there was a good result in Leicester East, where Keith Vaz regained the seat lost by Labour in 1983. And, ironically in view of the NEC's pessimism, despite the recent difficulties, there was a swing to Labour also in Nottingham East.

Alongside these mixed results for Labour's black candidates, however, it is particularly interesting to note that *all* of the black candidates for the Conservative and Alliance parties, with one exception, suffered swings against them. The numbers of Conservative and Alliance candidates are relatively small and, as with Labour candidates, local factors may significantly have influenced certain results. M. Moghal, for example, suffered a 15.7 per cent drop in the Alliance vote in Bradford West (thus significantly affecting the average results for all black Alliance candidates); but this was the seat contested in 1983 by Edward Lyons, the sitting MP who had switched from Labour to the SDP. P. Nischal held the Conservative vote exactly to its 1983 level in Birmingham Small Heath when he had also been the candidate. No firm conclusions may safely be drawn, then, but the apparently worse results for Conservative and Alliance black candidates do give pause for thought. While the Labour Party as a whole (and, by extension, its candidates generally) may have suffered the effects of racism in 1987, it is possible that racism had implications for the other parties also in as much as it selectively undermined the chances of their black candidates.

Table 23.1. *Afro-Caribbean and Asian parliamentary candidates, 1987*

Candidate	Constituency	Swing (%)
Conservative		
R. Chandran	Preston	4.5 to Lab.
N. Deva	Hammersmith	4.5 to Lab.
N. Khan	Birmingham Sparkbrook	1.6 to Lab.
K. Nath	M. Blackley	4.1 to Lab.
P. Nischal	Birmingham Small Heath	1.6 to Lab.
J. Taylor	Birmingham Perry Barr	0.4 to Con.
Labour		
D. Abbott*	Hackney N.	1.8 to Con.
V. Anand	Folkestone	0.5 to Con.
M. Aslam	Nottingham E.	1.5 to Lab.
P. Boateng*	Brent S.	3.4 to Con.
B. Bousquet	Kensington	1.1 to Lab.
B. Grant*	Tottenham	6.8 to Con.
N. Hafeez	Stafford	1.2 to Con.
A. Patel	Eastbourne	0.5 to Lab.
P. Patel	Brent N.	0.9 to Con.
R. Profitt	Lewisham E.	3.2 to Con.
C. St. Hill	Mid-Staffs	1.9 to Lab.
M. Savani	Sheffield Hallam	2.5 to Lab.
K. Vaz*	Leicester E.	2.8 to Lab
V. Vaz	Twickenham	0.3 to Con.
Alliance		
M. Ali	Blackburn	4.8 to Lab.
B. Chahal	Liverpool Riverside	5.5 to Lab.
S. Fernando	Nottingham N.	7.0 to Lab.
Z. Gifford	Harrow E.	5.0 to Con.
L. Kamal	Wakefield	6.7 to Lab.
M. Moghal	Bradford W.	13.8 to Lab.
G. Sangha	Birmingham Ladywood	8.9 to Lab.

* elected

Table 23.2. *Black candidates' results compared with regional swing*

	% actual vote	% projected vote (on regional swing)	Difference
Seats fought by 5 Conservative candidates	31.60	34.14	−2.54
Seats fought by 14 Labour candidates	29.68	31.62	−1.94
Seats fought by 7 Alliance candidates	12.67	17.90	−5.23

Source: MORI British Public Opinion, August 1987

Table 23.3. *Afro-Caribbean and Asian voting intentions 1987*

Party	All	Concentration		A–C	Asian
		High	Low		
	%	%	%	%	%
Conservative	18	15	39	6	23
Labour	72	77	43	86	67
Alliance	10	8	17	7	10
	100	100	100	100	100

Source: Harris Research Centre Political Attitudes Survey for *Caribbean Africa and Asian Times*. Conducted 25–29 May 1987. The sample as a whole was weighted heavily towards Asian respondents (of whom there were 707, compared with 299 Afro-Caribbeans); 136 of the total sample lived in areas of low concentration; and, of these, all but three were Asian.

Black voters

Almost unnoticed now, black voters seem to have continued massively to support the Labour Party, although slippage continued among Asian voters and may be a pointer to the future. By tradition, however, there are public warnings of mass defections – even though politicians increasingly dismiss these as 'crying wolf' – and three such instances in 1987 call for comment.

The first was the publicity which surrounded a survey commissioned by the *Caribbean Africa and Asian Times* which was conducted by the Harris Research Centre and published on 2 June. This produced headlines such as 'Black Support for Labour Slipping' (*Independent*, 3 June) and a post-mortem on 'the swing to the Tories among Britain's blacks' (*Guardian* 19 June). In fact, the poll *for the first time* sampled black respondents in areas of low ethnic minority concentration; and it was here that a significant non-Labour black vote began to be revealed,[17] as table 23.3 shows.

The two other 'scares' concerned individual constituencies but also received national publicity. The first, inevitably, was Nottingham East where Sharon Atkin's supporters warned of the huge damage done to Labour by the NEC's action. As table 23.1 shows, the results suggested little evidence of this: M. Aslam, in fact, increased Labour's share of the vote by 4.9 per cent.

The second 'threat' was to Roy Hattersley in Birmingham Sparkbrook where, in May, a number of Asian Labour party members resigned, warning of massive Asian disillusion with Labour. At the same time, some Moslem religious leaders in the city were reported as urging their followers to support one of their own and vote for the Conservative candidate, Nasir Khan. In the event, there was no evidence of the Conservatives benefiting: their vote dropped by 2.2 per cent, slightly more than the average (0.6 per cent) for the West Midlands region.

Only detailed local studies of black people at the polls in constituencies which had similarly been surveyed in 1983 could demonstrate trends in black party support and their impact – if any – on local results. This time, none had been undertaken. But the Harris survey does confirm earlier suggestions that black voters may be more likely to turn out where there is a black candidate standing for the party they usually support.[18] Were this the case, it could, of course, mask the extent of white backlash against such candidates in areas where the black electorate was significant *and* where their turnout was significantly enhanced. Given a marked trend to abstain among Afro-Caribbeans,[19] one would expect any such effect to show up in constituencies with black Labour candidates and a relatively high proportion of Afro-Caribbean voters. However, in the two instances which met these criteria in 1987, no obvious conclusions can be drawn. Turnout in Hackney North (black population 31 per cent) was up 3 percentage points on 1983; but in Brent South (black population 46 per cent, the highest in the country) the rise was only just over 1 percentage point. Both, in any case, are constituencies with large Labour majorities and the results would not have been significantly affected even had such an effect been noticeable. Of more interest, however, was the Conservative marginal of Leicester East where Asian voters seem to have demonstrated an extraordinary level of support for Keith Vaz and where the turnout rose by over 5 percentage points.

The issue of black sections appears to have had a far more potent effect on Labour's standing with white voters (see above) than on its black support.[20] There is now evidence that black people who have any opinion on the subject tend, on balance, to disapprove of black sections (see table 23.4). But it is unreasonable to assume that these opinions had a significant influence on their support for Labour, especially as the main drop was among Asians who were, according to Harris, less likely to approve of black sections.[21]

The potential for an anti-Labour vote based on this form of 'coded' or 'sanitised' racism[22] was vigorously cultivated by the popular press throughout the 1983–7 parliament, and intensified after the riots of 1985. Its main guises were references to its two main targets – Labour-controlled local authorities and black Labour parliamentary candidates. And Conservatives, both inside and outside parliament, actively fuelled the fire. By the time of the general election, it was inconceivable that they would forego the electoral advantage thus created.

In the 1987 campaign, then, the race card was played again in British politics, but this time the card had a non-racial gloss and was palmed with unprecedented skill. It has put Labour on the defensive about its commitments on racial equality and may further have undermined black politicians' chances in British national politics. Ironically – and unnoticed amid the fanfare (however discordant) about the election of four new black MPs in 1987 – there was already a black MP at Westminster. Jonathan Sayeed – who is half Indian – fought the 1983 general election on a straight party platform,

Table 23.4. *Afro-Caribbean and Asian attitudes to setting up Black Sections in the Labour Party*

	All	Concentration		A–C	Asian
		High	Low		
	%	%	%	%	%
Approve	33	36	20	39	31
Disapprove	45	43	58	44	46
DK	21	21	22	17	23
	100	100	100	100	100

Source: Harris Political Attitudes Survey

eschewing any reference to his race. He beat Labour's Tony Benn to win Bristol East for the Conservatives. Had he not been able to pass as white, had the media highlighted his ethnic origin, had his political opponents chosen to exploit it, and had he been standing as a new candidate in the changed climate of 1987, it is possible that his chances would have been less than even.

For the future, it would appear that there are Asian votes to be won over by the Conservatives, particularly in areas of low black concentration. On balance, however, there are more votes to be gained from white people alienated by the identification of race equality policies and black politicians with the 'extreme left' of the Labour Party.'

Notes

1 Peter Griffiths won the seat with a swing of 7.5 per cent to the Conservatives after a campaign in which the slogan 'If you want a nigger for a neighbour, vote Labour' was used.

2 The term 'black' is used throughout to refer to people of Afro-Caribbean or Asian ethnic origin, except where it is necessary to differentiate between and within the groups collectively referred to as 'black'.

3 According to Lord Pitt, his opponents canvassed Labour supporters saying 'You're not really going to vote for a black man, are you?' (Personal interview, 1983).

4 The argument was first publicised in the Community Relations Commission's *Participation of Ethnic Minorities in the General Election, October 1974* (London: Community Relations Commission, 1975).

5 According to the BBC Gallup poll, 21 per cent of black Labour supporters defected in 1987, compared with 31 per cent overall. It suggested that no fewer than 64 per cent of black voters supported Labour.

6 A primary head teacher, Ms Maureen McGoldrick, was suspended after allegedly saying she did not want any more black teachers. See M. Fitzgerald, 'Immigration and race relations: political aspects-No. 16', *New Community*, 13 (1987), 442–9.

7 On 26 February, Rosie Barnes turned a Labour majority of 1,211 into an SDP majority of 6,611 after Labour had run a 'hard left' candidate against the wishes of the leadership.

8 There were three Asian MPs before the period of post-war immigration, the last of whom, S. Saklatvala, represented Battersea between 1924 and 1929.

9 Paul Boateng had been a GLC councillor; Bernie Grant was Labour Leader of Haringey Council; Dianne Abbott and Sharon Atkin were councillors in Westminster and Lambeth respectively; Russell Profitt had been a councillor in Lewisham and was Principal Race Adviser in Brent; and Keith Vaz (the only non-councillor among them) had stood as parliamentary candidate for his own constituency of Richmond in 1983 and had worked for Islington Council.

10 The letter, addressed to Linda Bellos, read:
We understand that you are coming to Birmingham on Tuesday 7 April to attend a meeting organised by a small, unrepresentative group of people who claim to be concerned about the problems of some ethnic communities within our city.

As Labour MPs in Birmingham, fully committed to racial equality and ending discrimination, we want to make it clear that neither Birmingham District Labour Party nor the city council needs any advice from you or Haringey and Lambeth councils.

Indeed, we would have thought that you had more than enough to do in your own area
. . .
But if you do have spare time, you should come to Birmingham to learn how a sensible and progressive council . . . is dealing with this problem instead of coming to give us the doubtful benefit of your advice.

11 She is alleged to have said the Labour Party had black blood on its hands.

12 The full-time post was created to service Labour's Black and Asian Advisory Committee which the NEC set up after rejecting the working party report on Black Sections.

13 See M. FitzGerald, 'Immigration and race relations political aspects – no. 16'.

14 *Daily Mail, Sun*, 20 May 1987; *Times, Today, Daily Telegraph*, 1 June 1987.

15 Birmingham's Perry Barr was a particularly good result for Labour in 1983 and would have required a 7.3 per cent swing for the Conservatives to win in 1987, whereas Hammersmith only needed 3.1 per cent.

16 *Daily Mail*, 6 June 1987.

17 However, a GLC political attitudes survey of Londoners in 1984 had already suggested much higher levels of Conservative support among East African Asians than other black groups. But Asians from the Indian subcontinent in the top socio-economic group were more likely than matched white voters to have switched party between 1979 and 1983.

18 The GLC survey found 22 per cent of both Afro-Caribbean and Asian respondents saying they would be more likely to vote if they had a black candidate to vote for; Harris's figures were 38 per cent and 30 per cent respectively.

19 See M. Fitzgerald, *Black People and Party Politics in Britain*, Runnymede Trust, 1987, pp. 6–7.

20 A MORI poll for Midlands Independent Radio of 761 voters in Midlands marginal seats during the campaign showed that 73 per cent of respondents disapproved of the idea of Black Sections in the Labour Party. (The figure for Labour voters was 63 per cent.)

21 In a larger survey conducted in October 1984, Harris found that only 18 per cent of both Asians and Afro-Caribbeans agreed that it was 'right' for political parties to set up sections exclusively for Black and Asian supporters.

22 See Frank Reeves, *British Racial Discourse* (Cambridge: Cambridge University Press), pp. 189ff.

NINA FISHMAN and ANDREW SHAW

24 TV87: The campaign to make tactical voting make votes count

The months leading up to the 1987 general election witnessed the greatest ever level of publicity for 'tactical voting'. The phenomenon itself was not remotely new nor had it just been discovered, although some may have mistakenly believed this to be the case. However, the existence of an organised campaign promoting a particular tactical voting strategy was original. Known as TV87, it was formed to encourage tactical voting with the objective of producing a more representative House of Commons and thus preventing Mrs Thatcher forming a third government on the basis of a minority of the popular vote.

This paper discusses TV87's campaign. We avoid details on the political beliefs and arguments underlying the campaign, or on the merits of the overall strategy, since this was debated extensively prior to the election. Instead we concentrate on the development of TV87's activities and comment on certain difficulties which were encountered. We also offer a brief evaluation, in the light of the results, of aspects of TV87's campaign and conclude with a summary of the significance of tactical voting in the 1987 election.

Formation and launch

The origins of TV87 can be traced back to the last months of 1986. It was then that the Conservative Party re-established a lead in the opinion polls. The likelihood of Mrs Thatcher securing a third term seemed high. However, the Conservatives continued to command the support of well under one-half of the electorate. In this political environment the concept of tactical voting attracted serious consideration as a possible means of preventing another victory for the largest minority.

TV87 was formed in January, 1987 following letters to *The Guardian* by Nina Fishman and then Paul Ekins (with Jeremy Seabrook).[1] As others committed their support a Steering Committee was formed, which collectively gave direction to a campaign with three main foci. Firstly, national publicity was clearly required to raise awareness of both the concept of tactical voting and TV87's specific objectives. This would aim to provide the foundation for the second and central task of disseminating information about the crucial Conservative marginal constituencies where tactical voting could prove decisive. This meant producing a list of these vulnerable seats, with accompanying recommendations about which opposition party to support. Thirdly, the potential benefits of local activity were recognised. This might involve persuading candidates to use TV87's endorsement: letters and phone-calls by supporters to the local media; canvassing on the doorstep; and the promotion of constituency opinion polls.

The public launch of TV87 on 11 February promoted the straightforward theme of the campaign: tactical voting could make votes count in the crucial Conservative marginals and the relevant electoral information should be made available to the public for their consideration. Substantial media coverage resulted, followed by broadcasts which examined the potential of tactical voting in detail. It was shown that large numbers of people understood tactical voting and that in the coming general election many were likely to use their vote in this way.

In the light of the launch, good legal advice was obtained on the implications of the Representation of the People Act for TV87. This was vital not only to ensure that TV87 fulfilled its commitment to work within the law, but also because of the reaction of some Conservatives to the emergence of the organisation. Although the running of a general campaign for tactical voting to beat the Conservatives was clearly lawful, in individual constituencies TV87 could not campaign in a way that meant spending money without the consent of the chosen candidate's agent. Any such expenditure had to be included in details of the candidate's election expenses.

Meanwhile, TV87's list of supporters and available funds were growing steadily.[2] Supporters began to put their viewpoint across through the local media. In April, regional press conferences were held in Manchester, Bristol and Birmingham and on the day Nina Fishman brought greetings to the Edinburgh launch of The Campaign for a Tory-free Scotland, TV87's sister Scottish organisation, Mrs Thatcher named the election day.

The election campaign

By the time the election date was set, TV87's campaign was developing along the lines of the original strategy. The following sections explain and examine each of TV87's areas of activity in turn. Since an autonomous Scottish campaign had been established and a Welsh organiser appointed for the principality, we do not deal with Scotland and Wales in detail, although

TV87 in London was responsible for British-wide media coverage and for any coordination between these groups.

The list of target seats

The TV87 list or index of target seats aimed to be the best source of advice to anti-Thatcher voters who were considering a tactical vote. The objective was to provide a full list of Conservative-held seats in which tactical votes might help to secure victory for an opposition party, with recommendations stating, where possible, which of these parties had the best chance of success in each case. In compiling this list, the opposition parties were to be treated with complete impartiality.

The first list produced for TV87's public launch demonstrated the concept of supplying information at the constituency level on seats which, collectively, would be crucial to the election outcome.[3] At that time it was obviously far from certain that there would be a June poll and so it was most sensible to provide a lengthy list based on the 1983 election results. TV87 made it clear that there would be a second, more definitive list for the election campaign, although this would clearly draw upon the experience of the first. Thus, we concentrate here upon the second list (hereafter simply the list).[4]

Over 250 seats in England were considered for inclusion in the list of target seats. In effect, there are two distinct questions involved in drawing up such a list – 'who is running second?' and 'is this seat a realistic target?' This may seem obvious but amidst the work to determine who is the leading challenger it is easy to overlook the fact that the seat may be effectively safe for the Conservatives.

A basic assumption behind the list was a fall in the Conservative share of the vote of at least 3 per cent from its 1983 figure. In this circumstance a significant amount of tactical voting could make the difference between a Conservative majority and a hung parliament. It certainly seemed possible that the Conservatives would lose this proportion of votes; indeed, to many it appeared likely, as the polls put the Conservatives, on average, over three per cent below their level of support during the 1983 campaign. Secondly, it was assumed that Alliance voters would be more likely to switch to Labour than to Conservative, even if only marginally. Fortunately, poll findings continued to indicate that this was indeed true.[5]

The 1983 results provided the base for the analysis, as net changes in the parties' support since then appeared to be small. From these results models of change on the basis of uniform swing were produced in conjunction with figures about the amount of tactical voting, as a percentage of third party support, which would be needed to unseat the Conservatives. This was useful as an initial assessment of the prospects in each seat.

Although the 1983 results were the best base, they had to be checked to identify those which were in some way unusual and so did not provide a reliable guide to the present. This was done using regression estimates of the shares of the vote each party might have been expected to get in each seat on the basis of its social structure, with an adjustment being made for the average regional effect. In addition, the 1983 results were compared to the notional 1979 figures to check for changes which were out of the ordinary. Thus seats were identified which appeared either more or less vulnerable than the 1983 results suggested.

These data were enhanced by considering regional trends since 1983, as recorded by the Marplan 9000 in April 1987, which provided what turned out to be a good indicator of relative regional strengths.

Next, local election results were used as important evidence of the standing of the parties in many individual seats. TV87 collected what was almost certainly the most extensive set of May 1987 results aggregated at the constituency level, with the possible exception of the party HQs. For London, the most recent figures were those of May 1986. Although these figures indicated the change since 1983 in the relative support for the opposition parties in certain seats, they could not properly help to diminish the uncertainty about the overall situation in the capital.

Overall, the 1987 figures were useful, but not uniformly so. For example, given a knowledge of the local results it was not such a surprise that the Alliance managed to increase its share of the vote in Eastleigh, Leeds North-West, and Wyre Forest; equally, good Labour performances in Oxford East, Rossendale and Darwen and Wallasey were preceded by strong local showings; and an inkling that the Conservatives would easily hold Bury North, Keighley and Norfolk North-West could be found in the local results. Yet in other cases there seemed to be no benefit derived from increased support in local elections, which were thus only able to mislead.[6]

Finally, special local factors were considered, such as the retirement of the sitting MP. These local factors, however, did not include subjective judgements about the candidates who were fighting the seat for the opposition parties.

With the different pieces of evidence available about the seats *a judgement* had then to be made about which party was the leading challenger in each and how good a prospect (or 'winnable') it was.[7] At this stage, the stated commitment to treat the opposition parties even-handedly becomes influential, since it was judged that this was best fulfilled by including an equal number of recommendations for Labour and the Alliance. Thus one had to decide how many target seats would be listed for each;[8] how bold to be with difficult decisions; and also how to deal with the seats where the opposition parties really could not be separated at that stage.

It was to cope with such problems that the list was divided into two parts. This had a number of advantages: 1) attention could be focussed upon the

Table 24.1. *Target seats in the 1987 general election*

	Labour	Alliance	Local poll crucial	Total
Key targets (main list)	52	52	8	112
Worth a good fight (subsidiary list)	26	26	18	70

100–125 crucial seats without dropping altogether other 'hopefuls'; 2) bold decisions could be made for the main list while 'playing safe' in the second – there was little point in provoking arguments about marginal judgements on seats which the Conservatives would probably hold with ease anyway; 3) dividing the list in two provided flexibility, since seats could be promoted from the subsidiary list to the 'main battleground', if and when evidence came to light to justify this. The list was finalised on 17 May and published in the *New Statesman* on 22 May.[9] Offprints were distributed to many journalists and to TV87 supporters. The breakdown of seats in England was as shown in table 24.1.

The decision to put the label 'local poll crucial' to seats in which a recommendation was not to be made at that stage was done to tie in with TV87's promotion of constituency opinion polling and to identify the seats where it was most important for this to be done. The term was also used in the subsidiary list, but in the event most of these seats were easily retained by the Conservatives.

Initial protests about the recommendations were certainly less than anticipated. This may have been due to the limited amount of publicity received and the preoccupation of those concerned with their own campaign. Yet we were often surprised at the level of awareness of the recommendations. Certainly, most if not all of the 'contentious' decisions were soon 'brought to our attention', which tends to suggest that there was little dissent about the judgements which were not challenged.

The list was never viewed as a 'tablet of stone'. TV87 was prepared to make amendments and correct errors wherever new evidence made a convincing case for doing so. The fact that the campaign developed so as to put Labour about 10 points ahead of the Alliance naturally affected the recommendations. Yet out of 112 'key targets' TV87 decided that it had to swap sides in only two – Calder Valley and Stockport.[10] The general position in the other 50 Alliance key targets was summed up in a press release issued on 8 June: 'Despite their poor showing nationally, the Alliance is still the party best able to defeat the Conservatives in all other seats designated Alliance 'key targets' . . . In these seats, increased Labour support at the expense of the Alliance only means the main opposition party is further behind the Conservatives. This simply makes it more likely that the Conservatives will win them again.'

In the 'local poll crucial' target seats, we pointed out as polling day neared that Labour could generally be expected to be running second. We advised looking at the late polls in Cambridge and Norwich South and said that TV87 could not give a recommendation in just one of the 112 key targets, Erith and Crayford.[11]

TV87 and the media

Given that TV87's campaign relied on the media, the relationship with these organisations and their treatment of TV87 was of central importance. Summed up simply, TV87 received a good deal of attention in the run-up to the campaign and in the very early stages of it, but little coverage as 11 June approached. This was not altogether surprising, although in consequence there was less interest at a national level in the revised list of targets seats than we might have hoped for. Hence, getting specific information over to the electorate about individual constituencies was very troublesome. However, the problems were partially offset by the number of local newspapers and, at first, local radio stations who covered TV87's campaign.

Attempts were made to counteract TV87's diminishing national profile by continuing to provide the national media with letters and frequent TV87 press releases. Along with campaign updates, the latter attempted to capture attention by providing interesting, well researched, information. For example, the 'tactical factor' was introduced, providing a simple measure indicating the level of tactical voting required to deprive Mrs Thatcher of a third term. We also pointed out that extensive tactical voting could affect the election result while hardly altering the overall shares of the vote obtained by the parties, which undermined one of the arguments raised against the strategy. In addition, some keen supporters issued press releases about their own areas.

However, the national media appeared to focus on the image of a single three-horse race, making it difficult to impart constituency-level information to the electorate. Of course, in most constituencies the standing of the parties is quite different to that which prevails nationally. In deciding how to use their quadrennial cross, voters can clearly be put in a dilemma by a combination of national and local factors. This consequence of the British electoral system was not, we believe, adequately reflected in the amount of reliable information about individual seats which was reported.

In view of this, it is perhaps not so surprising that according to the *Newsnight* Election Panel the campaign produced only a slight increase in awareness of the basic electoral facts about the constituencies in which voters lived. At the outset of the campaign, 51 per cent of Labour supporters in Conservative–Alliance seats thought that Labour would finish first or second in their constituency. The equivalent figure for Alliance supporters in

Conservative–Labour seats was 48 per cent. By the last week-end of the campaign the former figure had not changed significantly (49 per cent), whilst the latter had fallen to 30 per cent.[12] In other words, as polling day approached up to half of those intending to vote Labour in Conservative–Alliance seats believed that Labour would not be behind both the other two main parties and over half of those actually thought Labour would win! For these voters, there was no logic in considering a tactical anti-Thatcher vote.

A further issue was raised by the treatment of TV87 by the broadcasting media, particularly the BBC. It became clear that the framework within which the BBC was organising its election coverage was unable to cope with an organisation which was not affiliated with or solely working in support of a single party, but which was openly campaigning in opposition to a particular party.[13] There did not seem to be any idea of how to count time spent covering TV87 in the equations used to ensure balance between the parties. Because the system could not cope, TV87 was effectively 'off-air' from sometime early in the campaign onwards.

It may be that as the election campaign progressed TV87 was judged not to be 'newsworthy'. In view of the earlier coverage, and the potential extent of tactical voting shown by the campaign polls, we wonder whether this was the case. Nevertheless, we certainly do not dispute the right of those with the editorial responsibility to make such judgements.

Our more fundamental concern is whether the broadcasting media should be closed to non-party groups which attempt to impart information to the electorate and to persuade them of the merits of a specific voting strategy. As far as we can infer, TV87 representatives would not have been interviewed as election day approached, whatever the extent or impact of the campaign. Should only those seeking election have access to the public through the broadcasting media during election campaigns, or does a genuine democracy demand a more open structure? And if so, what framework should govern the process so as to ensure both a fair hearing for all concerned and the maintenance of the impartiality of the broadcasting media?

Candidates and supporters

Candidates representing the party named by TV87 as most likely to defeat the Conservatives in the key target seats were offered TV87's endorsement, help where possible and the use of a logo kit of materials. TV87 could not make great efforts to cultivate the candidates, simply because it had neither the time nor the resources to do so. Yet, to our knowledge, TV87 had a specific involvement in at least 18 seats.[14] For example, TV87 representatives accepted invitations to speak in four constituencies in support of recommended candidates; over half-a-dozen candidates made use of TV87's recommendation in election leaflets; and in a few places TV87 supporters organised canvasses with the agreement of the candidate, whereby attempts were made to persuade those identified as intending to vote for the third-placed party of the merits of tactical voting.

TV87 supporters were encouraged to do what they could at local level. They had been supplied with a 'supporters' pack' containing suggestions for activity and details of the legal constraints upon them. Since large institutional funding was not obtained, it is only because of the commitment of these people that TV87 was able to campaign right up to 11 June. And many were more than willing to back up their financial support with campaigning work of their own. Coordinators were appointed in as many areas as possible, enabling them to contact local media and other TV87 supporters in the area on TV87's behalf. This enthusiasm produced local press conferences and press releases along with some of the canvassing and leaflets mentioned above. The potential importance of such activity to the latter stages of the campaign became apparent as the national organisation found it much harder to achieve media coverage.

Constituency opinion polls

TV87 encouraged polling as a means of establishing the 'tactical position'. The importance of the quality of any such polls was emphasised, since they provide information which some of the electorate are likely to take into account when voting (or choosing not to bother). Indeed, for the purpose of tactical voting this was the very objective. However, TV87's promotion of local opinion polling proved troublesome for three reasons.

Firstly, the resources available did not stretch to promoting constituency polling in a thorough and coordinated manner. Literature included reference to the advantages of a poll and when asked to explain TV87's campaign we were able to introduce this element, but little beyond that was possible.

Secondly, whilst some organisations, such as Granada TV, took the opportunity to enhance the information they provided to the public by commissioning polls in selected marginal seats, many did not consider this part of their responsibilities. So, in our view, far too few constituency polls were conducted.

The third problem arose unexpectedly during the campaign. The Harris organisation produced figures for Calder Valley which were frankly incredible – Labour on 45 per cent and the Conservatives on just 30 per cent. This placed TV87 in a difficult position. It would have been hard to attack a poll published by such a major agency without seeming to question the validity of all such polls – 'Yes, local polls are crucial, but this one just happens to be wrong' is hardly convincing, especially as we had no evidence in support.[15] Yet these figures certainly raised doubts about the reliability of constituency polls.[16] In retrospect, the *overall* record of the constituency polls was not so poor.[17] However, since a misleading poll is worse than no poll at all, the validity of constituency polls remains a matter of serious concern.

Evaluation and impact

It is quite impossible to analyse the election results to assess TV87's impact. Tactical voting has a long history and it is certain that many people would have voted tactically on 11 June if there had been no organised campaign to promote its merits, nor any media coverage of the concept.

However, the attention tactical voting received indicated that it was 'an issue' in the 1987 election. The fact that this was so may be regarded as a significant achievement for TV87. The coverage attracted by TV87's launch suggests both that there was a good deal of underlying interest to be tapped and that TV87 did play a major role in bringing tactical voting to the forefront of political debate. Yet once again, without knowing what might have happened otherwise, TV87's precise importance is difficult to assess. For example, one cannot say whether or not *Today* and *The Observer* would have published their own lists of seats with recommendations for tactical voting had not TV87 provided the lead.

What we can do is to comment upon the accuracy of the list of target seats in its own terms; and to review the overall impact of tactical voting.

The list can be evaluated in the light of the results by examining both the individual recommendations and whether the group of key targets contained the right seats on the basis of the original criteria. However, although the vast majority of decisions were clearly right and a few wrong, it is difficult to make a definitive judgement in all cases. Defining the criteria for establishing a 'wrong' decision is problematic. For example, the fact that the recommended party occasionally finished behind the other opposition party is not a satisfactory criterion. The fact that the Alliance is the second choice of far more Labour voters than Labour is of Alliance voters should be taken into account when assessing the 'tactical position'.[18] However, for the record, there were eleven listed seats in England where it was recommended to vote for the Alliance, but Labour actually finished second. Eight were key targets, with three in the subsidiary list. In three cases, we acknowledged the error during the campaign and changed the advice. In six of the other eight it is a matter of debate whether the recommendation was 'right' or 'wrong'.[19] Finally, in Birmingham Yardley and Pendle the Alliance was recommended on the basis of the local election results. The Alliance did manage to increase its vote very slightly in each, but Labour proved to be the leading challenger, as was shown in Yardley by a late opinion poll.

Judging which seats actually constituted the best prospects is no less difficult. In the case of the Alliance targets in particular, the conclusion one draws about a seat can vary wildly depending on which set of statistics, all

Table 24.2. *The poorer results in key targets and better results in subsidiary list seats (with the change in the Conservative lead over the relevant party, as a percentage of the total vote, in brackets)*

Poorer results in key targets		Better results from subsidiary list	
Labour targets			
Amber Valley	(+10.6)	Barrow in Furness	(− 1.8)
Bury North	(+ 7.0)	Birmingham Selly Oak	(− 5.6)
Derby North	(+ 4.8)	Coventry South-West	(− 6.8)
Edmonton	(+ 2.5)	Elmet	(− 5.7)
Hayes and Harlington	(+ 3.3)	Lancashire West	(−10.2)
Mitcham and Morden	(− 0.9)	Luton South	(+ 1.0)
Norwich North	(+ 3.4)	Nottingham South	(− 7.6)
Putney	(+ 3.8)	Rossendale and Darwen	(− 7.0)
		Streatham	(− 9.3)
Alliance targets			
Bedfordshire North	(+ 3.4)	Birmingham Hall Green	(− 7.6)
Carshalton and Wallington	(+ 6.0)	Hastings and Rye	(− 8.8)
Harrow East	(+10.1)	Hexham	(− 2.1)
Hendon South	(+13.6)	Stroud	(− 0.5)
Penrith and the Border	(+ 0.6)	Taunton	(− 3.1)
		Westbury	(+ 1.2)

apparently reasonable, forms the basis of judgement. In addition, although it is beyond our present scope, it would be useful to distinguish mistakes which might have been avoided by more thorough research from those which were exposed only by an election result which could not have been foreseen using all the available evidence. In table 24.2, therefore, we simply list key targets which on the basis of the election result alone, were not amongst the 50 best chances for each party (however one looks at the figures). In addition, seats in the subsidiary list with particularly good results relative to other targets are listed.[20]

Some of the good performances were anticipated and mentioned in pre-election press releases and it should be noted that only in three of these seats did Labour come within 5 per cent of victory, and that the Alliance came within 10 per cent in none of the subsidiary list seats where it was the challenger. Only in Lancashire West was TV87 caught out in the sense of having no idea that Labour would be so close to victory.

In the case of Alliance targets, after a relative handful of very good prospects there were and are a lot of seats where they run a fairly distant second and which are difficult to choose between, even in the light of the election results.

Two general themes can be found among the seats listed above. In many cases the effect of candidates seemed to be important. In particular we did not generally foresee that significant personal votes were built up by many Tory

MPs first elected in 1983. Sometimes this 'incumbency effect' was magnified by the fact that Labour's vote in 1983 included a personal vote for their sitting MP, which was lost with his or her defeat. In only one of the eight poor performances in Labour key targets did the conditions for a new incumbency effect not exist.[21] Equally, four of the six relatively good results for the Alliance from amongst the secondary list came in seats where the sitting Tory MP retired.

The second point is that the assessment of the prospects in London was over-optimistic. Over half of the poor key target results were in the capital, with the Conservatives proving particularly strong in the North-West quadrant of Greater London.

It makes little sense to attempt to draw a conclusion on how good the TV87 list was. We simply stand by our assertion that TV87 provided the best available advice to anti-Thatcher tactical voters.

The overall election result does not mean, of course, that extensive tactical voting did not take place. The ITN/Harris Exit Poll asked respondents whether they voted for their first choice party or if they voted tactically to defeat another party. No less than 17 per cent said that they had voted tactically. This seems an extraordinarily high figure, although obviously what many voters describe as a tactical vote may differ from our definition. Nevertheless, over a quarter of Alliance voters claimed to have voted tactically, which may reflect the element of protest at the other parties in their vote. More significant is that Labour attracted more tactical votes than the Conservatives. Among Conservatives 11 per cent said that they voted tactically; among Labour voters, 17 per cent.

Table 24.3 gives changes in the shares of the vote for each party, 1983–7, within each group of target seats. *Prima facie* evidence of significant anti-Thatcher tactical voting is provided by the variation in the average changes for Labour and the Alliance. Labour was able to advance in both the seats where it was clearly the challenger at the outset and those where it seemed to be evenly matched with the Alliance at the start of the campaign. However, where the Alliance was best placed to beat the Conservatives its average share of the vote hardly fell and Labour's increase was very small.

We have also averaged the changes in shares of the vote for the recommended parties in seats in which TV87 had a higher profile than elsewhere.[22] In the Alliance key targets where this was so, their vote actually rose by an average of about one per cent; in Labour's key targets the average increase for Labour was 4 per cent. One cannot say whether TV87's support made a noticeable difference or not. Indeed, quantifying the net effect of tactical voting, let alone TV87's impact, is difficult, due to the other variables for which one has to control. In the statistical appendix to the 1987 Nuffield election study Curtice and Steed reveal a complex picture.[23] They point out

Table 24.3. *The results (average change) in the groups of constituencies on the TV87 list*

Type of seat	Average change in share of the vote, 1983–7		
	Conservative	Labour	Alliance
Key Targets			
Labour	+2.6	+3.4	−5.5
Alliance[24]	−0.2	+1.1	−0.8
'local poll crucial'	+1.5	+4.8	−5.8
Worth a good fight			
Labour	+1.1	+4.0	−4.7
Alliance	+0.5	+0.7	−1.2
'local poll crucial'	+0.5	+3.5	−3.8
(All seats in England	+0.1	+2.9	−2.7)

the importance of distinguishing different motivations for switching from the Alliance. Otherwise one can be misled into concluding that tactical switching from the Alliance benefited the Conservatives more than Labour, when this is not necessarily the case at all. Rather they suggest that it is likely

> that Labour were the net beneficiaries of tactical voting by Alliance voters, but in many constituencies this was negated by the incumbency effect. If this conclusion is correct it would suggest that the tactical voting campaign did have an impact on the behaviour of some Alliance voters. Certainly, this is the first general election since 1964 at which there has been any evidence that a squeeze on the Liberals/Alliance disproportionately favoured Labour.[25]

Secondly, they discover a clear geographical divide in the extent of tactical voting, with Labour and Alliance supporters more prepared to switch to each other's party in the North and West of Britain, than in the South and East where 'the incidence of new tactical voting was patchy'. Since the majority of the Alliance target seats were in the South and East, this geographical correlation clearly limited the net benefit to them of tactical voting. Finally, the most extensive tactical voting appears to have occurred 'in seats where there was potential for an Alliance squeeze on a Nationalist candidate or vice versa'.[26]

With the Conservative vote holding up, it was not surprising that the effect of tactical voting in terms of seats was limited. Curtice and Steed suggest that Labour won Oxford East because of tactical voting, with the importance of switching 'debatable in only two or three other cases'. However, although there were not many of them, '[every] one of the seven Alliance and Nationalist gains were at least in part assisted by tactical voting'.[27]

Therefore, although no substitute for national shifts in popular support, this does show that tactical votes can count and that in a close finish they could be decisive.

Notes

1 Paul Ekins is a Research Fellow at the University of Bradford. He is former Co-chair of the Green Party Council.

2 TV87 initially sought support through an advertisement placed in *The Guardian* to coincide with the Press conference launch. Later, TV87 placed one further advert in *The Guardian*, took a series of small advertisements in *Private Eye*, and kept its address and phone number on display in the *New Statesman* classifieds. There was no further paid promotion. The campaign enrolled about 500 supporters and received and spent over £12,000 in donations.

3 The first list was produced by Tim Johnson and Dick Pountain in consultation with the Steering Committee. Tim Johnson is a consultant and writer on information technology, a former journalist and a member of the Liberal Party. Dick Pountain studied biochemistry at Imperial College and is a technical author, currently European Editor of *Byte Magazine*.

4 The second list was researched and prepared by Andy Shaw.

5 The evidence on how the Alliance vote would split if squeezed was somewhat variable, presumably due to differences in question format, the base of respondents, sampling errors as well as possible substantive changes over time. But the overall pattern suggested that Labour would be the net beneficiaries. Certainly we can recall no figures which suggested that the Conservatives would gain most. An illustrative example was provided by the *Newsnight* Election Panel. In the second wave (29 May–1 June) respondents were asked to name their party of second choice, if any. On this measure, the Alliance voters did split evenly between Conservative (35 per cent) and Labour (37 per cent). However, about half the Alliance voters said that they would seriously consider switching votes to keep out the party they most dislike, if they thought that their party had no chance of winning. Amongst this group, those who said that they would vote Labour if they switched amounted to over 1.5 times the total of those who would go over to the Conservatives. Furthermore, the pattern was similar amongst the sub-group of Alliance voters in the Conservative–Labour marginals (although limited numbers mean that this finding has to be viewed cautiously).

6 On the basis of the local results Labour looked set to win Basildon, Harlow and Swindon amongst others. In the event, the Conservatives increased their majority in each case. Maidstone and Warrington South are examples of seats in which the Alliance recorded a lower share of the vote than in 1983, having performed strongly in the local elections. The relationship between local and general election results, with the clear evidence of variations in different seats, is a subject which would seem likely to repay further research.

7 It is important to grasp that although the individual pieces of research can be and were done thoroughly and fairly 'scientifically', one cannot with any sense put all the evidence into a computer which will turn out 'the answers'. For many seats the various sources did not all point to the same conclusion and hence the need for judgement. We had great confidence in these because of the effort that went into making them, but one can never be certain in all cases.

8 Deciding upon the number of seats to put in a list means drawing a 'credibility line', which provides the cut-off point for realistic prospects. Clearly, the last seat included is unlikely to be very different from the first excluded, so the line is somewhat arbitrary. The practical problem for the TV87 list was that if considered separately this line would have been drawn under significantly less Alliance targets than Labour ones. Hence, balancing the list meant, at the margin, determining which 'extra' Alliance hopes to include and which Labour targets to leave out.

9 The list was published in the *New Statesman* due to the support for tactical voting of the then editor, John Lloyd. His commitment was displayed prior to the election campaign by the appearance of TV87's first list in the *New Statesman*.

10 In both cases constituency polls were published in the last week, which would probably have had more impact than the TV87 recommendation. We also said that the initial view that Northampton North was 'worth a good fight' for the Alliance should be ignored, as Labour seemed to be a clear second.

11 In Erith and Crayford, the national position suggested a close result between Labour and Alliance, and we saw no evidence of a considerable Labour upsurge (unlike in Croydon North-West). This proved to be true but what we had not anticipated was the large drop in the Alliance vote to the benefit of the Conservative MP, which suggested a significant double incumbency effect.

12 The respondents in the *Newsnight* panel were first interviewed between 14–17 May (wave I); the last interviews were conducted on 8–9 June (wave III). It has to be pointed out that in three of the twenty seats defined in this panel as Conservative–Alliance seats, Labour did actually finish second, so not every Labour voter who thought this would happen was wrong. Hence, the figures slightly exaggerate the extent of misperception.

13 The most striking example of this problem occurred when *Breakfast Time* arranged to interview Nina Fishman, and then cancelled well into the evening beforehand.

14 These seats were the Labour key targets of Derby North, Hampstead and Highgate, Lincoln, Oxford East, Putney, and Tynemouth; the Alliance key targets of Bath, Congleton, Cheltenham, Derbyshire West, Harrow East, Leeds North-West, Oxford West and Abingdon, St Albans, Stevenage, and Wyre Forest, along with Stroud and Westbury from the subsidiary list. Clearly this excludes any other seats where a candidate used a TV87 recommendation without informing us or in which TV87 gained particularly prominent local media coverage.

15 Fortunately, in the case of Calder Valley we did believe Labour to be running second because of the national position and so were willing to acknowledge the initial error and swap sides.

16 Later, MORI produced the following figures for Littleborough and Saddleworth (the figures in brackets show the actual result): Conservative 44 (43), Labour 31 (26), Alliance 25 (31). Although not beyond the realms of possibility, the Alliance and Labour figures were judged 'unlikely' at the time. The problem in this case, then, was the reversing of the positions of the opposition parties, which confused the tactical position. See also p. 251 of this book.

17 See the accompanying chapter by Robert Waller.

18 Take the case of Birmingham Hall Green, where the result was: Conservative 44.9, Labour 28.2, Alliance 27.0. Even if one could have known in advance that this was the standing of the parties one could not draw the conclusion that it was a mistake to recommend tactical voting for the Alliance, as TV87 did. For one must consider the percentage of the other's support that each opposition party would have required to overtake the Tories. Labour would have needed 62 per cent of all Alliance votes, or the Alliance 63 per cent of Labour votes to beat the Conservatives. On this basis, the Alliance seems the best tactical option, since it is unlikely that Labour are the second preference of over 60 per cent of Alliance voters, whereas the reverse is probably true. Even so, the target percentage cannot be used uniformly – if the Conservatives have just under 50 per cent support in a seat, then either opposition party would require the votes of all of the other if it was to have a hope. But if

one of them stands at 40 per cent, it is clear which is the best option. This note gives an idea of why it is often difficult to decide whether a decision was wrong, even in retrospect.

19 Naturally, we are inclined to a view that the recommendations in these seats were generally correct. The seats concerned are Birmingham Hall Green, Gloucestershire West, Harrow East, High Peak, Luton North, Watford.

20 We have not gone through the process of drawing up new lists on the basis of the results, to see exactly which seats should have been included as key targets and which 'relegated' to the second section, so these lists should not be regarded as definitive judgements.

21 This was in Putney, where David Mellor benefited from the Conservatives' strong showing in Wandsworth; his rise up the political ladder probably did no harm to his personal vote either.

22 The three Alliance key targets which were included on the basis of by-election results – Derbyshire West, Penrith and Stafford – were excluded from the calculations for this line of the table.

23 J. Curtice and M. Steed, 'Appendix 2 Analysis' in David Butler and Dennis Kavanagh (eds.), *The British General Election of 1987* (London: Macmillan, 1988).

24 These seats are the key targets detailed in note 14, with the exception of Derbyshire West, which is excluded from the calculation due to the apparent influence of the intervening by-election.

25 Curtice and Steed, in Butler and Kavanagh (eds.), *The British General Election of 1987* p. 339.

26 Curtice and Steed, in Butler and Kavanagh (eds.), *The British General Election of 1987*, p. 339.

27 Curtice and Steed, in Butler and Kavanagh (eds.), *The British General Election of 1987*, p. 340.

The list of participants at Conference on Political Communications: the Media, the Parties and the Polls in the 1987 Election Campaign, University of Essex, 23–25 October 1987.

Name	Affiliation
Linda Anderson	BBC TV
Max Atkinson	Wolfson College, Oxford
Barrie Axford	Oxford Polytechnic
Denis Balsom	University College of Wales
Anthony Barker	University of Essex
John Brown	Scottish Television
Philip Brown	University of Liverpool
Simon Brownholtz	MORI
Hilary Bryan	
David Butler	Nuffield College, Oxford
Roger Carroll	*Sunday Telegraph*
Jean Charlot	Fondation Nationale de Science Politique
Monica Charlot	Maison Française, Oxford
Peter Charlton	Portsmouth Polytechnic
Roger Corke	Granada TV
David Cowling	ITN
Ivor Crewe	University of Essex
Veronica Crichton	Goldsmith's College, London
James Curran	Goldsmith's College, London
Sir Robin Day	BBC
David Dubow	FDS (Market Research) Ltd
Andrew Ellis	The Liberal Party
Len England	Market Research Society
Maya Even	TV-am
Nina Fishman	TV87
Marian Fitzgerald	Runnymede Trust
Winston Fletcher	Delaney Fletcher Delaney

Donna Foote	*Newsweek Magazine*
Liz Forgan	C4 Television
Nigel Forman	MP
Bob Franklin	University of Leeds
Harold Frayman	The Labour Party
Ivor Gaber	Goldsmith's College, London
Chris Game	INLOGOV, University of Birmingham
Brian Gosschalk	MORI
Philip Gould	Philip Gould & Associates
Tony Halmos	SDP
Vincent Hanna	Viewpoint Productions
Robert Hargreaves	IBA
Martin Harrop	University of Newcastle upon Tyne
John Heritage	University of Warwick
Alastair Hetherington	University of Stirling
Patricia Hewitt	Opposition Leader's Office
Hilde Himmelweit	LSE
Richard Holme	Constitutional Reform Centre
Sarah Horack	Horack & Associates
John Hosker	Market Research Society
Peter Hutton	MORI
Nigel Jackson	Hull University
Meril James	Audience Selection
Peter Jenkins	*The Independent*
Sandy Johnstone	FDS (Market Research) Ltd.
Claudia Josephs	C4 Television
Dennis Kavanagh	University of Nottingham
Peter Kellner	*The Independent*
Anthony King	University of Essex
Raymond Kuhn	Queen Mary College, London
Chris Ledger	BBC-TV
Jacques Leruez	Fondation Nationale de Science Politique
Steven Link	FDS (Market Research) Ltd.
David Lipsey	*New Society*
Chris Long	ITN
Brian MacArthur	*The Sunday Times*
David Marsh	University of Essex
Linda McDougall	Central TV
Robin McGregor	BBC-TV
Paul McKee	Yorkshire Television
David McKie	*The Guardian*
Peter Madgwick	Oxford Polytechnic
Peter Mandelson	The Labour Party

Glyn Mathias	ITN
Philip Mercicca	Harris Research Centre
Lewis Minkin	Manchester University
Austin Mitchell	MP
Nick Moon	NOP Market Research
Hilary Muggeridge	Constitutional Reform Centre
Richard Newby	SDP
Ken Newton	University of Essex
Pippa Norris	Newcastle Polytechnic
Robin Oakley	*The Times*
Jim Orpe	
John Pardoe	Sight & Sound Education Ltd
Jim Parish	The Labour Party
Clive Payne	Oxford University
Gillian Peele	Lady Margaret Hall, Oxford
Max Perkins	HTV Wales
Anthony Piepe	Portsmouth Polytechnic
Cynthia Pinto	Harris Research Centre
Michael Pinto-Duschinsky	Brunel University
Chris Powell	Boase Massimi Pollitt
Colin Rallings	Plymouth Polytechnic
Adam Raphael	BBC-TV
Peter Riddell	*Financial Times*
Chris Rogers	Television South West
Michael Rudin	Constitutional Reform Centre
Richard Ryder	MP
Susan Scarrow	Oxford University
David Scott	Scottish Television
John Sharkey	Saatchi & Saatchi
Andrew Shaw	University of Liverpool
Anne-Marie Sieghart	*The Economist*
Peter Snow	BBC-TV
Michael Svennevig	IBA
Kevin Swaddle	Nuffield College, Oxford
Eric Tanenbaum	University of Essex
Norman Tebbit	CH, MP
Sarah Thane	IBA
David Thompson	*The Daily Mirror*
Michael Thrasher	Plymouth Polytechnic
Paul Tyler	Good Relations Public Affairs
Rodney Tyler	*News of the World*
Robert Waller	Harris Research Centre
Debbie Walter	Audience Selection Ltd

Graham Watson   The Liberal Party
Paul Whiteley   University of Bristol
John Wilson   BBC
Mallory Wober   IBA
Robert Worcester   MORI

General Index

Index of authors